Summary of Contents

THE ASP.NET 2.0 ANTHOLOGY
101 ESSENTIAL TIPS, TRICKS & HACKS

BY **SCOTT ALLEN**
JEFF ATWOOD
WYATT BARNETT
JON GALLOWAY
PHIL HAACK

The ASP.NET 2.0 Anthology: 101 Essential Tips, Tricks & Hacks

by Scott Allen, Jeff Atwood, Wyatt Barnett, Jon Galloway, and Phil Haack

Expert Reviewer: Wyatt Barnett

Managing Editor: Simon Mackie

Technical Editor: Matthew Magain

Technical Director: Kevin Yank

Printing History:

   First Edition: August 2007

Editor: Georgina Laidlaw

Editor: Hilary Reynolds

Index Editor: Fred Brown

Cover Design: Alex Walker

Notice of Rights

Notice of Liability

Trademark Notice

Published by SitePoint Pty. Ltd.

424 Smith Street Collingwood
VIC Australia 3066
Web: www.sitepoint.com
Email: business@sitepoint.com

ISBN 978-0-9802858-1-9
Printed and bound in the United States of America

About the Authors

Scott Allen is a consultant and founder of OdeToCode.com. Scott is also an instructor for Pluralsight—a premier Microsoft .NET training provider and home to many of the top authorities on .NET today. In 15 years of software development, Scott has shipped commercial software on everything from 8 bit embedded devices to 64 bit web servers. You can reach Scott through his blog at http://www.OdeToCode.com/blogs/scott/.

Jeff Atwood lives near Berkeley, California with his wife, two cats, and far more computers than he cares to mention. His first computer was the Texas Instruments TI-99/4a. He's been a Microsoft Windows developer since 1992. Most of his programming was in Visual Basic, although he spent significant time with early versions of Delphi, and now he's quite comfortable with C# or VB.NET. Jeff is particularly interested in best practices and human factors in software development, as represented in his blog, http://www.codinghorror.com/.

Wyatt Barnett leads the in-house development team for a major industry trade association in Washington DC. He also writes for SitePoint's .NET blog, Daily Catch, and worked as the Expert Reviewer for this book.

After working hard as a submarine lieutenant, Jon Galloway was amazed to find that people would pay him to goof off with computers all day. He spends most of his time with ASP.NET and SQL Server, but likes to keep involved with a variety of other technologies, including Silverlight, Mono, vector graphics, web technologies, and open source .NET development. Jon co-founded the Monoppix project, has contributed to several open source projects, including SubSonic, and regularly releases open source utilities (late at night, when his wife and three daughters are fast asleep). He's a senior software engineer at Vertigo Software, and blogs at http://weblogs.asp.net/jgalloway/.

Phil Haack has over eight years of experience in software development, consulting, and software management, which he puts to good use as the CTO and co-founder of VelocIT. In his spare time, he leads the Subtext open source blogging engine and contributes to various other open source projects. To keep his sanity, he also plays soccer regularly.

About the Technical Editor

Before joining the SitePoint team as a technical editor, Matthew Magain worked as a software developer for IBM and also spent several years teaching English in Japan. He is the organizer for Melbourne's Web Standards Group,[1] and enjoys candlelit dinners and long walks on the beach. He also enjoys writing bios that sound like they belong in the personals column. Matthew lives with his wife Kimberley and daughter Sophia.

---

[1] http://webstandardsgroup.org/

About the Technical Director

As Technical Director for SitePoint, Kevin Yank oversees all of its technical publications—books, articles, newsletters, and blogs. He has written over 50 articles for SitePoint, but is best known for his book, *Build Your Own Database Driven Website Using PHP & MySQL*. Kevin lives in Melbourne, Australia, and enjoys performing improvised comedy theater and flying light aircraft.

About SitePoint

SitePoint specializes in publishing fun, practical, and easy-to-understand content for web professionals. Visit http://www.sitepoint.com/ to access our books, newsletters, articles, and community forums.

Table of Contents

Chapter 11 **Working with Email** 339

Chapter 12 **Rendering Binary Content** 355

Preface

This is the book I *wish* I had when I was starting out with ASP.NET. Now, if you'd be so kind as to hop into a time machine, go back five years, and give me a copy, I'd be eternally grateful.

What's that? Time machines haven't been invented yet? Drat. I guess we're stuck in the here and now.

Many ASP.NET books try to be complete, exhaustive references. They're dense, fat books with an inflated sense of self-importance—books that take up lots of room on your bookshelf. But who actually *reads* these giant tomes of universal knowledge? Even if you could read one cover to cover, would it really be complete or exhaustive? The .NET framework is vast. As much as I've learned, I still discover new features of ASP.NET and the .NET Framework on a daily basis. And the platform itself is still actively evolving and growing. .NET 3.0 is already here, and .NET 3.5 is on the horizon.

This book is different from the rest. It doesn't pretend to be a complete reference. It won't waste your time with hundreds of pages on every obscure feature of ASP.NET. And it won't insult your intelligence by suggesting that it contains every last detail of ASP.NET.

Instead, this book will be your native guide to the ASP.NET jungle. As its authors, we'll share with you our cumulative experience in building ASP.NET sites large and small, commercial and open source, and all flavors in between. We're seasoned veterans with more than our share of scars, bumps, and bruises. We'll show you the most practical features, the best approaches, the useful features that are off the beaten path—in short, *the stuff that matters*. We absolutely, positively promise not to bore you with the same tired old tourist attractions that everyone else gets herded through.

Each chapter of this book is laid out in a problem–solution format. We'll start with a common problem that an intermediate ASP.NET developer may face, then provide a concise solution to that problem. In some cases, when the topic warrants it, we'll include a brief discussion of the solution to provide context.

We've grouped the chapters of this book to cover major areas of ASP.NET functionality. Inside, you'll find solutions to the most common challenges that ASP.NET developers face—at least in our experience.

Who Should Read this Book?

This book is for beginner and intermediate ASP.NET developers who want to get more out of the ASP.NET 2.0 framework. It's also for those programmers who have always just stumbled their way through ASP.NET without really understanding how things worked, or when it's appropriate to bend the rules or sidestep the "normal" way of building web applications. Finally, this book should serve ASP.NET 1.x developers who want to learn what's new in ASP.NET 2.0 (I'll give you a hint—a lot!)

This book assumes a few things. For one, it assumes that you are across the basics of ASP.NET—web forms, C# syntax, code-beside structure, and basic web project configuration. Readers of SitePoint's beginner ASP.NET book, *Build Your Own ASP.NET 2.0 Web Site Using C# and VB, 2nd Edition*, will find that this book fills in a lot of the gaps left by that title. This book also assumes that you're using Visual Studio 2005. You might be able to get by with the free Visual Web Developer Express Edition, but we offer no guarantees—this book is firmly targeted at serious ASP.NET 2.0 developers who use serious tools.

What's Covered in this Book?

Chapter 1: Introductory Topics

This chapter lists some of the solid skills that every ASP.NET developer should have—how to set up and use a source control repository, choose a web project model, and deploy a project. If you're confident that you've got this stuff under control you can skip this chapter, but you'd want to be absolutely certain—there's some good stuff here, trust me!

Chapter 2: .NET 2.0 Core Libraries

In this chapter we dissect some of the primitive classes that many developers take for granted, just to see what makes them tick. We look at the most efficient way to manipulate strings and generic collections, and how best to implement recursive logic.

Chapter 3: Data Access

The most exciting web applications are data-driven—but you have to store all that data somewhere. Here we look at common problems surrounding storing, retrieving, modifying, and displaying data stored in a database, and suggest some solutions for you to try in your own projects.

Chapter 4: Pushing the Boundaries of the `GridView`

The `GridView` control is one of the most frequently used data controls in the ASP.NET arsenal, and for good reason—it's flexible, it's reliable, and it displays tabular data admirably. But every now and then you hit a ceiling above which you doubt the `GridView` is capable of moving … and that's when you turn to this chapter.

Chapter 5: Form Validation

Forms are the key to interactivity on the Web … but they can also be extremely daunting and difficult for developers to get right. In this chapter we look at ways of synchronizing client-side and server-side validation, and we discuss approaches for building custom validation tools, so that form validation is never daunting again!

Chapter 6: Maintaining State

ASP.NET's built-in state management is a double-edged sword. In some situations, it can make handling the state of a user session a breeze, but there are times when it's more trouble than it's worth. This chapter reveals when you should use it, and when you should resort to alternative methods of maintaining state.

Chapter 7: Membership and Access Control

This chapter will show you how to utilize the built-in controls in ASP.NET 2.0 to add a membership system to your site that's both secure and flexible. We'll cover registration, forgotten passwords, remote user management, and more.

Chapter 8: Component-based Development

Good developers know that separating code into stand-alone components makes it more reusable and maintainable—but can this philosophy be applied to master pages and user controls? Luckily for you, the answer is "yes," and this chapter will show you how it's done.

Chapter 9: ASP.NET and Web Standards

The ASP.NET framework is not necessarily synonymous with the term "web standards," but there's no reason why your applications can't produce valid, semantic, standards-compliant markup. In this chapter we'll look at the CSS-friendly Control Adapters toolkit and learn how it can help ensure that our application's markup stays on the straight and narrow.

Chapter 10: Ajax and JavaScript

Mostly as a result of the rising popularity of Ajax as a means to enhance an application's interactivity and responsiveness, JavaScript is presently the new black. In this chapter we'll see how you can improve the custom JavaScript that you write, and investigate a number of libraries that can make your client-side scripting tasks a whole lot easier.

Chapter 11: Working with Email

There's a lot you can do with ASP.NET's built-in email functionality—you can send it, receive it, parse it, and add attachments. You can make it look pretty using HTML, or keep it as plain old text. Whatever your email needs, this chapter has the advice you're after!

Chapter 12: Rendering Binary Content

In this chapter we'll look at how ASP.NET makes it possible to deal directly with binary files, such as Microsoft Excel spreadsheets, and images. We'll create these types of files from scratch, as well as processing and modifying existing files. Who said the Web was just about text?

Chapter 13: Handling Errors

Even the best programmers make mistakes—but they also know how to find them and deal with them swiftly. This chapter will show you how to establish a strategy for writing log messages, handling exceptions, and debugging your application.

Chapter 14: Configuration

The **Web.config** file enables you to store configuration information for your application in one central location. In this chapter we'll explore some techniques for simplifying this file when it grows to be unmanageable, learn to secure the file through encryption, and understand how to get the most out of the ASP.NET configuration API.

Chapter 15: Performance and Scaling

We all want our applications to be fast and responsive to users, but this noble goal can be difficult to achieve when your application is voted the Next Big Thing™ and membership skyrockets! This chapter will show you how best to scale, and introduce a strategy for optimizing your application.

Chapter 16: Search Engine Optimization

Your ground-breaking web application might contain pages and pages of inspiring content, but your efforts creating it will all be in vain if nobody can find it. In this chapter we'll look at ways to ensure that your content can be found by both search engines and humans.

Chapter 17: Advanced Topics

This chapter contains a collection of random tips and techniques that didn't fit neatly into the previous chapters. We'll look at everything from screen scraping and creating portable data access layers to poking around the internals of the ASP.NET framework itself.

In short, this book is about getting things done in ASP.NET 2.0. There's a lot to cover, so let's get started!

The Book's Web Site

Located at http://www.sitepoint.com/books/aspnetant1/, the web site that supports this book will give you access to the following facilities.

The Code Archive

As you progress through this book, you'll note file names above many of the code listings. These refer to files in the code archive, a downloadable ZIP file that contains all of the finished examples presented in this book. Simply click the **Code Archive** link on the book's web site to download it.

Updates and Errata

No book is error-free, and attentive readers will no doubt spot at least one or two mistakes in this one. The Corrections and Typos page on the book's web site, at http://www.sitepoint.com/books/aspnetant1/errata.php, will provide the latest information about known typographical and code errors, and will offer necessary updates for new releases of browsers and related standards.

The SitePoint Forums

If you'd like to communicate with other web developers about this book, you should join SitePoint's online community at http://www.sitepoint.com/forums/. The ASP.NET forum, in particular, at http://www.sitepoint.com/launch/dotnetforum/, offers an abundance of information above and beyond the solutions in this book, and a lot of fun and experienced .NET developers hang out there. It's a good way to learn new tricks, get questions answered in a hurry, and just have a good time.

The SitePoint Newsletters

In addition to books like this one, SitePoint publishes free email newsletters, including *The SitePoint Tribune*, *The SitePoint Tech Times*, and *The SitePoint Design View*. Reading these newsletters will keep you up to date on the latest news, product releases, trends, tips, and techniques for all aspects of web development. If nothing else, you'll receive useful CSS articles and tips, but if you're interested in learning other technologies, you'll find them especially valuable. Sign up to one or more SitePoint newsletters at http://www.sitepoint.com/newsletter/.

Your Feedback

If you can't find an answer through the forums, or if you wish to contact us for any other reason, the best place to write is `books@sitepoint.com`. We have an email support system set up to track your inquiries, and friendly support staff members who can answer your questions. Suggestions for improvements as well as notices of any mistakes you may find are especially welcome.

Conventions Used in this Book

You'll notice that we've used certain typographic and layout styles throughout this book to signify different types of information. Look out for the following items:

Code Samples

Code in this book will be displayed using a fixed-width font, like so:

```
<h1>A perfect summer's day</h1> <p>It
    was a lovely day for a walk in the park. The birds were
    singing and the kids were all back at school.</p>
```

If the code may be found in the book's code archive, the name of the file will appear at the top of the program listing, like this:

```
                                                                example.css
.footer { background-color: #CCC; border-top: 1px
    solid #333; }
```

If only part of the file is displayed, this is indicated by the word *excerpt*:

```
                                                          example.css (excerpt)
border-top: 1px solid #333;
```

Some lines of code are intended to be entered on one line, but we've had to wrap them because of page constraints. A ➥ indicates a page-break that exists for formatting purposes only, and should be ignored.

```
URL.open.("http://www.sitepoint.com/blogs/2007/05/28/user-style-shee
➥ets-come-of-age/");
```

Tips, Notes, and Warnings

 Hey, You!

Tips will give you helpful little pointers.

 Ahem, Excuse Me ...

Notes are useful asides that are related—but not critical—to the topic at hand. Think of them as extra tidbits of information.

 Make Sure you Always ...

... pay attention to these important points.

 Watch Out!

Warnings will highlight any gotchas that are likely to trip you up along the way.

Chapter 1

Introductory Topics

Okay, so you've picked up this book with the aim of solving some ASP.NET problems. Great! But before we set off trying to solve any and every problem an ASP.NET developer might face, let's lay down a little groundwork.

This chapter covers some of the critical elements that you might want to consider *before* rushing off to furiously code your next web site.

Which web project model should I choose?

Starting with Visual Studio 2005, Microsoft introduced a new type of web project known as the **Web Site** project. A Web Site project is a radically simplified version of the more complex Web Application project. For instance, a Web Site project has no project file: in a Web Site project, the file system *is* the project.

Although Web Site projects are pleasingly simple on the surface, so many limitations were inherent in the file system model that developers soon demanded the old Web Application model back. And Microsoft evidently thought the issue was important enough to warrant action because, as of Visual Studio 2005 Service Pack 1, we can choose between two different web project models:

- Web Application project
- Web Site project

Selecting a project model is one of the first things you'll need to do on any .NET web project.

Solution

Choice is good. But to make an informed decision, you'll need to understand the differences between these two project models. This is an important choice that will have many repercussions for your project, so you should be familiar with how both models work.

Web Site Projects Versus Web Application Projects

Let's take a moment to investigate the differences between the two project models.

- Web Site projects are special cases. They do not behave like any other project type in Visual Studio.

- Web Application projects have a project file. Web Site projects do not.

- Web Application projects compile into one monolithic assembly DLL; to run and debug pages, the entire project must be compiled every time. Web Site projects compile dynamically at the page level; each page can be compiled and debugged independently.

- Web Application projects are deployed "all at once," as a single DLL, along with necessary static content files. Web Site projects are deployed as a set of files, each of which can be updated independently.

Each project type has its strengths and weaknesses, and Visual Studio 2005 will continue to fully support *both* project types, so either is a valid choice.

That said, web forums are overflowing with complaints about, and criticisms of, the Web Site project model. I've experienced enough problems with the Web Site project model myself to avoid using it. And there's definitely a reason why Microsoft did such a quick about-face and retrospectively added support for Web Application projects with the release of Service Pack 1.

The Web Site project's complete reliance on the file system as its statement of record makes it a little too "magical" for its own good, at least in my opinion. For example, the only way to exclude a file from a Web Site project is to rename it with the **.exclude** file extension. In a Web Application project, a file can be easily excluded—we simply remove the reference to it from the project file.

In general, I recommend that you avoid the Web Site project model. If you're starting a new project, you should choose the Web Application project by default. Web Sites seem like a good idea on paper, but in practice, they're too simplified and, ultimately, too limiting.

That said, there are a few cases in which the Web Site project type remains the best option:

- The Express editions of Visual Studio do not support the Web Application project type. So if you're using Visual Web Developer Express Edition, or planning to share code with developers who only have access to this tool, you should use Web Site projects.

- For small, demonstration projects, the Web Site model is often more appropriate than a full-blown Web Application. If your project is simple, choose the simple Web Site project type.

Creating Web Projects

The process you'll use to create a web project will depend on the type of project you need.

Creating a Web Site Project

Web Site projects are the default web project type in Visual Studio 2005 and (Visual Web Developer 2005 Express Edition). To create a new Web Site project, open the **File** menu and select **New > Web Site...**, as I've done in Figure 1.1.

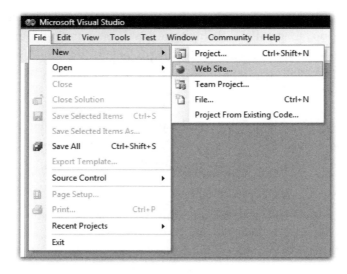

Figure 1.1. Creating a new Web Site project in Visual Studio

Next, you're presented with the **New Web Site** dialog, which lets you choose where you want the Web Site project to be stored—either on the local file system, or in a remote location via HTTP or FTP, as Figure 1.2 shows.

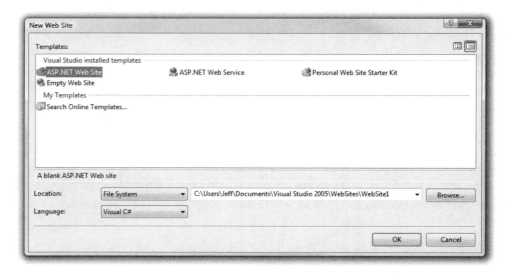

Figure 1.2. Choosing the location of our new Web Site project

Click **OK** to create the project. Once you've done this, the name of the solution displayed in the **Solution Explorer** reflects the location of the solution in the file system, as demonstrated in Figure 1.7.

Figure 1.3. The project as viewed in the Solution Explorer

If we right-click the solution and select **Properties**, the Web Site project's properties are displayed, as shown in Figure 1.4.

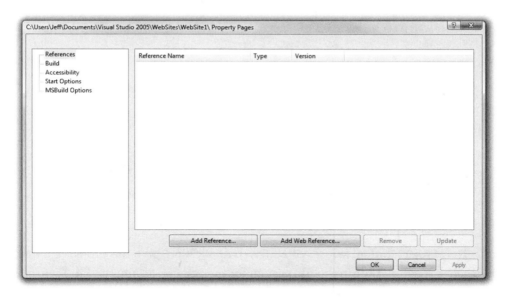

Figure 1.4. Displaying the Web Site project's properties

Web Site project properties are radically different from the properties for every other Visual Studio project type. Only a small subset of the options you'd expect to be here are present.

Creating a Web Application Project

Visual Studio 2005 Service Pack 1 Required!

You *must* have Visual Studio 2005 Service Pack 1 or later to create a Web Application project. If you're wondering why you can't create or open Web Application projects, you probably haven't installed Service Pack 1 yet, or you may be running the free Visual Web Developer 2005 Express Edition.

Use the **File** > **New** > **Project…** menu to create a new Web Application project, as shown in Figure 1.5.

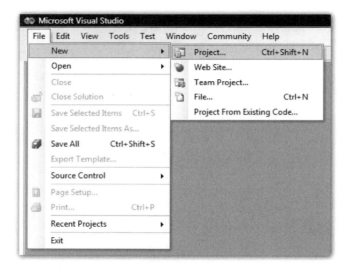

Figure 1.5. Creating a new Web Application project

In the **New Project** dialog, select **ASP.NET Web Application**, give the project a name, and select a location within the file system for the project, as depicted in Figure 1.6.

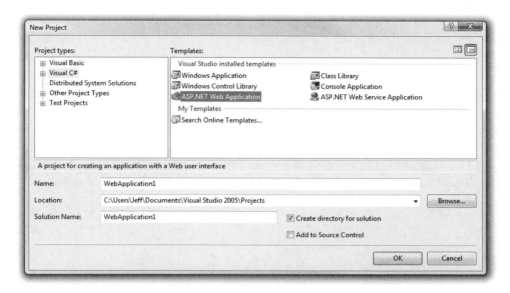

Figure 1.6. Specifying a name and location for a Web Application project

Once you've created the Web Application project, the title of the solution will reflect the name that you specified for the project, as Figure 1.7 shows.

Figure 1.7. Viewing the Web Application project in Solution Explorer

Note that a Web Application project has quite a few more elements than the simpler Web Site project. It has:

- a **Web.config** file
- an **AssemblyInfo.cs** file
- a **References** folder containing a number of items

This is consistent with the way other project types—such as the Console and Windows Forms project types—work in Visual Studio. If you right-click the project and select **Properties**, you can browse the project properties, as Figure 1.8 shows.

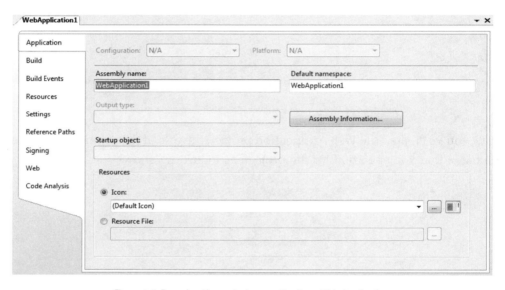

Figure 1.8. Browsing the project properties for a Web Application

Web Application projects behave almost identically to other Visual Studio project types, though Web Application projects offer the new **Web** tab for the management of web-specific settings.

How do I deploy my web site?

If you've chosen to build your ASP.NET project as a Web Site project, your compilation and deployment options are limited to the **Publish Web Site** menu option, the details of which are illustrated in Figure 1.9.

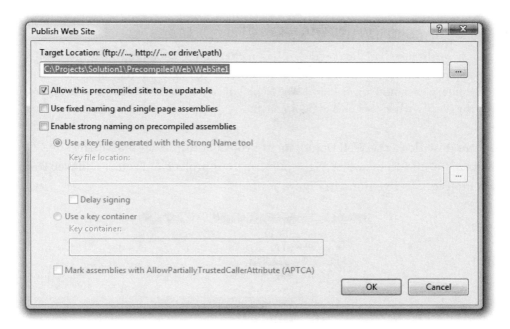

Figure 1.9. Deploying a Web Site project using the **Publish Web Site** option

While there's nothing wrong with the publish functionality that's built into Visual Studio 2005, the available deployment options are rudimentary at best.

Solution

One of the biggest weaknesses of Web Site projects is that they lack a **project file**—an umbrella file that keeps track of every other file in the project. For better or worse, Web Site projects are completely file system-based, so there's only one way to deploy a Web Site, and that's to copy *everything* in the file system to the target location.

This sounds convenient at first, but in practice it can be incredibly annoying—you don't always want every file in the file system to be deployed.

That's where a **Web Deployment project** comes in handy. Web Deployment projects add the sorely missed project file to your Web Site project. Having an explicit project file provides much more robust and flexible support for deployment.

Don't Leave Home Without One!

As we discussed in the previous solution, Web Application projects are definitely the preferred option for most sites. However, if you do need to go the Web Site route, you should *always* add a Web Deployment project to your solution to ensure flexibility when it comes to deployment.

You can download the Web Deployment project add-in from the MSDN site.[1] Once you have the add-in installed, right-click on your project and select **Add Web Deployment Project...**, as I've done in Figure 1.10.

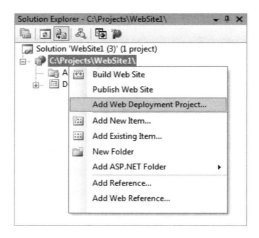

Figure 1.10. Adding a Web Deployment project

A new Web Deployment project will appear in your solution, along with its own set of property pages. Figure 1.11 shows how it displays.

---

[1] http://msdn2.microsoft.com/en-us/asp.net/aa336619.aspx

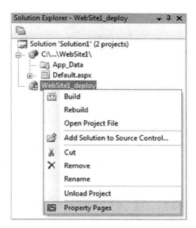

Figure 1.11. The Web Deployment project as viewed in the Solution Explorer

I won't elaborate on the Web Deployment project property pages here, but they offer lots of functionality that you won't get out of the box with a standard Web Site project, including:

- integration with the standard MSBuild process for complete and precise control over how your Web Site is compiled

- the ability to build a single named assembly, or one assembly per folder

- the ability to take advantage of build configurations in Visual Studio, such as Debug, Release, and custom build configurations

- the ability to modify **Web.config** at deployment, so that you can use different configurations for each deployment target (development, testing, staging, production, and so forth)

When you build the project, you'll see the following structure in your file system:

```
\Solution1\Solution1.sln
\Solution1\WebSite1
\Solution1\WebSite1\Default.aspx
\Solution1\WebSite1\Default.cs
\Solution1\WebSite1_Deploy
\Solution1\WebSite1_Deploy\WebSite1_deploy.wdproj
\Solution1\WebSite1_Deploy\Debug
```

```
\Solution1\WebSite1_Deploy\Debug\Default.aspx
\Solution1\WebSite1_Deploy\Debug\PrecompiledApp.config
\Solution1\WebSite1_Deploy\Debug\bin
```

I think you'll agree that this is quite an improvement on the default build options for a Web Site project, which produce no output whatsoever during deployment.

To deploy your Web Site project, simply copy the contents of the folder with the correct build configuration (Debug, in this example) to the target location.

How do I choose a third-party web host?

Most of the sites built by professional developers are hosted on servers that are completely under the developer's (or the company's IT department's) control. For large companies, the servers tend to be managed dedicated servers.

However, for smaller companies and personal web sites, large hosting companies are prohibitively expensive. Fortunately, plenty of smaller hosting companies offer hosting for very reasonable prices, and focus on the special hosting requirements of ASP.NET web applications.

Every application will have different needs and requirements, so you should shop around for a web hosting provider that best meets your specific needs. This solution will provide some guidelines and considerations to keep in mind as you look for a hosting provider.

In addition, this section will discuss some of the unique challenges and "gotchas" that you should be aware of when using the services of a hosting provider. In this section, we'll discuss how to choose a hosting provider and some points you might need to take into consideration in your code.

Solution

The costs of web site hosting can range from being free, to a couple dollars a month, to several hundred dollars a month. The first step is to identify what your application needs—you can then compare this list against what each host can offer for their price. Make a list of the technologies and requirements for your application, paying special attention to the following questions:

How much disk space does your application require?

If you plan to stream music or video, you will want to find a web hosting provider that offers large amounts of disk space.

How much bandwidth will your application require?

This can be a difficult figure to estimate, but most small business and personal web sites will be under 4GB a month.

What type of database does your application require?

Many hosting providers will provide a SQL Server database or two as part of the package, which is great for those who can't afford a full license to SQL Server: you can develop against the free SQL Server Express Edition and deploy to SQL Server when your application goes live. An option that many hosting providers provide for free is MySQL: a full-featured, open source database engine. Many ASP.NET developers are unfamiliar with MySQL, so be sure to read up on it before you make this choice.

How much space does your database require?

Generally, web hosting providers charge less per megabyte of file storage then they do for each megabyte of database storage. This may affect whether you design your application to store images and other binary data in a BLOB (Binary Large Object) field of your database, or on a file system.

Do you need an SSL certificate to process credit card orders securely?

If so, you may want to look for a host that can acquire and install a certificate for your site at a reasonable price. This approach may be more straightforward (and possibly cheaper) than acquiring a certificate on your own, then handing it over to the host.

Does your application need to send email to members?

Make sure the hosting provider supplies a mail server you can use for sending email.

Do you need to receive email through the same domain as the web site?
>   Most providers will offer free email services to customers, but check to make
>   sure the number of mailboxes and the mail management features meet your
>   needs.

Keep your list handy while working through the sites of web hosting providers.
Discard those providers that don't meet your needs for ASP.NET hosting, or don't
have flexible bandwidth and storage plans.

Narrowing the Field

Once you've narrowed the potential hosting providers down to four or five candidates, it's time to drill into specifics. You should consider calling or emailing your
short-listed web hosting providers with any questions that may arise from the following material. You'll want to get an idea of how easy the provider is to work with,
how quickly they can respond, and how technically accurate their answers are. If
they cannot impress you as a potential customer, chances are that they won't impress
you once you've signed up and sent them your hard-earned dollars.

Here are several areas in which you'll want to evaluate each web hosting provider.

Backups

Ask for details of your hosting provider's backup strategy. Find out how often they
back up the file system and the database, and ask about the average turn-around
time for restoring a site.

Reliability

You might want to know a bit about the provider's infrastructure. First, find out if
they have redundant connections to the Internet. You might also ask about a provider's reliability in newsgroups and email forms, but take any third-party feedback
from an untrusted source with a grain of salt. People are more likely to complain
about small problems than they are to praise small successes.

Deployment and Management

What will you do when the time comes to get your application to the hosting provider? Most hosts offer FTP access, and Visual Studio 2005 provides you the ability
to deploy a web project to a remote server over FTP. Some hosting providers require
you to use a web-based file manager to deploy files, but you should avoid these

kinds of services. They're usually quite cumbersome and won't allow you to use Visual Studio 2005 for deployment.

For SQL Server, hosting providers should allow SQL Server users to connect directly to their databases with a tool like Visual Studio .NET 2005, SQL Management Studio, or Query Analyzer. If the hosting provider offers only a web interface, you may find it challenging to use standard tools and scripts when installing, maintaining, and updating your database.

Statistics

You'll want to know the who, what, when, and where of the traffic that reaches your site. Most web hosting providers will provide reports built from the web server's logs to let you know how many hits you receive. Ask the web host for a sample of these reports to see if they give you information that you can use. Reports that include referrers (how people reached your site) and 404 errors (so you know when you have a bad link on the site) can be extremely useful. Some providers will also let you download the raw log files if you want to build your own reports—check whether the host offers this capability if you believe you'll need it.

Security

As an ASP.NET developer, you'll want to make sure your web host is using Windows Server 2003 and keeps up to date with the application of patches. Also ask the provider about how and when they apply security fixes.

Keep in mind that, in many cases, the hosting provider is allowing your code to execute on a server that hosts web sites that belong to others. As such, the hosting providers need to trust that your code won't do anything obnoxious. In reality, they don't. Many hosting providers (unless they provide a dedicated server or dedicated virtual server), will make sure that your web application runs in a partial trust environment, which is also known as Medium Trust within ASP.NET.

The best way to prepare your site for Medium Trust hosting is to set your trust level to medium and test the site thoroughly. This setting is altered via the `trust` element in `Web.config`:

```
<system.web>
  <trust level="Medium" />
</system.web>
```

If your web site makes outgoing HTTP requests, be sure to set the `originUrl` attribute of the `<trust />` section like so:

```
<system.web>
  <trust level="Medium" originUrl="*" />
</system.web>
```

Note that, in the **machine.config** file, your hosting provider may dictate which web sites your site may make requests to. So if you run into problems when making requests, be sure to contact your hosting provider's technical support team.

For more information on partial trust, see the Microsoft document *Using Code Access Security with ASP .NET.*[2]

Special Needs

Does your application make use of any components or services outside the .NET Framework? Do you rely on MSXML 4 or WSE 2, or on running a scheduled task every night? If so, you'll want to ask the web hosting provider if these components and services are available.

Perhaps your application uses an `HttpModule` or `HttpHandler` for URL rewriting or other special processing tasks. In such cases, you'll want to check if the web host allows these technologies.

Free Stuff

Most web hosting providers will offer free components and controls with your hosting package. Many of the controls are already free, so evaluate each package with a critical eye. Other web hosts may offer additional services, like SQL Server Reporting Services, for a fee.

How do I use source control?

Source control is one of the pillars of modern software engineering. A sane software developer would no sooner work outside source control than a climber would climb without safety ropes, or a fireman enter a fire without flame retardant clothing and breathing apparatus.

---

[2] http://msdn2.microsoft.com/en-us/library/aa302425.aspx

But before we dive into the wonderful world of source control, let's start with a true story that exemplifies its importance in real terms.

On April 30, 1999, US taxpayers lost over $1.2 billion due to a small mistake in software configuration management. It was on this day that a Titan IVB rocket was scheduled to put the US Air Force's most advanced communication satellite into orbit. The Titan rocket track record includes over 300 successful launches, but on this day the Titan failed to deliver the satellite into the desired orbit at 22,300 miles from earth. Flight controllers had to put the satellite into an ineffective elliptical orbit of 2,781 by 592 nautical miles, drain the electrical power, and disable all functions before the satellite ever performed service.

Why did this error occur? Because somebody forgot to put a parameter file under source control and the file was lost. When an engineer modified a similar file to recreate the lost file, the engineer typed in a value of -0.1992476 instead of the correct value: -1.992476. This small error meant an $800 million satellite and a $400 million rocket launcher produced zero payoff. Fortunately, for the majority of us, the cost of not using (or misusing) source control software will be orders of magnitude smaller—yet the cost is still there.

Solution

It's a common misconception that the only purpose of source control software is to enable a team of developers to work on source code without overwriting one another's changes. While a source control system does facilitate this kind of method of working, there's much more to the tools known as source control or version control systems.

The Elements of Source Control

In this section, we'll review the basic features that are common to source control systems and see how they work in the software development process.

The Repository

All source control systems feature a **repository** where source code and other files related to the software product are stored. Developers retrieve source code from the repository, make changes, perhaps add some new files, and finally commit (or check in) those changes to the repository.

Not only does the repository store the current version of the source files, it also tracks every single change that's made to a file as developers commit new versions of files to the repository. If you use a source control system, you can look at the entire history of any file in the repository to get a clear idea of the specific changes that have been made to it over time. Sometimes, just knowing what's changed since yesterday can help you track down an elusive bug that appeared today.

Perhaps if an engineer had checked in the parameter file, the Titan mission would have been successful—it's hard to say with 100% certainty, but I'm sure the chances of success would have been better. Likewise, you can dramatically decrease the risks to your software project by keeping the assets required by that project in a repository. The repository should be located on a secure machine and backed up regularly, of course.

Labeling

Labeling, also known **tagging**, is a feature of source control systems that allows you to apply a friendly name to a specific version of your files. It's a good idea to label files every time a product is built—perhaps with just the name of the product and an auto-incremented build number (WhizzBang.1186, for instance). If a problem is found during a test, you can delve into the repository and identify the exact set of files that were used to build the version of the software you're testing.

Another great time to apply a label is whenever you deliver your software to the outside world. Imagine, for example, that build 1186 of WhizzBang has passed all tests and is ready to be delivered to customers. You can apply another label to this set of files, perhaps calling it Whizz Bang 1.2 if you've already delivered versions 1.0 and 1.1. Now, if, in six months' time, one of your customers calls with a severe bug report for version 1.2, you'll know exactly what was deployed to the customer, because the files were labeled. A developer can simply retrieve all the files labeled Whizz Bang 1.2 and reproduce the problem.

Branching

The most common development workflow involves every developer always retrieving the latest version of code from the repository, making changes, and checking those changes back into the repository. If you think of your project as a source control tree, the latest version of the files represents the **trunk** of the tree.

Sometimes it's necessary to branch away from the trunk to perform parallel development on the product. Fortunately, source control also provides the ability to **branch** your project. For instance, suppose you've identified the problem in Whizz Bang 1.2, and now you need to get a fix to the customer. You could apply the fix to the latest version of the code (the trunk), but the rest of the product may not be ready for deployment. Perhaps you're already one month into a three-month project plan for version 2.0, and many new features are still incomplete. You can't send an incomplete version to the customer, so you can't build the latest version as a fix.

In this scenario, it would be prudent to apply the change to the stable version of the product labeled as version 1.2. Source control will allow you to branch the main tree at the version 1.2 label. While some developers begin to work on delivering version 1.2.1 from the branch, the rest of the team can continue working on the main trunk to finish the version 2.0 features. A good source control system will automatically merge changes made on a branch back into the trunk, in effect adding the fix to version 2.0 also.

The scenario above is just one example of branching in action. Branching is a powerful feature and there are many different ways to use branching to meet the style of your development, so make yourself familiar with the capabilities of the versioning system you choose.

Who Should Use Source Control?

Obviously, source control is valuable for teams of developers, and those working in a professional capacity for paying clients. Perhaps you're a solo software developer, or just experimenting at home with some code. If you've read this far, hopefully you've already realized that source control isn't just for big development teams. How many times have you started to make massive changes to a code base, but after an hour, decided that you don't like the new approach, and wished you could roll back to what was working before? Well, if you use source control, that wish is easily granted.

It's also advantageous to use a repository for storing all of your code, and to perform backups of this repository regularly. Tracking history, versioning, and labeling are all there to help you manage your code—even if you're "just tinkering!"

Source Control Tools

Source control products are available to fit every project and budget. If you're not using source control today, I hope we have convinced you to start using it tomorrow. Once you've embraced source control, you'll find it to be just like oxygen—you won't notice once you have it in place, but you'll be acutely aware of how much you rely on it once it's gone.

Figure 1.12 shows TortoiseSVN,[3] a client for the SubVersion source control tool.[4]

Figure 1.12. Revision control with SubVersion and the TortoiseSVN client

TortoiseSVN is popular because it integrates well with the Windows Explorer shell, but many other options—open source and commercial—are available.

---

[3] http://tortoisesvn.tigris.org/
[4] http://subversion.tigris.org/

How do I go about using open source code?

ASP.NET is a huge platform with amazing functionality. You'll find yourself continually discovering new features, even after several years spent working with the framework. Even so, it doesn't take long to start bumping into the limits of what ASP.NET does well. While it may be a large platform, the developers who create ASP.NET can't think of everything, nor supply every feature.

An active and thriving industry has sprung up around building components and libraries for use with ASP.NET, and .NET in general. If your company is willing to shell out the money to purchase these components, it's often a good investment—the well polished components can provide a great deal of functionality. Of course, not all companies understand the business need to purchase such components, which can leave developers in a bind. Even if you do purchase components, many of the commercial libraries don't come with source code. So the component that you thought would solve your needs may not—though it could if you were able to change just a couple lines of code. If only!

Fortunately, a large community of open source developers is actively building tools, applications, and libraries that fill the gaps for many common tasks. These projects provide developers with source code, allowing us to make tweaks and even to contribute patches to the original code base.

Solution

Using open source projects involve some licensing considerations, which we discuss below. Once you have a basic understanding of licensing, you can start looking around for suitable projects!

Open Source Licensing

A **license** is permission granted by a copyright holder to others to allow them to reproduce or distribute a work. It's a means by which the copyright holder can allow others to have some rights when it comes to using the work, without actually assigning the copyright to those other users.

Although there's a huge variety of licenses that could be used to manage the rights associated with open source projects, most tend to employ one of the Open Source Initiative, or OSI, approved licenses.[5]

The GNU GPL (General Public License) is the most widely used of these licenses, but it's often shunned by those producing commercial products. GPL is often called a **viral license** as it requires that any changes that developers make to the code must be released to the public. If you wish to use GPL in your code, I recommend that you consult your company lawyer, or avoid it unless your company wishes to make its code public.

A range of licenses, such as the LGPL, Apache, MIT, and New BSD licenses, do not place any such "give back" restrictions on code usage, which explains why they tend to be very popular among corporate users and those developing proprietary software.

Most of these licenses allow any and all use of the code (commercial or otherwise), as long as a set of requirements is met. Typically, the developers are required to keep the copyright notice in the code, and provide proper attribution.

Finding Open Source .NET Resources

If you think you'd like to use an open source library to solve a particular problem, where do you go to find that code? The Google search engine is a good starting point,[6] though you may spend a lot of time sifting through commercial products looking for the open source options. In my experience, though, open source projects tend to rank well in the search results because the community involvement in their development usually results in a lot of links to the project.

Another great place to look is SourceForge—the single largest repository of open source code.[7] For Microsoft-specific technologies, CodePlex is an excellent resource.[8] Google also recently deployed an open source code hosting service called Google Code.[9]

---

[5] http://www.opensource.org/licenses/alphabetical
[6] http://google.com/
[7] http://sourceforge.net/
[8] http://www.codeplex.com/
[9] http://code.google.com/

Recommended Open Source Projects

A huge number of useful open source libraries exist out there in the wild. In fact, we'll cover several of them in this very book. But for easy reference, the list below includes a few open source projects with which the authors of this book are familiar.

Log4Net (http://logging.apache.org/log4net/)

Log4Net is a port of the popular Log4J logging framework for Java. Log4Net is extremely extensible, allowing logging to a variety of output targets. It's also extremely fast, as performance is a major consideration for the Log4Net team.

NUnit (http://www.nunit.org/) and MbUnit (http://www.mbunit.com/)

NUnit is a port of the JUnit unit-testing framework for Java. NUnit is useful for automatic regression testing and Test Driven Development. MbUnit deserves special mention for the innovations it introduces to unit testing such as row-based testing, combinatorial testing, and transactional rollbacks.

NHibernate (http://www.nhibernate.org/)

NHibernate is a port of the Hibernate OR/M mapping tool for Java (are you noticing a theme here?). NHibernate provides mapping capabilities between your objects and the underlying database store. It dynamically generates the SQL necessary to load and persist your objects.

SubSonic (http://subsonicproject.com/)

SubSonic is a lightweight data access layer and code generator. It's often called OR/M Light, as it's designed to improve a developer's productivity by being really quick and easy to use. We've included an overview of SubSonic in Chapter 17.

DotNetNuke (http://www.dotnetnuke.com/)

DotNetNuke—DNN for short—is a free, open source, web portal application that has a very large and active community of contributors and supporters. Many companies have formed solely to build web sites on DNN, and sell custom modules and support.

FCKeditor (http://www.fckeditor.net/)

FCKeditor is an open source rich text editor for web sites that works with multiple web platforms, including ASP.NET. As a user, authoring content using FCKeditor is very similar to using Microsoft Word.

Where can I find more information about ASP.NET?

I'd love to tell you that this book contains all you'll ever need to know about ASP.NET, but I'd be lying. Any book that even tried to make such a quixotic claim would be too large a reference to hold in one's hands, much less read.

This book provides some valuable solutions to some of the common, tricky problems that we've run into—things we wish we had discovered in a book, rather than learned the hard way. But the true secret to navigating the jungles of ASP.NET is knowing where to look for answers when the books on your shelves fall short.

Solution

A number of detailed and well-maintained resources are available to ASP.NET developers. So when you run into what seems to be a dead-end, use these references to help move your project forward.

Searching for Information

When you're stuck on a problem, one of the first things you should do is fire up your favorite search engine. But don't just randomly type in search terms—to get good search results, *think* before you type. Consider what you're searching for, and what keywords are likely to produce the most relevant results.

For example, you might consider adding the word `ASP.NET` to your search terms to focus the scope of your search. So rather than searching for `GridView is not working`, search for `ASP.NET GridView is not working`. Better still would be to search for `ASP.NET GridView SqlDataSource no data displayed`, because a specific search phrase is much more likely to get you a helpful answer.

If you're searching for information on a specific class, conduct your search on the fully qualified type name to find the class's documentation. In fact, this may prove to be a faster way to locate the MSDN documentation for a type than navigating through the MSDN site.

Another option is to use a customized .NET search engine that searches specific sites. You can add as search providers any sites that support the OpenSearch standard (including IE 7 and Firefox), which allows you to run a .NET-focused search from your browser's search bar. Dan Appleman's searchdotnet.com is a good example of a .NET-centric search site, and Dan's also been nice enough to list some of the other top .NET search providers on the site.[10]

When your code has an unexpected exception, it's often helpful to search using the error message—this can be the quickest way to find information that may help to fix the problem. And if your search isn't generating good results, look through the near misses in your search results and see if any of the terms on those pages make good candidates for your next search attempt.

When in doubt, search. And if you're feeling generous, start your own blog and write about the solutions you found, so your fellow coders can find your results in their future searches. It's a virtuous cycle!

Google Groups

Before the World Wide Web—before web forums and blogs—the only online forum for public discussion was the USENET newsgroups. Although their importance has diminished over time, USENET newsgroups are still useful as a secondary search target.

If a regular Google search doesn't turn up the information you're looking for, try a quick search of Google Groups, which is a huge database of USENET newsgroup posts. It's quite possible that someone has run into the same problem you're having, and has posted a solution in a newsgroup posting.

The ASP.NET Web Site

The ASP.NET forums web site,[11] which is managed by Microsoft, is much like Google groups in that it's a place for users to post questions and receive answers from other members of the coding community.

Unlike Google Groups, these forums are solely focused on ASP.NET, which makes them a more targeted place to search for information. The rest of the ASP.NET domain is fairly good, too—there's a lot of great content and tutorials, especially under the Learn[12] and Resources categories.[13]

---

[10] http://www.searchdotnet.com/

[11] http://forums.asp.net/

[12] http://asp.net/learn/

[13] http://asp.net/resources/

ASP.NET–focused Blogs

The blog isn't just a fad format that gives people an outlet to write about the wacky antics of their cats. In the .NET world, there are many Microsoft bloggers—and Microsoft technology-focused bloggers—who provide a real service to the community via their blogs. These blogs are full of useful tips, tricks, and in-depth information about ASP.NET.

Table 1.1 contains a list of some blogs that we recommend for learning more about ASP.NET and .NET, selfishly starting with the authors' very own blogs, of course!

Table 1.1. Essential Blogs About ASP.NET and .NET

Blog	Description
http://codinghorror.com/	Jeff Atwood's blog is very highly regarded in the software development community. His blog tends to focus on software usability and high-level issues regarding software development.
http://odetocode.com/blogs/scott/	Scott Allen's blog is a rich source of in-depth information about ASP.NET. He also covers Windows Workflow Foundation (WF) and other ins and out of .NET technologies.
http://haacked.com/	Phil Haack tends to cover all sorts of information regarding software development in general, and ASP.NET in particular.
http://weblogs.asp.net/jgalloway/	Like the others in this list, Jon Galloway's blog covers .NET technologies, but he also likes to delve into SQL Server, providing useful advanced tips.
http://weblogs.asp.net/scottgu/	Scott Guthrie is a General Manager within the Microsoft Developer Division. He's in charge of ASP.NET, among many other technologies, and his blog is a great resource for learning about new features of ASP.NET.
http://hanselman.com/blog/	Scott Hanselman's blog is very popular among the .NET crowd. He likes to delve really deep into the intricacies of ASP.NET and other technologies.
http://www.pluralsight.com/blogs/fritz/	Fritz Onion wrote the book on ASP.NET—well, not the only book, but one of the best ones. His blog is a great resource on ASP.NET.

Reference Books

Table 1.2 lists a number of books that should be on every ASP.NET developer's bookshelf.

Table 1.2. Essential ASP.NET 2.0 Reading List

Book	Description
Build Your Own ASP.NET 2.0 Web Site Using C# & VB by Cristian Darie and Zac Ruvalcaba (Melbourne: SitePoint, 2006)	This introductory title from SitePoint represents assumed knowledge for the book you're currently reading. It introduces readers to programming with ASP.NET, and touches on the most commonly used aspects of the framework.
Essential ASP.NET with Examples in C# (Boston: Addison-Wesley Professional, 2003) and *Essential ASP.NET 2.0* (Boston: Addison-Wesley Professional, 2006) by Fritz Onion	These two books cover ASP.NET 1.0 and ASP.NET 2.0 respectively. The reason they're both listed here together is that the second book only covers features of ASP.NET 2.0 that weren't covered in the first book. Together they make a complete volume.
Professional ASP.NET 2.0, Special Edition by Bill Evjen, Scott Hanselman, Devin Rader, Farhan Muhammad, and Srinivasa Sivakumar (Hoboken: Wrox Press, 2006)	If you're going to get one big ASP.NET tome, this is the one. It's huge, but it's a solid reference. It's nice to have this one on hand when your web searches are coming up empty.
CLR via C#, 2nd Edition by Jeffrey Richter (Redmond: Microsoft Press, 2006)	Not strictly about ASP.NET, this book is essential for developers who wish to understand how the CLR and .NET work under the hood. Being armed with this knowledge is very helpful when debugging odd problems you may encounter with ASP.NET.
Code Complete, 2nd Edition by Steve McConnell (Redmond: Microsoft Press, 2004)	This book isn't about .NET, but no list of software-related books is complete without *Code Complete*. It's the essential guide to writing better code.

Summary

In this chapter, we've discussed some of the decisions and information you need to consider before starting your next application. We've seen how to decide between using a Web Site and a Web Application project, investigated the topic of source control, discussed choosing a hosting provider, explored the considerations involved in the use of open source code, and listed some great sources of ASP.NET information.

This information lays strong foundations from which you can build your ASP.NET knowledge, whether it comes from reading this book, or from using other books and online materials.

The topics we've covered in this chapter will likely come into play in any project you may encounter, so the knowledge you've gained here will serve you well in your .NET career.

.NET 2.0 Core Libraries

ASP.NET 2.0 is part of a very large and extensive application framework—the .NET Framework 2.0—and many of the great new features in ASP.NET 2.0 are closely related to improvements to the .NET core libraries. You may have put off learning some of these newer features because they're fairly complex and they don't provide the immediate feedback that you get from a data-bound `GridView`. Think of it this way, though—if these features power ASP.NET, they can really help power your applications.

In this chapter, we'll show you how to use some of our favorite features of the core libraries to solve common problems.

How do I use strings?

One of the simplest ways to render an object to the screen is to convert it to a human-readable string. But how do we do that? And why do we do it? I know these questions seem basic—maybe too basic—but strings are as fundamental to programming as are objects themselves. Allow me to illustrate.

Brad Abrams was a founding member of the .NET common language runtime team way back in 1998. He's also the co-author of many essential books on .NET, including both volumes of the *.NET Framework Standard Library Annotated Reference*.[1] I attended a presentation Brad gave to the Triangle .NET User's Group in Durham, North Carolina, early in 2005. During the question-and-answer period, an audience member—and a friend of mine—asked Brad, "What's your favorite class in the .NET 1.1 common language runtime?"

His answer?

"The string class."

That statement comes from a guy who will forget more about the .NET runtime than I will ever know about it. I still have my .NET class library reference poster, with Brad's autograph right next to the `String` class.

Solution

I've always felt that the string is the most noble of data types. Computers run on ones and zeros, sure, but people don't. They use words, sentences, and paragraphs to communicate. People communicate with strings. The meteoric rise of HTTP, HTML, REST, serialization, and other heavily string-oriented, human-readable techniques vindicates—at least in my mind—my lifelong preference for the humble string.

Of course, you could argue that, as we have so much computing power and bandwidth available today, passing friendly strings around in lieu of opaque binary data is actually practical and convenient. But I wouldn't want to be a killjoy.

Guess what my favorite new .NET 2.0 feature is. Go ahead—guess! Generics? Nope. Partial classes? Nope again. It's the `String.Contains` method. And I'm awfully fond of `String.IsNullOrEmpty`, too.

What I love most about strings is that they have a million and one uses. They're the Swiss Army Knife of data types.

---

[1] Brad Abrams, *.NET Framework Standard Library Annotated Reference* (Boston: Addison-Wesley Professional, 2004).

Regular expressions, for example, are themselves strings:

```
RegEx = "<[a-z]|<!|&#|\Won[a-z]*\s*=|(script\s*:)|expression\(";
```

SQL queries are strings, too:

```
Sql = "SELECT * FROM Customers WHERE State = 'NY'
    ORDER BY ZipCode";
```

Regular Expressions and SQL are mini-languages that wield considerable power—all inside a humble string. I love strings, and so should you. The String class is an integral part of any programmer's toolkit—mastering it is essential.

How do I display an object as a string?

Numeric types, enumerated types, exceptions ... they all serve their purpose in a web application, but none of them is as good as strings at displaying content to users. Luckily, we have a few options for taking the content of these objects and writing it out to a string.

Solution

Every class in .NET should have a meaningful ToString method. ToString magically and automatically converts an object into a human-readable string representation of itself. It's not quite **serialization**, but it's certainly a close cousin.

One classic example of the utility of ToString can be seen in the task of trapping exceptions:

ToStringExample1.cs

```
// Compile and execute from the command line
using System;
class ToStringExample1 {
  public static void Main()
  {
    int x = 0;
    int y = 0;

    try
    {
```

```
    y = 10/x;
    }
  catch (DivideByZeroException ex)
  {
    Console.WriteLine(ex.Message);
  }
  }
}
```

If you do this, all you'll get is the exception message `Attempted to divide by zero`. Good luck troubleshooting your application on that meager bit of information! But what if we change the last line to use `ToString` instead?

ToStringExample2.cs

```
// Compile and execute from the command line
using System;
class ToStringExample2 {
  public static void Main()
  {
    int x = 0;
    int y = 0;

    try
    {
      y = 10/x;
    }
    catch (DivideByZeroException ex)
    {
      Console.WriteLine(ex.ToString());
    }
  }
}
```

When compiled in debug mode, we now get an automatically generated string representation of that particular `Exception` object:

```
System.DivideByZeroException: Attempted to divide by zero.
at ConsoleApplication1.Program.Main(String[] args)
in C:\Program.cs:line 15
```

That's a lot more helpful—you could actually diagnose a problem with this detailed exception information by exploiting the ability of ToString to force the computer to provide human-readable output.

Discussion

Unfortunately, not all .NET classes have good ToString methods. If you have a DataSet, you might naturally try calling DataSet.ToString. Guess what you'll get when you do?

```
System.Data.DataSet
```

That's utterly useless. You might've expected something like this:

```
+-----------------------------------------------------------+
| DataSet1                                                  |
+-----------------------------------------------------------+
| Table1                                                    |
+-----------------------------------------------------------+
| field01 | field02 | field03 | field04    | field05       |
+-----------------------------------------------------------+
|    1    | first   | NULL    | NULL       | NULL          |
|    2    | second  | foo     | 2006-10-31 | 10:30:00      |
|    3    | third   | bar     | 2006-10-31 | 10:30:01      |
+-----------------------------------------------------------+
```

This seems perfectly logical to me, but DataSet.ToString doesn't work that way out of the box.

When you're creating your own classes, include ToString methods that make sense and produce human-readable output, even if the only human who will ever see that output is another programmer. If you're working with someone else's classes, consider overriding the ToString implementation to obtain the proper behavior that should have been present in the first place.

How do I display formatted strings?

When providing user feedback, site elements, or error reporting, you won't just echo data to the user as strings. Along with those strings, you'll echo all kinds of variables: numbers, dates, times, enumerations, and so forth. How do we specify the format of these variables so they display correctly as strings?

Solution

We looked at the `ToString` method very briefly in the previous solution. Considering that it can leverage standard .NET string formatting, you may well be tempted to use `ToString` in conjunction with the concatenation operator (+), as I've done in the following example:

```
"Date is " + DateTime.Now.ToString("MM/dd hh:mm:ss");
```

Here, I'm using `ToString` to specify the format of the `DateTime` object. It might be intuitive, but it's not the best solution. A much more efficient approach that produces identical output is to call the `String.Format` method on that `DateTime` object, as I've done here:

```
String.Format("Date is {0:MM/dd hh:mm:ss}", DateTime.Now);
```

This is reminiscent of one of the classic uses for a string that dates back to the days of C and `sprintf`—for specifying an output format. String formatting is incredibly powerful, but it doesn't have to be complicated—in fact most of the time you'll find yourself performing only simple types of string concatenation.

Here's another example:

```
d.SelectSingleNode("/a/b[value='" + value + "']");
```

While this approach works, it gives us a lot of plus signs and broken string fragments to keep track of. You may forget to close the quotes, or you might lose track of the number of brackets because they're separated by multiple plus signs. Moreover, should you use this code often, there may be serious implications for the performance of your application.

Let's replace that concatenation with a single `String.Format` command:

```
d.SelectSingleNode(String.Format("/a/b[value='{0}']", value));
```

We now have one unbroken string with a simple replacement operation. It's unambiguous, and it performs well.

Some people feel so strongly about using `String.Format` that they vow *never* to use + to concatenate strings ever again. I don't feel quite that strongly about it—I believe that concatenation has its place for very simple tasks. But you should definitely use `String.Format` whenever possible, for these reasons:

- Your code will be cleaner.
- You'll avoid potential concatenation performance problems.
- Using `String.Format` is a far more powerful approach than concatenation.

String Concatenation Versus String Builder

For more information about the performance implications of string concatenation, see the MSDN article titled *Improving String Handling Performance in .NET Framework Applications.*[2]

How Powerful is `String.Format`?

We've only encountered the very simplest string formatting option so far, which is quite basic—direct, numbered replacement:

```
String.Format("I like {1}, {0}, and {2}", "ninjas", "pirates",
    "cowboys");
```

In the example above, the first variable replaces the {0}, the second variable replaces the {1}, and so forth. This code may be easy to understand, but it's not particularly exciting. Let's add some features to make it more compelling.

We'll start by adding the `Format` identifier to specify alignment. A positive value indicates that the string should be right-justified, while a negative means it should

---

[2] http://msdn2.microsoft.com/en-us/library/aa302329.aspx

be left-justified. The value specifies the total length that the resulting string should take when padded with spaces:

```
String.Format("{0,-10}", "left"); // "left      "
String.Format("{0, 10}", "right"); // "     right"
```

Another common way to use the **format string**—the characters to the right of the colon—is to specify the formatting of numbers, dates, and enumerations:

```
String.Format("{0,-8:G2}", 3.14159); // "3.1     "
```

Here's where the real power of `String.Format` reveals itself. `String.Format` has a number of built-in number formatting specifiers, which are shown in the code listing below. Note that each specifier has a relatively easy-to-remember, case-insensitive, single-letter mnemonic associated with it: d for decimal, x for hexadecimal, and so forth:[3]

```
int i = 32768;
String.Format("{0:c}", i); // $32,768 (currency)
String.Format("{0:d}", i); // 32768 (decimal)
String.Format("{0:e}", i); // 3.276800e+004 (scientific notation)
String.Format("{0:f}", i); // 32768.00 (fixed-point)
String.Format("{0:g}", i); // 32768 (general)
String.Format("{0:n}", i); // 32,768.00 (number with commas)
String.Format("{0:p}", i); // 32,768% (percent)
String.Format("{0:r}", i); // 32768 (round trip)
String.Format("{0:x}", i); // 8000 (hexadecimal)
```

We can add a digit to some of the built-in numeric format specifiers to indicate how many decimal places we want the output to display; however, d and x cannot take a numeric format specifier because they require the number to be an integer:

```
String.Format("{0:c3}", i); // $32,768.000
String.Format("{0:c2}", i); // $32,768.00
```

In addition to the pre-built number formatting specifiers, ASP.NET permits the use of custom number formatters. A complete description of all the formatters is beyond

---

[3] Complete descriptions of each of the standard numeric format strings can be found in the online MSDN documentation: http://msdn2.microsoft.com/en-us/library/dwhawy9k.aspx.

the scope of this book, but here are a few examples to give you a glimpse of the possibilities:

```
double d = 1234.56;
String.Format("{0:00.0000}", d); // 1234.5600 (zero placeholder)
String.Format("{0:(#).##}", d); // (1234).56 (digit placeholder)
String.Format("{0:0.0}", d); // 1234.6 (decimal point)
String.Format("{0:0,0}", d); // 1,235 (thousands)
String.Format("{0:0,.}", d); // 1 (number scaling)
String.Format("{0:0%}", d); // 123456% (percent)
String.Format("{0:00e+0}", d); // 12e+2 (scientific notation)
```

These are some of the more common combinations that are available; you can view a more detailed list on the MSDN site.[4]

But what about dates and times? Let's see one of the built-in date formatters in action:

```
String.Format("{0:g}", DateTime.Now);
```

This outputs the current date and time in the following format:

```
8/05/2007 11:13 AM
```

There's a plethora of ways in which a date and time can be formatted, as shown by the following examples (note that I've omitted the call to `String.format` for brevity). These date formatters also come with single-letter mnemonics, although they're perhaps not quite as intuitive as those used to format numbers. The default date format is the general format used in the example above. Formats include:

```
"{0:d}" // 8/21/2007 (short date)
"{0:D}" // Tuesday, 21 August 2007 (long Date)
"{0:f}" // Tuesday, 21 August 2007 11:13 AM (full short)
"{0:F}" // Tuesday, 21 August 2007 11:13:17 AM (Full long)
"{0:g}" // 21/08/2007 11:13 AM (general)
"{0:G}" // 21/08/2007 11:13:17 AM (General long)
"{0:m}" // 21 August (month day)
"{0:o}" // 2007-08-21T11:13:17.4687500+10:00 (round trip)
"{0:R}" // Tue, 21 August 2007 11:13:17 GMT (RFC1123 pattern)
"{0:s}" // 2007-08-21T11:13:17 (sortable)
```

---

[4] http://msdn2.microsoft.com/en-us/library/0c899ak8.aspx

```
"{0:t}" // 11:13 AM (short time)
"{0:T}" // 11:13:17 AM (long Time)
"{0:u}" // 2007-08-21 11:13:17Z (universal)
"{0:U}" // Tuesday, 21 August 2007 1:13:17 AM (Universal GMT)
"{0:Y}" // August 2007 (Year month)
```

Whew, that's quite a list! If you're *still* not quite satisfied with any of the predefined date and time format specifiers, you can use the custom date formats to create your own. Here are a few examples:

```
"{0:dd}"          // 06 (day)
"{0:ddd}"         // Sat (day abbr)
"{0:dddd}"        // Saturday (day full)
"{0:fff}"         // 692 (second fraction)
"{0:gg}"          // A.D. (era)
"{0:hh}"          // 07 (12 hour)
"{0:HH}"          // 19 (24 hour)
"{0:mm}"          // 21 (minute)
"{0:MM}"          // 01 (month)
"{0:MMM}"         // Jan (month abbr)
"{0:MMMM}"        // January (month full)
"{0:ss}"          // 29 (seconds)
"{0:tt}"          // PM (am/pm)
"{0:yy}"          // 07 (year)
"{0:yyyy}"        // 2007 (year full)
"{0:zz}"          // -08 (timezone)
"{0:zzz}"         // -08:00 (timezone full)
"{0:hh:mm:ss}"    // 07:21:29 (separators)
"{0:MM/dd/yyyy}"  // 01/06/2007 (separators)
```

 ### Months and Minutes

Watch out for the minutes and month mnemonic (go on, say that three times fast—I dare you!). The standard, single-letter formatter (m or M) is case-insensitive and means *month*. However, when you begin specifying your own custom format string (using multiple letters, such as mm or MMM), you'll soon discover that case *does* matter.

For custom format strings, a lowercase m means *minutes*, and an uppercase M means *month*. Here's how I remember that: months are "larger" than minutes.

Dates are Culture-sensitive

There is one very important caveat to keep in mind whenever you're working with dates. All date and time output is heavily dependent on the system's current regional settings. Don't assume that because you live in the Eastern Time Zone the names you use for months will be identical to those used by a person living in Kazakhstan, for example. If you're worried about culture-independent date display, use the overloaded version of `String.Format` that accepts a culture:

```
String.Format(
    System.Globalization.CultureInfo.InvariantCulture,
        "{0:d}", d
)
```

If you pass in `InvariantCulture`, you're guaranteed that the date and time output will be universally understood, no matter where your code happens to be running in the world. Tim Berners-Lee would be proud of you for putting the "world" back into World Wide Web!

Discussion

If you need to use a reserved character in a formatting string, you can surround it with single quotes to escape it; your character will show up verbatim in the output. In the example below, I've escaped the percentage symbol:

```
String.Format("{0:##.00'%'", 1.23) // "1.23%"
```

If you still doubt the power of string formatting, consider this little nugget:

```
int i = 1;
String.Format("{0:yes;;no}", i);
```

The output of this line of code depends on the value of the variable i—a value of zero outputs no, and a non-zero value outputs yes. What we have here is an example of **conditional formatting**—an output that is conditional on the value of the variable passed in. Conditional formats take the following form:

```
String.Format("{0:positive;negative;zero}", variable);
```

As you can see, the three possible outputs of a conditionally formatted string are separated by semicolons. If *variable* has a value that is positive, the first string following the colon is displayed (in this case, *positive*); if *variable* is negative, the second string (*negative*) is displayed; and if *variable* has a value of 0, the third string (*zero*) is displayed.

Here's another example—one that's used quite often:

```
String.Format("{0:$#,##0.00;($#,##0.00);Zero}", d);
```

This conditional format string follows the accountant's convention of placing negative values in parentheses, and replaces the value 0 with the string Zero.

As you can see from the large number of examples listed in this solution, ASP.NET contains two extremely powerful tools for formatting strings: String.Format and, to a lesser degree, ToString. Yet these methods are just two small parts of the String class.

Strings, I've fallen in love with you all over again.

How do I use generics?

The biggest language change in the .NET 2.0 Framework was the introduction of **generics**—object types that allow us to define properties and methods without locking them down to a specific class. This gives us the ability to reuse code in a very efficient and type-safe manner.

Solution

You'll want to become really handy with generics for two reasons:

1. The framework makes heavy use of generics, so you'll need to understand them in order to put the .NET Framework to good use.

2. Generics can really supercharge and streamline your code. Doing more with less code is a great thing—after all, writing less code means writing fewer bugs!

Using generic collections, you can make your code more powerful and simpler at the same time. You don't even need to rewrite your container code to benefit! The .NET 2.0 Array object implements some interfaces—including IList, ICollection, and IEnumerable—in System.Collections.Generic, giving a lot of new power to old Array-based code without any additional effort on your part.

Prior to .NET 2.0, the .NET Framework offered two kinds of collection objects: we could store objects in untyped collections (like the ArrayList), or typed containers (like a StringCollection or an integer array). Both options had their problems.

Untyped containers provided flexibility and features, but at a heavy price: developers who used them had to give up type safety. We always needed to cast objects to retrieve the containers, and each addition or retrieval incurred a performance hit. Typed containers were safer and offered better performance, but they required code to be repeated for each object that the container held. Developers had to write a CustomerCollection, an OrderCollection, a ProductCollection, and a SupplierCollection, even though they all did the same things! Additionally, since each container had to re-implement each feature, typed containers generally weren't as rich in features as their untyped counterparts.

Generic containers give us the best of both worlds—we can store groups of objects using the flexibility of untyped containers, and gain the type safety and performance benefits of typed containers. The generic class is implemented only once, but can be declared and used with any type.

The best way to illustrate these benefits is with an example that compares the ways in which ASP.NET 2.0's generic collections are better than those of ASP.NET 1.1. Suppose we were building an application to display our comic book collection to the world. We'd probably start with a ComicBook class:

```
public class ComicBook
{
  public ComicBook(string title)
  {
    this.title = title;
  }

  public string Title
  {
    get
    {
      return this.title;
    }
  }
```

```
  }
  string title;
}
```

With .NET 1.1, we might create our comic book collection using an `ArrayList`:

```
ArrayList comics = new ArrayList();
comics.Add(new ComicBook("The Amazing Spiderman #1"));
comics.Add(new ComicBook("X-Men #3"));
```

This might seem fine on the surface, but imagine someone came along and added the following code:

```
comics.Add(new BaseBallCard("Mickey Mantle Rookie"));
```

Hey! That's not a comic book!

No, it's not. But as far as the `ArrayList` is concerned, it's perfectly valid—the `ArrayList` is a collection of `Object` instances. Since every class is derived from `Object`, the `ArrayList` isn't very discriminating. Ideally we'd like our classes to be more strongly typed.

It was possible to create strongly typed classes back in the days of .NET 1.1, but it typically required a lot of code. Not only that, but you had to write a lot of repetitive code if you planned on using strongly typed collections for *every* type that you wanted to aggregate. Amit Goel's article from 2003 gives an insight into just how much code was required to implement generics in .NET 1.1.[5]

With .NET 2.0, we can avoid all this repetitive code *and* gain type safety using a **generic collection**—a container that can be used to store objects of any class. We can specify a generic version of the `ArrayList` above using the syntax `List<T>`. The *T* between the brackets is called a **type parameter**, and it indicates that the type of the member objects in the list has not yet been specified. This could be any object class at all—which is why its container is called a generic collection.

We only specify the type of object to be held by the list at the time we create an instance of `List<T>`. For example, we could specify that our list should only contain

---

[5] http://www.ondotnet.com/pub/a/dotnet/2003/03/10/collections.html

`ComicBook` instances (or instances of classes that inherit from `ComicBook`). Here's how we'd do that:

```
List<ComicBook> comics = new List<ComicBook>();
comics.Add(new ComicBook("Sandman"));
comics.Add(new ComicBook("Arkham Asylum"));

// The following line does not compile.
comics.Add(new BaseBallCard("Kirby Pucket Rookie"));
```

With this additional level of detail in place, we can no longer slip a `BaseBallCard` instance into our `List<T>`—it won't compile. Providing the same type safety for an `ArrayList` would have required a considerable amount of additional code.

Generic collections have other advantages over untyped collections; for instance, they offer improved performance when storing value types in the collection. Here's an example:

```
ArrayList randomNumbers = new ArrayList();
randomNumbers.Add(8); //boxing occurs
randomNumbers.Add(8);
randomNumbers.Add(8);
int firstNumber = (int)randomNumbers[0];
```

In the above code listing, the `Add` method for the `ArrayList` accepts a parameter of type `Object`. This means that every time you add a value type (like an integer, as we've done here), the value type has to be cast to an instance of type `Object`—a process known as boxing.

When we retrieve a value, unboxing occurs. Because boxing and unboxing are expensive operations, doing them too often can hurt your application's performance.

Boxing and Unboxing your Objects

The terms **boxing** and **unboxing** refer to the way that C# handles the conversion between value types (primitive types such as integers) and reference types (such as classes and more complex data structures). Converting from a value type to a reference type is referred to as boxing, because the value is copied to a container in memory (a "box") where it is stored. Converting from a reference type back to a value type is called unboxing, as the value is copied out of the container and into the appropriate location.

While the handling of types in this manner is convenient, both the boxing and unboxing operations take a small amount of time. For large numbers of objects, this can cause a performance bottleneck.

We can avoid the performance penalty incurred in the above code by using a generic collection. Here's the same example rewritten as a generic collection:

```
List<int> randomNumbers = new List<int>();
randomNumbers.Add(8); // no boxing occurs
randomNumbers.Add(8);
randomNumbers.Add(8);
int firstNumber = randomNumbers[0]; // no casting necessary
```

Not only does the above code perform better than our previous attempt, which used an ArrayList, but it's also cleaner: when retrieving a value from the generic list, as we've done in the last line of code above, there's no need to manually cast the object.

Generics: Under the Hood

How do generic containers work? The type conversion magic is performed by the JIT, or Just In Time, compiler at runtime. For example, if your application uses a generic List object to store integers, then the first time your application references that class, the JIT compiler will create a List that's strongly typed to hold only int objects. From then on, every time you reference a List of ints, the JIT compiler will simply reuse the integer-typed List, rather than create a new class from scratch. Collections of custom classes (such as, for example, Customer objects) are even simpler—the JIT compiler only needs to create a single List for storing objects of the generic class object. The List can then be reused to store any reference object that we choose.

What's a Predicate?

Some of the most powerful utility methods provided by generic collections make use of predicates. But what *is* a predicate?

A **predicate** is a function that takes an element from a generic list and returns a Boolean result. When used as a hook for accessing a collection of generic objects, a predicate makes it easy for us to perform bulk operations on the objects without needing to know their types.

One example of a predicate in use is the `Find` method. To use `Find` on a generic collection, you must write code for the body of the method to return `true` if a matching element in the collection is found. The .NET runtime takes over the grunt work of looping through the collection—all we have to do is fill in the business logic.

Other functions in the `System.Delegate` library—actions, converters, and comparers—have been defined for use in generic collection methods, but in this chapter we'll focus most heavily on predicates.

How do I filter items in a generic collection?

The benefits we gain from using generics are all well and good, but how do we filter and retrieve groups of items from a generic collection?

Solution

To filter items in a generic collection, we use the `FindAll` method with a **match predicate**—a predicate that returns true when an item in the collection meets our custom filter criteria.

Let's dig into some examples. To begin with, we'll look at how we can use the `List.FindAll` method to find all employees who are managers by filtering them from a collection of `Employees`; we'll name this method `GetManagers`. The syntax for defining the collection of employees is `List<Employee>`.

To keep things simple, we'll assume that we have in place a basic `Employee` class, and a method called `GetEmployees` for retrieving `Employee` objects from the database:

```
                                                    Employee.cs (excerpt)
public class Employee : Person {
  public int EmployeeID;
  public bool IsManager;
}

public List<Employee> GetEmployees() {
    return new List<Employee>();
}
```

Our `GetManagers` method will first retrieve all employees. We'll then call `FindAll` and pass the `IsManager` method as the match predicate:

```
public List<Employee> GetManagers()
{
  List<Employee> employeeList = GetEmployees();
  return employeeList.FindAll(IsManager);
}
public bool IsManager(Employee emp)
{
  return emp.IsManager == true;
}
```

Great! The `FindAll` method iterated through the collection and jumped into the `IsManager` function for each `Employee` in the list. Every time the function returned `true`, `FindAll` added the `Employee` to the list of managers.

We can simplify this process slightly by replacing that `IsManager` method with an anonymous delegate.

Whoah—the jargon is flowing thick and fast now! Let's break that down:

■ A **delegate** is a type of function pointer. Unlike the function pointers that are used in languages such as C and C++, delegates are both object oriented and type-safe. For a deeper understanding of delegates, read the MSDN article "An Introduction to Delegates" by Jeffrey Richter.[6]

■ An **anonymous delegate** is a delegate function that is declared *inline*.

---

[6] http://msdn.microsoft.com/msdnmag/issues/01/04/net/default.aspx

Some predicates don't offer any values as reusable functions, so using an anonymous delegate allows us to specify a return value that we can actually use, while at the same time keeping our code simple. Here's how our `GetManagers` function looks once we introduce an anonymous delegate predicate:

Predicates.aspx.cs (excerpt)

```
public List<Employee> GetManagers()
{
    List<Employee> employeeList = GetEmployees();
    return employeeList.FindAll(
        delegate (Employee emp)
        { return emp.IsManager == true; }
    );
}
```

As you can see, the result is identical functionality that's achieved using less code.

There's another case that might cause you to use anonymous delegates: the situation that arises when a predicate needs additional parameters. List methods like `Find` and `FindAll` take a single parameter of type `Predicate<T>`. In English, this means that the predicate doesn't have access to anything other than the item in the collection to which it's being passed.

To see what I'm talking about, let's experiment with a function that looks up an `Employee` by the `Employee`'s id. Here's how you might try to write this function without using an anonymous delegate:

```
public static Employee Get(int id)
{
    List<Employee> EmployeeList = GetEmployees();
    return EmployeeList.Find(
        EmployeeMatch(Employee employee, int id)
    );
}

// THIS DOESN'T COMPILE - NOT A VALID PREDICATE
public static bool EmployeeMatch(Employee employee, int id)
{
    return employee.EmployeeID == id;
}
```

Unfortunately, that code won't compile—try, and you'll receive a series of errors. The compiler can't make sense of our attempt to pass two parameters to the predicate, and goes looking for additional parentheses and semicolons to compensate. This is because Find(Predicate<T>) method can accept only one parameter—the generic type object (in this case, Employee). Here, we can use an anonymous delegate to write our logic inside the Get function, and give us access to the id parameter:

Predicates.aspx.cs *(excerpt)*

```
public Employee Get(int id)
{
    List<Employee> employeeList = GetEmployees();
    return employeeList.Find(
        delegate(Employee emp)
        { return emp.EmployeeID == id; }
    );
}
```

This procedure is referred to as **local variable capturing**; in this case it's the id that has been "captured."

How can I get more use out of my custom logic?

In the section called "How do I use generics?", we promised we'd show you how to get more out of the code you've already written. Let's look at two solutions to the "Too Much Code" conundrum.

Solutions

In making the most of your code, you have two options: you can use generic methods or reusable delegates.

Using Generic Methods

Of course, one of the benefits of generic methods is that they can be reused with collections of different types. A very simple example is a function that sorts a collection and writes it to the console window:

```
static void WriteSortedValues<T>(List<T> list)
{
  list.Sort();
  list.ForEach(
    delegate(T item) { Console.WriteLine(item); }
  )
}
```

 ForEach Uses Action Delegates

In the above example, we're using the ForEach method with an **action delegate**. An action delegate is another type of anonymous delegate, only it doesn't return anything. The idea behind an action delegate is that it defines an action to be performed for each item in the collection. This compares with predicate delegates, which contain the decision logic. This action delegate uses the same logic that we saw with Find and FindAll in the section called "How do I filter items in a generic collection?".

The WriteSortedValues function is generic, as indicated by the <T> parameter that follows the function name. When we call WriteSortedValues and pass it a List<int>, .NET knows to replace those Ts with ints. And as WriteSortedValues is generic, we can use it with lists of any type that .NET knows how to sort. The following example shows the function in action, handling three different types of objects—a string, an int, and a DateTime:

Predicates.aspx.cs *(excerpt)*

```
private void SortingDemonstration()
{
  string[] names = { "Bob", "Sue", "Jim", "Edgar" };
  int[] values = { 456, 234, 567, 123, 890 };
  DateTime[] dates = {
      new DateTime(1950,2,3),
      new DateTime(1970,4,5),
      new DateTime(2000,1,1)
  };
  WriteSortedValues(new List<string>(names));
  WriteSortedValues(new List<int>(values));
  WriteSortedValues(new List<DateTime>(dates));
}
```

We can't necessarily use this solution with a collection of custom objects, such as `List<Employee>`, since the `List` object doesn't know how to sort them. An attempt to call `WriteSortedValues(List<Employee>)` would compile, but it would throw the runtime error: `Failed to compare two elements in the array`. It's not tough to fix that problem, though—we can either implement the `IComparable` interface in our `Employee` class, or we can call the overloaded `Sort` method and pass it a `Comparison` or `IComparer` delegate.[7]

Using Reusable Delegates

Most of our samples so far have implemented predicates and actions as anonymous delegates. We looked at the reasons for this (simpler code, local variable capturing) in the section called "How do I filter items in a generic collection?". However, you should keep an eye out for delegates that can be reused, and promote them to methods.

For example, let's assume that an application we've written for our employer consists of multiple classes, including `Customers`, `Employees`, `Stores`, and an `Address` structure.[8] This `Address` contains a `Region` property.

Our company is headquartered in California, so for various reasons (sales tax, employee taxes, benefits, and so on), we may want to filter our different lists so that our results include only items whose `Region` is California.

As such, our delegate method for retrieving Californian employees might look like this:

```
return employeeList.Find(
    p.Address.Region == "California"
);
```

We can move this into a reusable delegate method as follows:

---

[7] For more information on implementing the `IComparable` interface, see David Hayden's excellent blog post [http://codebetter.com/blogs/david.hayden/archive/2005/03/06/56584.aspx].

[8] A structure, represented by the keyword `struct` in C#, is a composite data type. A structure can contain fields, methods, constants, constructors, properties, indexers, operators and other structure types.

```
                                              Predicates.aspx.cs (excerpt)

public static bool IsCalifornian(Person p)
{
  return (p.Address.Region == "California");
}
```

Now we can use that method with *any* list that contains the Address structure—for example, a list of Employees or Customers:

```
                                              Predicates.aspx.cs (excerpt)

public List<Employee> GetCaliforniaEmployees()
{
  List<Employee> employees = GetEmployees();
  return employees.FindAll(Person.IsCalifornian);
}
public List<Customer> GetNonCaliforniaCustomers()
{
  List<Customer> customers = GetCustomers();
  customers.RemoveAll(Person.IsCalifornian);
  return customers;
}
```

In the above code listing, we're using the same predicate in two different ways. In the first example, GetCaliforniaEmployees, we're using it with FindAll to return all employees who have a Californian address. In the second example, GetNonCaliforniaCustomers, we're using the predicate with RemoveAll to remove all Customers with Californian addresses from the customer list.

How do I convert generic lists to specific classes?

It's all very well to make the most of our code using generic lists. But once our objects are in a generic list, how do we get them back out again?

Solution

Using the ConvertAll function with a **converter delegate** is the easiest way to convert a list of generic objects into specific types. As you might have inferred from its name, a converter delegate is yet another incarnation of anonymous delegates, but one that performs the conversion of each item in a list from a generic object to a specific class.

To see `ConvertAll` in action, let's convert a list of `DateTime` values to a list of other types. First let's build up a quick `List<DateTime>`:

Predicates.aspx.cs (excerpt)

```
List<DateTime> dates = new List<DateTime>();
for (DateTime d = DateTime.Now;
              d < DateTime.Now.AddMonths(10);
              d.AddDays(2)
  ) { dates.Add(d); }
```

Now we'll call `dates.ConvertAll` with a few different converter delegates to show how easy this approach to converting objects is:

Predicates.aspx.cs (excerpt)

```
// Convert date list to short date (string) list
List<string> strings = dates.ConvertAll<string>(
  delegate(DateTime value)
    { return value.ToShortDateString(); }
  );

// Convert date list to day of year (int) list
List<int> ints = dates.ConvertAll<int>(
  delegate(DateTime value)
    { return value.DayOfYear; }
  );

// Convert date list to daylight savings time (bool) list
List<bool> bools = dates.ConvertAll<bool>(
  delegate(DateTime value)
    { return value.IsDaylightSavingTime(); }
  );
```

Note that we're taking advantage of type inference to simplify the syntax a little. You can define the converter source and destination types explicitly if you want, like this:

```
List<string> strings = dates.ConvertAll<string>
  (new Converter<DateTime, string>
    (
      delegate(DateTime d) { return d.ToShortDateString(); }
    )
  );
```

However, as the compiler can see what you're converting from and to, it will infer those types for you.

How do I concatenate delimited strings from object properties?

The sample code we've looked at so far has been reasonably simple. Let's look at a more difficult problem—building a delimited list composed of values that are calculated from object properties.

Suppose we have a simple class named `Party`:

```
public class Party
{
  public Party(DateTime partyDate)
  {
    this.partyDate = partyDate;
  }

  public DateTime PartyDate
  {
    get
    {
      return partyDate;
    }
  }

  DateTime partyDate;
}
```

Consider the scenario that we need to concatenate instances of this class together. The desired output is a pipe-delimited list of the number of days between now and the `SomeDate` value.

Solution

Our first step is to determine where to place the logic that will perform the calculation and concatenation. The best place for this logic is in a predicate method that's called from the collection's `Join` method.

Performing predicate-based operations on your generic collections can really simplify and enhance your code.

The following example, in which we concatenate our `Party` objects, is not only useful on its own—it should also help to demonstrate the thought process behind moving from loop-based logic to clean, simple code that leverages predicates.

Let's start by defining a new `Join` method that can take in a delimiter, an enumeration, and an instance of the converter delegate. The converter delegate has the following signature:

```
delegate TOutput Converter<TIn,TOutput> (TIn input)
```

As an argument to the `Join` method, we specify that `TOutput` should be a `String`, leaving the input as a generic object:

PartyDemo.cs *(excerpt)*

```
public static string Join<T>(string delimiter
                           , IEnumerable<T> items
                           , Converter<T, string> converter)
{
  StringBuilder builder = new StringBuilder();
  foreach(T item in items)
  {
    builder.Append(converter(item));
    builder.Append(delimiter);
  }
  if (builder.Length > 0)
  {
    builder.Length = builder.Length - delimiter.Length;
```

```
  }
  return builder.ToString();
}
```

With this method defined, we can concatenate an `Array` or collection of `Party` instances, like so:

PartyDemo.cs *(excerpt)*

```
Party[] parties = new Party[]
{
  new Party(DateTime.Parse("1/23/2006"))
    , new Party(DateTime.Parse("12/25/2005"))
    , new Party(DateTime.Parse("5/25/2004"))
};
string result = Join<Party>('|', parties
    , delegate(Party item)
  {
    TimeSpan ts = DateTime.Parse("11/24/2006") - item.PartyDate;
    return ((int)ts.TotalDays).ToString();
  });
Console.WriteLine(result);
```

Note that we make use of an anonymous delegate that examines an instance of `Party` and calculates the number of days that have passed since `PartyDate`. This calculation returns a string that will be concatenated to the previous item in the list.

That code produces the following output: `305|334|913`.

Discussion

Here's what you'll gain by moving from "dumb" loops to predicate-based operations:

▨ Your code will be more reusable, since you can reuse generic methods with different objects. A good example of this is the ActiveRecord implementation in SubSonic, an open source Data Access Layer that we'll be exploring in detail in Chapter 17.[9]

---

[9] http://www.codeplex.com/actionpack/Wiki/View.aspx?title=ActiveRecord

▓ Your code will leverage framework methods rather than require you to write your own repetitive code. Less custom code means fewer custom bugs.

▓ Your library code will be likely to perform better, since it will be strongly typed.

Where to Sort and Filter

In this solution, and those prior to it, we've looked at ways to sort and filter objects in the application layer. But don't take this to mean that you should necessarily handle tasks like this in your application code rather than in the database. Generally, databases will be more efficient when it comes to sorting and filtering, although complex operations like string manipulation are better handled by application code.

How do I batch operations with large collections?

Every now and then, we run into programming situations in which we need to perform an action on a large amount of data. Such large operations can really put a strain on system resources, such as memory, if we're not careful.

Suppose, for example, that you have a blog engine with thousands of blog posts stored in a database. You decide to build an export page that allows the site's users to export every post in the system to a file using a serialization format such as BlogML.[10]

Solutions

A couple of solutions are available to address this problem. We'll first take a look at a naïve solution, and then explore an improved version that uses iterators.

The Naïve Solution

First, let's look at a naïve solution. Since we don't have the space or time to build an entire blog engine just for this demonstration, we'll have to do some hand-waving

---

[10] BlogML is an XML format designed for storing the entire content of a blog—most often for the purpose of transferring content from one blog to another. Read more at http://www.blogml.com/.

here and pretend that we've already defined a `BlogPost` class and created a database consisting of thousands of blog post records.

In this solution, we'll need a method to retrieve every blog post:

```
static ICollection<BlogPost> GetAllBlogPosts()
{
  // returns all blog posts
}
```

We'll also need a method for serializing a blog post to a file via a `TextWriter` instance:

```
public void Serialize(BlogPost post, TextWriter writer)
{
  // Serializes post to the writer.
}
```

In our naïve solution, we simply load a collection containing every blog post and iterate over each one, serializing it to the file:

```
ICollection<BlogPost> allPosts = GetAllDataBatch();
using(TextWriter writer = CreateXmlStream())
{
  int i = 0;
  foreach (BlogPost post in allPosts)
  {
    SerializeBlogPost(post, writer);
    writer.Flush();
  }
}
```

The Naïve Solution's Pitfalls

There are two problems with this naïve approach. First, we have to load every blog record into memory before we can start writing posts to a file. If there are a lot of records, this could use up a lot of memory and damage the site's performance. The other problem is that we're flushing each post to the file, one at a time. Ideally, we should only be writing to the file in batches.

To Flush or to Batch?

Note that classes that implement `TextWriter` usually handle the task of flushing contents to the file appropriately—the developer doesn't need to worry about this detail.

But imagine if, instead of flushing contents to a file, we were calling SQL statements. In this case, it might be better to batch groups of statements together.

The `BatchIterator` Class Solution

There are a few techniques that we could use to improve the memory usage and performance issues discussed in our naïve solution. One optimization we could make to that solution would be to pull in records from the database one batch at a time. Let's look at using iterators to implement this optimization in a clean and re-usable manner.

The iterator is a new language feature that was introduced with C# 2.0. As an example, we could use iterators to create a class to iterate over "batches" of data, pulling each batch of data from the database when we need it, rather than loading it all at the start. Allow me to explain.

Our first step is to define a generic delegate that will return a collection containing a "batch" of blog posts:

BatchIterator.cs *(excerpt)*

```
public delegate ICollection<T> BatchSource<T>(int batchIndex);
```

This method returns a generic collection that corresponds to the specified `batchIndex`.

Next, we'll define our new `BatchIterator` class:

BatchIterator.cs *(excerpt)*

```
public class BatchIterator<T> : IEnumerable<ICollection<T>> ❶
{
  BatchSource<T> batchDataSource;
  private int batchIndex = 0;
  public BatchIterator(BatchSource<T> batchSource) ❷
```

```
  {
    this.batchDataSource = batchSource;
  }
  public IEnumerator<ICollection<T>> GetEnumerator() ❸
  {
    // First batch.
    ICollection<T> nextBatch = this.batchDataSource(0);
    while(nextBatch != null)
    {
      yield return nextBatch;
      nextBatch = this.batchDataSource(++batchIndex);
    }
  }
  IEnumerator IEnumerable.GetEnumerator()
  {
    return GetEnumerator();
  }
}
```

Let's walk through some of the specifics of this class:

❶ You'll notice that the BatchIterator class itself is a generic class. It implements the generic interface IEnumerable<T>, but in this case T just happens to be ICollection<T>. Confusing? Yes, especially when you're not very familiar with generics. But if you think of a BatchIterator as a collection of collections, this approach should start to make sense.

❷ The constructor of this class takes a BatchSource<T> delegate as a parameter. As you'll recall, earlier we defined this delegate to return an instance of ICollection<T>. This constructor method will be used to populate the collections that we are iterating over with this class.

❸ Finally, we get to the GetEnumerator method, which we need in order to implement the IEnumerable<T> interface. This method defines the approach we'll take to iterate over the contents of the BatchIterator. First, we populate a collection using batchDataSource, which is our delegate of type BatchSource:

```
    ICollection<T> nextBatch = this.batchDataSource(0);
```

Then, we start a loop while `nextBatch` is `null`. At this point we reach what appears to be a particularly odd line of code—especially if you've never used an iterator before:

```
yield return nextBatch;
```

This tells the iterator to place a bookmark at that line of code, and returns the `nextBatch` instance. Then, when the code asks for the next item in the enumeration, code execution begins again right where it left off at the bookmark.

To help solidify this concept, let's rewrite our naïve solution using the `BatchIterator` class. First, we'll need to define a method that meets the `BatchSource` delegate method signature:

Iterators.aspx.cs (excerpt)

```
static ICollection<BlogPost> GetPostBatch(int index)
{
  // Gets the next batch of blog posts from
  // the database corresponding to the index.
}
```

Then, we simply create an instance of the batch iterator, passing in the method we used to populate each batch of blog posts:

Iterators.aspx.cs (excerpt)

```
BatchIterator<BlogPost> batches =
  new BatchIterator<BlogPost>(GetPostBatch);
```

Finally, we can iterate over each collection of blog posts:

Iterators.aspx.cs (excerpt)

```
using (TextWriter writer = CreateXmlStream())
{
  foreach (ICollection<BlogPost> blogPostBatch in batches)
  {
    // At this point, the iterator is stopped at the following
    // line in the method GetEnumerator()
```

```
    // yield return nextBatch;
    // The next time GetEnumerator() is called,
    // it will execute the next line of code:
    // nextBatch = this.batchDataSource(++batchIndex);
    foreach (BlogPost post in blogPostBatch)
    {
      SerializeBlogPost(post, writer);
    }
    writer.Flush();
  }
}
```

The beauty of this code is that rather than loading all blog posts into memory at once, the BatchIterator only loads a few blog posts at a time, depending on how many blog posts are returned by the method GetPostBatch. It also calls the Flush method after each small collection of blog posts—a more efficient way of streaming all the blog post records into a file.

As it uses generics, this BatchIterator class can be used any time you need to iterate over a large set of data and perform an action on that data in small chunks.

How do I choose the right collection?

Making effective use of data collections is an essential skill of software developers. Nearly all computer science programs require students to take one or more courses focused solely on data structures.

The various collection types within the .NET Framework implement many of the most common data structures. The MSDN reference site lists the following as the most commonly used collection types:[11]

- Array
- ArrayList and List
- HashTable and Dictionary
- SortedList and SortedDictionary
- Queue
- Stack

---

[11] http://msdn2.microsoft.com/en-us/library/0ytkdh4s.aspx

Of course, there are more collection types than these, but for the most part, you can get a lot done with just the types presented here. The big question is, how do we choose one collection over another?

Solutions

Your choice of collection should, of course, be based on the role it will serve. Performance and memory considerations should also influence your decision. Some of the questions you need to ask yourself before you choose a collection include:

- Do I need to access elements at random, or will I only need to access them sequentially?
- If I need random access, is it good enough to access them using an index, or will I need to access them with a key?
- Does the collection need to grow, or do I know its size in advance?
- Do I need to be able to sort elements?

The Array

The lowly but powerful Array is the simplest of collection types. It's represented in memory as a sequence of values or references (depending on whether the array is storing value types or reference types, respectively).

An Array is useful when performance is an issue and you know how many elements you will need to store in advance.

The .NET Framework Design Guidelines recommend that you don't use an Array as the return type of a public property.[12] Most of the time, arrays are used in low-level programming as parameters to methods—for example, when working with streams:

```
byte[] data = new byte[] {0x0f, 0x0e, 0x13};
data[0] = 0xff; // random access
MemoryStream stream = new MemoryStream(data);
```

As the above code demonstrates, one benefit of using arrays is that the syntax for instantiating an Array in C# is very human readable.

---

[12] http://msdn2.microsoft.com/en-us/library/k2604h5s.aspx#ctl00_LibFrame_ctl18img

The `ArrayList` and the `List<T>`

The `Array` quickly loses its charm when you don't know in advance the number of items that you need to store. The `ArrayList` object fills this void; it's a replacement for an `Array` that's capable of growing dynamically.

The `ArrayList` basically implements the same interface as the `Array`, but includes methods for adding new items:

```
ArrayList items = new ArrayList(new byte[] { 0x0f, 0x0e, 0x13 });
items[0] = 0x00; // Random access
items.Add(0xff); // Dynamically growing the ArrayList
```

Notice that instantiating an `ArrayList` is not as syntactically clean as it is with an `Array`. However, because the constructor of an `ArrayList` takes in an `ICollection`, and `Array` implements the `ICollection` interface, you can achieve the desired result with something that vaguely resembles our nice, neat `Array` syntax, as I've done above.

One problem with this code is that the `ArrayList` accepts items of type `Object`. This means that storing and retrieving values causes boxing and unboxing to take place, which can create a performance bottleneck. It's in situations like this that the generic `List<T>` class can be particularly useful.

In fact, the `List<T>` class possesses so many improvements under the hood that the Microsoft Framework team recommends it over the `ArrayList` in almost all cases. Let's revisit the previous code snippet, which I've rewritten to use the `List<T>` class:

```
List<byte> items = new List<byte>(
    new byte[] { 0x0f, 0x0e, 0x13 });
items[0] = 0x00;
items.Add(0xff);
```

As you can see, the code basically looks the same, but now it's also type-safe, the result of which is that we've avoided the boxing and unboxing of each item in the list.

The `Hashtable` and the `Dictionary`

One potential problem with accessing elements via an index is that the index for a given item in the collection can change over time. Consider the following code sample:

```
List<int> scores = new List<int>(new int[] {962, 175, 238});
Console.WriteLine("At index 0 we have: " + scores[0]);
scores.Insert(0, 23);
Console.WriteLine(scores[1] + " is now t index 1.");
```

The code adds three integers (in this case, high scores in a video game) to the `List` instance, then writes out the value at index 0—the value 962—to the console. We then insert another value at index 0, and write out the value stored at index 1. As you can see, the value 962 is now stored at index 1. This situation is problematic if your application relies on a stored value being retrieved from the same index at which it was inserted.

Using a `Hashtable` instead of a `List<T>` would allow us to associate a key with each value. We might choose to use the person's name as the key, to ensure that our key-value relationship is maintained, as I've done in the following code listing:

```
Hashtable scores = new Hashtable();
scores.Add("Phil", 196); // boxing occurs
scores.Add("Jon", 250);
scores.Add("Scott", 750);
scores.Add("Jeff", 901);
Console.WriteLine("Phil's Score is: " + scores["Phil"]);
```

While lookups are extremely fast, the speed at which a `Hashtable` performs the lookup comes at the cost of increased memory usage.

The `Dictionary` class is the generic equivalent of the `Hashtable`; while a `Hashtable` only stores an `Object` for the key and value, a `Dictionary` allows us to specify the type of both the key and value, and thereby create a strongly typed hash table. Because storage and retrievals from a `Dictionary` are not subject to boxing or unboxing, the performance of these operations is greatly increased. Let's see `Dictionary` in action:

```
Dictionary<string, int> scores = new Dictionary<string, int>();
scores.Add("Phil", 196); //no boxing occurs.
scores.Add("Jon", 250);
scores.Add("Scott", 750);
scores.Add("Jeff", 901);
Console.WriteLine("Phil's Score is: " + scores["Phil"]);
```

SortedList and SortedDictionary

Continuing the example of video game scores that we discussed above, let's imagine that our application needed to access a score both by index *and* by key. For example, suppose we wanted to keep the scores in an alphabetical order based on user names—using a Hashtable would give us no guarantee that the items would remain in any particular order.

The SortedList and SortedDictionary classes, both of which come in generic and non-generic flavors, are perfect for such a situation. While the interfaces for these classes are largely the same, for this discussion we'll focus on SortedList. The following code demonstrates a SortedList in action:

```
SortedList<string, int> scores = new SortedList<string, int>();
scores.Add("Phil", 196);
scores.Add("Jon", 250);
scores.Add("Scott", 750);
scores.Add("Jeff", 901);
Console.WriteLine("Scores in alphabetical order");
foreach(string key in scores.Keys)
{
  Console.WriteLine("{0}: {1}", key, scores[key]);
}
// I can still access score by key.
Console.WriteLine("Phil's Score is: " + scores["Phil"]);
```

Although this code has added our name-score combinations in random order, when we iterate over the sorted list, the scores will be displayed in alphabetical order:

```
Jeff: 901
Jon: 250
Phil: 196
Scott: 750
```

We can pass in an `IComparer` instance to apply a different sort to our items. For example, suppose we wanted to sort the items on the basis of the lengths of the users' names, rather than in alphabetical order. We could write a quick class that implements `IComparer` to achieve this:

```
public class KeyLengthComparer : IComparer<string>
{
  public int Compare(string x, string y)
  {
    return x.Length.CompareTo(y.Length);
  }
}
```

We'd then pass this class into the constructor for `SortedList`:

```
SortedList<string, int> scores =
    new SortedList<string, int>(new KeyLengthComparer());
```

So, how can you choose between using `SortedList` and `SortedDictionary`? According to the MSDN documentation,[13] these two classes have very similar object models, although the `SortedDictionary` does not support the efficient random access of its `Key` and `Value` collections by index.

These classes' performance in retrieving items is also similar, though the `SortedList` uses less memory than the `SortedDictionary`. If your collections are quite large, and memory usage is a concern, the `SortedList` is the class to use. However, for smaller collections that don't need to be accessed by an index, a `SortedDictionary` is the way to go.

Queue

A **queue** is a **First In, First Out (FIFO)** collection. It's easy to think of queues in terms of waiting in line to enter a theater—the first person to get into line is the first person to enter the theater.

In thinking about the circumstances under which we might use a queue, we need to consider why queues form in the real world. Queues usually form because there

---

[13] http://msdn2.microsoft.com/en-us/library/ms132319.aspx

is more demand for a particular action or item than the system can meet. So there may be fifty people waiting to go into the theater, but only two people selling tickets.

In software development terms, queues are useful when we need to store messages in the order in which they were received so that we can handle them sequentially.

As a demonstration, let's look at some code for an imaginary blog engine. Every comment in the system needs to be submitted to a third-party web service that will determine whether the comment is spam or not.

First, we instantiate a `Queue<Comment>` as a private static instance:

```
static Queue<Comment> queue = new Queue<Comment>();
```

Our method for adding comments to the `Queue` needs first to obtain a lock on the `Queue` for thread safety, because we'll be using another thread to read from the `Queue`. Here's how we obtain that lock:

```
public void AddToFilterQueue(Comment comment)
{
  lock(queue)
  {
    queue.Enqueue(comment);
  }
}
```

Every time a user submits a comment, the `AddToFilterQueue` method is called, which immediately adds the comment to the queue. We need to create a method to process this queue in a separate background thread:

```
public void ProcessQueue()
{
  Queue<Comment> localQueue = new Queue<Comment>();

  // Keep the queue locked for as short as possible.
  lock (queue)
  {
    // Put comments from global queue into local queue.
    while(queue.Count > 0) localQueue.Enqueue(queue.Dequeue());

    // Tell any waiting threads we're done with the queue.
```

```
    Monitor.PulseAll(queue);
  }
  while(localQueue.Count > 0)
  {
    CommentService.Filter(comment);
  }
}
```

One thing to notice here is that we copy the queue to a separate local `Queue` instance:

```
  while(queue.Count > 0) localQueue.Enqueue(queue.Dequeue());
```

We do this because we don't want to hold the lock on the `Queue` any longer than we have to, since sending the comment to the comment filter service could take a while. Other parts of our application cannot add new entries to the `Queue` while we're holding a lock on it.

After we've pulled the comments into the local queue from the global queue, we notify any waiting threads that they can proceed to add new comments to the global `Queue`:

```
  Monitor.PulseAll(queue);
```

Stack

In contrast to the queue, which, as we saw, is a First In, First Out (FIFO) collection, a stack implements a **Last In, First Out (LIFO)** collection. Stacks are used extensively by modern operating systems, as well as by the .NET Framework. For example—and this is a simplification—calling a method involves placing the parameters on the stack one after the other, in the order in which they're encountered in the code. As the method is executed, each parameter is popped from the top of the stack—starting with the parameter that was added most recently, then working backwards through the added parameters—and processed in turn.

Stacks can also be useful for implementing recursive logic. One problem with recursive method calls is that the code can become to difficult to read. In fact, any recursive algorithm can be rewritten to use a stack. For example, a method I've found myself writing countless times is one that finds a control with a specific ID within a nested control hierarchy. Since web controls form a tree structure, one natural way to implement a method to find a specific control would be to use recursion. The following method accomplishes this by using a `Stack`:

```
public static Control FindControlUsingStack(Control root,
    string id)
{
  // Seed it.
  Stack<Control> stack = new Stack<Control>();
  stack.Push(root);

  while(stack.Count > 0)
  {
    Control current = stack.Pop();
    if (current.ID == id)
      return current;

    foreach (Control control in current.Controls)
    {
      stack.Push(control);
    }
  }
  return null;
}
```

Using a stack to implement recursion results in code that is much easier to follow than code containing a method that calls itself.

Summary

It's always good to spend some quality time with the .NET core libraries. In this chapter, we showed how to leverage core features like strings and generics to solve real world problems, then took a look inside the .NET core libraries to get a better understanding of how they work.

We'll continue to build on these core features as we solve ASP.NET problems in the following chapters.

Data Access

Just about every ASP.NET application needs to deal with data access, but the topic's not a highlight of most developers' days. You need effective, efficient data access for your sites, but you'd rather spend your time on features your users will notice, right? I'm with you.

Data access in ASP.NET 2.0 can be a little overwhelming due to the large range of access options available. It's important to know how to pick the right data access strategy for your application—you want one that meets your current needs and can scale to meet future requirements. We'll start this chapter with a review of the available options; then we'll explore some practical tips for selecting and applying data access techniques that fit your current application.

How can I get started using ADO.NET?

Visual Studio provides a rich set of tools for building data access code quickly. Before we dig into them, though, let's review some of the underlying ADO.NET technologies on which those tools are built. Even if you don't think you'll ever need to dive under the hood in order to write your own data access code, it's important to know how ASP.NET works with your data—with this knowledge, you can make smart choices every time you use the ASP.NET data access controls.

Solution

The ADO.NET components in ASP.NET 2.0 offer two main methods of data access:

connected (`DataReader`-based)

> This method uses a **firehose cursor** connection, meaning that it returns only one row of data at a time. `DataReader` gives you fast, no-frills access to the data.

disconnected (`DataSet`-based)

> This approach grabs a local, in-memory copy of the data, then disconnects from the database. Since the data is held in memory, you can do more with it (such as sorting and filtering), but this method's not as efficient as using a `DataReader`. The `DataSet` class also supports hierarchies composed of multiple data tables with foreign-key relationships. These hierarchies are serializable, and they allow you to perform disconnected data updates that are synchronized on the next connection.

So, you ask, which approach should *you* use? Well, it's true that many developers select a preferred method for data access, ignoring the other. A more pragmatic approach is to see the two options as different tools at your disposal. Carpenters don't argue that drills are better than hammers; they understand that these tools serve different purposes.

Psst! Don't tell anyone, but a `DataSet` gets its data the same way every other object does—it uses a `DataReader`.

Discussion

Back in the ASP.NET 1.x days, some programmers saw the benefit of accessing their data via a rich-object wrapper, but weren't happy with the way the `DataSet` worked. What emerged were several third-party data access frameworks that use a `DataReader` behind the scenes, while still providing some of the convenience of a `DataSet`.

In ASP.NET 1.x, any operation other than stock-standard data access—such as using data integration features like declarative data binding—was not well supported. Microsoft recognized that developers wanted flexibility in their data access, and as a result, ASP.NET 2.0 supports data-source controls such as the `ObjectDataSource`. This control acts as an interface for data-aware controls, should you decide to use your own data access layer.

How do I configure my database connection?

A database isn't much good to us if we can't connect to it to extract our data. Creating a database connection used to be a lot more difficult during the reign of ASP.NET 1.1, but fortunately, it's dead simple in ASP.NET 2.0.

Solution

You can use a Data Connection component to configure a database connection. A Data Connection makes it easy to store and use database connection string information. Best of all, the component stores the information in a separate section in the **Web.config** file, called (appropriately enough) `connectionStrings`.

The easiest way to add a Data Connection is through the Server Explorer, which can be accessed via the **View** menu, and displays as shown in Figure 3.1.[1]

Figure 3.1. Viewing the Server Explorer in Visual Studio

Click the **Connect to Database** button to display the dialog shown in Figure 3.2. After selecting a server and a database, it's a good idea to click the **Test Connection** button to make sure that your application and database are able to talk to each other.

---

[1] If you're using the free Visual Web Developer Express Edition tool, you can instead add a new data connection through the Database Explorer.

Figure 3.2. Adding a database connection

There are a few points to note here:

- If you're developing against a database that's running on your development machine, it's a good idea to type in **(local)** rather than to select your computer's name from the **Server name** drop-down. **(local)** is a generic way to refer to the default instance of SQL Server running on the same machine as the web server. It's helpful to keep this value generic so that your data connection setting can work as-is on other computers that have different names (for instance, on machines belonging to other developers on your team).

- One benefit of the new `connectionStrings` section of the **Web.config** file is that it allows you to use named connection strings. This is useful for deployment purposes, as your **Web.config** file can contain the connection string for every environment to which you wish to deploy your application (for example, development, staging, and production). When you're deploying the site to a new environment, you can specify which connection string you want to use by adding an `appSetting` section to the file, or using the `dataConfiguration` section if you're using the latest Microsoft Data Access Application Block.[2]

- If possible, try to connect using the **Use Windows Authentication** option. While this approach can take a little more work to configure, it's much more secure than listing your username and password in your **Web.config** file, since the connection string doesn't include a username or password.

Don't Connect as sa!

Unfortunately, it's an all-too-common practice to connect to the database as the **sa** SQL Server user account during development. While this option is usually chosen for the sake of convenience, this potentially disastrous setting has a habit of finding its way into the production site.

Connecting as the **sa** user violates the security principle of **least privilege**, which states that, generally speaking, your web application shouldn't require permissions to drop a database or perform other system administration operations. A bug in the application that allowed an SQL injection attack, for instance, would be disastrous if the **sa** user was in use in production—in that case, your system would lack a safety net of database permissions that could to prevent the attack.

I've even seen clients use the **sa** account with *no password* on production web sites. A double no-no!

If you're using a Web Application project, then clicking the **OK** button will result in your connection string information being added to the **Web.config** file:

---

[2] http://msdn2.microsoft.com/en-us/library/aa480458.aspx

Web.config *(excerpt)*

```
<connectionStrings>
  <add name="NorthwindConnectionString"
       connectionString="Data Source=WORK;Initial Catalog=Northwind;
➡Integrated Security=True"
       providerName="System.Data.SqlClient"/>
</connectionStrings>
```

Of course, if you'd rather add these connection settings manually, you can edit the **Web.config** file directly. I recommend using the dialog to do so, since the drop-down menus and **Test Connection** button in that dialog can help you avoid errors, but either method should work if you enter the settings correctly.

Note that many of the data-related examples throughout this book utilize the Northwind example database that ships with Microsoft SQL Server. If you don't have Northwind installed, you can download it from the project's download site.[3]

 ### A Useful `connectionString` Resource

I tend to write my connection strings by hand for no good reason. Fortunately, I keep my browser closely focused on the ConnectionStrings web site.[4] This resource provides the formats for connection strings to nearly every type of data source.

Once you've configured a data connection, ASP.NET makes the data source easily accessible to your code in either code-behind or code-front approaches. You can reference a connection string from the code-behind file like this:

```
string northwindConnectionString = ConfigurationManager.ConnectionSt
➡rings["NorthwindConnectionString"].ConnectionString;
```

It's even easier to read a connection string using code-front code, since it's exposed as an expression:

---

[3] http://www.microsoft.com/downloads/details.aspx?FamilyId=06616212-0356-46A0-8DA2-EE-BC53A68034/

[4] http://connectionstrings.com/

```
ConnectionString =
    "<%$ ConnectionStrings:NorthwindConnectionString %>"
```

You'll notice that the data-source controls (which are discussed in detail in the section called "How can I perform data binding without having to write all that repetitive code?") use this syntax to configure their connections.

How do I read data from my database?

What use is a data connection if we don't do anything with it? In this solution, we'll read data from our database for a very simple case—we want to fill an array with values from a table in our database.

Solution

A DataReader is an efficient solution for instances when you just want to read some data. This code shows the DataReader in action:

SimpleDataAccess.aspx.cs *(excerpt)*

```
using System;
using System.Data;
using System.Configuration;
using System.Collections;
using System.Web;
using System.Web.Security;
using System.Web.UI;
using System.Web.UI.WebControls;
using System.Web.UI.WebControls.WebParts;
using System.Web.UI.HtmlControls;
using System.Collections.Generic;
using System.Data.SqlClient;

public partial class SimpleDataAccess : System.Web.UI.Page
{
  protected void Page_Load(object sender, EventArgs e)
  {
  }
  protected List<string> GetProductList()
  {
    List<string> products = new List<string>();
    string connectionString =
```

```
      ConfigurationManager.ConnectionStrings["NorthwindConnectionStr
      ➥ing"].ConnectionString;
    string query = "SELECT * FROM Products";
    using (SqlConnection connection =
      new SqlConnection(connectionString))
    using (SqlCommand command = new SqlCommand(query, connection))
    {
      connection.Open();
      IDataReader dr =
        command.ExecuteReader(
          CommandBehavior.CloseConnection
          );
      while (dr.Read())
      {
        products.Add(dr["ProductName"].ToString());
      }
    }f
    return products;
  }
}
```

Notice anything unusual about this code? (I'll give you a hint—I've highlighted the interesting lines in bold!) While we're using an instance of SQLDataReader, we're talking to it through an IDataReader interface. Talking to objects through interfaces makes our code more portable—for instance, it could more easily be converted to work with a data provider other than SQL Server—so use IDataReader unless you need additional functionality that the basic IDataReader interface doesn't support.

Look at the documentation for the System.Data.Common namespace to see the full list of classes shared by .NET Framework data providers.[5]

You can work with three primary classes to retrieve data directly from a SQL Server database via a DataReader:

SqlConnection

This class allows us to specify the server and database to which we want to talk, and to provide login information for them.

---

[5] http://msdn2.microsoft.com/en-us/library/system.data.common.aspx

SqlCommand

Once we've connected to a database, we use a `SqlCommand` to do the actual work.

SqlDataReader

The `SqlDataReader` allows us to read through the command's results. The `SqlDataReader` stays connected to the database while we're using it, and it only has access to one row of data at a time. A component that provides this kind of data access is often described as a firehose cursor, as we first learned in the section called "How can I get started using ADO.NET?", because the `DataReader` "sprays" the data one row at a time. Don't bother to ask it about anything other than the current row—it can't tell you.

How do I sort and filter data?

Usually the best place to undertake sorting and filtering is in the database, but there are times where this approach isn't practical—for instance, when the data is being returned by a stored procedure that can't be changed easily because of its complexity, or because of the impact such a change might have on other areas of the application.

Solution

When we're faced with the challenge of sorting data on the server, the best solution is to use a `DataTable`:

DataReaderSample.aspx.cs

```csharp
using System;
using System.Data;
using System.Data.SqlClient;
using System.Collections.Generic;

public class DataReaderSample
{
  public static void Main()
  {
    List<string> products = GetProductList();
    products.ForEach(delegate(String name)
      {
        Console.WriteLine(name);
      }
    );
```

```
    }
  public static List<string> GetProductList()
  {
    List<string> products = new List<string>();
    string connectionString =
      ConfigurationManager.ConnectionStrings["NorthwindConnectionStr
      ➥ing"].ConnectionString;

    string query = "SELECT * FROM Products";

    using(SqlConnection connection =
        new SqlConnection(connectionString))
    using(SqlCommand command = new SqlCommand(query,connection))
    using(SqlDataAdapter adapter = new SqlDataAdapter(command))
    {
      DataTable table = new DataTable();
      adapter.Fill(table);
      string sort = "UnitPrice";

      string filter = "ProductName LIKE 'T%'" +
        " AND UnitsInStock > 0";

      // Using the current time to randomly alter the filter.
      if(System.DateTime.Now.Second % 2 == 1)
        filter = "ProductName LIKE 'E%'" +
        " AND UnitPrice > 5";

      foreach (DataRow dataRow in table.Select(filter, sort))
      {
        products.Add(
          string.Format("{0}\t{1}",
                          dataRow["ProductName"].ToString(),
                          dataRow["UnitsInStock"].ToString()
          )
        );
      }
    }
    return products;
  }
}
```

Discussion

The disconnected data access model is built on DataTables; a DataSet can hold one or more DataTables and manage links between them. In this case, though, we didn't need to support a rich hierarchy, so we used a single DataTable.

Note that the DataTable.Select method allows for both sorting and filtering tasks. In the example above, for instance, we randomly select between two different criteria to filter our data. This randomness is implemented by inspecting the value of the current time—if the final digit of that value is even, then products beginning with T that are in stock are displayed; if the digit is odd, then the application will display products beginning with E that have a unit price greater than $5.00. This method is a lot simpler than the implementation of dynamic sorting and filtering in the database, but you should keep in mind that it's also a less efficient one, since it retrieves all products from the database, then sorts them on the web server.

In this example, it would have been more efficient to vary the SQL query so that the sorting and filtering were handled by the database, for two reasons:

1. Databases are more efficient than application code at processes such as sorting, aggregation, and filtering.

2. Filtering data in the database cuts down on network traffic between the database and the web server.

However, if the query was to select the output from a stored procedure or view, changing the sort and filter expressions might be a lot more complex. It's also possible to add processing power to the web layer by adding another server—you generally can't scale an SQL Server database very easily.

We've hit a problem that has two competing solutions. The right choice will depend on the needs of your application.

How do I fill a DropDownList from a database table?

The DropDownList control is super-useful for allowing users to make a selection from a list of options. But what's the best way to get those options out of the database and into the list?

Solution

The optimal way to populate a `DropDownList` from a database is to use **data binding**, which is best suited to controls containing visual elements that are tied to a database table. To kick off this solution, I'll show you how to bind your data to a control manually; then, in the section called "How can I perform data binding without having to write all that repetitive code?", we'll see how we can perform the same exercise using a new ASP.NET 2.0 feature: the `DataSource` control.

The following code shows how to set up a data source manually, using an example **Default.aspx** file that contains a single `DropDownList` that's set to `AutoPostBack`:

```
<%@ Page Language="C#" AutoEventWireup="true"
    CodeFile="Default.aspx.cs" Inherits="_Default" %>
<!DOCTYPE html PUBLIC "-//W3C//DTD XHTML 1.0 Transitional//EN"
    "http://www.w3.org/TR/xhtml1/DTD/xhtml1-transitional.dtd">

<html xmlns="http://www.w3.org/1999/xhtml" >
<head runat="server">
    <title>Data Access — DropDownList — Manual Binding</title>
</head>
<body>
    <form id="form1" runat="server">
    <div>
        <asp:DropDownList ID="productDropDown" runat="server"
            AutoPostBack="true">
        </asp:DropDownList>
    </div>
    </form>
</body>
</html>
```

To keep things simple, we'll do all of the data loading in the `Page_Load` method:

```
protected void Page_Load(object sender, EventArgs e)
{
  if (!Page.IsPostBack)
  {
    string connectionString =
      ConfigurationManager.
      ConnectionStrings["NorthwindConnectionString"].
      ConnectionString;
    string query = "SELECT * FROM Products";
```

```
  using (SqlConnection connection =
    new SqlConnection(connectionString))
  using (SqlCommand command = new SqlCommand(query, connection))
  {
    connection.Open();
    IDataReader dr =
      command.ExecuteReader(CommandBehavior.CloseConnection);
    productDropDown.DataSource = dr;
    productDropDown.DataValueField = "ProductID";
    productDropDown.DataTextField = "ProductName";
    productDropDown.DataBind();
  }
}
else
  Response.Write ("You picked " +
      productDropDown.SelectedItem.Text);
}
```

Here, we're using the same basic data access code that we used earlier to retrieve a `DataReader`, but instead of putting the values into a list, we've bound them to a control. That's as good as it got in ASP.NET 1.1, and it's worth knowing how to wire this up in case you're dealing with a complex control that requires you to get your hands dirty. Most of the time, though, it's better if you can take advantage of the ASP.NET 2.0 Data Source Controls. We'll explore those features next.

How can I perform data binding without having to write all that repetitive code?

ASP.NET 1.1 developers soon began to realize that data binding code was fairly repetitive. While the specifics change—connection, query, fields, and so on—the data access code was always the same. Developers found ways to encapsulate the code manually, but ASP.NET 2.0's `DataSource` controls make this encapsulation really simple.

Solution

The most efficient way to perform data binding is to use declarative data binding with a `DataSource` control.

`DataSource` controls are well named, as they provide a source of data for other data-bound controls. Although they're commonly used in a declarative context, they are standard .NET controls and can be manipulated programmatically as well.

You'll find the `SqlDataSource` in the **Toolbox** under the **Data** heading. Drag it onto your web form (either in Design or Source View), as shown in Figure 3.3.

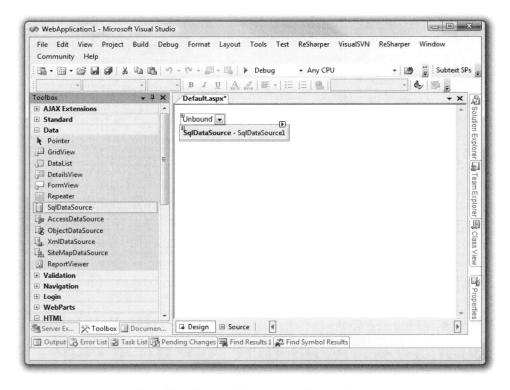

Figure 3.3. Adding a `SqlDataSource` object to the page

Click on the small button in the upper right-hand corner to show the smart tag task menu associated with the `SqlDataSource` control; it's shown in Figure 3.4.

Figure 3.4. Displaying the control's smart tag task menu

We'll select the only option, **Configure Data Source**…. The first page of the **Configure Data Source** wizard allows us to select an existing data connection or to create a new one. If you're creating a new data connection, you'll be presented with the dialog that we saw previously, in the section called "How do I configure my database connection?".

Press **OK** to accept your settings, and press **Next** > to go to the next page in the wizard. By default, the wizard will save your connection string using the name of the database—in the example shown in Figure 3.5, it will select **NorthwindConnection-String**. You can change the string if you like, then press **Next** >.

Figure 3.5. Choosing a Data Connection

The purpose of the **Configure the Select Statement** wizard screen depicted in Figure 3.6, is self-explanatory. You can either specify a SQL query or stored procedure to call, or use the user interface to design one. I generally avoid tools that generate SQL for me, but this one works well because it displays the query text as the query is constructed. Here I've selected the `Products` table and the two columns that I'll be data binding to my `DropDownList`.

It's tempting to use `SELECT *` (all columns), or to manually select all columns, in case you might want them later, but restrain yourself! Remember that you want to return the minimum information necessary from your database to eliminate unnecessary work—on both the database server and the web server. It's very easy to add a column to the query at a later stage, once the data source has been configured.

SqlCacheDependency Won't Work with SELECT * Queries

Here's one more reason to avoid SELECT * queries: you can't make use of the SqlCacheDependency on a data source that uses such queries. We'll talk more about the SqlCacheDependency in Chapter 15.

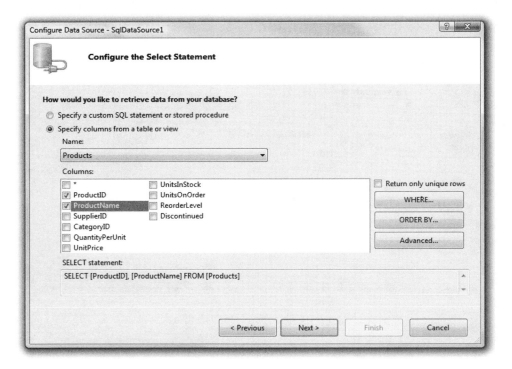

Figure 3.6. Configuring the SELECT statement for data binding

Finally, we'll test the query—click the **Test Query** button shown in Figure 3.7. If you don't receive any error messages, you're done! Click **Finish** and the wizard will close. If you're having trouble connecting, double-check that your SQL Server instance is indeed running, and that your connection details are correct.

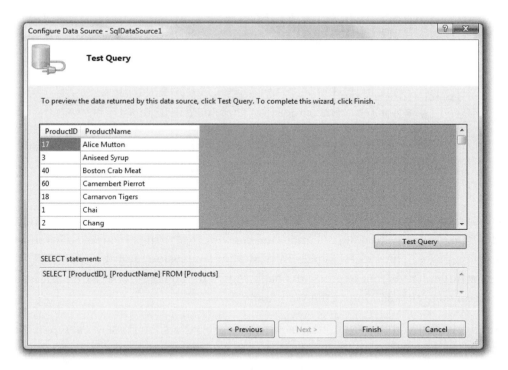

Figure 3.7. Testing the data bind query

Now, that may seem like a lot of work compared to just cranking out the data binding code. Trust me, it's not!

■ First of all, we had to set up our database connection. However, remember that this is a one-off task; the next time you add a SqlDataSource control to a page, you can just select the database connection and move on.

■ Secondly, the **Configure the Select Statement** screen is really simple, so you can breeze through it in seconds. If you're better at writing SQL by hand, select the first option on that page and knock yourself out.

■ Finally, if you're a fast typist, you can avoid the wizard altogether and just type out the control properties. Here's the ASPX source that we just built with the wizard—it's not all that difficult to type this if you're so inclined:

```
                                                    DropDownList.aspx (excerpt)
<asp:SqlDataSource
  ID="SqlDataSource1"
  runat="server"
  ConnectionString=
      "<%$ ConnectionStrings:NorthwindConnectionString %>"
  SelectCommand=
      "SELECT [ProductID], [ProductName] FROM [Products]">
</asp:SqlDataSource>
```

Notice that the ConnectionString information isn't included here. Visual Studio
added that to our **Web.config** file under the connectionStrings section, so it's shared
between pages. The <%$ %> syntax indicates an expression, and the ASP.NET
parser understands that expressions beginning with ConnectionStrings indicate
a reference to that section of the **Web.config** file.

Finally, we'll need to wire up the DropDownList to the SQLDataSource. Open the
Smart Tab task menu and select **Choose Data Source...**, as depicted in Figure 3.8.
The dialog shown in Figure 3.9 will appear.

Figure 3.8. Viewing the SmartTab task menu for our data source

This page is quite simple—we need to take just three actions:

1. Select the data source that we just configured.

2. Select the database table to be displayed. This will control the values that appear
   in the DropDownList.

3. Select the database table to use for identifying each value in the list. It's possible
   to use the same column that you selected for the **Display** field here, but it's much
   better practice to use an ID column to represent the value if one is available.

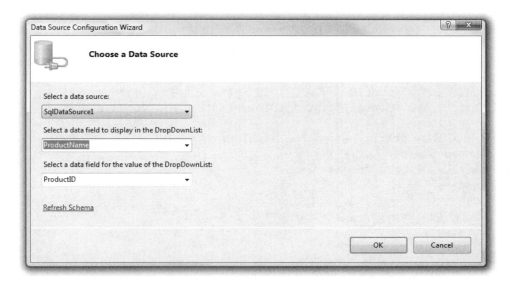

Figure 3.9. Choosing a data source

Great, we're done … almost. There's one more setting to tweak, and it's not visible in the wizard. The `DataSourceMode` property (available in the **Properties** grid, and editable manually in the Source View) defaults to `DataSet`. It's fine to use that default setting if you need the advanced capabilities a `DataSet` provides—for instance, if you're going to enable sorting or paging on a `GridView`. For simple binding scenarios, however, it's a good practice to switch your `DataSourceMode` from `DataSet` to `DataReader`. If you're not sure whether or not you need a `DataSet`, just set your data source to `DataReader` and test it out—if you're attempting to use functionality that requires a `DataSet`, you'll get an error message which tells you just that:

```
The SqlDataSource 'SqlDataSource1' does not have paging enabled. Set
the DataSourceMode to DataSet to enable paging.
```

That's reasonably straightforward, huh?

Since we've been "coding by clicking," let's take a look at the code that we've generated. First, the ASPX code:

```
<%@ Page Language="C#" AutoEventWireup="true"
    CodeFile="DataSourceControl.aspx.cs" Inherits="_Default" %>

<!DOCTYPE html PUBLIC "-//W3C//DTD XHTML 1.0 Transitional//EN"
  "http://www.w3.org/TR/xhtml1/DTD/xhtml1-transitional.dtd">

<html xmlns="http://www.w3.org/1999/xhtml" >
<head runat="server">
  <title>Sql Data Source</title>
</head>
<body>
  <form id="form1" runat="server">
    <div>
      <asp:DropDownList
          ID="productDropDown"
          runat="server"
          AutoPostBack="True"
          SelectedIndexChanged="OnSelectedIndexChanged"
          DataSourceID="SqlDataSource1"
          DataTextField="ProductName"
          DataValueField="ProductID">
      </asp:DropDownList>
      <asp:SqlDataSource ID="SqlDataSource1"
          runat="server"
          DataSourceMode="DataReader"
          ConnectionString=
          "<%$ ConnectionStrings:NorthwindConnectionString %>"
          SelectCommand="SELECT [ProductID], [ProductName]
                         FROM [Products]">
      </asp:SqlDataSource>
    </div>
  </form>
</body>
</html>
```

As the data access and binding is done in code, our `Page_Load` method doesn't require any additional code in order to work. We just need to add an event handler method to handle the `SelectedIndexChanged` event, as follows:

DropDownList.aspx.cs *(excerpt)*

```
protected void OnSelectedIndexChanged(object sender, EventArgs e)
{
  Response.Write ("You picked " +
      productDropDown.SelectedItem.Text);
}
```

Figure 3.10 shows the page in action.

Figure 3.10. The DropDownList populated with data

How do I display the contents of a database table?

Writing SQL queries is one way of exploring the contents of your database table, but surely there are more flexible ways to access this data? I'm glad you asked …

Solution

To dump the contents of a database table into a format that's useful, use a GridView bound to a SqlDataSource. The easiest way to do this is to find the table in the **Server Explorer** window, then to drag and drop it onto your web form. Let's walk through this process first, then look under the hood to see how it works.

1. Ensure you've set up a data connection to your database.

2. Locate the table in the **Server Explorer**, as shown in the section called "How do I configure my database connection?".

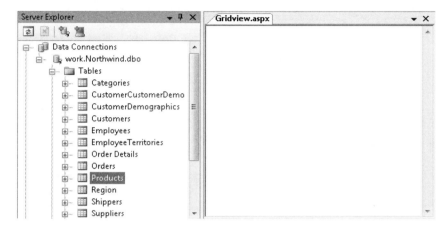

Figure 3.11. Selecting a table to display

3. Drag and drop the table onto the design surface for your web form, as depicted in Figure 3.12. You can do this in either Design or Source View. Design View is fine for a simple or empty page, but if you're adding the GridView to an existing page with a complex structure, you'll probably find that it's easier to use the Source View instead.

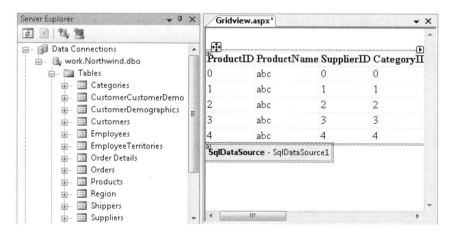

Figure 3.12. Placing the table on the page

4. Configure the GridView. When you first add the table, the GridView's smart tag task menu will automatically expand, as Figure 3.13 demonstrates. If you're like me, browser popups may have conditioned you to close this menu automatically, but resist the urge and keep the menu open for a moment. You can fine-tune most of the important GridView features from this menu—that's probably a good approach until you become familiar enough with the properties to be confident to do your editing in the Source View.

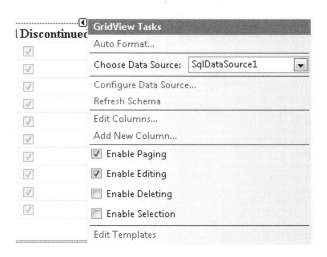

Figure 3.13. Configuring the table using the smart tag task menu

Discussion

Let's take a look at the grid options. You can enable paging, sorting, editing, deletion, and selection via the checkboxes. As I mentioned in the section called "How can I perform data binding without having to write all that repetitive code?", paging and sorting require you to keep the SqlDataSource's DataSourceMode in DataSet, which is not terribly efficient. I've selected **Enable Paging** and **Enable Editing**.

Next, we'll look at the **Fields** dialog shown in Figure 3.14, which can be launched by selecting the **Edit Columns...** menu item from the GridView's smart tag task menu. The default GridView column settings might be okay for a basic administration page, but there are a few aspects that you'll want to change before you unveil the grid for the world to see:

■ By default, all columns are shown, including ID columns. Users probably don't
  need to see those IDs, though.

■ The grid column titles are generated from the table column names—that spells
  bad news for most database tables. For instance, the `Products` table in the
  Northwind example database has column names like `ProductID` and `Quanti-
  tyPerUnit`. At a minimum, we'd want to put some spaces between the words—for
  example, `Quantity Per Unit` is much nicer for our users to see than `Quanti-
  tyPerUnit`.

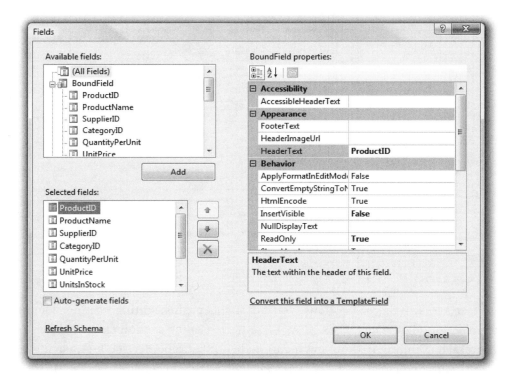

Figure 3.14. Default settings in the **Fields** dialog

Keep these points in mind when you're working with the **Fields** dialog:

■ **Auto-generate fields** is unchecked by default. This is a good thing—it tells you
  that Visual Studio generated the columns for the table and stored them with the
  `GridView`'s source, rather than just relying on ASP.NET to auto-generate the
  columns every time the page is displayed.

■ All table columns are added by default. The user interface for correcting this is fairly intuitive—to remove a field, select it in the **Selected fields** list and click the red **X** button to delete it.

■ You can configure a column by selecting it in the **Selected fields** list, then making changes in the **BoundField properties** grid on the right. For example, you'll probably want to change the **HeaderText** to be a little more presentable. This interface is fine for making a small number of changes, but in most cases you're going to need to edit *all* of the columns. Using this interface to make all those changes will become tiresome very quickly. For that reason, I recommend that you make column-by-column changes in the Source View.

Close the **Edit Columns** dialog and switch to Source View, where we'll do the rest of the grid configuration. Your page's source should look something like this:

Gridview.aspx (excerpt)

```
<asp:GridView ID="GridView1"
  runat="server"
  AutoGenerateColumns="False"
  DataKeyNames="ProductID"
  DataSourceID="SqlDataSource1"
  EmptyDataText="There are no data records to display.">
    <Columns>
    <asp:BoundField DataField="ProductID"
          HeaderText="ProductID"
          ReadOnly="True"
          SortExpression="ProductID" />
    <asp:BoundField DataField="ProductName"
          HeaderText="ProductName"
          SortExpression="ProductName" />
    <!--Additional columns omitted from listing-->
    </Columns>
</asp:GridView>
```

This view of our column mapping makes it easier to make bulk changes, so it's the best place for editing your `HeaderText` values to add those spaces.

The `GridView` default formatting properties are generally reasonably good, but you'll want to make sure that date and currency fields have appropriate formatting. For instance, the `Northwind Products` table has a `Decimal` valued `UnitPrice` column, which will display with four decimal places rather than two. We can take care of this issue by setting the column's `DataFormatString` value as follows:

```
DataFormatString="{0:c}"
```

There's just one small gotcha to be aware of: when a column's `HtmlEncode` property is `true` (which it is by default) the associated format string isn't applied. So when you set a `DataFormatString`, make sure to set `HtmlEncode` to `false`.

There is one more setting I'd like to discuss before we give our table a run: Auto Format styling. To view the styles available, select your `GridView`, click on the smart tag to open the object's task menu, and choose **Auto Format...**.

Auto Format styling works by hard-coding style values into each `tr` *and* a element. I don't like this approach for several reasons:

 The correct way to style a `GridView` (from an HTML purist's viewpoint) is to set the `CssClass` property of the `GridView` and do your styling where it belongs: in a style sheet.

 Auto Format repeats the same style attributes for each row, which is unnecessarily inefficient. Assigning a class to the `GridView` allows you to define your styles once for the entire site.

 Last but certainly not least, Auto Format settings are a bit ugly. They're better than no formatting at all, but they're not going to win you any design awards.

That said, an Auto Format style may be appropriate for a quick, internal page. If you do decide to use Auto Format styling, you have a selection of styles to choose from. Select one from the list on the left—in Figure 3.15, I've selected the **Professional** style.

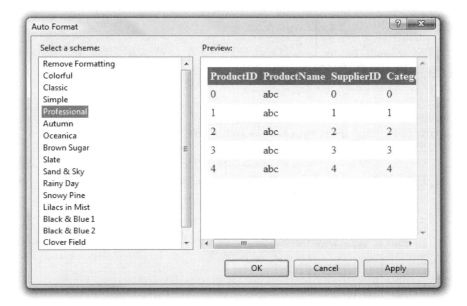

Figure 3.15. Using the **Professional** Auto Format style option

Figure 3.16 shows the result of our work.

	Product ID	Product Name	Quantity Per Unit	Unit Price	Units In Stock	Units On Order	Reorder Level	Discontinued
Edit	31	Gorgonzola Telino	12 - 100 g pkgs	$12.50	0	70	20	☐
Edit	32	Mascarpone Fabioli	24 - 200 g pkgs.	$32.00	9	40	25	☐
Update Cancel	33	Geitost	500 g	2.5000	112	0	20	☑
Edit	34	Sasquatch Ale	24 - 12 oz bottles	$14.00	111	0	15	☐
Edit	35	Steeleye Stout	24 - 12 oz bottles	$18.00	20	0	15	☐
Edit	36	Inlagd Sill	24 - 250 g jars	$19.00	112	0	20	☐
Edit	37	Gravad lax	12 - 500 g pkgs.	$26.00	11	50	25	☐
Edit	38	Côte de Blaye	12 - 75 cl bottles	$263.50	17	0	15	☐
Edit	39	Chartreuse verte	750 cc per bottle	$18.00	69	0	5	☐
Edit	40	Boston Crab Meat	24 - 4 oz tins	$18.40	123	0	30	☐
				1 2 3 4 5 6 7 8				

Figure 3.16. The **Professional** Auto Format style option in action

While I tend to steer away from using Auto Format styling, I'm happy to concede that this is not a bad result for dragging a table onto a form and setting a few properties! Visual Studio configured a `SqlDataSource` and added a `GridView`, and we fixed up the column headers and cleaned up the style a little. Nice!

Styling the `GridView` in CSS

Earlier, we said that the correct way to style a `GridView` is with CSS. The best way to do that is with the CSS Friendly Control Adapters, which we'll explore in more detail in Chapter 9.

In the meantime, though, here are the general steps you'd take to convert your `GridView` styling from Auto Format styling to CSS:

1. Use the CSS Friendly Gridview Adapter. The download page for the CSS Friendly Control Adapters Toolkit contains an example of the Gridview Adapter,[6] and Fritz Onion has published an excellent overview of the adapter.[7]

2. Remove your Auto Format styles by applying the **Remove Formatting** Auto Format scheme (yes, this *is* kind of like clicking **Start** to shut your computer down).

3. Modify an existing **gridview.css** style sheet to match your site's design and color scheme, rather than tackling the style for your table from scratch. You can download a working **gridview.css** file from the CSS Friendly Control Adapters tutorial mini-site, which comes bundled with the toolkit. See Fritz Onion's article (noted in Step 1 above) for information on how to go about this.

Two-way Data Binding?

Windows Forms developers have long enjoyed the ability not only to bind controls to a data source, but to have the data source automatically updated to reflect user changes to the values in the controls. Such two-way data binding capabilities are not natively supported in ASP.NET Web Forms.

Fortunately, Rick Strahl has developed a control that addresses this shortcoming; the details were published in *MSDN Magazine* as an article titled "Simplify Data Binding In ASP.NET 2.0 With Our Custom Control."[8] Rick makes great use of control extenders to build a rich control for two-way data binding and validation.

---

[6] http://www.asp.net/cssadapters/gridview.aspx
[7] http://www.pluralsight.com/blogs/fritz/archive/2007/03/27/46598.aspx
[8] http://msdn.microsoft.com/msdnmag/issues/06/12/ExtendASPNET/default.aspx

How do I allow the modification of a single record?

The GridView is handy for displaying lots of data at once, but in many cases a grid is not the right interface for viewing, editing, or updating individual records. To achieve this in ASP.NET 1.1, developers had to write detailed forms by hand (we also had to walk barefoot seven miles to school in the snow, uphill both ways, but that's another story!). ASP.NET 2.0 delivers a much better solution.

Solution

The best way to modify a single record in a modern ASP.NET application is to use the DetailsView control.

The DetailsView control does just what you'd expect—it binds to a single row in a database table, and has modes for viewing, editing, and deleting the row.

We'll demonstrate this method by hooking up a DetailsView control to a DropDownList populated by our Northwind Products list. Select a **Product Name** in the drop-down, and the details of that product will be displayed in the DetailsView.

The simplest way to set up this control is to use two SqlDataSources. The one we use to populate the Products DropDownList only needs the product name and ID, so we'll set it to only select those columns. We'll then place a DropDownList on the page and bind it to that control.

The resulting markup for those two controls looks like this:

```
                                    DetailsView.aspx (excerpt)
<asp:DropDownList
  ID="productDropDown"
  runat="server"
  AutoPostBack="True"
  DataSourceID="dataSourceProductNames"
  DataTextField="ProductName"
  DataValueField="ProductID">
</asp:DropDownList>
<asp:SqlDataSource ID="dataSourceProductNames"
  runat="server"
```

```
ConnectionString=
    "<%$ ConnectionStrings:NorthwindConnectionString %>"
SelectCommand="SELECT [ProductID], [ProductName] FROM [Products]">
</asp:SqlDataSource>
```

Next we'll create an `SqlDataSource` that pulls all the details for a selected `Product`, and uses a `WHERE` clause to tie the `SqlDataSource` query parameter for `ProductID` to the product that has been selected in the `DropDownList`.

First we select from our `Products` table the columns we want to use in our query. As Figure 3.17 shows, I've selected eight.

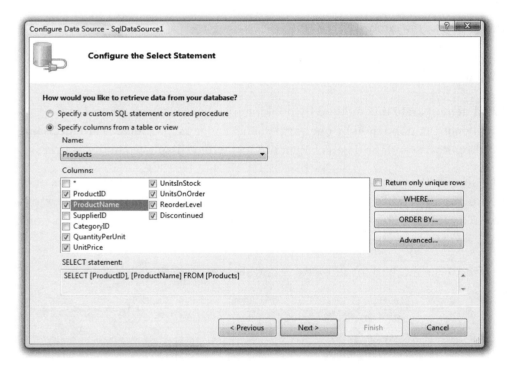

Figure 3.17. Configuring the SELECT statement for our query

Now click the **WHERE…** button on the right-hand side to show the **Add WHERE Clause** dialog. Set the `ProductID` column to equal the value of the Product's `DropDownList`, as shown in Figure 3.18.

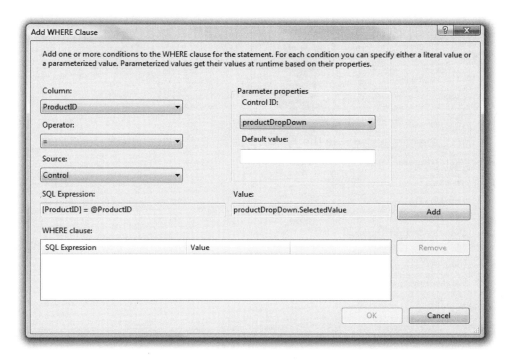

Figure 3.18. Building the WHERE clause for our query

 Other Ways to Select a Row

In our example, we'll be selecting the row we want to display via a `DropDownList`. Other common ways to select a row are to use a `QueryString` parameter or to select a row in a `GridView`. Keep in mind that you can easily adapt the technique demonstrated here to other GUI controls by changing the way the `SelectParameter` for the `SqlDataSource` is set. It's very straightforward to declaratively bind it to a control or `QueryString` value; you can also set it programmatically if needed.

It's all downhill from here—we just place a `DetailsView` control on the page and select the Product's `SqlDataSource` as the `DataSourceID`. I applied an Auto Format style for the `DetailsView`, which produces the table shown in Figure 3.19.

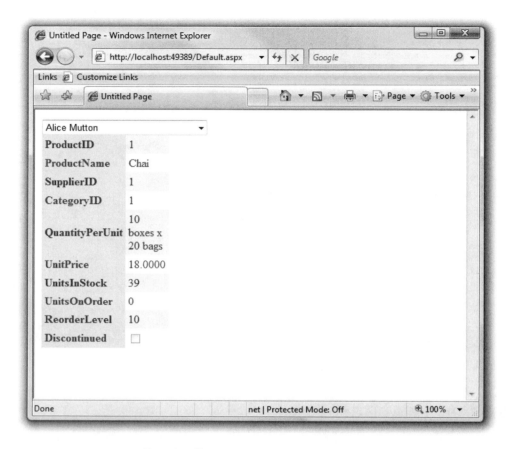

Figure 3.19. The DetailsView, styled and populated

We can turn on **Edit**, **Delete**, and **New** buttons for the control, but we'll need to make sure that the data source has the appropriate queries defined. For example, I need do two things to allow deletion:

1. Define a DELETE query for the data source.

2. Set the DetailsView's AutoGenerateDeleteButton value to true.

To define the DELETE query, select the SqlDataSource associated with the Product, and click the ellipsis button in the DeleteQuery field of the **Properties** grid. You'll see the **Command and Parameter Editor** pictured in Figure 3.20, with a **DELETE command** specified.

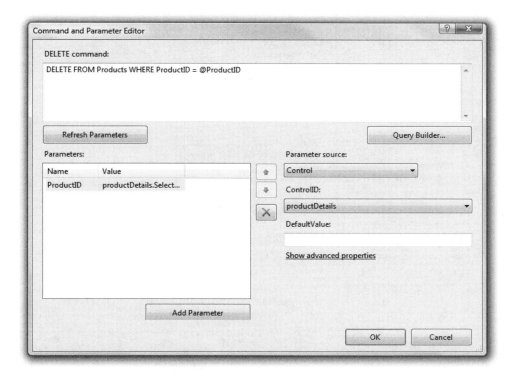

Figure 3.20. Defining the DELETE query

Foreign Keys and Stored Procedures

This query is just a sample—in the actual Northwind sample database, a foreign key from the `Products` table to the `Orders` table prevents the deletion of a product associated with orders. The correct way to handle this deletion would be to write a stored procedure that handles the deletion of products, then call that procedure in the `DataQuery`.

The source for the page ends up looking like this (I've removed the Auto Format style for the `DetailsView` to clear up the markup):

```
                                                        DetailsView.aspx

<%@ Page Language="C#" AutoEventWireup="true"
    CodeFile="DetailsView.aspx.cs" Inherits="DetailsView" %>

<!DOCTYPE html PUBLIC "-//W3C//DTD XHTML 1.0 Transitional//EN"
  "http://www.w3.org/TR/xhtml1/DTD/xhtml1-transitional.dtd">
```

```
<html xmlns="http://www.w3.org/1999/xhtml" >
<head id="Head1" runat="server">
  <title>DetailsView Sample</title>
</head>
<body>
  <form id="form1" runat="server">
  <div>
    <asp:DropDownList ID="productDropDown"
        runat="server"
        AutoPostBack="True"
        DataSourceID="dataSourceProductNames"
        DataTextField="ProductName"
        DataValueField="ProductID">
    </asp:DropDownList>
    <asp:SqlDataSource ID="dataSourceProductNames"
    runat="server"
    ConnectionString=
        "<%$ ConnectionStrings:NorthwindConnectionString %>"
      SelectCommand=
          "SELECT [ProductID], [ProductName] FROM [Products]">
  </asp:SqlDataSource>
    <asp:SqlDataSource ID="dataSourceProductDetails"
    runat="server"
    ConnectionString =
        "<%$ ConnectionStrings:NorthwindConnectionString %>"
      SelectCommand="SELECT [ProductID], [ProductName], [UnitPrice],
          [QuantityPerUnit], [UnitsInStock], [UnitsOnOrder],
          [ReorderLevel], [Discontinued], [CategoryID],
          [SupplierID]
          FROM [Products] WHERE ([ProductID] = @ProductID)">
      <SelectParameters>
        <asp:ControlParameter ControlID="productDropDown"
          Name="ProductID" PropertyName="SelectedValue"
          Type="Int32" />
      </SelectParameters>
  </asp:SqlDataSource>
    <asp:DetailsView ID="productDetails" runat="server"
      AutoGenerateRows="False" DataKeyNames="ProductID"
      DataSourceID="dataSourceProductDetails">
      <Fields>
        <asp:BoundField DataField="ProductID"
                      HeaderText="ProductID" InsertVisible="False"
            ReadOnly="True" SortExpression="ProductID" />
        <asp:BoundField DataField="ProductName"
```

```
                    HeaderText=
                        "ProductName" SortExpression="ProductName" />
        <asp:BoundField DataField="UnitPrice"
                    HeaderText="UnitPrice" SortExpression="UnitPrice" />
        <asp:BoundField DataField="QuantityPerUnit"
                    HeaderText="QuantityPerUnit"
                    SortExpression="QuantityPerUnit" />
        <asp:BoundField DataField="UnitsInStock"
                    HeaderText="UnitsInStock"
                    SortExpression="UnitsInStock" />
        <asp:BoundField DataField="UnitsOnOrder"
                    HeaderText="UnitsOnOrder"
                    SortExpression="UnitsOnOrder" />
        <asp:BoundField DataField="ReorderLevel"
                    HeaderText="ReorderLevel"
                    SortExpression="ReorderLevel" />
        <asp:CheckBoxField DataField="Discontinued"
                    HeaderText="Discontinued"
                    SortExpression="Discontinued" />
      </Fields>
    </asp:DetailsView>
  </div>
  </form>
</body>
</html>
```

Using the `FormView` to Control your Layout

If you want more control over the HTML than the `GridView` provides, use the `FormView`. It's similar to the `GridView` control, but provides additional functionality; for instance, it allows you to take control of data-bound output by defining templates—much like the `Repeater` control. Scott Mitchell's tutorial is a good place to get started on using the `FormView`.[9]

---

[9] http://asp.net/learn/data-access/tutorial-14-cs.aspx

How can I data bind without using the `SqlDataSource`?

The `SqlDataSource` control makes it easy to hook directly into your SQL Server database. This approach may be fine for small or simple applications, but as your application grows, you'll probably want to funnel your data access through some other layers, such as business and data objects.

Solution

Abandoning the SqlDataSource control doesn't mean abandoning the convenience that comes with declarative data binding. You can still use declarative data binding with your objects by utilizing the `ObjectDataSource` control.

Binding to Objects that Support IEnumerable

In ASP.NET 1.1, it was common to write code to bind data to objects that implemented the IEnumerable interface. For instance, you could create a custom collection that implemented IEnumerable, or just use a native .NET collection that already implemented IEnumerable (you could store `Customer` instances in an `ArrayList`, for example).

Of course, this approach still works in ASP.NET 2.0. However, while binding to such an object works to *display* data, it can't take advantage of some of the more advanced features exposed by data-aware controls—features such as being able to insert, update, and delete records. Unfortunately, there is no way for an IEnumerable object to indicate to the data-aware controls whether or not the object supports in-place editing (and if so, which method to call to take advantage of this).

Instead of using the IEnumerable interface, use an `ObjectDataSource`—it provides far more flexibility.

If you've ever implemented an object that supported data-binding, you may be expecting that your object will need to implement some difficult interfaces to support declarative data-binding. Not in this case! The `ObjectDataSource` is really flexible—it allows you to declaratively map data-binding functions to your existing class methods without having to implement any new interfaces. It's very likely that your existing entity objects can work as `ObjectDataSources` without any changes.

There are some gotchas, though. The `ObjectDataSource` can be configured to work with most entity objects, but advanced features like paging and sorting will require code changes. In this solution, we'll start with a simple data-binding case; then we'll talk about some advanced usage scenarios.

Take a look at this simple `Customer` entity object:

Customer.cs *(excerpt)*

```csharp
using System;
using System.Web;
using System.Data;
using System.Collections.Generic;

[Serializable]
public class Customer
{
  private int customerID;
  public int CustomerID
  {
    get { return customerID; }
    set { customerID = value; }
  }
  private string firstName;
  public string FirstName
  {
    get { return firstName; }
    set { firstName = value; }
  }

  private string lastName;
  public string LastName
  {
    get { return lastName; }
    set { lastName = value; }
  }

  private string address;
  public string Address
  {
    get { return address; }
    set { address = value; }
  }
```

```
    private string city;
    public string City
    {
      get { return city; }
      set { city = value; }
    }

    private string state;
    public string State
    {
      get { return state; }
      set { state = value; }
    }

    public Customer()
    {
    }

    public Customer(int customerID,
      string firstName,
      string lastName,
      string address,
      string city,
      string state)
    {
      this.CustomerID = customerID;
      this.FirstName = firstName;
      this.LastName = lastName;
      this.Address = address;
      this.City = city;
      this.State = state;
    }
}
```

What we've done here is define a simple `Customer` class with some bare-bones properties and getter/setter methods.

Next, we'll implement a business object, named `CustomerData`, that provides access to the `Customer` entity:

```csharp
public class CustomerData
{
  public CustomerData()
  {
    if (Customers.Rows.Count == 0)
    {
      FetchCustomers();
    }
  }

  public void Update(int customerID,
    string firstName,
    string lastName,
    string address,
    string city,
    string state)
  {
    Customer c = Get(customerID);

    c.CustomerID = customerID;
    c.FirstName = firstName;
    c.LastName = lastName;
    c.Address = address;
    c.City = city;
    c.State = state;
  }

  public IEnumerable<Customer> GetCustomers()
  {
    foreach (DataRow row in Customers.Rows)
      yield return CustomerFromRow(row);
  }

  public Customer Get(int id)
  {
    return FetchCustomerById(id);
  }

  public void Add(Customer c)
  {
    Customers.Rows.Add(
      c.CustomerID,
      c.FirstName,
```

```
        c.LastName,
        c.Address,
        c.City,
        c.State
        );
  }

  public void Delete(int id)
  {
    DataRow[] rows = Customers.Select("CustomerID = " + id);
    if (rows.Length == 1)
      Customers.Rows.Remove(rows[0]);
  }

  public void Delete(Customer c)
  {
    Delete(c.CustomerID);
  }

  public int Count()
  {
    return Customers.Rows.Count;
  }

  // For simplicity, we're reading from internal DataTable.
  // The following methods populate and manipulate our test data.
  // These methods could be working against any data source,
  // including webservices, files, etc.

  private void FetchCustomers()
  {
    string[] First = new string[] {
        "Bob", "Phil", "Edna", "Sue", "George" };
    string[] Last = new string[] {
        "Smith", "Johnson", "Williams", "Jones", "Brown" };

    Random rng = new Random(Guid.NewGuid().GetHashCode());
    for (int i = 1; i < 50; i++)
      this.Add(
        new Customer(
        i, First[rng.Next(5)],
        Last[rng.Next(5)],
        rng.Next(1000) + " Main St.",
        "Dallas",
        "TX"));
```

```csharp
}

private Customer FetchCustomerById(int id)
{
  DataRow[] rows = Customers.Select("CustomerID = " + id);
  if (rows.Length == 1)
  {
    return CustomerFromRow(rows[0]);
  }
  return null;
}

private Customer CustomerFromRow(DataRow row)
{
  Customer c = new Customer(
    int.Parse(row["CustomerID"].ToString()),
    row["FirstName"].ToString(),
    row["LastName"].ToString(),
    row["Address"].ToString(),
    row["City"].ToString(),
    row["State"].ToString()
    );
  return c;
}

private DataTable Customers
{
  get
  {
    System.Web.HttpContext context =
        System.Web.HttpContext.Current;
    DataTable dt = context.Session["CustomerData"] as DataTable;
    if (context.Session["CustomerData"] as DataTable == null)
    {
      context.Session["CustomerData"] = CreateCustomerTable();
    }
    return context.Session["CustomerData"] as DataTable;
  }
  set
  {
    System.Web.HttpContext.
      Current.Session["CustomerData"] = value;
  }
}
```

```
private DataTable CreateCustomerTable()
{
  DataTable dt = new DataTable("Customers");
  dt.Columns.Add("CustomerID", typeof(Int32));
  dt.Columns.Add("FirstName", typeof(string));
  dt.Columns.Add("LastName", typeof(string));
  dt.Columns.Add("Address", typeof(string));
  dt.Columns.Add("City", typeof(string));
  dt.Columns.Add("State", typeof(string));
  return dt;
}
}
```

This implementation includes private methods that load and update sample data (a `DataTable` stored in the ASP.NET `Session`). This code is intended only for demonstration purposes—your data access object could be pulling data from a database, a file, or a web service. Don't be confused by the fact that we're using a `DataTable` internally to store our state. The `CustomerData` object never publicly exposes the `DataTable` control; the `CustomerData` object communicates via `Customer` objects, `Customer` properties, and `List<Customer>` generic types.

Now let's hook up that `ObjectDataSource` and see how it performs. Drop an `ObjectDataSource` on a web form and select the **Configure Data Source...** task, as shown in Figure 3.21.

Figure 3.21. Selecting the configuration screen from the smart tag task menu

The general flow of the `ObjectDataSource` configuration wizard is similar to the `SqlDataSource` configuration wizard (see the section called "How can I perform data binding without having to write all that repetitive code?"), but it has a focus on business objects.

The first screen in the wizard is shown in Figure 3.22; begin by selecting a business object from the drop-down menu.

Figure 3.22. Choosing a Business Object to bind to

After clicking **Next** >, you're presented with a screen that allows you to configure SELECT, UPDATE, INSERT, and DELETE methods for your object, as shown in Figure 3.23. The wizard does a fairly good job of guessing the appropriate methods based on the parameter and return types required for each operation.

Note that the only required method is SELECT; if you leave UPDATE, INSERT, or DELETE methods unmapped, you can still bind to the ObjectDataSource. However, the data will be available for read-only purposes when it is retrieved.

Note also that the SELECT method can return either standard ADO.NET objects (DataSet and DataReader) or a strongly typed collection. In this case, our GetCustomers method returns an IEnumerable generic collection of Customers.

Figure 3.24, Figure 3.25, and Figure 3.26 show the wizard building UPDATE, INSERT, and DELETE methods respectively.

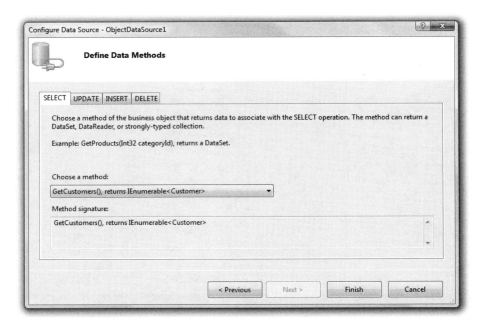

Figure 3.23. Configuring the SELECT method for our business object

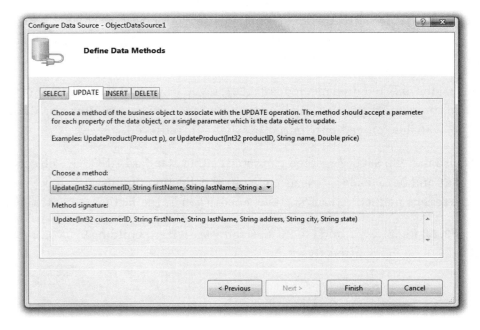

Figure 3.24. Defining the UPDATE method

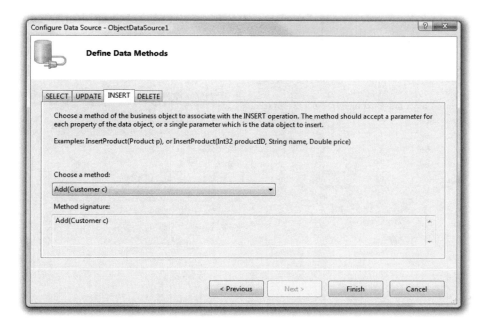

Figure 3.25. Defining the INSERT method

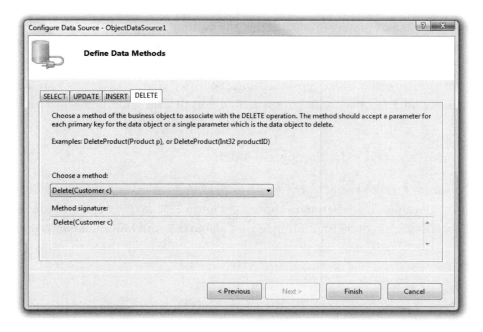

Figure 3.26. Defining the DELETE method

Now that we have our queries in place, we can go ahead and data-bind a `GridView` to the `ObjectDataSource`, as shown in Figure 3.27.

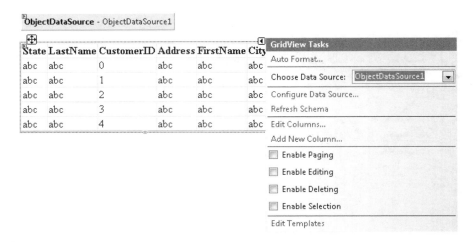

Figure 3.27. Binding the `GridView` to an `ObjectDataSource`

This data-binding experience that we've just stepped through is relatively pain-free, but it would be true to say that it's not as pleasant as binding to a standard data source. The biggest inconvenience is that the columns aren't in the order in which they appeared in the `Customer` class—the order in the final display looks as if it's random. When data-aware controls bind to a conventional data source, they can read the column order. Since the `ObjectDataSource` generates columns by reflecting the class's public properties, it isn't able to determine the intended order for those columns.

There are a few ways to fix the column order:

■ One approach is to select a column by clicking on the column header. The `GridView` smart tag task menu, shown in Figure 3.28, will be updated to include column-specific tasks, including **Move Column Left** and **Move Column Right**.

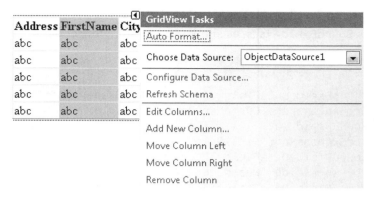

Figure 3.28. Correcting column order using the object's smart tag task menu

- Another option is to select the **Edit Columns...** task from the smart tag task menu. This displays the good old **Fields** editor, shown in Figure 3.29. In this dialog, you can choose a column in the **Selected fields** list and use the Up and Down arrow buttons to change the order.

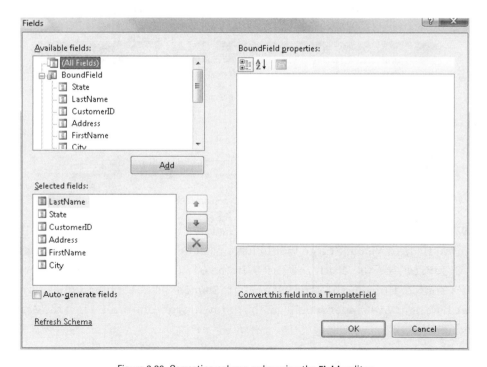

Figure 3.29. Correcting column order using the **Fields** editor

■ Yet another approach would be to just switch to **Source View** and manually reorder the <asp:BoundField> tags, as shown in the following code:

ObjectDataSource.aspx (excerpt)

```
<asp:BoundField DataField="CustomerID" HeaderText="CustomerID"
    SortExpression="CustomerID" />
<asp:BoundField DataField="FirstName" HeaderText="FirstName"
    SortExpression="FirstName" />
<asp:BoundField DataField="LastName" HeaderText="LastName"
    SortExpression="LastName" />
<asp:BoundField DataField="Address" HeaderText="Address"
    SortExpression="Address" />
<asp:BoundField DataField="City" HeaderText="City"
    SortExpression="City" />
<asp:BoundField DataField="State" HeaderText="State"
    SortExpression="State" />
```

Figure 3.30 shows our data-bound GridView with the correct column order.

	CustomerID	FirstName	LastName	Address	City	State
Edit Delete	1	Sue	Johnson	792 Main St.	Dallas	TX
Edit Delete	2	Sue	Williams	996 Main St.	Dallas	TX
Edit Delete	3	Edna	Johnson	737 Main St.	Dallas	TX
Edit Delete	4	George	Smith	255 Main St.	Dallas	TX
Edit Delete	5	Edna	Brown	240 Main St.	Dallas	TX

Figure 3.30. The GridView object with data populated from the ObjectDataSource

Now that we've got our column order correct, we're ready for the next hurdle. The user interface in Visual Studio would have us believe that we can enable paging for the GridView—on the GridView Tasks, in the GridView properties editor, or in the ASPX source. However, if your ObjectDataSource SELECT method doesn't return a DataSet or a DataReader, you'll get the following runtime error when the GridView is bound:

```
System.NotSupportedException: The data source does not support
server-side data paging.
```

To enable paging, you'll need to implement a new method, `GetCustomers`, which takes two parameters. The first parameter, *Rows*, represents the total number of rows to return. The second parameter, *StartIndex*, specifies the number of rows to return on a single page.

You may also expect that you could just make a simple modification to the existing `GetCustomers` method to implement the paging logic, as shown below:

```
//Won't work
public IEnumerable<Customer> GetCustomers(int rows, int startIndex)
{
    if (rows == 0) rows = Customers.Rows.Count;
    List<Customer> pageCustomers = new List<Customer>();
    for (int i = startIndex;
            i <= rows && i <= Customers.Rows.Count - 1;
            i++)
        yield return CustomerFromRow(Customers.Rows[i]);
}
```

An `IEnumerable` method with a yield return, such as we have here, is certainly an elegant and efficient solution—it streams the results to the calling function rather than evaluating the entire list and sending it *en masse*. However, the `ObjectDataSource` we used doesn't support paging against an `IEnumerable` select method. Instead, our paging select method will need to return a populated `List<Customer>` object:

Customer.cs (excerpt)

```
public List<Customer> GetCustomers(int rows, int startIndex)
{
  if (rows == 0)
  {
    rows = Customers.Rows.Count;
  }
  List<Customer> pageCustomers = new List<Customer>();
  for (int i = startIndex; i <= rows && i <=
      Customers.Rows.Count - 1; i++)
  {
    pageCustomers.Add(CustomerFromRow(Customers.Rows[i]));
  }
  return pageCustomers;
}
```

Another `ObjectDataSource` Gotcha

Since `ObjectDataSource` uses reflection to determine column fields, it can only bind to properties, not public fields. If the `Customer` class simply implemented `Customer` as a public integer field, the class wouldn't be exposed via the `ObjectDataSource`.

The `ObjectDataSource` also tries to use every public property in the object—even those that aren't intended to be used as data properties. For example, when it's trying to save changes to a property, `ObjectDataSource` will try to write to a read-only property, unless you specify otherwise.

We've highlighted a few of the potential issues you may face when mapping an existing business object to an `ObjectDataSource`. Performing a direct mapping works, but you end up having to modify your business objects to allow binding to them. If you can't (or don't want to) modify your existing business objects, you can use an adapter class that calls into your object and converts the output to an object type that the `ObjectDataSource` can handle easily. The benefit of this approach is that you don't need to change the way your business objects work in order to accommodate the `ObjectDataSource`; instead, you build your business objects as you'd like, then use the adapter to perform the mapping. If you take this approach, it's best to just return your data in standard ADO.NET objects (`DataSet`, `DataTable`, or `DataReader`).

For example, let's say we want to support paging with our `CustomerData` class, but we don't want to modify the way `CustomerData` works just to support advanced data binding. We decide to implement a `CustomerDataSource` class that has `ObjectDataSource`-friendly methods. For instance, it has a `GetDataTable` method, which calls the `GetData` method on the `CustomerData` class and converts the output to a `DataTable`.

One Final `ObjectDataSource` Gotcha

Providing data to the `ObjectDataSource` in `DataTable` objects simplifies a lot of issues such as paging and sorting. However, the `ObjectDataSource` won't automatically read your column names from the `DataTable`, so you'll need to configure this functionality yourself.

While the code in the adapter class itself might be a little ugly (simple to write, just ugly!), it allows you to use the `ObjectDataSource` without changing the way you write your business objects.

Summary

As you can see, the topic of data access is an involved one—it's impossible to do it justice in a single chapter. In fact, it's hard to do it justice in a single *book*, though many authors have made valiant efforts to do so. This just goes to show how extensive and rich data access functionality is within ASP.NET.

Data access is at the core of every significant web application. In this chapter, we refreshed our knowledge of some of the basics of data access, and quickly stepped through a number of examples that used the new data source controls, covering some of the common scenarios you may run into throughout your ASP.NET development career.

For more in-depth coverage of data access in ASP.NET, I recommend you start with the ASP.NET 2.0 Data Tutorials on the official ASP.NET web site.[10]

---

[10] http://www.asp.net/learn/dataaccess/

Pushing the Boundaries of the GridView

The introduction of the `GridView` control in ASP.NET 2.0 basically sent the `DataGrid` control to the dustbin of ASP.NET history. While the `DataGrid` served us well in its time, the `GridView` is the table control of choice now, as it boasts more functionality and extensibility than its predecessor.

Of course, there are still many situations in which `Repeater` or `DataList` controls are appropriate, but when you need rich sorting and paging, the `GridView` is hard to beat.

In fact, we like the `GridView` so much that we've dedicated this whole chapter to accomplishing various non-trivial tasks with the `GridView`. However, some of these techniques can be used with any of the table controls. For example, the following section covers nested data binding, which could also apply to a `Repeater` control.

How do I add a data-bound drop-down to a `GridView`?

Suppose you have a table of product details that you'd like to display to an administrative user so that he or she can edit the information about each product. This is a common task, and one that can easily be handled by binding a `Gridview` to your products table. Figure 4.1 shows a possible interface through which we could allow users to edit product details.

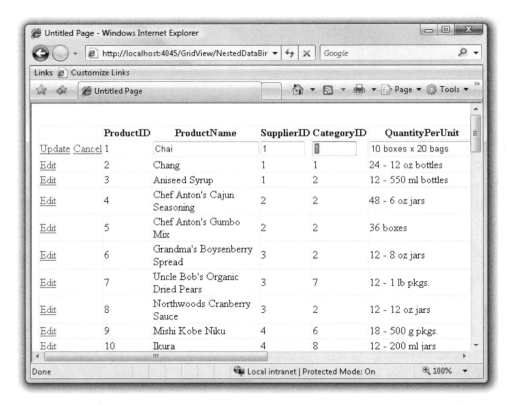

Figure 4.1. A simple UI to accompany a `GridView` control

You can see that the `Products` table contains a column called `CategoryID`, which is a foreign key into another table, namely `Categories`. You'll notice, however, that at present the `CategoryID` column requires that the user know the range of available category IDs.

It would be ideal if we could present users with a `DropDownList` containing the available category IDs. Let's look into how we can do this.

Solution

For this solution, we'll use the sample Northwind database that comes with SQL Server. If you don't have this database installed, the scripts are available for download from the Microsoft web site.[1]

In order to get up and running quickly, we'll use the designer and IDE to full effect here. For more detailed coverage of data binding a `GridView`, see Chapter 3.

Click on the **Server Explorer** and create a **Data Connection** to the Northwind database. Once this is set up, add a new **Web Form** to your project and make sure it's in Design View. Now expand the Northwind database in the **Server Explorer** and drag the `Products` table over to the **Web Form** designer. Visual Studio will automatically create a `GridView` that's bound to a `SqlDataSource`, as depicted in Figure 4.2.

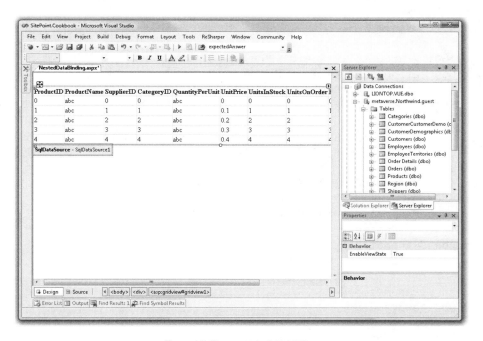

Figure 4.2. The generated `GridView`

---

[1] http://www.microsoft.com/downloads/details.aspx?familyid=06616212-0356-46a0-8da2-ee-bc53a68034&displaylang=en

If you click on the **Source** tab, you can see the markup that the designer generates. In the code below, I removed some of the columns and the commands for updating, deleting and inserting rows. Note that no source code is generated—it's just declarative markup:

NestedDataBinding.aspx *(excerpt)*

```
<asp:GridView ID="GridView1" runat="server"
    AutoGenerateColumns="False" DataKeyNames="ProductID"
    DataSourceID="SqlDataSource1" EmptyDataText="There are no data
    records to display.">
  <Columns>
    <asp:BoundField DataField="ProductID" HeaderText="ProductID"
        ReadOnly="True" SortExpression="ProductID" />
    <asp:BoundField DataField="ProductName" HeaderText="ProductName"
        SortExpression="ProductName" />
    ⋮
    <asp:CheckBoxField DataField="Discontinued"
        HeaderText="Discontinued" SortExpression="Discontinued" />
  </Columns>
</asp:GridView>

<asp:SqlDataSource ID="SqlDataSource1" runat="server"
    ConnectionString =
        "<%$ ConnectionStrings:NorthwindConnectionString1 %>"
    SelectCommand="SELECT [ProductID], [ProductName], [SupplierID],
        [CategoryID], [QuantityPerUnit], [UnitPrice],
        [UnitsInStock], [UnitsOnOrder], [ReorderLevel],
        [Discontinued] FROM [Products]" … >
  <InsertParameters>
    <asp:Parameter Name="ProductName" Type="String" />
    ⋮
    <asp:Parameter Name="Discontinued" Type="Boolean" />
  </InsertParameters>
  <UpdateParameters>
    <asp:Parameter Name="ProductName" Type="String" />
    ⋮
    <asp:Parameter Name="ProductID" Type="Int32" />
  </UpdateParameters>
  <DeleteParameters>
    <asp:Parameter Name="ProductID" Type="Int32" />
  </DeleteParameters>
</asp:SqlDataSource>
```

Switch back to Design View, and click on the upper right arrow of the GridView to display the GridView's smart tag. Be sure to check **Enable Editing**, as shown in Figure 4.3.

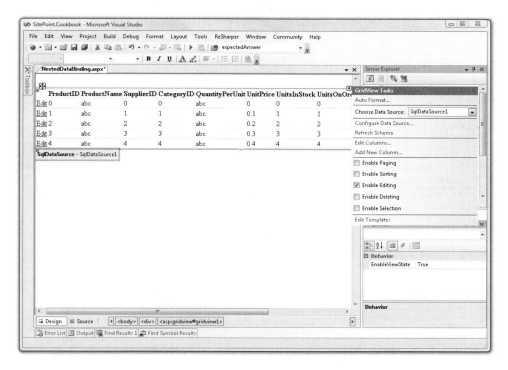

Figure 4.3. Enabling editing of the GridView

If you compile and run this page, you'll see the interface shown in Figure 4.1. Think it looks good? We're just getting warmed up!

Bring up the smart tag again and select **Edit Columns** to display the dialog shown in Figure 4.4.

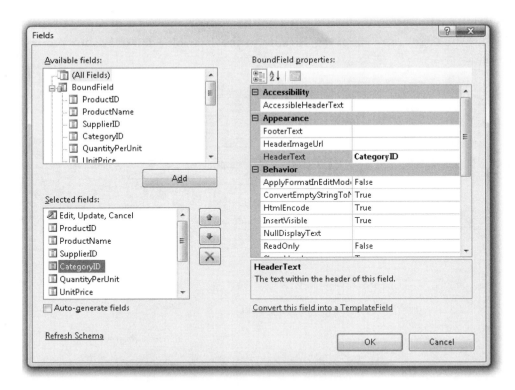

Figure 4.4. The **Fields** dialog

We need to convert the `CategoryID` column from a bound column to a template column. Select `CategoryID` in the **Selected fields** area, click the **Convert this field into a TemplateField** link, then click **OK**.

Once again, bring up the smart tag and click **Edit Templates.** This will display a dialog that will allow you to select a template for any of the template columns, though in this case, we're focusing on `CategoryID`. Select the **EditItemTemplate** for the `CategoryID` column.

Next, we remove the default `TextBox` from the template and replace it with a `DropDownList` control.

Now we need to add a data source for the `Category DropDownList`—a task that we can accomplish simply by dragging the `Categories` table to the web form. After you do so, delete the `Categories` grid view that was created by the designer. We need only the data source.

Switching to Source View, you should see the following additional markup for the new SqlDataSource. In the following snippet, I removed the `DeleteCommand`, `InsertCommand`, and `UpdateCommand` attributes as we won't need them:

NestedDataBinding.aspx (excerpt)

```
<asp:SqlDataSource ID="SqlDataSource2" runat="server"
    ConnectionString =
        "<%$ ConnectionStrings:NorthwindConnectionString1 %>"
    ProviderName =
  "<%$ ConnectionStrings:NorthwindConnectionString1.ProviderName %>"
    SelectCommand = "SELECT [CategoryID], [CategoryName],
        [Description], [Picture] FROM [Categories]"
    <InsertParameters>
        <asp:Parameter Name="CategoryName" Type="String" />
        <asp:Parameter Name="Description" Type="String" />
    </InsertParameters>
    <UpdateParameters>
        <asp:Parameter Name="CategoryName" Type="String" />
        <asp:Parameter Name="Description" Type="String" />
        <asp:Parameter Name="CategoryID" Type="Int32" />
    </UpdateParameters>
    <DeleteParameters>
        <asp:Parameter Name="CategoryID" Type="Int32" />
    </DeleteParameters>
</asp:SqlDataSource>
```

Now bring up the smart tag for the `DropDownList`—as shown in Figure 4.5—and select **Choose Data Source**.

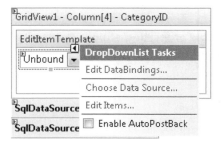

Figure 4.5. Choosing the data source for the DropDownList

Select the data source containing the `Categories` table data (it will still be name by its default filename, `SqlDataSource2`, unless you've renamed it), then select `CategoryName` as the display field and `CategoryId` as the value field for our new `DropDownList`.

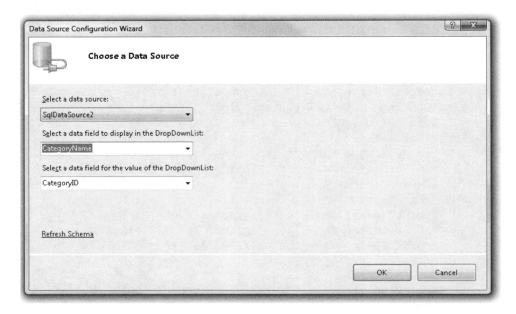

Figure 4.6. Using the Data Source Configuration Wizard to choose a data source

We're almost done: we just need to make sure that the value we selected for the `Category` drop-down is bound to the product's `CategoryID`.

Bring up the smart tag for the drop-down and click on **Edit** > **DataBindings**. The **DataBindings** dialog for the `DropDownList` will display.

From the list headed **Bindable properties**, choose **SelectedValue**. Then, in the right-hand column, select the field to which you want to bind this property—`Category-ID`—as shown in Figure 4.7.

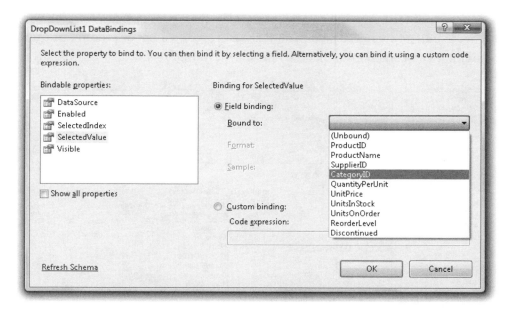

Figure 4.7. Binding a `DropDownList` control

When we switch to the Source View, we see the updated markup for the `CategoryID` column:

```
                                              NestedDataBinding.aspx (excerpt)
<asp:TemplateField HeaderText="CategoryID"
    SortExpression="CategoryID">
  <EditItemTemplate>
    <asp:DropDownList ID="DropDownList1" runat="server"
        DataSourceID="SqlDataSource2" DataTextField="CategoryName"
        DataValueField="CategoryID"
        SelectedValue='<%# Bind("CategoryID") %>'>
    </asp:DropDownList>
  </EditItemTemplate>
  <ItemTemplate>
    <sp:LookupLabel id="lookupLabel" runat="server"
        DataSourceID="SqlDataSource2" DataTextField="CategoryName"
        DataValueField="CategoryID"
        SelectedValue='<%# Bind("CategoryID") %>' />
  </ItemTemplate>
</asp:TemplateField>
```

We're now ready to build and run the page again. This time, when you click on the **Edit** link to edit a row in the table, you'll see a drop-down list of product categories from which you can choose, like the one shown in Figure 4.8.

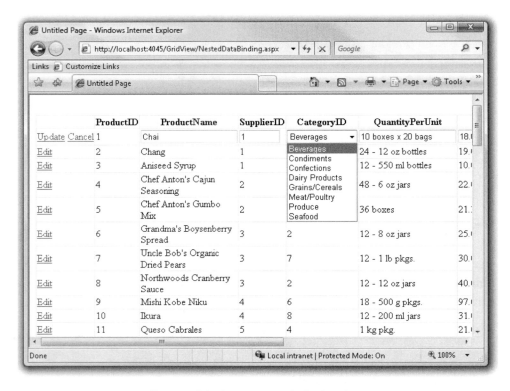

Figure 4.8. Selecting a category via the drop-down

Select a category, click the **Update** link, and you should see that the `CategoryID` has changed to reflect your new selection.

Discussion

A more generic term for the technique we demonstrated in this section is **nested data binding**. ASP.NET 2.0 Data Source controls make it easy to set up nested data binding declaratively.

Although we demonstrated nested data binding with a `DropDownList` control, it will work with any bindable control. For example, we could have swapped the `DropDownList` for a `RadioButtonList`, or even another nested `GridView` control.

How do I sort on multiple columns?

Enabling sorting with the `GridView` control is extremely easy—simply set the
`AllowSorting` property to `true`:

```
<asp:GridView ID="GridView1" runat="server"
    AllowSorting="True" />
```

The only problem is that this solution allows you to sort only one column at a time.
What if you want to sort on two columns? Well, as it turns out, this isn't too difficult.

Solution

The trick here is to handle the `Sorting` event of the `GridView` and set the sort expression via code. For this demonstration, we'll display the `Suppliers` table from
the Northwind sample database that comes with SQL Server.

The quick and easy way to display a `GridView` with the data from the `Suppliers`
table is to follow the instructions from the section called "How do I add a data-
bound drop-down to a `GridView`?".

Now, within the code behind, we need to attach an event handler to the `Sorting`
event:

MultiSorting.aspx.cs (excerpt)

```
protected void Page_Load(object sender, EventArgs e)
{
  this.GridView1.Sorting +=
      new GridViewSortEventHandler(GridView1_Sorting);
}
void GridView1_Sorting(object sender, GridViewSortEventArgs e)
{
  ⋮
}
```

Handling Events Declaratively

Another way to handle the `Sorting` event for the `GridView` is to declaratively specify the method in the markup for the `GridView`, like so:

```
<asp:GridView ID="GridView1" runat="server"
    Sorting="GridView1_Sorting" />
```

You'll find that some people are opposed to this approach because it hides what's really happening under the hood. While explicitly wiring up the event handlers avoids this "Magic behind the curtain" issue, the authors believe the choice of one or the other of these approaches to be primarily a matter of taste.

Some might bring up so called "performance" issues with this approach because it uses reflection. While it is true in theory that the page will execute slightly slower using this approach than it would if you explicitly wired up the event handling directly, unless you measure, you won't know whether the performance hit is significant. Compared to the performance of the data access code, it's probably negligible in most cases.

The next step is to fill in the `GridView1_Sorting` method with our implementation, which will track the columns we're sorting on and adjust the `SortExpression` accordingly:

MultiSorting.aspx.cs *(excerpt)*

```
void GridView1_Sorting(object sender, GridViewSortEventArgs e)
{
  string currentExpression = GridView1.SortExpression;
  if (currentExpression.Length == 0) return;
  //First column to sort, no need for anything special.
  //Want to keep the clicked on sort expression in the front.
  string[] sortedColumns = currentExpression.Split(',');
  string newSortExpression = e.SortExpression;
  foreach (string sortExpression in sortedColumns)
  {
    if(sortExpression != e.SortExpression) newSortExpression
        += "," + sortExpression;
  }
}
```

Notice that the method has a parameter of type GridViewSortEventArgs. This contains a property, SortExpression, which holds the value of the sort expression for the column the user clicked.

The basic idea is to build a sort expression by concatenating each SortExpression from the columns on which the user clicks. However, we want to keep the most recent column at the front of the expression.

Our first task is to grab the SortExpression from the GridView. This is the current full sort expression at the time the sort column was clicked. If this value is empty, then we know that this is the first time a sort column has been clicked (otherwise we would already have a sort expression), so we can just return from the method and let the default behavior apply. This procedure takes place in this snippet of code:

```
string currentExpression = GridView1.SortExpression;
if (currentExpression.Length == 0)
  return; //First column to sort, no need for anything special
```

The next section of code handles the situation after one or more sort columns has been clicked. In this situation, the GridView.SortExpression property will not be empty—it'll contain the current sort expression, which will be a comma-delimited list of column sort expressions.

First, we split this sort expression into an array using the comma as a delimiter. Then, we simply want to iterate through the existing sort expressions and append them to the end of the sort expression for the column the user clicked on, which we obtained via the GridViewSortEventArgs.SortExpression property. That's what this snippet of code accomplishes:

```
string[] sortedColumns = currentExpression.Split(',');
string newSortExpression = e.SortExpression;
foreach (string sortExpression in sortedColumns)
{
  if(sortExpression != e.SortExpression)
    newSortExpression += "," + sortExpression;
}
```

As we build this new sort expression, we must be careful not to include the sort expression for the currently active column twice—the conditional check within the `for` loop ensures that we avoid this.

Discussion

One drawback to this approach is that when the user sorts the data on multiple columns, the sort direction will always be ascending. Why?

The `SortDirection` property of the `GridView` control is an enumerated value of type `System.Web.UI.WebControls.SortDirection`. Since this property is not a string, we cannot append multiple sort directions to the value.

But even if you try to sort multiple columns in descending order by setting the `SortDirection` in the `Sorting` event handler, it won't work: the `SortDirection` property seems to ignore anything other than `Ascending`:

```
e.SortDirection = SortDirection.Descending;   //ignored
```

Changing the `SortDirection`

The `SortDirection` property of the `GridView` class is a read-only property. So how would you change the sort direction for a column? The only way to change it is within the event handler for the `Sorting` event. The event handler is passed an argument of type *GridViewSortEventArgs*, and you can change the sort direction by setting the `SortDirection` property of the *GridViewSortEvent-Args* argument.

How do I display the sort state?

When you enable sorting on a `GridView`, each column's title is displayed as a hyperlink. Click on the hyperlink, and the `GridView` sorts the table on the basis of that column, but it does not give any visual indication of which column is being used to sort the data, or in which direction the data is being sorted. Let's learn how to resolve this issue.

Solution

In this demonstration, we'll display the `Suppliers` table from the Northwind sample database that comes with SQL Server.

Figure 4.9 shows a `GridView` displaying the raw data from the `Suppliers` table with sorting enabled. In this case, we've sorted the data by `CompanyName`, but there's no indication that we've sorted the data by that column.

Figure 4.9. The display failing to indicate which is the sort-by column

In order to rectify this situation, we need to handle the GridView's Sorting event to create a visual indication of the sort-by column. In our Sorting event handler, we're passed an instance of GridViewSortEventArgs, which contains the SortExpression property that we can use to find the sorted column like so:

SortableGridView.aspx.cs *(excerpt)*

```
protected void Page_Load(object sender, EventArgs e)
{
  this.GridView1.Sorting += GridView1_Sorting;
}
void GridView1_Sorting(object sender, GridViewSortEventArgs e)
{
  foreach(DataControlField column in GridView1.Columns)
  {
    if(column.SortExpression == e.SortExpression)
    {
      column.HeaderStyle.CssClass = "sorted";
      column.HeaderStyle.BackColor = Color.Khaki;
    }
    else
    {
      column.HeaderStyle.CssClass = "";
      column.HeaderStyle.BackColor = Color.White;
    }
  }
}
```

Notice that when we find the sorted column, we set the CSSClass property to sorted, which allows us to style the sorted column via CSS. While this is my preferred approach, for the sake of this demonstration, I'll also set the background color to Khaki so that we don't have to set up an external style sheet to see the results.

Upon refreshing your browser, you should see something like Figure 4.10.

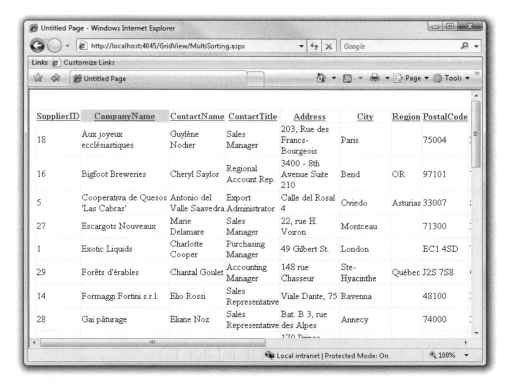

Figure 4.10. Indicating the sort-by column using color

This is helpful, but we're not done yet. How do we get the column to display the direction in which the data was sorted? This is a slightly trickier problem, but it's not too difficult.

Showing Sort Direction via CSS

One approach to showing users the sort direction of tabular content is to use the CSS trick we saw above, assigning a CSS class for an ascending sort, and a different CSS class for a descending sort. We can use these CSS classes to differentiate between the sort directions by using different styles—for example, setting a background image with an up or down arrow.

In this example, we'll simply append the words `[asc]` or `[desc]` to the end of the `HeaderText` of the column by which the data was sorted.

The only tricky part is that we need to store the original `HeaderText` value for all columns so that when we stop sorting the data on that column, we can return its `HeaderText` back to its original value.

In order to do this, we'll add the `HeaderText` for each column to the `ViewState` object, using the column's `SortExpression` as the key. Within the `OnLoad` method, we'll initialize the `ViewState` object to contain the original `HeaderText` values (the new code is shown in bold):

SortableGridView.aspx.cs *(excerpt)*

```
protected override void OnLoad(EventArgs e)
{
  AllowSorting = true;
  if (!Page.IsPostBack)
  {
    foreach (DataControlField column in Columns)
    {
      if (ViewState[column.SortExpression] == null)
        ViewState[column.SortExpression] = column.HeaderText;
    }
  }
  base.OnLoad(e);
}
```

Now, through our `GridView Sort` event handler, we'll append the word `[asc]` or `[desc]` to the column's `HeaderText`, depending on the sort direction (again, the new code is shown in bold):

SortableGridView.aspx.cs *(excerpt)*

```
protected override void OnSorting(GridViewSortEventArgs e)
{
  foreach (DataControlField column in Columns)
  {
    if (column.SortExpression == e.SortExpression)
    {
      column.HeaderStyle.CssClass = "sorted";
      column.HeaderStyle.BackColor = Color.Khaki;
      if (e.SortDirection == SortDirection.Descending)
        column.HeaderText = ViewState[column.SortExpression]
            + " [asc]";
```

```
      else
        column.HeaderText = ViewState[column.SortExpression]
          + " [desc]";
    }
    else
    {
      if (ViewState[column.SortExpression] != null)
      {
        column.HeaderText = ViewState[column.SortExpression]
          as string;
      }
      column.HeaderStyle.CssClass = "";
      column.HeaderStyle.BackColor = Color.White;
    }
  }
  base.OnSorting(e);
}
```

Now when we sort a column in ascending order, we'll see the word characters
[desc] to indicate that clicking on that column will sort the column in descending
order, as Figure 4.11 illustrates.

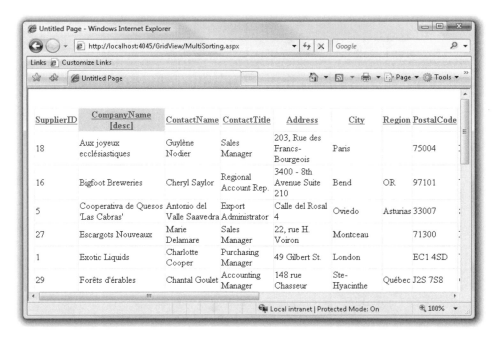

Figure 4.11. Identifying the sort-by column with color and label indicators

Discussion

It's worth mentioning that while it is possible to customize the GridView control by responding to its various events within the code for the host page, this isn't a very reusable approach.

Instead, it makes more sense to extend the GridView by writing a custom version of the control, which ensures that you only need to write that code once. For example, we might create a class called SortableGridView like so:

SortableGridView.aspx.cs *(excerpt)*

```csharp
using System;
using System.Drawing;
using System.Web.UI.WebControls;
namespace SitePoint.Cookbook.GridViews
{
  public class SortableGridView : GridView
  {
    // Classes that inherit from this class and override OnLoad
    // must be sure to call base.OnLoad or they lose this
    // functionality.
    protected override void OnLoad(EventArgs e)
    {
      AllowSorting = true;
      if (!Page.IsPostBack)
      {
        foreach (DataControlField column in Columns)
        {
          if (ViewState[column.SortExpression] == null)
            ViewState[column.SortExpression] = column.HeaderText;
        }
      }
      base.OnLoad(e);
    }
    protected override void OnSorting(GridViewSortEventArgs e)
    {
      foreach (DataControlField column in Columns)
      {
        if (column.SortExpression == e.SortExpression)
        {
          column.HeaderStyle.CssClass = "sorted";
          column.HeaderStyle.BackColor = Color.Khaki;
          if (e.SortDirection == SortDirection.Descending)
```

```
      {
        column.HeaderText = ViewState[column.SortExpression] +
           " [asc]";elsecolumn.HeaderText =
           ViewState[column.SortExpression] + " [desc]";
      }
    }
    else
    {
      if (ViewState[column.SortExpression] != null)
        column.HeaderText = ViewState[column.SortExpression]
           as string;
      column.HeaderStyle.CssClass = "";
      column.HeaderStyle.BackColor = Color.White;
    }
  }
  base.OnSorting(e);
  }
 }
}
```

How do I implement custom paging?

As in the previous two examples, we're going to begin by dragging a Northwind table onto the Web Form designer. In this discussion, let's mix things up by dragging the OrderDetails table to the form.

Enable sorting and paging on the GridView. Once you've built the project, view the page in the browser—you should see something that looks like Figure 4.12.

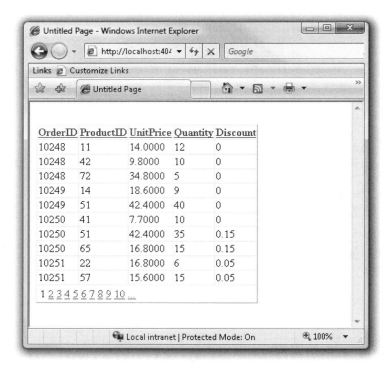

Figure 4.12. Default paging on a `GridView`

At the bottom of the grid is a paging control that allows us to click through the various pages of data. This is useful for navigating through the data, but it could be improved upon in a number of ways. Let's see how.

Using `PagerSettings`

The `PagerSettings` element within the `GridView` markup gives us a lot of control over the pager output without requiring us to deal with any custom programming, or modification of the pager template.

However, when you need total control, modifying the `PagerSettings` is the only way to go.

Solution

First, we need to edit the `PagerTemplate` within the `GridView`. In the designer, bring up the `GridView`'s smart tag and click **Edit Templates**. Select **PagerTemplate** as shown in Figure 4.13.

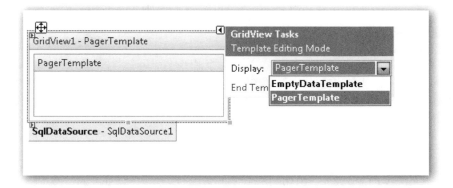

Figure 4.13. Selecting **PagerTemplate** from the drop-down

Within this template we're going to drag several LinkButton controls which will be used to navigate back and forth between pages, much like a WizardControl.

In fact, the paging in a GridView works exactly like a WizardControl. By specifying the appropriate CommandArgument property of each button, the GridView automagically wires up the button to the appropriate navigation event.

In Source View, the final result of the PagerTemplate should look like this:

Paging.aspx *(excerpt)*

```
<PagerTemplate>
  <asp:LinkButton ID="first" runat="server" Text="<< First"
      CommandArgument="First" CommandName="Page" />
  <asp:LinkButton ID="prev" runat="server" Text="< Previous"
      CommandArgument="Prev"
      CommandName="Page" />
  Page <asp:DropDownList ID="pages" runat="server"
      AutoPostBack="True"/> of <asp:Label ID="count"
      runat="server" />
  <asp:LinkButton ID="next" runat="server" Text="Next >"
      CommandArgument="Next" CommandName="Page" />
  <asp:LinkButton ID="last" runat="server" Text="Last >>"
      CommandArgument="Last" CommandName="Page" />
</PagerTemplate>
```

The LinkButton instances will navigate back and forth between pages, while the DropDownList will contain all the page numbers. When the user selects a page in the DropDownList, the control will AutoPostBack and navigate to the selected page.

With the paging UI set up, let's dig into the code to make the magic happen. The first step we need to take is to wire up the DataBind event of the GridView1 to an event handler and to the DropDownList's SelectedIndexChanged event:

Paging.aspx.cs *(excerpt)*

```
protected void Page_Load(object sender, EventArgs e)
{
  GridView1.DataBound += GridView1_DataBound;
  GridViewRow row = GridView1.BottomPagerRow;
  if (row == null) return;
  DropDownList pages =
      (DropDownList)row.Cells[0].FindControl("pages");
  pages.SelectedIndexChanged += OnSelectedIndexChanged;
}
void GridView1_DataBound(object sender, EventArgs e)
{
  //...
}
protected void OnSelectedIndexChanged(Object sender, EventArgs e)
{
  //...
}
```

Most of our work happens within the GridView.DataBound event handler. Take a look at the full code here, then we'll walk through it piece by piece:

Paging.aspx.cs *(excerpt)*

```
private void GridView1_DataBound(object sender, EventArgs e)
{
  GridViewRow row = GridView1.BottomPagerRow; ❶
  if (row == null) return;

  // get your controls from the gridview ❷
  DropDownList pages =
      (DropDownList)row.Cells[0].FindControl("pages");
  pages.SelectedIndexChanged += OnSelectedIndexChanged;
  Label count = (Label) row.Cells[0].FindControl("count");
```

```
if (pages != null)
{

  // populate pager
  for (int i = 0; i < GridView1.PageCount; i++) ❸
  {
    int pageNumber = i + 1;
    ListItem pageItem = new ListItem(pageNumber.ToString());
    if (i == GridView1.PageIndex)pageItem.Selected = true;
    pages.Items.Add(pageItem);
  }
}

// populate page count
if (count != null)
{
  count.Text = string.Format("<b>{0}</b>",
      GridView1.PageCount); ❹
}
LinkButton prev = (LinkButton) row.Cells[0].FindControl("prev");
LinkButton next = (LinkButton) row.Cells[0].FindControl("next");
LinkButton first = (LinkButton) row.Cells[0].FindControl("first");
LinkButton last = (LinkButton) row.Cells[0].FindControl("last");

// set the pager nav state based on the current page ❺
if (GridView1.PageIndex == 0)
{
  prev.Enabled = false;
  first.Enabled = false;
}
else if (GridView1.PageIndex + 1 == GridView1.PageCount)
{
  last.Enabled = false;
  next.Enabled = false;
}
else
{
  last.Enabled = true;
  next.Enabled = true;
  prev.Enabled = true;
  first.Enabled = true;
}
}
```

1   The first couple of lines check to make sure the `BottomPagerRow` exists, and grab a reference to it.

This is a defensive coding technique that we'll use to protect us just in case someone later deletes the `PagerTemplate` from the markup, or we find we don't have any data to data bind to.

2   The next step is to retrieve the `DropDownList` and label defined in the `PagerTemplate`. At this point, we know we'll find the controls within the first cell of the `Pager` row. We also attach an event handler to the `DropDownList`.

3   Now we populate the `DropDownList` with an item for every page of data. In this loop we simply iterate over an index and create a `ListItem` for each page number. Notice that the `PageIndex` property is a zero-based index, but obviously, for the purposes of presentation, we want our page numbers to be a one-based index.

4   As a convenience, we populate the `Label` control with the total count of pages.

5   The final step is to obtain a reference to each of our navigation buttons, and set their `Enabled` properties on the basis of the current page. This approach ensures that when the user is on the first page, the **First Page** and **Previous** links are not enabled—it wouldn't make any sense for them to be usable at that point.

Now we can implement the event handler for the `SelectedIndexChanged` event of the `DropDownList`:

```
protected void OnSelectedIndexChanged(Object sender, EventArgs e)
{
  GridViewRow pager = GridView1.BottomPagerRow;
  DropDownList pages =
      (DropDownList)pager.Cells[0].FindControl("pages");
  GridView1.PageIndex = pages.SelectedIndex;
  // a method to populate your grid
  GridView1.DataBind();
}
```

All we're doing here is setting the `GridView`'s page index to the same index as the drop-down list, then rebinding the `GridView`. It's fairly straightforward. Figure 4.14 shows the results of our work.

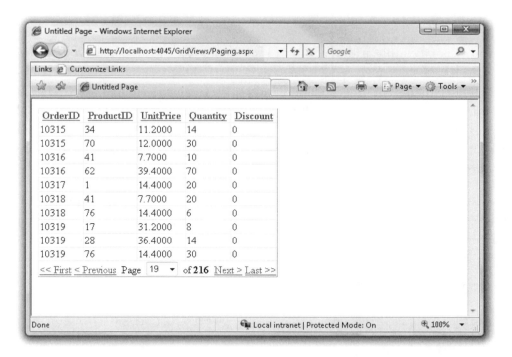

Figure 4.14. Our custom paging controls

Discussion

As we just demonstrated, the GridView's extensibility enables us to create just about any kind of paging user interface we'd want. Although it may seem unorthodox to use a DropDownList control, one minor benefit of this approach is that the user can tab into the DropDownList, quickly type a page number, and hit the **Enter** key to be taken directly to a specific page.

How can I allow users to download tabular data as a Microsoft Excel file?

It's a common requirement—we show pretty tabular data on a web page, and Wilbur, that pencil pusher in accounting, immediately says he needs to export it to Microsoft Excel. Fine, we can do that.

Solution

If you've got a simple grid that will fit into a single Excel worksheet, you can use the old HTML table trick, which takes advantage of the fact that Excel can read HTML documents and interpret tabular data. We'll create a standard `GridView`, but when we send the output to the browser, we'll make sure the content is as simple as possible and set the content type to that of an Excel file. Wilbur's browser will see an Excel file downloading and pass the buck to Excel, which will display the document.

First, we'll need a simple `GridView` that we can preview before the export takes place. To keep things simple, we'll be working with a default `GridView` generated by dragging the Northwind `Products` table onto an empty form. The only change we'll make to the form is to add a button:

ExcelExport.aspx *(excerpt)*

```
<asp:Button ID="btnExport"
  runat="server"
  OnClick="btnExport_Click"
  Text="Export to Excel"
/>
```

Great! Now let's handle the export:

ExcelExport.aspx.cs *(excerpt)*

```
using System;
using System.Data;
using System.Configuration;
using System.Web;
using System.Web.Security;
using System.Web.UI;
using System.Web.UI.WebControls;
using System.Web.UI.WebControls.WebParts;
using System.Web.UI.HtmlControls;
using System.IO;
public partial class _Default : System.Web.UI.Page
{
    GridView gridToExport = null;
    protected void btnExport_Click(object sender, EventArgs e)
    {
```

```
        gridToExport = grdProducts;
    }
    protected override void Render(HtmlTextWriter writer)
    {
        if (gridToExport as GridView != null)
            ExportGridToExcel(gridToExport, "Products.xls");
        base.Render(writer);
    }
    private void ExportGridToExcel(GridView grid, string filename)
    {
        if(string.IsNullOrEmpty(filename))
            throw new ArgumentException(
                "Export filename is required");
        if(!filename.EndsWith(".xls"))
            filename += ".xls";
        grid.AllowPaging = false;
        grid.AllowSorting = false;
        grid.DataBind();
        StringWriter tw = new StringWriter();
        HtmlTextWriter hw = new HtmlTextWriter(tw);
        Response.Clear();
        Response.ContentType = "application/vnd.ms-excel";
        Response.AddHeader(
            "content-disposition",
            "attachment;filename=" + filename);
        Response.Charset = string.Empty;
        Page.EnableViewState = false;
        grid.RenderControl(hw);
        Response.Write(tw.ToString());
        Response.End();
    }
    /// <summary>
    /// Need to override this to prevent checking that controls are
    /// in a webform, since we're rendering the gridview by itself.
    /// </summary>
    /// <param name="control"></param>
    public override void VerifyRenderingInServerForm(
        Control control)
    {
    }
}
```

Discussion

This task used to be simpler in ASP.NET 1.1; ASP.NET 2.0's improved security complicates things a little. First of all, you'll notice that the button `click` event isn't directly calling the export; it's just setting it up to be called in the `Render` method. That's because ASP.NET's event validation doesn't allow us to modify controls that participate in event validation outside the `Render` method. The simplest workaround is to add `EnableEventValidation="false"` to your `@Page` declaration, but that's not the best solution. Event validation checks provide additional security for your site, so it's best to leave them in place if possible. We're working with the event validation mechanism by modifying our page controls inside the `Render` method.

There's more information on exporting a `GridView` to Excel at the site of Grid-ViewGuy.[2]

Numeric Formatting and Formulæ

It's only natural that, once we're exporting our tabular data in Excel files, those Excel users will want their numbers to be formatted correctly.

No problem! The trick is to set up an Excel file with the formatting you need, export the file to HTML, and check the HTML source. When you do that, you'll see that each table cell has a `class` attribute assigned to it, and that the CSS rule-set for that class includes Excel-specific formatting instructions. In order to duplicate the formatting when you export, you'll need to write out the style information to define the cell format, then assign the style to each table cell to which you want it to apply.

For example, let's say we want to format the Unit Price column as a US currency value rather than a simple numeric value. Instead of values like 18 and 23.5, we want to see $18.00 and $23.50.

Start by exporting the `GridView` as an Excel file without any special formatting, then open it in Excel, select all the cells in the Unit Price column, and set the format to Currency.

Next, export the Excel file as HTML, and open the HTML file in a text editor, like Notepad. You'll need to dig through some pretty dense HTML code, but you'll find that the cells in the Unit Price column have a class named something like `x126`:

---

[2] http://gridviewguy.com/ArticleDetails.aspx?articleID=197

```
<td class=x126
    align=right
    width=65
    style='border-top:none;border-left:none;width:49pt'
    x:num="9.2">
$9.20
</td>
```

Now, scroll to the top of the file and find the definition of that style:

```
.x126 {
  mso-style-parent: style0;
  mso-number-format: "\0022$\0022\#\,\#\#0\.00";
  border: .5pt solid black;
  white-space: normal;
}
```

The only thing we care about right now is that format line, but if you want to apply fancy formatting like borders or cell colors, you'll need to include those declarations as well.

Let's add a method that applies the formatting for a grid. The method takes the grid as a parameter, so we could support the export of different grids if needed. Note that we had to escape several characters in that format string. The one that's not obvious is the \0, which, while it will compile, will write out null characters. It needs to be replaced with a \\0:

ExcelExport.aspx.cs *(excerpt)*

```
private string GetExcelStyle(GridView grid)
{
  if(grid == grdProducts)
    return
      "<style>" +
        "excelCurrency{mso-number-format:" +
        "\"\\0022$\\0022\\#\\,\\#\\#0\\.00\";" +
      "</style>";
  return string.Empty;
}
```

We call the new `GetExcelStyle` method from our `Render` method, right before we write out the rest of the HTML:

ExcelExport.aspx.cs *(excerpt)*

```
grid.RenderControl(hw);
Response.Write(GetExcelStyle(grid));
Response.Write(tw.ToString());
Response.End();
```

The last step is to add the `class` attribute of `x126` to the cells we want to style. The cleanest way to add a `class` attribute to a `GridView` cell is to set its `ItemStyle-CssClass` property:

ExcelExport.aspx.cs *(excerpt)*

```
<asp:BoundField
    DataField="UnitPrice"
    ItemStyle-CssClass="excelCurrency"
    HeaderText="UnitPrice"
    SortExpression="UnitPrice" />
```

Figure 4.15 depicts our work so far, when viewed in Excel.

E	F	G
QuantityPerUnit	**UnitPrice**	**UnitsInStock**
10 boxes x 20 bags	$18.00	39
24 - 12 oz bottles	$19.00	17
12 - 550 ml bottles	$10.00	13
48 - 6 oz jars	$22.00	53
36 boxes	$21.35	0
12 - 8 oz jars	$25.00	120
12 - 1 lb pkgs.	$30.00	15
12 - 12 oz jars	$40.00	6
18 - 500 g pkgs.	$97.00	29
12 - 200 ml jars	$31.00	31
1 kg pkg.	$21.00	22
10 - 500 g pkgs.	$38.00	86
2 kg box	$6.00	24
40 - 100 g pkgs.	$23.25	35

Figure 4.15. Viewing the styled content in Excel

While we're at it, we can even dress our data up a little—Wilbur will love it! Let's add autofilters to those columns. By adding autofilter to the headers and viewing the HTML, we can see that we need to add an x:autofilter attribute to the header cells. Since we're adding a non-standard attribute, we'll need to handle it in the RowDataBound of our GridView event:

ExcelExport.aspx.cs *(excerpt)*

```
protected void grdProducts_RowDataBound(
    object sender, GridViewRowEventArgs e)
{
  if (e.Row.RowType == DataControlRowType.Header)
  {
    foreach (TableCell cell in e.Row.Cells)
    {
      cell.Attributes.Add("x:autofilter", "all");
    }
  }
}
```

The x: at the beginning of the x:autofilter attribute shows that we'll need to declare an XML namespace for the HTML document. We'll do that in the Render method, right before we write out our cell format:

ExcelExport.aspx.cs *(excerpt)*

```
grid.RenderControl(hw);
Response.Write(
    "<html xmlns:x=\"urn:schemas-microsoft-com:" +
    "office:excel\" >");
Response.Write(GetExcelStyle(grid));
```

That explanation should give you enough detail to handle most Excel formatting issues. Using CSS you can include fonts, colors, borders—even formulas—in your made-for-Excel HTML. Just follow the pattern we used here: add a single feature, view the HTML, then duplicate it in your export.

Exporting Multiple Worksheets in One Excel File

After playing with Excel's HTML support for a bit, you might get the idea that you can implement any Excel feature by adding a few HTML attributes and styles. There's one feature that you can't implement with Excel HTML, though: exporting multiple worksheets in one Excel document.

If you need to do that, take a look at using Excel's XML format, which can contain multiple `Worksheet` elements. Obviously, including multiple worksheets is going to take more work than rendering the `GridView` to the response and tweaking it a bit.

In this case, you'll want to skip over the `GridView` and just convert a `DataSet` to XML, then convert it to Excel XML via XSLT.

Excel 2003 introduced Microsoft's first XML spreadsheet format, called SpreadsheetML.[3] Another method for creating SpreadsheetML is the free CarlosAG Excel Writer.[4] Wyatt Barnett has published a great introduction to this library on the SitePoint web site.[5] Using the CarlosAG Excel writer, you can create a spreadsheet programmatically:

```csharp
using CarlosAg.ExcelXmlWriter;

class TestApp
{
  static void Main(string[] args)
  {
    Workbook book = new Workbook();
    Worksheet sheet = book.Worksheets.Add("Sample");
    WorksheetRow row =  sheet.Table.Rows.Add();
    row.Cells.Add("Hello World");
    book.Save(@"c:\test.xls");
  }
}
```

While Excel 2007 continues to support the Excel 2003 SpreadsheetML format, Microsoft released a new XML-based spreadsheet format with Excel 2007. This was part of Microsoft's transition to using open, published XML formats, known as the Open XML formats, in Office 2007. Like the other Open XML formats, the

---

[3] http://support.microsoft.com/kb/319180/

[4] http://www.carlosag.net/Tools/ExcelXmlWriter/Default.aspx

[5] http://www.sitepoint.com/blogs/2006/08/22/making-excel-the-carlosag-way/

new Excel XSLX format is actually a zip file that contains one or more XML files as well as any images and other media that are included in the worksheet collection.

Whereas the SpreadsheetML format expresses the entire document in a single XML document (in which each worksheet is a node), the XSLX format uses a separate XML document for each worksheet. The end result is that the XSLX file format is very powerful, though it's also more complex to create from within an ASP.NET application. That's why you'll want to use the ExcelPackager, which is available on CodePlex.[6] OpenXmlDeveloper.org (sponsored by Microsoft) offers sample code that demonstrates the use of ExcelPackager to generate XSLX in a server-based application.[7]

Summary

A lot of the features we used to bolt onto the `DataGrid` come standard with the `GridView`. If you need to accomplish something `GridView` doesn't offer, you'll find that it's usually fairly easy to add the functionality—most of these tips, for example, didn't require much code.

We hope this chapter showed you more than a few slick tips for jazzing up `GridView`, and that you now feel confident to use the general techniques for extending this control.

---

[6] http://www.codeplex.com/ExcelPackage/

[7] http://openxmldeveloper.org/articles/Creating_Spreadsheets_Server.aspx

Form Validation

It's a commonly held belief that the point of validating user input is to ensure that valid, accurate data is entered into your database. To some degree this may be true, but search your user database for the number of users named Mickey Mouse and you'll soon realize that a determined user can always pass your validation rules with inaccurate data.

The real objective of form validation is to help users who want to enter accurate information to do so as easily as possible, while making as few mistakes as possible. For example, if you validate an email address, you may catch a typo that the user entered inadvertently. If you do so without requiring a post back to the server, you've made it easier for the user to enter valid information.

This chapter quickly reviews the basics of form validation before discussing some common and important tasks that must be addressed when you're implementing your own form validation controls.

How do I validate form input?

Let's start with the most basic example of ASP.NET form validation. Figure 5.1 shows a simplified version of a form that's extremely common on the web: the registration form. In a real application, the form would likely have more fields and validation rules, but the general principles we'll demonstrate here are common to most forms.

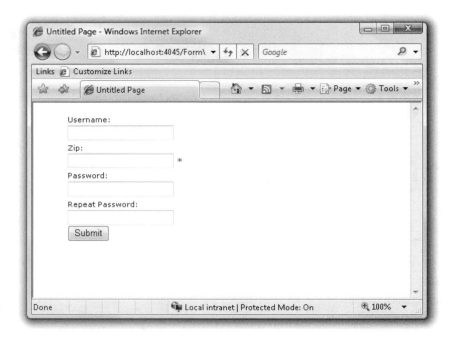

Figure 5.1. A simple form

For the purpose of this demonstration, the **Username**, **Password**, and **Repeat Password** are required fields. We'll also make sure that the **Password** and **Repeat Password** match exactly. The **Zip** field is not required, but if it's not left blank, we will make sure it has a valid zip code format (five digits optionally followed by a dash and four more digits).[1]

When the user clicks the **Submit** button, the page displays a red asterisk next to each invalid input and presents a list of error messages above the form.

---

[1] This example is designed for U.S. sites only. For international sites, we'd replace the zip code with a postal code and change the validation rule accordingly.

This example demonstrates the use of only a small selection of the validation controls. Visit the MSDN site to read up on the complete set of controls that come with ASP.NET.[2]

Solution

The following snippet shows the ASPX markup for the page:

SimpleForm.aspx *(excerpt)*

```
<asp:ValidationSummary ID="vldMessages" runat="server" />

<ul>
  <li>
    <label for="txtUsername">Username:</label>
    <asp:TextBox ID="txtUsername" runat="server" />
    <asp:RequiredFieldValidator ID="vldUsernameRequired"
        runat="server"
        Text="*"
        ErrorMessage="Username is Required"
        ControlToValidate="txtUsername" />
  </li>
  <li>
    <label for="txtZip">Zip:</label>
    <asp:TextBox ID="txtZip" runat="server" />
    <asp:RegularExpressionValidator ID="vldZip"
      runat="server"
      ValidationExpression="\d{5}(-?\d{4})?"
      ErrorMessage="The zip code is not valid."
      Text="*"
      ControlToValidate="txtZip" />
  </li>
  <li>
    <label for="txtPassword">Password:</label>
    <asp:TextBox ID="txtPassword" runat="server"
        TextMode="Password" />
    <asp:RequiredFieldValidator ID="vldPasswordRequired"
      runat="server"
      ErrorMessage="Password is Required"
      Text="*"
      ControlToValidate="txtPassword" />
```

---

[2] http://msdn.microsoft.com/library/default.asp?url=/library/en-us/cpgenref/html/cpconASPNETSyntaxForValidationControls.asp

```
    </li>
    <li>
       <label for="txtPasswordRepeated">Repeat Password:</label>
       <asp:TextBox ID="txtPasswordRepeated" runat="server"
         TextMode="Password" />
       <asp:CompareValidator ID="vldPasswordsMatch"
         runat="server"
         ErrorMessage="The passwords do not match"
         Text="*"
         ControlToValidate="txtPassword"
         ControlToCompare="txtPasswordRepeated" />
    </li>

    <li>
       <asp:Button ID="btnSubmit" runat="server"
         Text="Submit"
         OnClick="btnSubmit_Click" />
    </li>
  </ul>
```

The code-beside file is very simple. We just need to make sure that when the **Submit** button is clicked, we call the `Validate` method of the page:

SimpleForm.aspx.cs *(excerpt)*

```
public partial class ValidationExample : System.Web.UI.Page
{
  protected void btnSubmit_Click(object sender, EventArgs e)
  {
    if(Page.IsValid) //Calls Page.Validate()
    {
      //Register user.
    }
  }
}
```

When the `Validate` method is called, the page will recursively iterate through every control on the page looking for any control that implements the `IValidator` interface. The page then calls the `Validate` method on each of the validator controls it finds; this sets the `IsValid` property on each validator.

The `ValidationSummary` control's list of error messages will include the value of the `ErrorMessage` property of each validator control that's found to be invalid.

 Why Validate Again on the Server?

One question developers often ask about validator controls is, "Why do the controls validate on the server even when client-side validation is enabled?"

Client-side validation is for the benefit of the user and should *never* be used in place of server-side input validation. Any users who want to bypass client-side validation can do so very easily by turning off JavaScript, or even by replacing the validation functions on our live page within the context of their browsers. Add to this the fact that bots and other automated attacks won't have a JavaScript engine, and you begin to understand why relying on JavaScript for the validation of your data is foolish at best. The simple rule of thumb is "Never trust user input," regardless of where that input originates.

Discussion

The possible variations in the ways you can display form validation messages are innumerable. In the previous example, we displayed a red asterisk next to each field in which an error was detected, and used the `ValidationSummary` control to display a list of error messages on the page.

Some site owners prefer to display error messages next to the invalid input. This is easily accomplished by removing the `ValidationSummary` control and the `Text` attribute of each validator. Here's the code that demonstrates this technique:

SimpleFormWithSideMessages.aspx (excerpt)

```
<ul>
  <li>
    <label for="usernameTextBox">Username:</label>
    <asp:TextBox ID="usernameTextBox" runat="server" />
    <asp:RequiredFieldValidator ID="usernameRequiredValidator"
        runat="server"ErrorMessage="Username is Required"
        ControlToValidate="usernameTextBox" />
  </li>
  <li>
    <label for="zipTextBox">Zip:</label>
    <asp:TextBox ID="zipTextBox" runat="server" />
    <asp:RegularExpressionValidator ID="zipValidator"
```

```
        runat="server" ValidationExpression="\d{5}(-?\d{4})?"
        ErrorMessage="The zip code is not valid."
        ControlToValidate="zipTextBox" />
  </li>
  <li>
    <label for="passwordTextBox">Password:</label>
    <asp:TextBox ID="passwordTextBox" runat="server"
        TextMode="Password" />
    <asp:RequiredFieldValidator ID="passwordRequiredValidator"
        runat="server"
        ErrorMessage="Password is Required"
        ControlToValidate="passwordTextBox" />
  </li>
  <li>
    <label for="passwordRepeatedTextBox">Repeat Password:</label>
    <asp:TextBox ID="passwordRepeatedTextBox" runat="server"
        TextMode="Password" />
    <asp:CompareValidator ID="passwordCompareValidator"
        runat="server" ErrorMessage="The passwords do not match"
        Operator="Equal" ControlToValidate="passwordTextBox"
        ControlToCompare="passwordRepeatedTextBox" />
  </li>
  <li>
    <asp:Button ID="submitButton" runat="server" Text="Submit"
        OnClick="submitButton_Click" />
  </li>
</ul>
```

You can see the result of this approach in Figure 5.2.

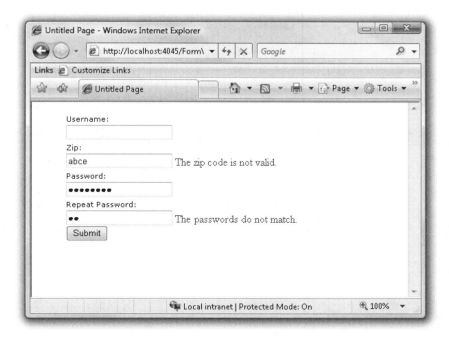

Figure 5.2. Displaying form input errors

How do I validate multiple forms?

A persistent search box is a handy widget to offer on a web site, which explains why search boxes are among the universal layout elements on so many web sites. The SitePoint web site shown in Figure 5.3 is a case in point—the search box appears in the header of the site.

In ASP.NET 1.1, many developers ran into a problem with the "One Method to Validate them All" approach when attempting to implement a search box on a page that included another form. The granularity of form validation in ASP.NET 1.1 is at its finest at the page level. So, when the user clicks the **Search** button, you'll want to validate the search box input, but validators for all other forms on the page will also be run concurrently.

Certainly, there are some workarounds for this scenario that are easy to implement, but there are many circumstances in which developers want to add multiple forms to a page, and have each of them validate independently.

Figure 5.3. A search field in the header of SitePoint's homepage

Solution

Luckily, ASP.NET 2.0 provides validation groups to solve this very problem. Let's see how they work. The following snippet is the stripped down markup for an ASPX page with a single form:

```
                                      WithoutValidationGroupExample.aspx (excerpt)

<p>
  <asp:ValidationSummary ID="vldMessages" runat="server" />
</p>
Search: <asp:TextBox id="txtSearch" runat="server" />
<asp:RequiredFieldValidator ID="vldSearchRequired" runat="server"
    ErrorMessage="Search" ControlToValidate="txtSearch"/>
<asp:Button ID="btnSearch" runat="server" Text="Search"
    OnClick="btnSearch_Click" />
<ul>
```

```
<li>
  <label for="txtFirstName">First Name:</label>
  <asp:TextBox ID="txtFirstName" runat="server" />
  <asp:RequiredFieldValidator ID="vldFirstRequired"
      runat="server" ErrorMessage="First Name"
      ControlToValidate="txtFirstName" />
</li>
<li>
  <label for="txtLastName">Last Name:</label>
  <asp:TextBox ID="txtLastName" runat="server" />
  <asp:RequiredFieldValidator ID="vldLastRequired"
      runat="server" ErrorMessage="Last Name"
      ControlToValidate="txtLastName" />
</li>
<li>
  <asp:Button ID="btnSubmit" runat="server" Text="Submit"
      OnClick="btnSubmit_Click" />
</li>
</ul>
```

Let's take a quick look at the code-beside file:

WithoutValidationGroupExample.aspx.cs

```
public partial class ValidatorsExample : System.Web.UI.Page
{
  protected void btnSubmit_Click(object sender, EventArgs e)
  {
    if(Page.IsValid) //Calls the Page.Validate() method.
    {
      //Do Search…
    }
  }
  protected void btnSearch_Click(object sender, EventArgs e)
  {
    if(Page.IsValid)
    {
      //Submit User Info…
    }
  }
}
```

Ideally, we'd like this page to be divided into two logical forms—the search form on top, and the form that collects user information beneath it.

If we load this page into the browser and submit the Search form, we'll see a result that looks like Figure 5.4.

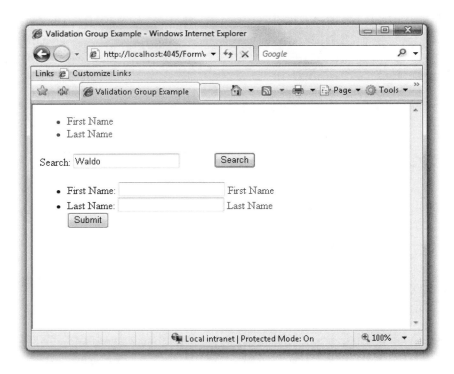

Figure 5.4. Validating both forms simultaneously

Notice that we receive an error message for the **First Name** and **Last Name** fields. We're used to seeing this behavior in ASP.NET 1.1, where calling the `Page.Validate` method will validate every `Validator` control on the page.

Fortunately, ASP.NET 2.0 introduces the `ValidationGroup` attribute. By applying this attribute to our form controls, we can create logical groupings of form elements.

Let's revisit the ASPX markup for this page and create two validation groups. We'll call the first group `Search` and apply this to the **Search** textbox and button:

```
Search: <asp:TextBox id="txtSearch" runat="server"
    ValidationGroup="Search" />
<asp:RequiredFieldValidator ID="vldSearchRequired" runat="server"
    ErrorMessage="Search"
    ControlToValidate="txtSearch"
    ValidationGroup="Search" />
```

We'll call the second group UserForm and apply it to the other form inputs:

```
<ul>
  <li>
    <label for="txtFirstName">First Name:</label>
    <asp:TextBox ID="txtFirstName" runat="server"
        ValidationGroup="UserForm" />
    <asp:RequiredFieldValidator ID="vldFirstRequired"
        runat="server" ErrorMessage="First Name"
        ControlToValidate="txtFirstName"
        ValidationGroup="UserForm" />
  </li>
  <li>
    <label for="txtLastName">Last Name:</label>
    <asp:TextBox ID="txtLastName" runat="server"
        ValidationGroup="UserForm" />
    <asp:RequiredFieldValidator ID="vldLastRequired"
        runat="server" ErrorMessage="Last Name"
        ControlToValidate="txtLastName"
        ValidationGroup="UserForm" />
  </li>
  <li>
    <asp:Button ID="btnSubmit" runat="server" Text="Submit"
        OnClick="btnSubmit_Click"
        ValidationGroup="UserForm" />
  </li>
</ul>
```

Don't Forget the Validation Group

Remember to apply the `ValidationGroup` attribute to the form inputs (such as `TextBox`, `RadioButtonList`, etc.) as well as the `Button` control that should trigger the validation (`CausesValidation` property set to `true`) for those inputs. It's common to forget to tell ASP.NET for which group a `Button` should trigger validation.

Once we've saved this change, we won't not need to change the code beside at all. Simply refresh the page, and when you perform a search, you'll see the result shown in Figure 5.5.

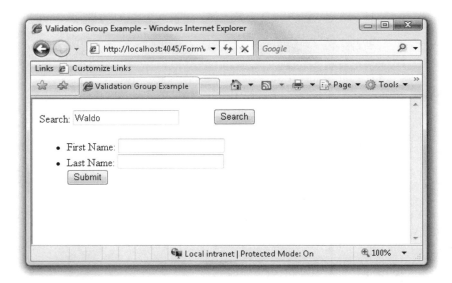

Figure 5.5. Forms validating independently thanks to `ValidationGroup`

Searching for **Waldo** no longer triggers the validation controls for **First Name** and **Last Name**.

How do I set up custom validation?

The basic validator controls are great for validating simple input, as they provide the validation logic for free, but they won't work in every situation. Consider, for example, a page that allows the user to change the PIN (or personal identification number) used to access a web site. For the sake of demonstration, we will keep this page extremely simple, as Figure 5.6 shows.

Figure 5.6. Our one-field form

See? It's *very* simple. However, we do need to apply some business logic here. For example, the user must enter between four and eight digits, and may not change the PIN to any of the last three PINs that he or she used.

We could simply use a `RegularExpressionValidator` to enforce the first of those rules. But for the second, we'll need to execute some custom logic.

Solution

The `CustomValidator` allows you to execute custom server-side logic in order to validate a field. Let's walk through the ASPX markup for this PIN submission page:

```
                                      CustomValidatorExample.aspx (excerpt)
<div>
  <asp:Label ID="pinLabel" runat="server" Text="PIN:"
      AssociatedControlID="pinTextBox" />
  <asp:TextBox ID="pinTextBox" runat="server" />
  <asp:RegularExpressionValidator ID="pinDigitValidator"
      runat="server" ControlToValidate="pinTextBox"
      ErrorMessage="Pin must contain four to eight digits"
      ValidationExpression="\d{4,8}" />
  <asp:CustomValidator ID="pinCustomValidator"
      runat="server" ErrorMessage="You used that PIN recently."
      ControlToValidate="pinTextBox"
      OnServerValidate="pinCustomValidator_ServerValidate"
```

```
        ClientValidationFunction="isValidPin" />
  <p>
    <asp:Button ID="submitButton" runat="server"
        Text="Change PIN" />
  </p>
</div>
```

In this example, we've added a `CustomValidator` control to the page and set its `ControlToValidate` property to point to `txtPin`. The `OnServerValidate` handler requires a server-side event handler for the `ServerValidate` event.

 The `CustomValidator`'s `ControlToValidate` Property

Notice that we set the `ControlToValidate` property to point to another control on the page. Strictly speaking, this is not necessary—it merely populates the `Value` property of the `ServerValidateEventArgs` instance passed to the validation method. However, nothing prevents you from accessing the properties of any of the controls directly. For example, if you need to compare the content of two text boxes, you can access them both via the `validator` method and leave the `ControlToValidate` property blank.

The `ServerValidate` event handler must have the following method signature:

```
void OnServerValidate(object source, ServerValidateEventArgs args)
```

The method takes in two parameters. The first is of type `object` and contains a reference to the custom validator itself. The second is of type `ServerValidateEventArgs` and contains information about the custom validation event.

The class `ServerValidateEventArgs` has two properties:

Value   if set, contains the value of the form field we are validating

IsValid   used to indicate whether or not the form data is valid

To implement a `ServerValidate` event handler, we perform our custom validation logic and set the `IsValid` of the `ServerValidateEventArgs` to `true` if the input is valid; otherwise, we set it to `false`.

The following code demonstrates this approach within our PIN changing example. In order to simulate the storage of the last three PINs used in the database, we simply store a `Queue` in the `Session`. When the user submits a PIN, we check the `Queue` to see if the PIN exists. If it does, we set the `ServerValidateEventArgs.IsValid` property to `false`. If the PIN does not exist, we add the PIN to the `Queue`, making sure to keep the `Queue` within a maximum size of three:

CustomValidatorExample.aspx.cs *(excerpt)*

```
protected void pinCustomValidator_ServerValidate(object source,
    ServerValidateEventArgs args)
{
  Queue<string> pins = Session["Pins"] as Queue<string>;
  if (pins == null)
  {
    pins = new Queue<string>(3);
    Session["Pins"] = pins;
  }
  foreach(string pin in pins)
  {
    if(pin == args.Value)
    {
      args.IsValid = false;
      return;
    }
  }
  if (pins.Count == 3)
  {
    pins.Dequeue();
    pins.Enqueue(args.Value);
  }
}
```

Discussion

Before we move on, there's an important point that you might like to note about this example. A mistake that's easy to make when we're using validators is to forget that, except for `RequiredFieldValidator`, the validators only validate controls when the value of the control is not empty.

So, if you leave the PIN field empty in this example, the custom validator control will not fire. In addition to the `CustomValidator` control, we should also use the

RequiredFieldValidator control to ensure that the PIN is not empty. It's common to use multiple validator controls to validate a single field in this way.

How do I perform custom client-side validation?

Validator controls support the validation of form fields on the client via Java-Script—an approach that can save the user from waiting on round-trips to the server. However, since we can never fully trust the browser, the server-side logic for every validator still fires on PostBack even if the client script deems the form field to be valid. This is a prudent security measure.

ASP.NET 2.0 has some great client-side validation features—so great, in fact, that we'd be crazy not to take advantage of them in our PIN example. So, just how do we validate the control on the client?

Solution

In the same way that we provide a server validation function, we can also specify a client validation function through the aptly named ClientValidationFunction property. Let's add this to our earlier example:

CustomValidatorExample.aspx *(excerpt)*

```
<asp:CustomValidator ID="pinValidator" runat="server"
    ErrorMessage="You used that PIN recently."
    ControlToValidate="pinTextBox"
    OnServerValidate="pinValidator_ServerValidate"
    ClientValidationFunction="isValidPin" />
```

We now need to write the JavaScript function that will validate this control. Keep in mind that the client-side validation function is sent to the browser, so we definitely *do not* want to send the user's last three PINs embedded as values in the function. One way to handle this potential security hole would be to use the XMLHttpRequest object, as shown below.

The Difference Between XMLHttp and XMLHttpRequest

The XMLHttp object was first introduced by Microsoft in Internet Explorer 5 as an ActiveX control. Since then, it's been adopted by every major browser under the name XMLHttpRequest. As of Internet Explorer 7, Microsoft's implementation matches that of Firefox, Opera, and Safari and is no longer dependent on ActiveX.

The XmlHttpRequest object enables JavaScript to make an Ajax request—we'll look at Ajax in more detail in Chapter 10.

CustomValidatorExample.aspx *(excerpt)*

```
<script type="text/javascript">
function isValidPin(source, args)
{
  var pin = args.Value;
  var xmlhttp;
  if (window.XMLHttpRequest)
  {
    // if IE 7, Mozilla, Safari, Opera, etc.
    xmlhttp = new XMLHttpRequest()
  }
  else if (window.ActiveXObject)
  {
    // use the ActiveX control for IE 5.x and IE 6
    xmlhttp = new ActiveXObject("Microsoft.XMLHTTP")
  }
  xmlhttp.open('GET', '/IsPinValid.aspx?pin=' + pin, false);
  xmlhttp.send(null);
  args.IsValid = eval(xmlhttp.responseText);
}
</script>
```

This script makes an XMLHttpRequest call to a page named **IsValidPin.aspx**, and adds a timestamp string to the request URL to ensure that we never receive cached results. The code for the page checks the validity of the PIN and writes either true or false to the response, as you can see below.

Dealing with Sensitive Data

You may be asking yourself why we didn't just append the PIN to the request URL in the previous example. The reason is simple, and very important: for the sake of security. If you were to submit a PIN via GET (that is, by placing it in the request URL), it would appear as plain text in server and proxy logs, compromising your customer's privacy and putting you in a prime position to face legal action in a worst-case scenario.

When you're dealing with private customer information, such as PINs, it's essential that your form and processing pages are served from an HTTPS server, otherwise the information is transferred in plain text, which can be spied on by malicious hackers during transit.

InPinValid.aspx.cs *(excerpt)*

```
protected void Page_Load(object sender, EventArgs e){
  string pinFromJS = Request.Form["pin"];
  Queue<string> pins = Session["Pins"] as Queue<string>;
  if (pins != null)
  {
    foreach (string pin in pins)
    {
      if (pin == pinFromJS)
      {
        Response.Write("false");
        return;
      }
    }
  }
  Response.Write("true");
}
```

The response from this page is evaluated by the following line of code in the client validation function:

CustomValidatorExample.aspx *(excerpt)*

```
args.IsValid = eval(xmlhttp.responseText);
```

Discussion

Notice that the method signature for the client validation function is very similar to its server-side equivalent. The code for these methods is basically the same too.

Such code duplication is one drawback of this approach. However, various methods are available to help us avoid duplicating code between the client and server. One approach uses an Ajax request to call from the client script the method we use for server-side validation. Another approach is to generate the client script using the server-side code—an experimental approach that Nikkhil Kothari takes with his Script# framework.[3]

How do I build my own validator control?

The `CustomValidator` control can handle just about every validation scenario you can throw at it. You'd be forgiven if you stopped right there and read no further in this chapter. However, I should warn you that the `CustomValidator` control is not a panacea.

At some point, you're going to want to reuse that validation logic on another page, or even another site. Perhaps a fellow developer admires the work you've done and wants to use that validation logic in his or her own project. Cutting and pasting the control declaration and associated back-end code will be a real pain. Is there a better solution?

Solution

There is! When you want to reuse or share validation logic, building your own validator control is the way to go. It's common to refer to any `Validator` control that you build as a **custom validator control**.

---

[3] http://www.nikhilk.net/ScriptSharpIntro.aspx

Custom Validator Versus `CustomValidator`

Be careful not to confuse a custom validator control with the `CustomValidator` control. Unfortunately, these two concepts share very similar names, so it's easy to get the two mixed up.

In this section, when we use the two words together—`CustomValidator`—we're speaking of the ASP.NET validator control included with ASP.NET. When we talk about a custom validator, we're referring to a validator control written by a third party, such as yourself, in order to provide custom validation.

Before we get started, we need to make a choice about how we'll implement our validator. The basic interface that all validators implement is the `System.Web.UI.IValidator` interface:

```
public interface IValidator
{
  void Validate();
  string ErrorMessage { get; set; }
  bool IsValid { get; set; }
}
```

Technically speaking, this is the only interface your validator control needs to implement in order to hook into the validation framework. But you'll notice that this interface doesn't provide you with the value of the control to validate. You'll need to use reflection to obtain that value. Using reflection introduces processing overhead and is worth avoiding unless your application can gain substantially from it.

Fortunately, there's a better approach to validation that works in most situations. By having your class inherit from the abstract `BaseValidator` class instead, you'll be free to focus on your validation logic and not worry about the validation plumbing.

`BaseValidator` has one abstract method that you must implement—`EvaluateIsValid`, which has the following method signature:

```
protected abstract bool EvaluateIsValid();
```

ASP.NET uses the result of this method to determine whether a form input is valid or not. `BaseValidator` also defines many methods and properties that are useful for implementing a validator control.

For example, to find out the name of the control you're validating, you can look at the `ControlToValidate` property. To get the value of the control you're validating, call the `GetControlValidation` method. Let's put all this together in the implementation of our custom PIN validation control:

PinValidator.cs *(excerpt)*

```
public class PinValidator : BaseValidator
{
  protected override bool EvaluateIsValid()
  {
    Queue<string> pins = HttpContext.Current.Session["Pins"]
        as Queue<string>;
    if (pins == null)
    {
      pins = new Queue<string>(3);
      HttpContext.Current.Session["Pins"] = pins;
    }
    string pinFromForm = GetControlValidationValue(
        ControlToValidate );
    foreach (string pin in pins)
    {
      if (pin == pinFromForm)
      {
        return false;
      }
    }
    if (pins.Count == 3)
    {
      pins.Dequeue();
    }
    pins.Enqueue(pinFromForm);
    return true;s
  }
}
```

Now we can drop the `PinValidator` control onto any page, set its `ControlToValidate` property, and reuse this validation logic anywhere.

How do I perform client-side validation with my custom validator control?

We're not quite done with the control we defined in the section called "How do I build my own validator control?" just yet—we haven't dealt with client-side validation in our custom validator control.

As we saw in the introduction to this chapter, the primary purpose of form validation is to make it easy for the user to enter accurate data. If we require the user to submit a form and wait for the post back to find out whether or not a field is valid, we've raised the difficulty and annoyance factors for the user.

However, if we do as much validation as possible on the client, via JavaScript, the application appears more responsive and the user remains happy.

With that in mind, let's delve into the task of building client-side validation for a custom validator control.

Solution

This solution assumes that you've already written a custom validator control with working server-side validation logic, like the one we developed in the section called "How do I set up custom validation?". Here, we're going to focus on the steps necessary to add client-side validation logic.

The process of adding client-side validation logic to our custom validator control takes three steps, which we will cover in more detail in a moment:

1. Write a JavaScript validation function.

2. Make sure the JavaScript validation function is available anywhere the control is used.

3. Register the client validation function with the validation framework.

Understanding the Client Validation Function

In the previous section, we wrote a client validation function referenced by a `CustomValidator` control. The client validation function for a custom validator control will look similar, but not exactly the same.

For this function to be able to be called by the ASP.NET Form Validation framework, it needs to have the following signature:

```
function FunctionName(val)
{
  //Return true or false based on validation logic.
  return true|false;
}
```

As you can see from the method signature, the client validation function takes in a parameter and returns either `true` or `false` depending on whether or not the input is valid.

The parameter for this method represents the custom validator control. To get the value of the control we're validating, we use the `ValidatorGetValue` method. Here's the full code for the client validation function:

PinValidatorEvaluateIsValid.js (excerpt)

```
function PinValidatorEvaluateIsValid(val)
{
  var pin = ValidatorTrim(
      ValidatorGetValue(val.controltovalidate));
  var xmlhttp;
  if (window.XMLHttpRequest)
  {
    xmlhttp = new XMLHttpRequest()
  }
  else if (window.ActiveXObject)
  {
    xmlhttp = new ActiveXObject("Microsoft.XMLHTTP");
  }
  var date = new Date();
  var pinParam = "pin="+pin;
  xmlhttp.open('POST', '/FormValidation/IsPinValid.aspx?rnd='
      +date.getTime(), false);
  xmlhttp.setRequestHeader('Content-Type',
      'application/x-www-form-urlencoded');
  xmlhttp.send(pinParam);
  return eval(xmlhttp.responseText);
}
```

As in the previous solution, this code makes an `XMLHttpRequest` request to a page to determine the validity of the user-specified PIN. If you were to use this code in a project, you'd be wise to consolidate your `XMLHttpRequest` conditional logic in a function and call it when you need a new instance, like so:

```
function getXmlHttp ()
{
  var xmlhttp;
  if (window.XMLHttpRequest)
  {
    xmlhttp = new XMLHttpRequest()
  }
  else if (window.ActiveXObject)
  {
    xmlhttp = new ActiveXObject("Microsoft.XMLHTTP");
  }
  return xmlhttp;
}

//usage:
var httpRequest = getXmlHttp();
```

Embedding the Client Validation Function

Now that we've written our client function, we need to make sure it's available on any page that uses this control. We could place this script in a **.js** file and expect the developer to remember to link to the script using the `script` element in any page where the developer calls the function, but that solution wouldn't be very re-usable.

Instead, we want the control to cause the page to render a link to the script automatically. We can accomplish this easily by embedding the script as a **web resource**—a static file that is embedded into an assembly, and is therefore available for your pages to reference.[4]

One common strategy for handling such resources is to create a **Resources** folder in your project as the root folder for embedded resources. In Figure 5.7, you can see that I've added a **Scripts** folder to contain embedded scripts. This folder contains

---

[4] While a complete discussion of the ins and outs of web resources is beyond the scope of this book, if you're interested in exploring the web resources feature of ASP.NET 2.0, the article "Working with Web Resources in ASP.NET 2.0" should serve you well. [http://support.microsoft.com/kb/910442/]

the file **PinValidatorEvaluateIsValid.js**, which contains the method we wrote in the previous solution.

Figure 5.7. The project's directory structure

After you add this file to the **Scripts** directory, select the file and make sure the **Build Action** is set to **Embedded Resource**, as shown in Figure 5.8.

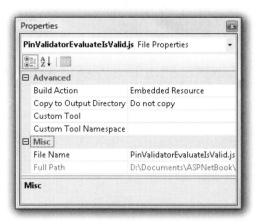

Figure 5.8. Adding our validation function as an **Embedded Resource**

We need to register this web resource via the `WebResourceAttribute` assembly-level attribute as shown here:

```
[assembly: WebResource("SitePoint.Cookbook.Resources.Scripts.PinVali
➥datorEvaluateIsValid.js", "text/javascript")]
```

This assembly-level attribute can be placed in any class within the assembly in which it resides. I prefer to place it within the control that uses the resource, but others may prefer to put it within **AssemblyInfo.cs**.

This attribute tells ASP.NET that it's safe to make the resource described in the attribute value accessible via a URL. Finally, we need to register this resource so that ASP.NET will render a proper `script` element using the URL described in the call to `WebResource`. The `OnPreRender` method is a good place to do this:

PinValidator.cs (excerpt)

```
protected override void OnPreRender(EventArgs e)
{
  base.OnPreRender(e);
  if(EnableClientScript)
  {
    string scriptUrl = Page.ClientScript.GetWebResourceUrl(
        this.GetType(),
        "FormValidationExamples.Resources.Scripts.PinValidatorEvalua
        ➥teIsValid.js");
    if (!Page.ClientScript.IsClientScriptIncludeRegistered(
        "PinValidatorEvaluateIsValid"))
    {
      Page.ClientScript.RegisterClientScriptInclude(this.GetType(),
          "PinValidatorEvaluateIsValid", scriptUrl)
    }
  }
}
```

Registering the Client Validation Function

Great! Our client validation script will be included on the page. But how does the client validation framework know to call our client validation method when it's time to validate the form input?

We need to register the method by adding the `evaluationfunction` attribute to our validator control within the `AddAttributesToRender` method:

PinValidator.cs *(excerpt)*

```
protected override void AddAttributesToRender(
    HtmlTextWriter writer)
{
  base.AddAttributesToRender(writer);
  if(RenderUplevel)
  {
    Page.ClientScript.RegisterExpandoAttribute(this.ClientID,
        "evaluationfunction", "PinValidatorEvaluateIsValid");
  }
  else
  {
    writer.AddAttribute("evaluationfunction",
        "PinValidatorEvaluateIsValid");
  }
}
```

The `ClientScriptManager.RegisterExpandoAttribute` method call probably deserves an explanation. This method uses JavaScript to add custom properties (or attributes) to an element in the DOM.

We can add attributes to an element in two ways. The first is to simply render the attributes in the HTML like so:

```
<span id="vldPin"
    evaluationfunction="PinValidatorEvaluateIsValid" />
```

One problem with this approach is that `evaluationfunction` is not a valid attribute of the span element. However, by calling `ClientScriptManager.RegisterExpandoAttribute`, the `evaluationfunction` attribute is added to the span through JavaScript. This renders the following HTML for the validator control:

```
<span id="vldPin" />
```

The JavaScript that adds the `evaluationfunction` attribute looks like this:

```
<script type="text/javascript">
  var vldPin = (document.getElementById) ?
      document.getElementById("vldPin") :
      document.all["vldPin"];
  vldPin.controltovalidate = "txtPin";
  vldPin.errormessage = "You used that PIN recently.";
  vldPin.evaluationfunction = "PinValidatorEvaluateIsValid";
</script>
```

 Preparing Custom Controls for Validation

We've learned how to build custom validator controls that are useful for validating standard form controls. But what happens when you try to validate a composite control that you've built?

Perhaps the "value" of your control is composed of the values of several controls, or is based on a click selection such as the `Calendar` control. How do you use the validation controls with your custom control?

You'll need to add the `ValidationPropertyAttribute` to the start of your class to specify which property of your control is the "value" of the control for the purposes of validation. The following code snippet demonstrates this point:

```
[ValidationProperty("MyControlValue")]
```

Also, our client-side validation function will look for an attribute named `value`. You can use the ever-useful `ClientScriptManager.RegisterExpandoAttribute` method to supply this value as follows:

RegisterExpandoAttributeExample.aspx (excerpt)

```
ClientScriptManager.RegisterExpandoAttribute(this.ID,
    "value", MyControlValue);
```

Figure 5.9 shows our new custom validator control in action. We need to seed the control by submitting a couple of PINs (I've added 1234 and 1235). Afterwards, we can clear the textbox, type in "1234", and then press **Tab** and wait a moment to see the client validation at work.

Figure 5.9. Our new custom validator control in action

Summary

The solutions we covered in this chapter range from the simple validation of required fields, to the challenge of validating input based on complex custom business rules. In all cases, the goal of validation is to make it easy and pleasant for the user to enter accurate information into the form.

One common theme we've seen among the validator controls we've worked with in this chapter is that they all provide a means to validate data on both the client and server sides. Validating data on the client side using JavaScript provides a smooth user experience, while validating on the server side helps to keep bad data entered by malicious user agents out of our databases.

You now have the tools to build a rich library of reusable custom validator controls for validating various user inputs that are specific to your business needs.

6

Maintaining State

The Web is built upon HTTP—a stateless protocol. But what exactly do the terms "state" and "stateless" mean?

The **state** of a web application is a sort of snapshot of an application's configuration values, which change over time. The fact that HTTP is **stateless** means that it does not have the mechanism for maintaining any kind of history of a user's interactions with your application. When you make a request for a web page, and the server sends a response back, that connection to the web server is closed. The transaction is over. The very next request of the server could come from anyone, anywhere, and HTTP wouldn't know the difference between one request and the next. This is the typical way in which requests are made over the Web, which is why it's seen as being stateless.

Yet we experience state all the time when we work with web applications—when I add an item to a shopping cart, the next page on the site shows that item's still in the cart. If the Web we use is truly stateless, how is this information maintained?

Web developers work around the limitations of a stateless Web by storing state-related information at the application level. Some of this information is sent in small chunks between the browser and the server; these bits of data are more commonly known as **cookies**. Cookies contain identifiable data that informs the server about the source of the request and whether the request is part of a multi-request operation.

In other instances, the application maintains state by storing information within hidden form fields, and then posting that data back to the server on subsequent requests.

ASP.NET provides many different means for maintaining state at all levels, from global application state to the state of a single request. Let's look at how to make sense of all the options available to you as an ASP.NET developer.

How do I maintain per-request state in a web application?

A **request**—also known as a "hit"—refers to the process by which a user's browser asks the web server for an object. That object may be an HTML file, an image, a script, or some other media file. **Per-request state** is therefore state that's stored during the processing of a single request. Let's look at how per-request state is maintained in an ASP.NET application.

Solution

In ASP.NET 2.0, the `Page` class contains an `Items` property that allows you to store data as name-value pairs in a similar manner to the `HttpContext` object's `Items` property. Using the `Page.Items` property, you can store data for a request within the scope of the page. You can therefore retrieve the data from within the page or from any control nested in that page.

The following code measures the time between the point at which ASP.NET calls our page's `OnInit` method and the moment it calls a control's `OnPreRender` method. It measures this time frame by storing a `DateTime` value during the initialization of the page, and then calculating the difference between it and the current time within the `OnPreRender` method:

State.aspx.cs *(excerpt)*

```
public partial class Default : System.Web.UI.Page
{
  protected override void OnInit(EventArgs e)
  {
    Page.Items["InitTime"] = DateTime.Now;
    base.OnInit(e);
  }
  protected override void OnPreRender(EventArgs e)
  {
    double elapsed = (DateTime.Now -
        (DateTime)Page.Items["InitTime"]).TotalMilliseconds;
    Response.Write(elapsed + " seconds elapsed.");
    base.OnPreRender(e);
  }
}
```

If you paid attention as you read through this code, you might be wondering why we didn't use a private member variable in this case. Good question!

I chose to use `Page.Items` here purely for demonstration purposes. However, suppose for a minute that we were performing the same calculation for a deeply nested control within the `Page`'s control hierarchy. If we used a private member variable, we'd need to pass the variable down the control hierarchy somehow to ensure it was accessible within the scope of the nested control. Rather than passing the start time to the control, we can instead store it in the `Page.Items` collection, so the control can retrieve the value directly.

We can also accomplish this task with the `HttpContext.Items` property. One benefit of using the `HttpContext.Items` property is that state for the current request can be stored in the `Items` collection very early in the request life cycle. For example, you might add an HTTP module to store the data you're after during the `OnAcquireRequestState` method, like so:

HttpModuleTest.cs *(excerpt)*

```
public void Init(HttpApplication context)
{
  context.AcquireRequestState +=
      new EventHandler(context_AcquireRequestState);
```

```
}
void OnAcquireRequestState(object sender, EventArgs e)
{
  HttpContext.Current.Items["AcquireRequestState"] = DateTime.Now;
}
```

With this information safely stowed away, you can use the `HttpContext.Items` property to store the data, which can be included in various calculations. For instance, the calculation I've created below records the time that elapses between the application acquiring request state and the initialization of the page:

PageInitialization.aspx.cs *(excerpt)*

```
protected override void OnInit(EventArgs e)
{
  if (HttpContext.Current.Items["AcquireRequestState"] != null)
  {
    DateTime acquired =
        (DateTime) HttpContext.Current.Items["AcquireRequestState"];
    double interval = (DateTime.Now - acquired).TotalMilliseconds;
  }
}
```

Choosing Between `Page.Items` and `HttpContext.Items`

Don't confuse `Page.Items` with the `HttpContext.Items` property. Unlike other `Page` properties that are simply wrappers around similarly named `HttpContext` properties, the `Page.Items` collection is *not* a wrapper to the `HttpContext` variable—it bucks the convention established by properties such as `Request` and `User`.

Personally, I think it's best to avoid `Page.Items` in favor of `HttpContext`, as its use has the potential to cause confusion. Besides, the `HttpContext.Items` property has a slightly larger scope, so it's more useful in the long run.

How can I maintain session state in a web farm using a state server?

In comparison with per-request state, which we looked at in the previous solution, **session state** is state that's maintained across a series of requests. The most useful implementation of session state for a web application begins from the moment a user begins to use the application (or logs in), and ends when the user leaves the application (either by explicitly logging out, or by timing out due to inactivity).

The `Session` object is a useful container for storing user-specific data for the duration of a user's session on a web site. The `Session` object exists in memory by default, which makes it extremely useful for storing information such as the contents of a user's shopping cart, or the step a user is currently at in a multi-step operation.

However, what happens when your application becomes enormously popular, and you're forced to load-balance your site across more than one server (in a so-called **web farm** environment)? Storing session state in memory can be problematic—many load balancers are not sticky, and should your server require rebooting, the information is lost anyway.

What is Sticky Load Balancing?

Sticky load balancing is the act of distributing user requests across multiple servers so that requests from a given user are consistently sent to the same server. The result of implementing sticky load balancing is that you are able to maintain session state for all of your users, despite the fact that your application is distributed across several machines.

We can use two approaches to maintain session state in a web farm environment. One option is to use a **state server**, whereby all the session variables for the entire web farm are stored on a single server. The other option is to store the session variables in a database. We'll see how to implement a state server in this solution, and look at the database storage approach in the section called "How can I maintain session state in a web farm using a database?".

Solution

Setting up a state server is fairly easy: first, be sure to set the same `machineKey` value for each server in your web farm.

Setting the Machine Key

Whenever you set up a web farm, it's generally a good idea to synchronize the `machineKey` across every web server, whether you plan to implement a state server or not—this element is also used by other features that make use of encryption.

You'll find the `machineKey` setting in the **Web.config.comments** file on each web server. By default, the `machineKey` section looks like this:

```
<machineKey validationKey="AutoGenerate,IsolateApps"
  decryptionKey="AutoGenerate,IsolateApps"
  validation="SHA1"
  decryption="Auto" />
```

To synchronize the machine keys, you'll need to generate some keys and turn off the `AutoGenerate` feature. The end result should look something like the following:

```
<machineKey validationKey="ABD2EE0B66...E566D8AC5D1C045BA60"
  decryptionKey="1F090935F6...67F451CE65D0F2ABE9B"
  validation="SHA1" />
```

Generating Machine Keys

The MSDN Documentation recommends using the `RNGCryptoServiceProvider` class to generate strong keys, but this seems like a lot of unnecessary work to me.

It's far easier to point your browser to the ASP.NET Resources online machineKey generator.[1] This online service will generate the entire `machineKey` section for you!

The next step is to make sure that the ASP.NET state service is running. The service is installed as part of the ASP.NET and .NET Framework installation, so, on the

---

[1] http://aspnetresources.com/tools/keycreator.aspx

machine that will operate as your session state server, type the following command at the command prompt (from any directory):

```
C:\> net start aspnet_state
```

This will start the service listening, by default, on port 42424.

 Automatically Starting the State Server

> If you're using the state service, you'll probably want it to start automatically—that way, you don't need to start it manually every time the machine reboots. Open the Windows **Services** management console, and set the **Startup** type for the **ASP.NET State Service** to **Automatic**.

Now add the following few lines into the `system.web` section of each web server's `Web.config` file, replacing *StateServerName* with the name of your server:

```
<sessionState mode="StateServer"
  stateConnectionString="tcpip=StateServerName:42424"
  cookieless="false"
  timeout="20" />
```

That's it—you've configured your state server! However, there's one final and very important step that we need to take to ensure that our machines can pass requests among each other.

Since we're now storing session state on another machine rather than in memory, we'll need to make sure that every object we store in the session is serializable. The failure to perform this step is probably the most common mistake that developers make when implementing sticky load balancing.

ASP.NET handles the serialization of some of the primitive types such as int, byte, decimal, string, and so on. For other objects, ASP.NET will attempt to use its built-in `BinaryFormatter` to serialize the object. Be sure to mark your types as `[Serializable]` to avoid an unwelcome surprise when you deploy your application to the production environment.

If performance is crucial for your application, you may want to consider storing all session state information using only primitive types. For example, suppose we were storing our session data in memory on a single server environment. Our code might look something like this:

```
Person person = null;
if (Session["User"] != null)
{
  person = Session["User"] as Person;
}
```

Once we move to a web farm environment, we could instead use the following approach, thus reducing the traffic and CPU cycles being sent to and from our state server:

```
Person person = null;
if (Session["UserId"] != null)
{
  person = new Person((int)Session["UserId"]
  , (string)Session["UserName"]);
}
```

How can I maintain session state in a web farm using a database?

In the previous topic, we explored how to set up out-of-process session state using a state server. One of the disadvantages of using a state server is that, should the server require rebooting, the session state for all users would immediately be lost.

An alternative approach to maintaining state in web farms is to store session state in the application's database.

Solution

There are several important steps to perform when you use a database for state storage. Let's work through them together.

Configuring SQL Server

The first step is to set up the necessary database tables within SQL Server. To start the SQL Server Setup Wizard, type the following at the command prompt:

```
C:\> aspnet_regsql -W
```

Alternatively, you can double-click the file **aspnet_regsql.exe**, located in the directory **%SystemDrive%\Windows\Microsoft.NET\Framework*version***, from within Windows Explorer. Figure 6.1 shows the first screen of the wizard.

Figure 6.1. The ASP.NET SQL Server Setup Wizard

This wizard is used to install various ASP.NET features that rely on SQL Server. Click the **Next >** button to move to the next step, shown in Figure 6.2.

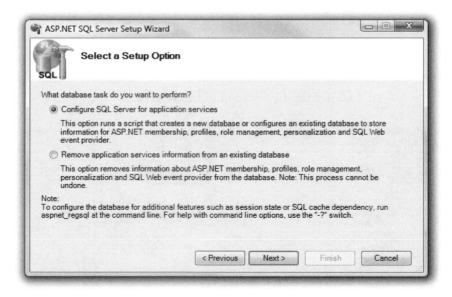

Figure 6.2. Configuring SQL Server to store session data

Since we're installing the tables and scripts necessary for storing session data in the database, select the first option and click **Next** >. You'll be presented with the database connection details screen shown in Figure 6.3.

Figure 6.3. Configuring database and user credentials

Replace *SERVERNAME* with your database server name and fill in your connection credentials. When you click **Next >**, you'll see a confirmation screen and have one last opportunity to change your mind before the wizard executes the script.

If you're curious, the actual script that the wizard executes is named **InstallSqlState.sql** and it's located within the following directory: **%SystemDrive%\Windows\Microsoft.NET\Framework\version**.

When the wizard finishes its work, you'll have a brand new database named ASP-STATE.

Configuring ASP.NET

The next step is to configure ASP.NET to use the database to store its session data. Modify the `sessionState` section within the **Web.config** file to include a `mode` attribute with a value of `SQLServer` as well as a database connection string, as follows:

```
<sessionState mode="SQLServer"
  sqlConnectionString=
    "Server=SERVERNAME;Trusted_Connection=True;"
  cookieless="false"
  timeout="20"/>
```

Trusted Connections

If you plan to use trusted connections to connect to the session state database, take a moment to make sure that the user account you use to connect to the database has sufficient permissions to use that database.

This step is often overlooked because the developer (okay, this author) is liable to forget that the session database is yet *another* database for which permissions need to be set.

In this scenario, I would recommend avoiding impersonation (a configuration setting that allows you to tell ASP.NET to run as particular user), because if you do, you may not be able to take advantage of connection pooling to the session database.

The final step in the process is to make sure that every web server in the web farm has the same application path (for example **\LM\W3SVC\1**). The Microsoft Knowledge Base article *Session State Is Lost in Web Farm* goes into more detail on this issue.[2]

Discussion

The storing of session state in the database has a number of advantages:

- Session state can be persisted across user visits, which is useful for applications that allow users to save their positions within a multistep operation.

- If SQL Server Clustering is employed, the storage of session state scales well in comparison to using a simple state server.

- Session state persists even after a server reboot.

Disadvantages of this approach include:

- Storing session state in the database can increase the load on an already heavily loaded database.

- Storing state in the database is significantly slower than using in-memory state storage or a state server. However, the database storage approach is more scalable, and has the potential to increase the overall performance of your application.

- As with the state server, all session objects that are stored in the database must be serializable.

Even with the disadvantages I've acknowledged here, storing session state in a database is an excellent option should you need to persist session state across user visits and reboots. As with all architectural choices, the decision of where to store your session state will depend upon a number of factors, such as the features your application will offer its users, the number of concurrent users the application will have at any time, and the budget you have available for buying extra hardware.

---

[2] http://support.microsoft.com/default.aspx?scid=KB;EN-US;325056&ID=KB;EN-US;325056

Where should I store application state?

A common question ASP.NET developers ask is where global data and global application state should be stored. The reason why this is such a common question is that no absolutely correct answer is available. The answer to this—as to so many of life's questions—is, "well … it depends."

That said, developers can follow certain guidelines to make sure they don't store application state in the wrong place. Where *is* the wrong place, you ask? The wrong place is any location that makes using the data more challenging than it needs to be.

Solutions

There are a couple of factors to consider when you're storing global data:

frequency
> The frequency with which the data needs to be changed is important—read-only global data is much easier to deal with than global data that can be both read and written to.

concurrency
> If the global data can be written to, then concurrency is also an extremely important factor that will need to be taken into account.

Based on these factors, three avenues are available to us to store global data: static variables, the cache, and application variables.

Storing Data in Static Variables

For read-only data that only needs to be created once (perhaps when the application starts), but is read often, I recommend simply using a static private member. The following code demonstrates the use of this approach using a collection of the countries of the world.

Countries.cs (excerpt)

```
public sealed class CountryHelper
{
  private static ReadOnlyCollection<Country> _countries =
      GetAllCountries();
```

```
public ReadOnlyCollection<Country> Country
{
  get
  {
    return _countries;
  }
}
private static ReadOnlyCollection<Country> GetAllCountries()
{
  IList<Country> countries = new List<Country>();
  countries.Add(new Country("Afghanistan"));
  countries.Add(new Country("Albania"));
  countries.Add(new Country("American Samoa"));
  :
  countries.Add(new Country("Zimbabwe"));
  return new ReadOnlyCollection<Country>(countries);
}
}
```

With this code, the list of countries can be referenced in a thread-safe manner at any time like so:

```
Console.WriteLine(CountryHelper.Countries.Count);
```

Our use of a ReadOnlyCollection<Country> class ensures that no one can change this collection (for example, to add a new, non-existent country). However, one drawback to using static private members is that the data is stored in memory until the application is terminated. This mode of storage wastes memory if the volume of data is large and not read frequently.

Storing Data in the Cache

The cache is a good place to store global data that may be accessed frequently. Let's look at an example:

CountryHelper.cs (excerpt)

```
public sealed class CountryHelper
{
  CountryHelper()
  {
    HttpContext.Current.Cache["countries"] =
```

```
      LoadCountries();
  }
  public static IList<Country> GetCountries()
  {
    IList<Country> countries = null;
    Cache cache = HttpContext.Current.Cache;
    countries = cache["countries"] as IList<Country>;
    if (countries == null)
    {
      countries = LoadCountries();
      cache["countries"] = countries;
    }

    return countries;
  }
  static IList<Country> LoadCountries()
  {
    //pretend this came from the database.
    IList<Country> countries = new List<Country>();
    countries.Add(new Country("Afghanistan"));
    countries.Add(new Country("Albania"));
    ⋮
    countries.Add(new Country("Zimbabwe"));
    return countries;
  }
}
```

Here we have a simple helper class that lists the countries of the world. Notice that
in the static constructor for this class, we populate the cache object with *all* the
countries. So why do we check for null when we try to retrieve the countries from
the cache in the GetCountries method?

We check for null in this case because the framework may have removed those
values. ASP.NET always clears infrequently used objects from the cache in order
to make room for data that is used more frequently, so when you attempt to retrieve
data from the cache object, there's no guarantee that it'll be there.

As well as being squeezed out of the cache by other objects, it's also possible for an
object to drop out of the cache because a timeline was set for it. The following example shows how a timeline for caching an object can be set explicitly:

```
                                        CounterHelper.cs (excerpt)
public sealed class UserOnlineHelper
{
  public IList<string> GetOnlineUsernames()
  {
    Cache cache = HttpContext.Current.Cache;
    IList<string> usernames = cache["online-users"]
      as IList<string>;
    if(usernames == null)
    {
      usernames = LoadOnlineUserNames();
      cache.Insert("online-users"
        , usernames
        , null
        , DateTime.Now.AddMinutes(1)
        , Cache.NoSlidingExpiration);
    }
    return usernames;
  }
  IList<string> LoadOnlineUserNames()
  {
    //some code to get usernames.
  }
}
```

In this case, we're caching the number of users in our application. Of course, we don't want to cache this value indefinitely, as the value changes constantly. Conversely, we don't want to calculate that number *every* time—for tasks such as displaying a count of site users to other users, having the exact figure is not a high priority.

We therefore set an expiration time that's one minute into the future—this way, the number of online users will be cached for one minute at a time. Even one minute of caching can help the performance of a very busy web site!

Storing Data in Application Variables

One final option for the storage of global data is to use an application variable. One of the benefits of storing data in an application variable is that you *know* it'll be there when you go back to retrieve it. Let's rewrite our previous `CountryHelper` example to demonstrate this point:

```
                                        CountryHelper.cs (excerpt)
public sealed class CountryHelper
{
  CountryHelper()
  {
    HttpContext.Current.Application["countries"] = LoadCountries();
  }
  public static IList<Country> GetCountries()
  {
    IList<Country> countries = null;
    HttpApplicationState application =
        HttpContext.Current.Application;
    countries = (IList<Country>)application["countries"];
    return countries;
  }
  static IList<Country> LoadCountries()
  {
    // Code to load countries from the database goes here.
  }
}
```

Note that we don't need to check for `null` when retrieving the `countries` application variable—it was populated in the static constructor, so we can be certain that it'll still be there.

The effectiveness of this approach is dependent on the frequency with which this data is accessed: if the countries aren't referenced often, we're storing a lot of data in memory that could be better used to store data that's more frequently accessed.

Another potential hurdle associated with using an application variable is that we've sacrificed the flexibility that the `Cache` object provided—for example, we can't specify an expiration time or `CacheDependency`. See Chapter 15 for more on using the ASP.NET cache.

What's the cleanest way to access a page's view state?

There's nothing to prevent a developer from deciding to access the view state directly from within a page. Yet experience shows that this approach can be error-prone, as the potential exists for typos to creep into your code.

For example, look at the following code:

```
ViewState["FirstKey"] = "Hello";
ViewState["Firstkey"] += " World";
Response.Write(ViewState["Firstkey"]);
```

At first glance, you might expect the output of this code to be Hello World. In fact, the output is just World. ViewState keys are case-sensitive, so it can be very easy to make small mistakes with them.

So, if accessing the view state directly from within a page is problematic, what's the best approach to use?

Solution

The best solution for accessing a page's view state is to create a **ViewState-backed property**, which is a property that stores its value directly in the view state.

For example, suppose you wanted to store a city name in the view state. Rather than using ViewState["city"] directly, you could type the following:

```
                                              ViewState.aspx.cs (excerpt)
public string City
{
  get { return (string)ViewState["City"]; }
  set { ViewState["City"] = value; }
}
```

Override the get and set methods for your string, as we've done in the code above. This code takes advantage of the object oriented concept of **data hiding**, where access to a store (in this case, the view state) is hidden behind a property. The consumer of the class accesses the `City` as if it were any other property of the class, rather than accessing the view state directly.

Now that's all well and good, but we're yet to account for the possibility that a value retrieved from the view state might be `null`. This might have been desirable in the above example, but what if you wanted to store a Boolean value in the `ViewState` object? In this case, a value of `null` would be meaningless!

Wherever it's necessary, be sure to check for `null` before you access your `ViewState`-backed variable. Here's one (admittedly long-winded) example that demonstrates how this check is performed:

```
public bool Enabled
{
  get
  {
    if (ViewState["Enabled"] == null)
      return false;

    return (bool)ViewState["Enabled"];
  }
  set
  {
    ViewState["Enabled"] = value;
  }
}
```

While the check works fine, that sure is a lot of typing for a simple property! To rewrite this code in a way that's cleaner and shorter, you can make use of the new *Null Coalescing Operator* in C# 2.0:

ViewState.aspx.cs *(excerpt)*

```
public bool Enabled
{
  get
  {
    return (bool)(ViewState["Enabled"] ?? false);
  }
  set
  {
```

```
    ViewState["Enabled"] = value;
  }
}
```

This code ensures that we'll never retrieve a null value, yet gives us the benefits of a clean syntax for reading and writing to the view state.

 Understanding the Null Coalescing Operator

Version 2.0 of the C# language introduced some new syntax—the ?? operator, which is called the Null Coalescing Operator.

Let's take a look at this operator in action. The expression z = x ?? y is roughly equivalent to the following code:

```
string tempX = x;    // Ensures thread safety by
                     // using a local variable.
if (tempX != null)
  z = tempX;
z = y;
```

Note that the coalescing operator is thread-safe—it copies the reference to a local, temporary variable before making the null comparison. If the coalescing operator didn't perform this step, it would be possible for another thread to modify the original reference between the comparison and the assignment.

Discussion

In order to keep the discussion in this section short and sweet, I've only explained this technique of accessing name-value information as it relates to the view state. However, the technique can be applied just as effectively to any name-value storage facility, including the Session, application variables, HttpContext.Items, and others. In fact, any time you retrieve a property value using a string key, consider wrapping access to that property with a strongly typed property.

A strongly typed property provides type safety and is less prone to the kinds of errors that may easily be introduced by small typos. If we use strongly typed properties, rather than a simple string key, gaining access to the Enabled property of the ViewState object, for example, becomes as easy as typing the following code:

```
bool enabled = this.Enabled;
```

This code is certainly a lot cleaner than the following awkward execution:

```
bool enabled = (bool)(this.ViewState["Enabled"] ?? false);
```

One additional benefit of this approach is that it allows the developer to take advantage of Microsoft's IntelliSense™ code completion functionality, rather than having to memorize which `ViewState` keys are in use.

 Dealing with an `InvalidCastException`

> Any time you attempt to cast a `ViewState` property to another value, as we've done in these examples, there's always the possibility that the result will throw an `InvalidCastException`.
>
> This could happen if another piece of code has overwritten your property's value with an object of a different type. In the code examples we've looked at so far, I haven't tried made any effort to handle such an exception—in general, if an exception like this was thrown, I would want to be notified immediately, as it could indicate a major logic error.
>
> I don't recommend catching such an exception and trying to handle it gracefully, because if you did so, your application could continue in an invalid state from the point at which the exception was thrown, causing even more damage than the simple failure thrown by this exception. We'll discuss error handling in detail in Chapter 13.

How can I make sure my custom control works when view state is turned off?

Many developers find developing with the view state to be more trouble than it's worth (we'll talk more about this issue in Chapter 16). While it does provide a convenient means of storing data between multiple requests for the same page, the view state data stored in the page can grow quickly to an unwieldy size, causing slow page loads and postbacks while all that data is shuttled back and forth over the network.

Ideally, controls would use the view state *only* to store data across postbacks (the data displayed by a GridView, for example), rather than using it to store information about how the control functions, which it does by default.

It's easy enough to turn the view state off, but if our custom control relies on it to store information between postbacks, our control will be crippled. How can we modify our control to remove its reliance upon the view state?

Solution

In the days of ASP.NET 1.1, developers either stored everything in the ViewState object, or spent a lot of time writing code to store values in hidden form fields. In ASP.NET 2.0, Microsoft introduced the **control state** to solve this problem. If view state is turned off in your application (for example, because you wanted to reduce your page weight), your custom control should use the control state to store information between postbacks.

The control state is a new addition to ASP.NET 2.0, and takes slightly more work to use than does the view state. What every responsible developer should *not* do, however, is simply dump *everything* into the ControlState object, which would create the same size-related problems of which the view state is often guilty.

 The Control State is Here to Stay

> Try to store as little as possible in the control state. Unlike the view state, there's no way to turn it off, so if the size of the control state balloons, you could end up with enormous pages, leading to slow page load times and poor overall performance.

Your control must override two virtual methods in order to take advantage of the control state:

LoadControlState

This method restores the control state from a previous page request. ASP.NET calls this method, passing in the ControlState object as a parameter.

SaveControlState

This method saves to the view state any changes made to the page since the page was loaded, or since the last postback. The method must return the status of your control as the return value for ASP.NET to store.

As well as having these two methods in place, your control must inform the `Page` that it will be using the control state. This step can be completed by calling the `Page.RegisterRequiresControlState` method.

Allow me to demonstrate the use of the control state with some code. Let's begin with a very simple control; here's the initial class definition:

ControlStateDemoControl.cs (excerpt)

```
public class ControlStateDemoControl : WebControl
{
  protected override void OnInit(EventArgs e)
  {
    // Let the page know this control needs the ControlState.
    Page.RegisterRequiresControlState(this);
    base.OnInit(e);
  }
  // The rest of the control implementation goes here
}
```

As you can see, the `OnInit` method is a good place to register this control's need to use the control state if it is to function correctly.

Let's add two properties to our class:

ControlStateDemoControl.cs (excerpt)

```
public int ViewPostCount
{
  get { return (int)(ViewState["ViewProp"] ?? 0); }
  set { ViewState["ViewProp"] = value; }
}
public int ControlPostCount
{
  get { return this.controlPostCount; }
  set { this.controlPostCount = value; }
```

```
}

private int controlPostCount;
```

The `ViewPostCount` property stores its value to, and retrieves its value from, the view state. This is an example of a `ViewState`-backed property, as discussed in the section called "What's the cleanest way to access a page's view state?".

The `ControlPostCount` property uses a private member variable to store its value. In order to store this value to, and retrieve it from, the `ControlState`, we'll need to implement the two methods discussed earlier in this section. Here's what those methods look like:

ControlStateDemoControl.cs *(excerpt)*

```
protected override object SaveControlState()
{
  return this.controlPostCount;
}
protected override void LoadControlState(object savedState)
{
  int state = (int)(savedState ?? 0);
  this.controlPostCount = state;
}
```

The `SaveControlState` method is called by ASP.NET late in the control's life cycle, when it's time to save changes to the control state (after `OnPreRender`, and just before `SaveViewStateRecursive` is called).

Your job as the control developer is to return an object that represents the current state of the control. That object will be reloaded on the next request. In this case, we store the value of `controlPostCount`.

The `LoadControlState` method is called by ASP.NET after a postback, and provides your control with the control state data from the previous request. The data is available in the form of an object named `savedState`.

In this example, since we're saving an int value into the control state (by returning `controlPostCount` in the `SaveControlState` method), we can simply cast it to an int and set `controlPostCount` to equal that value.

ControlState and Inheritance

In this example, we've inherited from the `WebControl` class, which doesn't have any state of its own. If we inherited from a control that made use of the `Control-State`, we'd have to be careful not to obliterate its `ControlState` with that of our custom control. We'll explore this very issue in the Discussion section for this solution.

Let's add our final methods:

ControlStateDemoControl.cs *(excerpt)*

```
protected override void OnLoad(EventArgs e)
{
  ViewPostCount++;
  ControlPostCount++;
  base.OnLoad(e);
}
protected override void Render(System.Web.UI.HtmlTextWriter writer)
{
  // Each time we render, we increment.
  writer.Write("<p>ViewState: " + this.ViewPostCount + "</p>");
  writer.Write("<p>ControlState:" + this.ControlPostCount + "</p>");
  base.Render(writer);
}
```

Since we intend for our control's property values to increment from one postback to the next, we perform this increment in the `OnLoad` method. The `Render` method writes out the value of each property to the response.

Let's take this control for a test-drive—we'll construct an ASP.NET page that includes the following markup:

ControlStateExample.aspx *(excerpt)*

```
<form id="form1" runat="server">
  <div>
    <sp:ControlStateDemoControl ID="demo" runat="server" />
    <asp:Button ID="button" runat="server" Text="Post Back!" />
  </div>
</form>
```

This simple page contains our control as well as a button that forces the page to perform a postback. Figure 6.4 shows the output after we click the button three times.

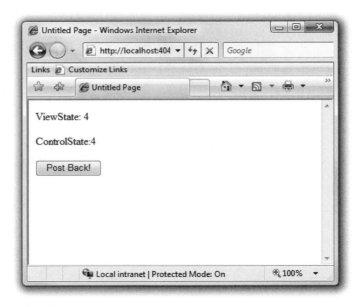

Figure 6.4. Storing state information with view state and control state

Now let's disable the view state for this page and try clicking four more times. Figure 6.5 shows the result.

Figure 6.5. Our custom control, this time with view state disabled

As you can see, the view state is no longer being persisted across postbacks, but the control state still is.

Where's the Control State Stored?

The control state is actually stored in a hidden form field named __VIEWSTATE. Sound familiar? It's the same field in which the view state is saved. Once the view state is disabled, the field is only used for the control state.

Discussion

I've deliberately kept the code in this solution simple in order to best demonstrate how to load and save the ControlState. However, there's one important question that I have yet to address: what's the proper way to implement the LoadControlState and SaveControlState methods when inheriting from a control that already makes use of the ControlState?

To demonstrate how this situation should be tackled, let's create a subclass of the ControlStateDemoControl control. Here's the basic implementation without the ControlState methods:

```
                                          SubControlStateDemo.cs (excerpt)
public class SubControlStateDemo : ControlStateDemoControl
{
  public int AnotherCount
  {
    get { return this.anotherCount; }
    set { this.anotherCount = value; }
  }
  private int anotherCount;

  protected override void OnLoad(EventArgs e)
  {
    AnotherCount++;
    base.OnLoad(e);
  }
  protected override void Render(HtmlTextWriter writer)
  {
    base.Render(writer);
    writer.Write("<p>AnotherCount:" + this.AnotherCount + "</p>");
  }
  // More implementation to come …
}
```

As you can see, all we've added here is a normal property, anotherCount, which contains get and set methods. We increment this property in the OnLoad method and display the value of the property in the Render method. So far, this control implementation is very similar to the control that we created earlier.

This might look straightforward to you right now, but our implementation of SaveControlState and LoadControlState is a little trickier—we have to be careful not to lose the state of the inherited class. The body of those methods is as follows:

```
                                          SubControlStateDemo.cs (excerpt)
protected override object SaveControlState()
{
  // Grab the state for the base control.
  object baseState = base.SaveControlState();

  // Create an array to hold the base control's state
  // and this control's state.
  object thisState = new object[] {baseState, this.anotherCount};
```

```
    return thisState;
}
protected override void LoadControlState(object savedState)
{
  object[] stateLastRequest = (object[]) savedState;

  // Grab the state for the base class
  // and assign it to the class.
  object baseState = stateLastRequest[0];
  base.LoadControlState(baseState);

  // Now load this control's state.
  this.anotherCount = (int) stateLastRequest[1];
}
```

Let's walk through what's happening here. In `SaveControlState`, we first grab the state from the base control. As you'll recall, this holds the value for `controlPostCount`. But since we want to add `anotherCount` to the `ControlState`, we create an array to store both values. This array is the object that's returned.

What Form Should `ControlState` Data Take?

Although we've used an array in this example, we could have chosen any serializable object—the key is to use a consistent object type each time you save information to the `ControlState` within your application.

In the `LoadControlState` method, we expect to be passed an array object. We grab the value that the base class is expecting, pass it to `base.LoadControlState`, and set `anotherCount` to the value of the state for this control.

I recommend using this approach whenever you write a custom control that makes use of `ControlState`. With the use of less comprehensive techniques, you never know when you might inadvertently override the `ControlState` for a base class.

Summary

The proper handling of state is an essential task for any non-trivial web application. Fortunately, ASP.NET provides a wealth of options and features for handling states of varying scope, including global state, session state, or the state within a single request.

In this chapter we've explored the most common and essential aspects of dealing with state. Table 6.1 displays some of the storage options we covered, along with the scope and lifetime of each.

Table 6.1. State Storage Options for an ASP.NET Page

State Store	Scope	Lifetime
Static Members	global per process	entire lifetime of the web application
Application Object	global per `AppDomain`	entire lifetime of the web application
`Session`	global per process for in-memory; global for state-server or database-backed session	lifetime of a user's session, which by default lasts 20 minutes after the user's last request
`HttpContext.Items`	single request	entire lifetime of a single request
`Page.Items`	single request	only accessible during the page life cycle
View State	typically for a single page, but cross-page postbacks are possible	lifetime spans multiple page requests as long as each page posts the view state data
Control State	typically for a single page, but cross-page postbacks are possible	lifetime spans multiple page requests as long as each page posts the view state data

We could certainly fill an entire book if we were to attempt to be absolutely complete and detailed with our coverage of state management in ASP.NET. But with the tools provided in this chapter, you're well equipped to make use of state reliably and efficiently in your next web application.

Membership and Access Control

Any site that provides a level of customization or interaction will need to be able to authenticate and authorize its users. **Authentication** is the act of determining the identity of a user, while **authorization** is the determination of whether a user is permitted to perform a certain action or not.

One type of site that implements authentication and authorization is a blog (or web log). Typically, *any* users have permission to read the content posted to a blog without having to identify themselves. However, the blog won't allow just anyone to create a new post on the site. A user must first log in (authentication) and have the correct permissions (authorization) before he or she can create a new post.

Despite the fact that authentication and authorization are such common functions, it used to be the case that developers had to implement these features from scratch in every project. With ASP.NET 2.0, developers have access to the membership API, which consists of a MembershipProvider class and a comprehensive set of web controls for authentication and authorization.

In this chapter's solutions, we'll be using the MembershipProvider class extensively. Let's get started!

What's the easiest way to add membership to my site?

The `MembershipProvider` is designed to accommodate most developer needs for managing users and roles, as it's extremely configurable.

Of course, with any configurable API, the further your situation lies from the use case upon which the class was designed, the more work it takes to use it properly.

In this section, we'll look at the basic, default case for the `MembershipProvider`'s implementation.

Solution

It only takes one line of configuration code to get started with the `MembershipProvider`. After creating a web site using Visual Studio (or Visual Web Developer), right-click the project, select **Add New Item** and then **Web Configuration File**. Then add the following line of code to the `system.web` section of **Web.config** file:

```
<authentication mode="Forms" />
```

The following snippet shows this setting in context, once all other **Web.config** elements and comments have been removed:

Web.config (excerpt)

```
<?xml version="1.0"?>
<configuration>
<system.web>
  <authentication mode="Forms" />
</system.web>
</configuration>
```

Discussion

That's all it takes! This web site will inherit its `MembershipProvider` configuration from the settings defined in **Machine.config**.

For very simple sites whose `MembershipProvider` doesn't need to diverge from the default settings, there is no need to add anything to **Web.config**.

Of course, there's more to be done once you add this line of code. You still need to create a means for creating users, and allowing those users to log in to your site. We'll look at these functions next.

Finding `machine.config`

The **machine.config** file is located in the **%SystemRoot%\Microsoft.NET\Framework\v2.0.50727\CONFIG** folder. For a default installation, that should be:

C:\Windows\Microsoft.NET\Framework\v2.0.50727\CONFIG\machine.config

In you take a look at the contents of this file, you'll find that it references a default connection named `LocalSqlServer`. This points to a SQL Server Express database called **aspnetdb.mdf**, which resides in the web site's **App_Data** folder:

```
<connectionStrings>
  <add name="LocalSqlServer"
    connectionString="data source=.\SQLEXPRESS;
    Integrated Security=SSPI;
    AttachDBFilename=|DataDirectory|aspnetdb.mdf;
    User Instance=true"
    providerName="System.Data.SqlClient" />
</connectionStrings>
```

The ASP.NET membership provider data access calls go through `System.Web.DataAccess.SqlConnectionHelper`. This helper class checks for the presence of a membership database; if such a database doesn't exist, it will be created.

Adding Membership to an Existing Database

Of course, you can specify a different membership database if you'd like. The easiest way to add membership to an existing SQL Server database is by running **aspnet_regsql.exe** from the Visual Studio 2005 Command Prompt. Scott Guthrie wrote a great walk-through of this procedure, which is available on his weblog.[1]

---

[1] http://weblogs.asp.net/scottgu/423703.aspx

Building your Own Membership Provider

What if your member details are stored in an existing database that can't be changed, or are returned to your application via a web service? In cases like this, the default ASP.NET membership provider probably won't work for you.

Fortunately, that doesn't mean that you have to write your own membership system from scratch. You can build a membership provider to allow the ASP.NET membership and personalization system to work against your existing membership store.

Building a custom membership provider is not a simple task, and is beyond the scope of this book. You can get an idea of what's involved by looking at the following MSDN examples:

- the `ReadOnlyXmlMembershipProvider` example at http://msdn2.microsoft.com/en-us/library/aa479031.aspx

- the `SqlMembershipProvider` at http://msdn2.microsoft.com/en-us/library/ms366730.aspx

How do I allow users to register for my site?

ASP.NET provides the `CreateUserWizard` control to facilitate registration. In this section, we'll walk through the process of using this control to allow users to register for your site.

Solution

To begin, add a new web form to the site. In this case, naming it `Default.aspx` should be fine.

Make sure you're in Design View for the page, and bring up the **Toolbox**. If you expand the **Login** section, you should see the list of controls shown in Figure 7.1.

Figure 7.1. The login controls available within the `MembershipProvider` class

That's quite a list of controls! Double-click on the `CreateUserWizard` control, which should add to the page the control with its smart tag options expanded, as shown in Figure 7.2.

Figure 7.2. Adding the control to the page

For now, we'll just leave the control as is, but as you can see, it's possible to make many customizations.

Press **Ctrl-F5** to run the web site. This should display the wizard, as shown in Figure 7.3.

Figure 7.3. The `CreateUserWizard` control in action

Go ahead: fill in the form and click **Create User**. Congratulations—you just success-fully created a user for your web site!

Discussion

Okay, so we created a user. But where exactly *is* this user?

By default, ASP.NET stores membership information in an instance of SQL Server Express 2005. ASP.NET creates the database when a user fills in the page generated by the `CreateUserWizard` control and clicks **Create User**.

Go ahead: right-click the Solution Explorer and select **Refresh Folder**. You should now see a new **App_Data** folder that contains a database named **ASPNETDB.MDF**, as Figure 7.4 shows.

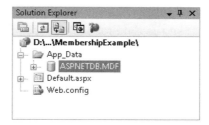

Figure 7.4. The new database as viewed in the Solution Explorer

Right-click on the database and select **Open**. This will expand the database in the Server Explorer and display the database objects, such as tables and views, which can be seen in Figure 7.5.

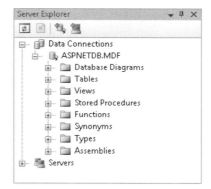

Figure 7.5. Viewing the new database in the Server Explorer

 Handling Connection Errors

The default database connection in the **machine.config** file is configured to use SQL Server Express, but it's possible that you may not have installed it. If you're receiving connection errors, first check that SQL Server Express is installed and the service is running. SQL Server Express will appear in your services list as "SQL Server (SQLEXPRESS)." If it's not installed, you can install it from the Visual Studio 2005 Installation media, but if you've got a fast Internet connection, it might be easiest to just grab the 35MB download.[2]

The other alternative is to change your **Web.config** to point to an existing SQL Server instance.

---

[2] http://msdn.microsoft.com/vstudio/express/sql/download/

Expand the **Tables** node and double-click on the `aspnet_Members` table—you can see your newly created user in the data for the table, as Figure 7.6 shows.

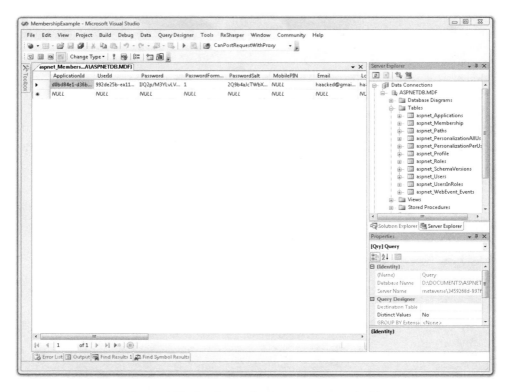

Figure 7.6. Viewing the user data in our newly created table

How do I manage users on my site?

Once your site has users, roles, and profiles, you'll need to manage them.

When you're developing your site, the simple answer to the management question is to use the **Web Site Administration Tool (WSAT)**—a browser-based tool for site configuration. The easiest way to access this tool is to open the **Project** menu in Visual Studio, and select **ASP.NET Configuration**. This option gives you access to a simple web site that lets you manage several aspects of your application, including users and roles. Figure 7.7 shows what the site looks like.

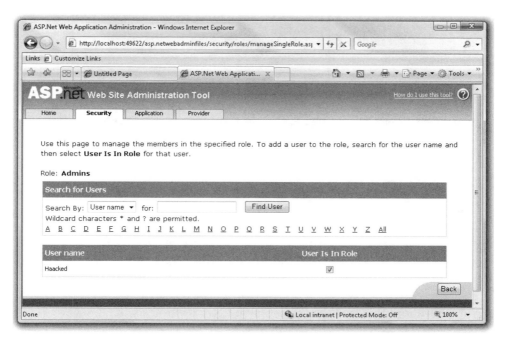

Figure 7.7. The Web Site Administration Tool, a browser-based tool for site configuration

This tool comes with one major restriction, though—it's only available on your local machine. What can we do when we need to administer a site on another machine?

Solution

We can administer a site from a remote machine in a few different ways.

My recommendation is to use Peter Kellner's Membership Editor, which was explained in an article published as a four-part series on MSDN.[3] Kellner's approach is a smart one—he uses `ObjectDataSource` objects to wrap the membership provider interfaces, and bind them to ASP.NET controls. You can use Peter's membership data providers to build your own editor if you like. Figure 7.8 shows the Membership Editor tool in action.

---

[3] http://msdn2.microsoft.com/en-us/library/aa479399.aspx

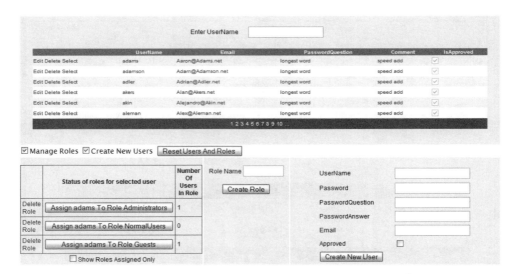

Figure 7.8. The Membership Editor, an administration tool that can be operated remotely

More details about this tool are available on Peter Kellner's site.[4]

If this solution isn't right for you, there are a few other options you can try:

- You can build your own administration interface. If you do, I'd recommend that you utilize the membership provider object interface rather than directly modifying data in the membership tables—the tables are a little complex.

- You can copy the membership data from the production server to your development machine, and use the Web Site Administration Tool to make the necessary changes before copying the files back again. This approach will only be practical if your membership database is small and changes only occasionally (and of course you'd want to formalize this process quite a bit if you were using it in a live production environment).

- It's possible to allow a remote user to access the **webadmin.axd** file.[5] Doing so will also make the Web Site Administration Tool available from a remote machine (see the warning below about this).

---

[4] http://peterkellner.net/2006/03/13/adding-personalization-via-profiles-to-the-objectdatasource-in-aspnet-20/

[5] http://weblogs.asp.net/jeffwids/archive/2005/07/26/420572.aspx

Security Concerns with webadmin.axd

Early beta releases of ASP.NET 2.0 allowed remote access to the WSAT, but the ASP.NET team removed this facility prior to release due to security concerns. As such, I'd only recommend that you use this approach on an a well-secured intranet application.

How do I require users to log in?

In the first two solutions in this chapter, we configured a web site to take advantage of the `MembershipProvider` class, and we created a page that allowed users to register for our site. This functionality isn't terribly useful on its own, though, since we're not actually doing anything with that user data.

Let's provide registered users with the ability to log in to our site. In this section, we'll create an `Admin` area for our site that only registered users can see.

Solution

To get started, add an **Admin** folder to your web site project. Within that folder, add a page named **Default.aspx**. For demonstration purposes, add to the page the text, "This page is only for registered users who have logged in."

If you right-click on this page and select **View in Browser**, you'll be able to view the contents of the page without logging in. Let's change this, so that the text is only visible to users who are logged in.

First, we'll add the following `location` section to our **Web.config** file:

Web.config *(excerpt)*

```
<?xml version="1.0"?>
  <configuration>
    <system.web>
      <authentication mode="Forms" />
    </system.web>
    <location path="Admin">
      <system.web>
        <authorization>
          <deny users="?" />
        </authorization>
```

```
    </system.web>
  </location>
</configuration>
```

Within the `location` section of the above code is an `authorization` section that denies access to all unregistered users (the group of users indicated by the question mark).

 Denying All Users

To deny *all* users access to the site, you could use the asterisk like so:

```
<deny users="*" />
```

Why would we deny access to all users? Well, we could use this facility to restrict all users by default, then allow users with certain roles to view a page:

```
<deny users="*" />
<allow roles="Administrator" />
```

Now we just need to add a new web form named **Login.aspx** to the root of the web site. In Design View for that page, drag the `Login Control` from the toolbar onto the page.

Now try right-clicking on **/Admin/Default.aspx** and viewing it in the browser again—you should now be redirected to the login page, as illustrated in Figure 7.9.

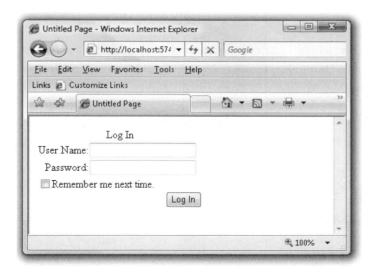

Figure 7.9. The login page to which users are redirected if they attempt to view the restricted page without logging in

Discussion

The LoginControl is one of several new ASP.NET 2.0 controls that are designed to work with the MembershipProvider class. Like many other controls, the layout of this control is easily configured via templates.

In designing these controls, their creators have been careful not to make any assumptions about the underlying data store for users and roles. By relying upon the MembershipProvider API, the LoginControl works whether an underlying user store exists or not.

How do I grant access to users who have forgotten their passwords?

It happens to everyone at some point, and it's embarrassing. No, I'm not talking about *that*! I'm talking about forgetting your password.

A web site that doesn't provide an means by which users can retrieve forgotten passwords automatically is just *asking* to be inundated with tech support calls. Fortunately, the ASP.NET team has you covered!

Solution

The `PasswordRecovery` control is extremely useful in this case. Be sure to add the control to a page that anonymous users are authorized to access—there's no point burying the password recovery page within a page that requires authentication.

To use the `PasswordRecovery` control, just drag it onto a page. Figure 7.10 shows the control appearing on the Login page—a perfectly suitable location.

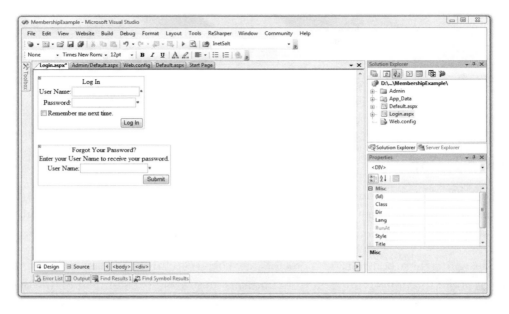

Figure 7.10. Adding the `PasswordRecovery` control to the Login page

Three templates need to be configured once this control has been added to a page:

UserName

This template asks for the user for a username.

Question

This template asks for the "challenge question" that was created by the user upon registration. Only the user should know the answer.

Success

This template defines a success message that's displayed when the password is recovered.

There's a fourth "view" of this control that needs to be considered—the email message that's sent to the user and contains the password. Expand the `MailDefinition` section of the **Properties** dialog to set the Subject, From address, and other email settings.

Figure 7.11. Configuring the settings for an email to be sent to users recovering passwords

At this point, you need to configure your application to use a mail server, so that it can actually send your email. Fortunately, ASP.NET makes this easy via the built-in web site administration utility.

Just click on the control's smart tag and select the **Administer Website** option. This will start the web-based Web Site Administration Tool (WSAT)—a tool that we looked at in the section called "How do I manage users on my site?". Click on the **Application** tab, then select the **Configure SMTP e-mail settings** link within the **SMTP Settings** section.

Clicking this link should display the screen shown in Figure 7.12.

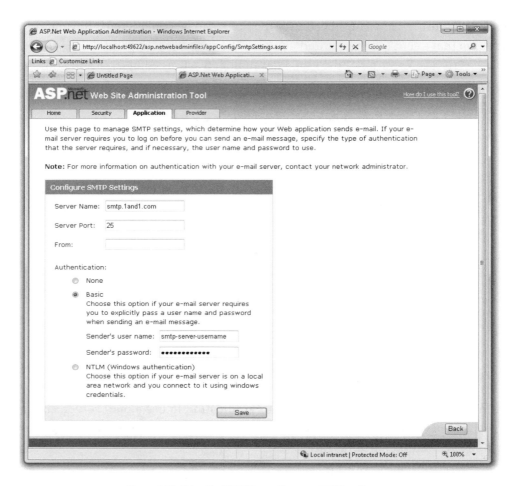

Figure 7.12. Using the WSAT to configure an SMTP mail server

Fill in your mail server settings and click **Save**. The administration tool will update your **Web.config** settings with the changes you made. The following sample shows the lines that were modified by the WSAT when I configured my application to use a mail server on my local machine:

Web.config *(excerpt)*

```xml
<?xml version="1.0"?>
  <configuration>
    <system.net>
      <mailSettings>
        <smtp>
          <network>
```

```
        host="localhost"
        port="25"
        userName="smtp-server-user-name"
        password="smpt-server-password"
        defaultCredentials="false"
      />
    </smtp>
  </mailSettings>
</system.net>
</configuration>
```

With these configuration changes complete, you're ready to test this control. Build the project and navigate to the login page in your browser. Enter your username in the second form, and click **Submit**. You should be presented with your challenge question, as shown in Figure 7.13.

Figure 7.13. Presenting the challenge question to the user

Once you answer the question correctly, a success message will be displayed, and an email will be sent to your email address containing a new password.

But that Wasn't my Original Password!

The default membership provider settings store cryptographic hashes of users' passwords rather than the passwords themselves.[6] Storing encrypted passwords is much more secure than storing the passwords in plain text—if your database is compromised, the passwords remain secure. Unfortunately, it means that ASP.NET is unable to provide users with their original passwords, and must generate new passwords for them.

Your users may not appreciate their new, random passwords, as they can be quite hard to remember, so it's a good idea to implement a `ChangePassword` control on your site, to allow them to change those freshly generated passwords to something they can remember.

It's possible to use plain text passwords, and if you do so, users' original passwords will be provided to them when they go through the password recovery process. However, because of the potential security issues associated with this approach, I strongly recommend that you stick with password hashes rather than storing users' original passwords.

Figure 7.14 shows the password recovery email that was sent to my address.

Figure 7.14. The password recovery email sent by the `MembershipProvider` class

---

[6] Hashing a value is a destructive process, so it's impossible to recover the original value from a hash. However, every time you hash a given value, you'll get the same result. By storing only password hashes, ASP.NET is able to verify that the user has entered the correct password without knowing what that password is.

And that's that! We've created a comprehensive password recovery system, without writing a line of code!

How do I display content based on roles?

One compelling reason for wanting to segment your users into different roles is to vary the content that you present to them based on the types of users they are. For example, suppose your site contained articles that were submitted by your users. You may want to allow *all* users to view the final, published articles, but restrict access to new articles that require approval to a team of administrators.

Let's assume that, in addition to the two standard `RoleGroups` (`LoggedIn` and `Anonymous`) our site has a custom `RoleGroup` called `Admin`. We learned how to restrict users from viewing pages in the section called "Solution", but how can we vary the content on a page based on a given user's role?

Solution

The (somewhat confusingly named) `LoginView` control lets us display particular content to users with particular roles.

After you add the `LoginView` control to a web form, the control's smart tag lets you select a view to edit. As you can see in Figure 7.15, each view in the drop-down list corresponds to a role (with the exception of `LoggedIn`, which corresponds to the user's current login status).

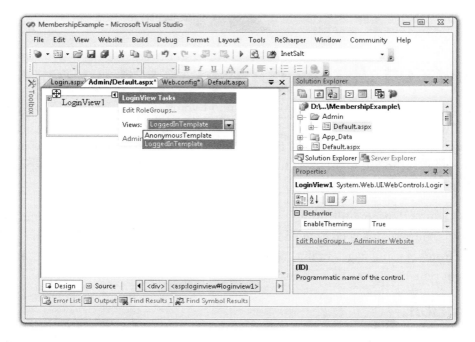

Figure 7.15. Selecting a role for the `LoginView` control

By default, only two templates are available: `Anonymous` and `LoggedIn`.

Since we want to show special content to users in the `Admins` role, we'll need to create an additional template. To do so, click **Edit RoleGroups…** to launch the `RoleGroup` Collection Editor dialog shown in Figure 7.16.

Figure 7.16. The `RoleGroup` Collection Editor

Click the **Add** button to add a role group for the `Admins` role. When you click **OK**, a new `LoginView` template named `RoleGroup[0]` — `Admins` will appear in your control's smart tags menu, as shown in Figure 7.17.

Order Matters

Keep in mind that the *first matching template* is always chosen, so it's important to pay special attention to the order of the `RoleGroup`s.

For example, if we were to use a `LoginView` control for users in roles of `Admins` and `Users`, and all `Admins` were also `Users`, we would want to list the `Admin` template first. Otherwise, both groups will inherit the `User` template.

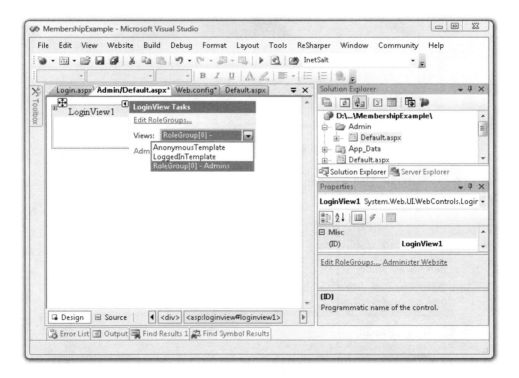

Figure 7.17. Our `LoginView` control containing a new `RoleGroup`

Select your new `RoleGroup` from the smart tag, and type your admin-specific content within the `LoginView` control, as shown in Figure 7.18. For the purposes of this demonstration, we'll just inform the members of the `Admins` role: "You are an admin!"

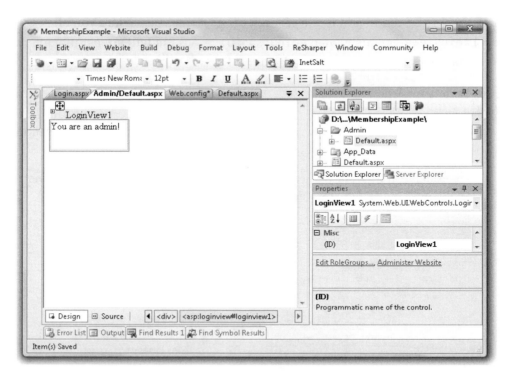

Figure 7.18. Adding content specific to the `Admins` role

Now, to test our page! Log in as an `Admin`, and you should see a page that looks like the one in Figure 7.19.

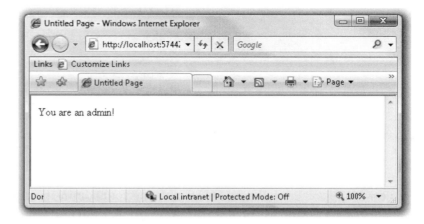

Figure 7.19. The page seen by those logged in as `Admin`

To complete this demonstration, we should break the bad news to those members who aren't in the `Admins` group. Our web content team confers for a few weeks and comes back with the following: "You are not an admin."

However, they've decided to soften the blow by at least greeting the user by his or her username. To display the username, we'll need to add a `LoginName` control to the page. So the complete template that we'll display to a user who's logged in, but is not an admin, is as follows:

Admin.aspx (excerpt)

```
<LoggedInTemplate>
  <p>
    Hello, <asp:LoginName id="loginName" runat="Server" />.
  </p>
  <p>
    You are not an admin.
  </p>
</LoggedInTemplate>
```

Yes—we *can* include HTML and other ASP.NET controls in a `LoginView` control template.

Now, when our lowly non-admin users log in, they'll see the page shown in Figure 7.20.

Figure 7.20. The page displayed to those logged in as `User`

As we've seen in this example, it's easy to use ASP.NET to deliver specific content to users depending on their roles, so long as you choose the right control for the job.

Summary

ASP.NET 2.0 includes a rich, extensible membership system. It can help you administer your users, control site access, and manage what users see and do based on roles that you can define. Additionally, the provider architecture that forms the basis of the membership system allows you to plug your own logic and data into the existing system, so that the user experience of your site's members is limited only by your imagination!

Chapter

8

Component–based Development

It's easy to succumb to a drag-and-drop mindset when working with ASP.NET and Visual Studio.

This mentality might apply to small applications, but becomes a problem in large applications built by teams of software developers. A drag-and-drop approach encourages developers to think of web forms as simple collections of server-side controls and HTML markup—we tend to write our code as if the names, types, and locations of the controls will never change, making the controls very closely intertwined and not particularly reusable. It's this tight coupling that can introduce bugs that result in late-night debugging sessions every time we need to make a change to our software.

In this chapter, we'll explore a **component-based approach** to web form development. In a component-based approach, we try to divide the user interface into independent black boxes. These black boxes can hide the details of how a component is implemented, resulting in increased flexibility should we need to change our code in the future. By isolating our code into independent components, we can identify more errors at compile time when changes are made; such compiler errors are far easier to locate and fix than runtime errors.

Also in this chapter, we'll see how properties, events, and interfaces can help us build loosely coupled components based on web forms, user controls, and master pages. Let's begin with one of the most misunderstood components in ASP.NET—the master page.

How can I use master pages?

Our first topic for discussion is the ASP.NET 2.0 implementation of master pages. You might question why we would cover such a low-level detail in a problem–solution style book such as this. The answer is that the majority of common master page problems arise because the master page implementation is widely misunderstood. Even the class name MasterPage is misleading. A master page is neither a *master* in charge of a web form, nor a *page* that can stand alone.

A **master page** is a template that we can use to maintain consistent markup across multiple web forms. A master page focuses on controlling the *structure* of the interface, leaving each web form responsible for displaying its own unique content.

Let's look at the code for a simple master page (Simple.master) with a single ContentPlaceHolder control:

Simple.master

```
<%@ Master Language="C#" AutoEventWireup="true"
   CodeFile="Simple.master.cs" Inherits="Simple" %>
<!DOCTYPE html PUBLIC "-//W3C//DTD XHTML 1.0 Strict//EN"
    "http://www.w3.org/TR/xhtml1/DTD/xhtml1-strict.dtd">
<html xmlns="http://www.w3.org/1999/xhtml" >
<head runat="server">
  <title>Untitled Page</title>
</head>
<body>
  <form id="form1" runat="server">
  <div>
    <asp:contentplaceholder id="ContentPlaceHolder1" runat="server">
      This is some default content.
    </asp:contentplaceholder>
  </div>
  </form>
</body>
</html>
```

The master page lays out the common elements, such as the server-side `head` and `form` elements. A web form that uses a master page is called a **content page**. The following code creates a content page that uses our simple master page:

```
Simple.aspx (excerpt)

<%@ Page Language="C#" MasterPageFile="~/Simple.master"
    AutoEventWireup="true" CodeFile="Simple.aspx.cs"
    Inherits="_Default" Title="Home" %>
<asp:Content ID="Content1" Runat="Server"
    ContentPlaceHolderID="ContentPlaceHolder1">
  This will override the default content.
</asp:Content>
```

Figure 8.1 shows this content page as it displays in the browser.

Figure 8.1. Viewing the simple content page

As you can see, the web form was able to plug its custom content into the master page's `ContentPlaceHolder`, almost as if by magic. Let's take a peek behind the magician's curtain to see how the trick works.

Solution

Analyzing the source code of the master page gives us a few hints about its behavior. The first hint is that we must associate a master page with a content page *before* the `Init` event of the page is triggered. Luckily, the ASP.NET 2.0 `Page` class gives us the `PreInit` event for just this purpose. This is particularly powerful when you consider the fact that we can use this event to programmatically define our master page. Thus we have the ability to, say, set the master page based on a user preference or other database setting:

Simple.master.cs *(excerpt)*

```
protected void Page_PreInit(object sender, EventArgs e)
{
  this.MasterPageFile = "~/Simple.master";
}
```

We can gain a second hint about master page behavior by looking at the control tree that's present when the page renders. You can view the control tree by adding `Trace="true"` in the `@ Page` directive. The control tree will appear in the trace output, as shown in Figure 8.2.

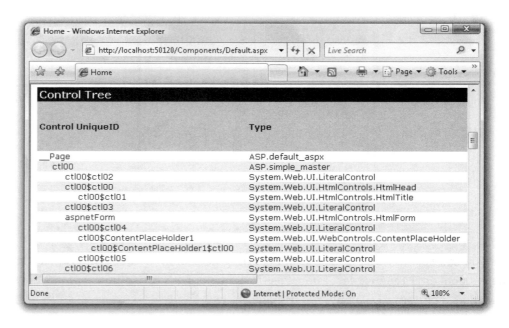

Figure 8.2. Tracing a web form to see the control tree

You may have assumed, quite reasonably, that the master page, being a *master*, would be the uppermost control in the tree. Instead, the master page appears as a child control inside the content page! This seems like a role reversal … until we look at the inheritance hierarchy for the `MasterPage` class conceptualized in Figure 8.3.

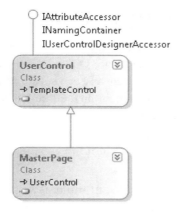

Figure 8.3. `UserControl` is the base class for `MasterPage`

It turns out that `MasterPage` inherits from the `UserControl` class, which yields yet another clue about the behavior of master pages. To find out what's going on behind the scenes, we can look through the source code in the ASP.NET framework's class library using a third-party tool like Reflector, which we'll look at in more detail in Chapter 17.

Just after the content page's `PreInit` event is triggered (but before the `Init` event is triggered), ASP.NET hands control to the master page. The master page attaches itself as a child control of the `Page` object, then walks through the content page's `Content` controls. The master page matches each `Content` control with a `ContentPlaceHolder`, and copies the controls *inside* the `Content` control into the placeholder. At this point the master page has finished working its magic, and is just another control inside the page (or just another rabbit in the hat, so to speak).

Discussion

We tend to think of master pages differently when we realize they are, for the most part, just another control inside the page. However, this way of thinking can be misleading. Master pages shouldn't be used to manage database connections, authorize users, or provide diagnostic and logging capabilities. These are all services that every page in our application might need to use, but providing these services through a central master page is not the best approach. A master page should be responsible for maintaining a consistent user interface, and nothing more.

Locating Diagnostic and Logging Code

If code to perform diagnostics and logging shouldn't be placed inside a `MasterPage` class, where *should* it go? One solution is to use an HTTP Module, which lives in the ASP.NET pipeline and can subscribe to events such as `BeginRequest` during the lifetime of the request. We can provide functionality inside the module that will be available in every request for a page, but without cluttering up pages themselves. Another solution is to create a base class (derived from the `Page` class) for all the web forms in an application.

There are times, of course, when we want the master page and content page to interact. For example, we might want our content page to respond to a button click event that occurs on the master page. When this requirement crops up, we should treat the master page like a component—a black box. We want a clearly defined interface to formalize the interaction between the two pages, rather than writing our content page so that it depends upon the existence of a specific control in the master page.

Keep these issues in mind as we talk about common master page scenarios in the next few solutions.

Master Page Voodoo and ClientIDs

One nasty side-effect of using a master page is the impact it has on the `ClientID` property of the controls inside a page. The `MasterPage` class implements a special ASP.NET interface: INamingContainer. When ASP.NET renders a control inside an INamingContainer, it prefixes the ID used in the client with the ID of the INamingContainer. This means that an input field with an ID of `myValue` will appear in the browser with an ID of `_ctl0_myValue`, where `_ctl0` is the ID of the `MasterPage` control. This naming scheme is important to remember if you use JavaScript or CSS that references an element by its ID. We'll revisit the INamingContainer in the section called "How do I treat user controls as components?"

How can my content page override data on my master page?

A content page can insert custom content into a master page, but only when the master page provides a placeholder for the content. Sometimes a content page doesn't need this level of control—it might just need to tweak one property of a control that's already inside the master page.

Let's examine an excerpt from another master page—`Interaction.master`:

Interaction.master (excerpt)

```
<form id="form1" runat="server">
<div class="header">
  <h1>
    <span runat="server" id="HeaderSpan">Welcome!</span>
  </h1>
</div>
<div>
  <asp:ContentPlaceHolder ID="ContentPlaceHolder1" runat="server">
  </asp:ContentPlaceHolder>
</div>
</form>
```

This master page defines a `form` element and a content place holder. The master divides the page into a header area and a content area. Inside the header is a `span` element that's processed on the server (as indicated by the `runat="server"` attribute). With a little CSS styling, a page that uses this master template might look like Figure 8.4.

Figure 8.4. Displaying a master page with header and content

The "Welcome!" text at the top of the page is held inside the server-side span. The master page could easily change the InnerText, InnerHtml, or other properties of this control at run-time. A content page can also tweak these properties, but it will first need to obtain a reference to the control.

One approach to obtaining this reference might be to use the master page's FindControl method, as shown in the following code:

```
HtmlGenericControl span;
span = Master.FindControl("HeaderSpan") as HtmlGenericControl;
if (span != null)
{
  span.InnerText = "Welcome Back!";
}
```

This code would allow our content page to change the "Welcome!" text on the master page, but is this the best approach? The code assumes that the control it needs to modify will always have the name HeaderSpan. It also assumes the control will always be of class HtmlGenericControl. If someone were to modify the master page, they could break this code and not know about the problem until the page executes. Fortunately, it's relatively easy for us to improve on this approach—let's see how.

Solution

For our improved solution, we'll treat the master page like a component. If we know that our content pages may need to modify the header text every now and then, we can expose a public property for the content page to read and write to the header text:

Interactions.master.cs *(excerpt)*

```
public partial class Interaction_Site : System.Web.UI.MasterPage
{
  public string WelcomeMessage
  {
    get { return this.HeaderSpan.InnerText; }
    set { HeaderSpan.InnerText = value; }
  }
}
```

This property allows a content page to modify the header text on the master page (and *only* the header text). We've hidden the fact that we're using a `span` element in the master page, and we can now change the implementation in the future if we feel the need. To use this property from the content page in an ASP.NET 2.0 Web Site project, we first apply a `@ MasterType` directive in our **aspx** file:

```
<%@ MasterType VirtualPath="~/Interaction/Interaction.master" %>
```

When ASP.NET is generating code for our content page and sees the `@ MasterType` directive, it will look at the master page specified by the `VirtualPath` attribute and generate a strongly typed `Master` property for our content page. The existence of this strongly typed property means that we don't have to cast object references or use control names to set the header text. All the content page needs to do is make use of the `Master` property, like this:

```
Master.WelcomeMessage = "Welcome Back!";
```

The end result is the same, as Figure 8.5 shows, but the solution we're using now is more robust.

Figure 8.5. Setting text through a strongly typed property

Discussion

There are a couple of points about this solution that warrant further discussion.

Using a Strongly Typed Property

Adding a public property to our master page, as we've done in the code above, formalizes the interaction between content pages and our master page. By doing so, we've hidden the implementation of our page's header in the master page.

Now, let's imagine a scenario where some developers replaced the span in the master page header with an ASP.NET Label control. If they were still using a FindControl approach to modify the header text, they wouldn't experience any problems until runtime, at which time casting the control to type HtmlGenericControl would fail and throw an exception.

If they used the property approach that I've outlined in this solution, the developers would instead see a compiler error in the master page's WelcomeMessage property (the error occurs because a Label control does not have an InnerText property). Fortunately, it's easy for the developer to modify the code to use the Text property of the new Label control—the application can continue running without error and without requiring any further changes.

Handling Multiple Master Pages

One common question that arises with this solution is how we should handle an application that uses *multiple master pages.* In such an application, we won't want our content pages to depend on a specific master page to be assigned at runtime. After all, we may want to change the master page depending on such factors as the user's preferences, or the time of day.

To solve the problem of changing the master page that a content page uses, we can create a base class for our master pages. The base class can define the public properties and methods available for content pages to use, and each master page can then inherit from this common base class.

It's important in this scenario to revisit the content page's @ MasterType directive, which in our solution points to a specific master page. The directive has another attribute, TypeName, which can be used in place of the VirtualPath attribute. By pointing TypeName to the master page base class, we'll give our content pages a strongly typed Master property that can reach the public API of all our master pages. The directive would look like the one shown below, where BaseMasterPage is the base class for all available master pages:

```
<%@ MasterType TypeName="BaseMasterPage" %>
```

In the next solution, we'll turn the tables and see how a master page can work with different content pages.

How can I have my master page interact with my content page?

Often when we work with master pages we need to communicate with the content page from the master page. As an example, let's suppose that we're building a web site and want to give our users the ability to email the content of any page to people they know. Since we'll need a button on every page, along with the text **Email This Page**, we'll want to place this button, and a text box into which the user can enter an email address, on the master page, as shown in Figure 8.6.

Figure 8.6. A master page that allows users to email content to friends

One approach to handling the event triggered by a button click—in this case, the sending of the email—is to place the code that sends the email in the master page. This method *might* work if all the content pages were to use the same code to send an email. However, suppose we were serving different types of content, and wanted to email each piece of content using the appropriate encoding for each type. For instance, if the user was viewing a photo album, we could email a ZIP archive containing image files, but if the user was viewing a resume, we could email a copy of the resume in PDF format. In this case, the code that would handle the email event might look like the following:

```
protected void SendEmailButton_Click(object sender, EventArgs e)
{
  if(Request.Url == "the url to a photo album")
  {
    // send a zip file
  }
  else if (Request.Url == "the url to a resume")
  {
    // send a pdf
  }

  // and so on ...
}
```

As you can imagine, code like this has the potential to become a tangled, unmaintainable mess of conditional logic and hard-coded strings. Let's take a look at a more robust solution that uses a component-based approach.

Solution

In an improved solution, we'll make the content pages responsible for mailing their own content. In this case, we need the master page to raise an event when the user clicks the button to send an email. Content pages that are interested in this event can subscribe to the event, and provide their own implementations for mailing content.

First, let's write a class that will define the event arguments:

SendEmailEventArgs.cs *(excerpt)*

```
public class SendEmailEventArgs : EventArgs
{
  public SendEmailEventArgs(string emailAddress)
  {
    _emailAddress = emailAddress;
  }
  private string _emailAddress;
```

```
  public string EmailAddress
  {
    get { return _emailAddress; }
    set { _emailAddress = value; }
  }
}
```

These event arguments represent all the information a content page will need in order to send out an email. We'll also need to define a delegate for the event handlers:

SendEmailEventArgs.cs *(excerpt)*

```
public delegate void SendEmailEventHandler(object sender,
    SendEmailEventArgs args);
```

With this code in place, we can write a new implementation of the button click event in our master page. We also need to define a public event in our master page:

Interaction.master.cs *(excerpt)*

```
protected void SendEmailButton_Click(object sender, EventArgs e)
{
  if (SendEmail != null)
  {
    SendEmailEventArgs args;
    args = new SendEmailEventArgs(AddressTextBox.Text);
    SendEmail(this, args);
  }
}
public event SendEmailEventHandler SendEmail;
```

Content pages can now subscribe to the public event defined in the master page. If we use the @ MasterType directive, as we did in the last section, the content pages can subscribe to the event through the strongly typed Master property. Here's the code for a content page:

MasterEvents.aspx.cs *(excerpt)*

```
public partial class Interaction_Default : System.Web.UI.Page
{
  protected override void OnInit(EventArgs e)
  {
    base.OnInit(e);
    Master.SendEmail += new SendEmailEventHandler(Master_SendEmail);
  }
  void Master_SendEmail(object sender, SendEmailEventArgs args)
  {
    string toAddress = args.EmailAddress;
    //
    // code to send the email ...
    //
  }
}
```

The page could use classes from the `System.Net.Mail` namespace to send the email. See Chapter 11 for more details on email and ASP.NET.

Discussion

We can examine our solution from two perspectives:

from the master page's point of view

All responsibility for mailing content has been removed from the master page. The master page is only responsible for raising an event. This separation of concerns keeps our master page clean and uncluttered.

from the point of view of the content page

The content page doesn't know how—or why—the master page is raising the `SendEmail` event. It only knows how to respond to the event. The event arguments carry all the information that the content page needs (in this case, just an email address). The master page could change the text box control to a drop-down control or a tree view—the change won't impact the content page at all. I'm sure you'll agree that being able to change the implementation of one part of our application without breaking code in another part is a huge benefit.

How do I use URLs in a master page?

There are not many web applications that can be written by placing all files into a single directory—typically, an application's pages are divided between multiple folders and subfolders. While relative URLs can make an application portable, they can also cause problems when they're used from within master pages.

Consider the following markup:

```
<img src="images/disco_night.png" alt="Disco night" />
```

Notice that the `src` attribute points to the image with a relative URL. If the master page and the content page live in the same directory, this approach will work fine. But should our project structure resemble that shown in Figure 8.7, we'll run into problems.

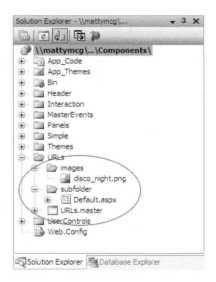

Figure 8.7. When relative URLs go wrong …

In this project we have a master page (`URLs.master`) and a content page (`Default.aspx`) residing in different folders. From the discussion at the beginning of this chapter, we can deduce that the master page will write the relative link for the image into the HTML output.

It's important to realize that the web browser knows *nothing* about master pages and content pages. The browser sees only the rendered HTML that the two objects produce in response to its request for a single resource (for example, `http://local-host/URLs/subfolder/Default.aspx`). The browser will process the HTML it retrieves from the server, and in doing so will attempt to retrieve an image from the address `http://localhost/URLs/subfolder/images/disco_night.png`. Unfortunately, the picture lives inside an images folder one directory higher, and the result will be a 404 error: **File Not Found**.

What can we do to fix these fragile links inside a master page?

Solutions

There are a few techniques that we can use to manage URLs in master pages. Let's look at the merits of each of them.

Using Absolute URLs

The immediately obvious alternative to relative URLs is to use absolute URLs, which remove any ambiguity as to the location of a resource. As an example, the following code would correctly retrieve the image successfully:

URLs.master (excerpt)

```
<img src="http://localhost/URLs/images/disco_night.png"
    alt="Disco night" />
```

However, this code is extremely inflexible—the machine name and application location may change over time, or between deployment environments, yet this static code won't reflect those alterations. That's why, generally speaking, absolute URLs should be avoided.

Using the `ResolveClientUrl` Method

A better solution is to use the `ResolveClientUrl` method. The master page class inherits this method from the `Control` class. `ResolveClientUrl` is aware of the difference between the locations of the master and content pages, and can adjust the URL parameter accordingly. Here's how we'd use `ResolveClientUrl` to refer to our image:

```
                                                    URLs.master (excerpt)
<img src="<%= ResolveClientUrl("images/disco_night.png")%>"
    alt="Disco night" />
```

The return value of the method will be a URL that can successfully fetch the image. In this example, the browser will see the following img element in the HTML:

```
<img src="../images/disco_night.png" alt="Disco night" />
```

You'll notice that this is still a relative URL, though it now points to the correct **images** directory.

Although this approach frees us from embedding absolute URLs in our master page, it still has one drawback: the image won't appear in the master page when we're using the Design view of Visual Studio, so the ResolveClientUrl method will only work at runtime. Being unable to see the images during the design phases can be a headache. Fortunately, we have one more trick up our sleeve!

Using URL Rebasing

ASP.NET attempts to solve the problem of relative paths leading to broken links with a feature called **URL rebasing** through which ASP.NET will examine URL-related properties at runtime, and adjust the paths for us.

So why doesn't this feature work with an img element? Because ASP.NET only performs URL rebasing on *server-side controls*. If we add runat="server" to our img element, as I've done below, we'll suddenly have a server-side control, and ASP.NET will automatically amend the relative URL to point to the correct location:

```
<img src="images/disco_night.png" runat="server"
    alt="Disco night" />
```

As the ASP.NET Image control is a server-side control, it will have its ImageUrl attribute rebased by ASP.NET. Therefore, the following markup will also correctly resolve the image location:

```
<asp:Image runat="server" ImageUrl="images/disco_night.png"
    ID="Image1" />
```

Although ASP.NET attempts to rebase all URLs for server-side controls, it doesn't catch every one. The following div element is a server control, but ASP.NET won't rebase the URL inside the style attribute:

URLs.master *(excerpt)*

```
<div runat="server"
    style="background-image:url(images/disco_night.png)">
```

However, we can explicitly rebase URLs by returning to the `ResolveClientUrl` method of the `Control` class. Here's how we'd rebase the URL in the above markup:

URLs.master *(excerpt)*

```
<div style="background-image:url(
    <%=ResolveClientUrl("images/disco_night.png")%>)">
```

The Ideal Approach

As both master pages and user controls can live in different folders from their `aspx` hosts, care must be taken when you're using relative URLs. When in doubt, it's possible to explicitly rebase a URL to ensure that it resolves correctly.

How do I modify header elements in a master page?

Since every page needs a `head` element, this element will usually be defined in a master page. Consider the following markup from a master page—the `head` element includes `link` and `meta` elements:

Header.master *(excerpt)*

```
<%@ Master Language="C#" AutoEventWireup="true"
CodeFile="Header.master.cs" Inherits="Header_Header" %>
<!DOCTYPE html PUBLIC "-//W3C//DTD XHTML 1.0 Transitional//EN"
    "http://www.w3.org/TR/xhtml1/DTD/xhtml1-transitional.dtd">
<html xmlns="http://www.w3.org/1999/xhtml">
<head runat="server">
  <link href="StyleSheet.css" rel="style sheet" type="text/css" />
  <meta name="description" content="Testing custom styles"/>
```

```
</head>
<body>
  <form id="form1" runat="server">
  <div>
    <asp:ContentPlaceHolder ID="ContentPlaceHolder1" runat="server">
    </asp:ContentPlaceHolder>
  </div>
</form>
</body>
</html>
```

It's often the case that a content page needs to change the header content provided by the master page—some content pages may need to add custom meta information, or link to a custom style sheet or external JavaScript file. How should a content page go about customizing the head element?

Solution

You'll notice the head element in the above master page contains a runat="server" attribute, making the head element a server control. Using runat="server" in the header is good practice, and is required in many scenarios (for instance, when using the ASP.NET AJAX Framework, which we'll look at in Chapter 10).

With the header now a server control, ASP.NET will expose that control as an Html-1Head object via the Header property of the Page class. And once we have access to it, we could potentially clear all the content from the head element by placing the following code inside our content page:

Header.aspx.cs (excerpt)

```
Header.Controls.Clear();
```

We can also use the Header property to add controls to the head element of the master page. For instance, the following code will add a meta element that redirects the page:

Header.aspx.cs *(excerpt)*

```
HtmlMeta meta = new HtmlMeta();
meta.HttpEquiv = "Refresh";
meta.Content = "2;URL=http://www.odetocode.com";
Header.Controls.Add(meta);
```

In addition to the `HtmlMeta` class that manages `meta` elements, ASP.NET provides the `HtmlLink` class to manage `link` elements. The following code injects a link to a style sheet into the header:

Header.aspx.cs *(excerpt)*

```
HtmlLink link = new HtmlLink();
link.Href = "customstyles.css";
link.Attributes.Add("rel", "style sheet");
link.Attributes.Add("type", "text/css");
Header.Controls.Add(link);
```

Remember, the `Header` property only works when `runat="server"` is present in the opening `head` tag.

Discussion

ASP.NET actually offers a built-in mechanism for style sheet injection—the **themes** feature in ASP.NET 2.0 can manage style sheets automatically, and when combined with master pages, can help to build a consistent and maintainable user interface. We'll look at themes in the next solution.

How do I use themes effectively in conjunction with CSS?

Just as master pages can manage the common *content* of multiple web forms inside an application, themes can manage the *appearance* and *layout* of controls inside an application. A theme uses style sheets and skin files to achieve this goal.

There's some overlap between the features provided by master pages and themes. Both can dictate the layout of a content page—for example, a master page could use a table-based design to organize the sections of a user interface into table cells.

However, while table-based designs are easy to create, they do present problems if we want to take a component-based approach to development. Table-based designs produce a page that entwines the content and structure of a page. For example, to create a new layout from a table-based design, we have to copy and paste table cells and table rows into new areas of the page—in other words, we have to rip apart the structure of a page.

Using a CSS-based design can help separate the page's content from its structure. And using a CSS-based design with ASP.NET 2.0 themes means that we can rearrange the layout of a page by simply changing the page's theme.

Solution

Let's look at some markup from a content page. Inside the page, we have two distinct pieces of content: links and news. Each piece of content lives inside a div element with an appropriate id attribute:

Themes.aspx (excerpt)

```
<form id="form1" runat="server">
<div id="links">
  <asp:BulletedList runat="server" ID="linkList"
     SkinID="LinkListSkin" >
    <asp:ListItem Value="http://www.odetocode.com/blogs/scott/">
      Scott's Blog
    </asp:ListItem>
    <asp:ListItem Value="http://haacked.com/">
      Phil's Blog
    </asp:ListItem>
    <asp:ListItem Value="http://weblogs.asp.net/jgalloway/">
      Jon's Blog
    </asp:ListItem>
    <asp:ListItem Value="http://www.codinghorror.com/blog/">
      Jeff's Blog
    </asp:ListItem>
    <asp:ListItem
        Value="http://www.sitepoint.com/blogs/category/net/">
      Wyatt's Blog
    </asp:ListItem>
  </asp:BulletedList>
</div>
<div id="news">
```

```
    "The ASP.NET Anthology" is now available!
</div>
</form>
```

Let's create a new theme to arrange the content on the screen. We'll name the first theme that we create "Plain." Inside the theme, we'll create a new style sheet that contains the following CSS rules:

Plain/StyleSheet.css *(excerpt)*

```
body, div
{
  margin: 0;
  padding: 0;
  background: #99cccc;
}
#links
{
  background: #cccc99;
  float: left;
  width: 25%;
}
#news
{
  float: right;
  width: 75%;
}
```

Notice that we've specified the layout and arrangement of our content using `float` and `width`. Figure 8.8 shows what happens when we assign the theme to our page using the directive @ `Page Theme="Plain"`. ASP.NET automatically applies all of the style sheets from the theme to the page.

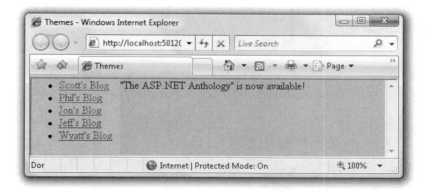

Figure 8.8. Applying the "Plain" theme

We can change our layout by creating a second theme—let's call this one "Crazy." Inside this theme, we'll create a new style sheet that contains the following rules:

```
Crazy/StyleSheet.css (excerpt)
body
{
  margin: 0;
  padding: 0;
  background: #CCFF11;
  font-family: Impact;
}
#links
{
  background: #11FFCC;
  float: right;
  width: 25%;
}
#news
{
  float: left;
  width: 75%;
}
.list
{
  list-style-image: url(images/beachball.gif);
}
```

Figure 8.9 shows our page display once the new theme has been applied using the directive @ `Page Theme="Crazy"`.

Figure 8.9. Applying the "Crazy" theme

As you can see, we've reversed the two columns of our page content without modifying the structure of the page at all. This flexibility is one of the benefits of a component-based approach to user interface design.

Discussion

Back in the Crazy theme style sheet, we defined the following style:

Crazy/StyleSheet.css (excerpt)

```
.list
{
  list-style-image: url(images/beachball.gif);
}
```

As we saw in Figure 8.9, our browser correctly applied this style to the bulleted list of links in our content.

A couple of questions come to mind about this behavior. The first question, given our previous discussion regarding relative URLs in master pages, is: "Isn't it dangerous to use a relative path to refer to the beach ball image?"

The answer is no—web browsers will *always* request the beach ball image *relative to the location of the style sheet*. We don't need to concern ourselves with the location of the style sheet relative to the location of the pages that use the style sheet. Typically, when we're using themes and style sheets with image references, we'd place those images inside a subdirectory of the theme. The Solution Explorer window depicted in Figure 8.10 shows the structure for the Plain and Crazy themes used in this solution.

Figure 8.10. Theme file locations in Solution Explorer

A second question about the list style is: "How was this style applied to the bulleted list?" We didn't specify a class name when we used the `BulletedList` ASP.NET control, as the following markup shows:

Themes.aspx *(excerpt)*

```
<asp:BulletedList runat="server" ID="linkList"
    SkinID="LinkListSkin" >
  <asp:ListItem Value="http://www.odetocode.com/blogs/scott/">
    Scott's Blog
  </asp:ListItem>
  <asp:ListItem Value="http://haacked.com/">
    Phil's Blog
  </asp:ListItem>
  <asp:ListItem Value="http://weblogs.asp.net/jgalloway/">
    Jon's Blog
  </asp:ListItem>
  <asp:ListItem Value="http://www.codinghorror.com/blog/">
```

```
    Jeff's Blog
  </asp:ListItem>
</asp:BulletedList>
```

The answer lies in the `SkinID` attribute. We've specified a skin for the bulleted list control, and each theme contains a skin file, named **SkinFile.skin**. The skin file for our Crazy theme contains the following code:

Crazy/SkinFile.skin (excerpt)

```
<asp:BulletedList runat="server" SkinID="LinkListSkin"
  DisplayMode="HyperLink" CssClass="list"
/>
```

A skin applies its properties to *all* the controls on given a page that have the same type and `SkinID`. If we were to omit the `SkinID`, the result would be a skin that was applied to all controls of the same type, regardless of `SkinID` value.

Since this skin sets the `DisplayMode` and `CssClass` properties for all `BulletedList` controls that have a `SkinID` of `LinkListSkin`, the `CssClass` assigns a `class` attribute with a value of `list`—hence the class name used to define the CSS rules.

Themes and skins are potent features in ASP.NET 2.0, but their real power is apparent when we use them in conjunction with CSS to build our applications. Many tools and UI designers already understand CSS; by applying default `CssClass` properties with skin files, and placing our style sheets in theme directories, we can enjoy the best of both worlds.

How do I treat user controls as components?

User controls and master pages have much in common. We saw earlier that master pages derive from the `UserControl` class, and both will ultimately position themselves as child controls inside a page.

Like master pages, we can treat user controls as black-box components, and our strategy for doing so should follow closely the strategy we used for master pages.

Solution

User controls are in fact a fantastic tool for packaging common UI elements into reusable components. Let's look at an example that demonstrates this point.

In this solution, we'll build a user control that we can use as the header for multiple web forms. We could place this control inside a master page to ensure the control appears on every page, but in this example we'll place the control inside a single web form.

Our control needs to provide:

- a customizable greeting message
- search functionality

Such a user control might look like this:

Header.ascx *(excerpt)*

```
<%@ Control Language="C#" AutoEventWireup="true"
    CodeFile="Header.ascx.cs"
    Inherits="UserControls_Header" %>
<div class="header">
  <div id="Greeting">
    <asp:Label runat="server" ID="GreetingLabel" Text="Welcome" />
  </div>

  <div id="Search">
    <asp:TextBox runat="server" ID="SearchTermTextBox"/>
    <asp:Button runat="server"
                ID="SearchButton" Text="Search"
                PostBackUrl="~/UserControls/SearchResults.aspx" />
  </div>
</div>
```

Using this control is as simple as dragging and dropping it onto a page. This drag-and-drop operation in Design View will automatically add the required @ Register directive to our page:

```
                                          UserControls.aspx (excerpt)
<%@ Page Language="C#" AutoEventWireup="true" Theme="Default" %>
<%@ Register Src="Header.ascx" TagName="Header" TagPrefix="uc1" %>
<!-- ... -->
<uc1:Header ID="Header" runat="server" Message="Greetings!"/>
<!-- ... -->
```

Notice that our web form can declaratively set the greeting message that the user control will display. It can do so because we've given our user control public properties that'll allow a page to get and set important values. Here's the code that facilitates this:

```
                                             Header.ascx.cs (excerpt)
public partial class UserControls_Header : UserControl
{
  public string Message
  {
    get { return GreetingLabel.Text; }
    set { GreetingLabel.Text = value; }
  }
  public string SearchTerm
  {
    get { return SearchTermTextBox.Text; }
    set { SearchTermTextBox.Text = value; }
  }
}
```

The SearchTerm property is an interesting case. When the user clicks the **Search** button, our control performs a cross-page postback to a new web form: **SearchResults.aspx**. A cross-page postback is controlled by the PostBackUrl property on the ASP.NET Button control.

Unfortunately, the SearchResults page doesn't know how to reach the SearchTerm property, because the user control is part of a different web form. Luckily, we can access the raw value of the TextBox control using the FindControl method. The following code shows what the Page_Load method of the SearchResults web form will look like if we use this approach:

```
                                         SearchResults.aspx.cs (excerpt)
protected void Page_Load(object sender, EventArgs e)
{
  if (PreviousPage != null)
  {
    Control header = PreviousPage.FindControl("Header"); ❶
    if (header != null)
    {
      TextBox searchBox = header.FindControl("SearchTermTextBox") ❷
        as TextBox;
      if (searchBox != null)
      {
        SearchResults.Text = "You searched for " + searchBox.Text;
      }
    }
  }
}
```

The `PreviousPage` property provides a reference to the original web form in an ASP.NET 2.0 cross-page postback. Notice that we make two calls to `FindControl`:

❶   The first call locates the user control on the page.

❷   The second call locates the `TextBox` inside the user control.

This approach is required because a user control implements the INamingContainer interface. Any control that implements this interface is known as a **naming container**. The scope of the `FindControl` method is limited to the current naming container, so when `FindControl` is traversing a control collection, it won't search within any controls that reside in a new naming container.

In other words, we couldn't use the following code:

```
Page.FindControl("SearchTermTextBox"); // returns null
```

This code wouldn't find the `TextBox` named `SearchTermTextBox` because the user control, being a naming container, would prevent `FindControl` from looking inside it.

In the section called "How can my content page override data on my master page?", we discussed the fragility of FindControl, and saw how a public property can formalize the communication between two UI components. We already have a public property on our user control, but the SearchResults page doesn't know how to gain access to that user control. Rather than depending on the PreviousPage class to always contain a specific user control, we can raise the level of abstraction by defining an interface for *all* pages that post back to the SearchResults page, like this:

ISearchTermSource.cs *(excerpt)*

```
public interface ISearchTermSource
{
  string SearchTerm
  {
    get;
  }
}
```

Our web form needs to implement this interface as follows:

UserControls.aspx.cs *(excerpt)*

```
public partial class UserControls_Default :
Page, ISearchTermSource
{
  public string SearchTerm
  {
    get { return Header.SearchTerm; }
  }
}
```

With an accessible public property in place, our SearchResults page doesn't care about user controls or text boxes—it simply looks for the ISearchTermSource interface, and performs the search:

SearchResults.aspx.cs *(excerpt)*

```
protected void Page_Load(object sender, EventArgs e)
{
  ISearchTermSource source = PreviousPage as ISearchTermSource;
```

```
  if (source != null)
  {
    SearchResults.Text = "You searched for " + source.SearchTerm;
  }
}
```

Once again, we've written some extra code to decouple our user interface components. The extra code required additional work up front, but will make our application much more maintainable in the end!

How do I embed resources into my components?

Web controls can require many different types of resources. For example, a tree view control might include a default set of images, or a custom grid view control may need to include JavaScript files.

We already store these custom controls in a separate library, so it's a reasonable jump to think of these controls as black-box components. Unlike user controls, which we build as a combination of markup (**.ascx** files) and code (**.cs** files), we build custom controls entirely in code. Take, for instance, the following custom control:

```
public class HilightPanel: Panel
{
  public string HilightCssClass
  {
    get { return _hilightCssClass; }
    set { _hilightCssClass = value; }
  }

  protected override void AddAttributesToRender(
      HtmlTextWriter writer
  ) {
    writer.AddAttribute("onmouseover",
    String.Format("setPanelStyle(this, '{0}');",HilightCssClass));
    writer.AddAttribute("onmouseout",
    String.Format("setPanelStyle(this, '{0}');", CssClass));

    base.AddAttributesToRender(writer);
```

```
    }
    private string _hilightCssClass;
}
```

This custom control is a panel that will change styles whenever the user moves the cursor inside the control's region. A page could use the control in the following manner:

```
<%@ Page Language="C#" AutoEventWireup="true" %>
<%@ Register Assembly="HilightPanel" Namespace="HilightPanel"
    TagPrefix="cc1" %>

⋮

<cc1:hilightpanel id="HilightPanel1" runat="server"
CssClass="dark" HilightCssClass="bright">

Frodo lives.

</cc1:hilightpanel>
```

If we define contrasting dark and light styles in CSS, the panel will appear to light up when a mouse enters the region:

StyleSheet.css *(excerpt)*

```
.bright
{
  background-color:#ffffff;
}
.dark
{
  background-color:#333333;
}
```

To switch styles during the `onmouseover` and `onmouseout` events, the `HilightPanel` uses JavaScript. The first pieces of JavaScript are the event handlers attached to the panel during the `AddAttributesToRender` method we listed earlier. These event handlers call a simple JavaScript function like so:

```
function setPanelStyle(panel, className)
{
  panel.className = className;
}
```

The amount of JavaScript that's required in this component is extremely small—we could therefore just inject the above code directly into the page using the `ClientScript` property and the `RegisterClientScriptBlock` method:

```
string script =
@"function setPanelStyle(panel, className) {
  panel.className = className;
}";

Page.ClientScript.RegisterClientScriptBlock(
    GetType(), "HilightScript", script
);
```

There are a couple of drawbacks to this approach, though. First, we're mixing our JavaScript code with C# source code, making it difficult to locate and maintain. Secondly, even though the amount of JavaScript code is small, we're still adding to the size of the page by inserting this code block into the page every time the web form renders.

If we were to keep our JavaScript code in a separate **.js** file, we'd reduce page bloat and give the browser a chance to cache the file, but unfortunately, keeping our script in a separate **.js** file makes our component difficult to share and reuse. Rather than copying a single binary file into one directory, we'd first need to copy each of the C# files, then make sure each JavaScript file was uploaded to its correct location on the web server. Surely there's an easier way?

Fortunately, there is—and it's a solution that'll give us the best of both worlds!

Solution

Version 2.0 of ASP.NET introduced a new HTTP handler by the name of **WebResource.axd**. This handler can retrieve resources embedded inside a .NET **assembly**—a binary file ending with the **.exe** or **.dll** extensions. The embedded resource can be a JavaScript file, an image file, an HTML file, or any other form of static content.

The first step in using **WebResource.axd** is to embed our JavaScript file into the assembly that holds our custom control. First, we add the JavaScript file to the custom control's project, as I've done in Figure 8.11. Open this project in the code archive if you'd like to follow along.

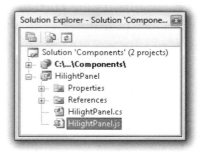

Figure 8.11. Adding a JavaScript file to a project

If we right-click the **HilightPane.js** file and examine its properties, we can tell Visual Studio what we want to happen to the file during a build. We want to embed the file as a resource in the assembly, so we'll set the **Build Action** to **Embedded Resource**, as shown in Figure 8.12.

Figure 8.12. Configuring our file as an embedded resource

WebResource.axd won't just serve up any old embedded resource—we have to formally advertise the resources available using one or more `WebResource` attributes on our assembly. A `WebResource` attribute defines the name and the content type of an embedded resource that we want to make available to the Web. To advertise the `HilightPanel` control, we can add the following code to the project's **Assembly-Info.cs** file:

```
[assembly: WebResource("HilightPanel.HilightPanel.js",
    "text/javascript")]
```

This is all the information we need to provide to **WebResource.axd** to ensure that our JavaScript file can be served. Back inside the `HilightPanel` custom control, we simply add a reference to the JavaScript file, rather than inserting a script block:

```
protected override void OnInit(EventArgs e)
{
  Page.ClientScript.RegisterClientScriptResource(GetType(),
      "HilightPanel.HilightPanel.js");
  base.OnInit(e);
}
```

Notice the `ClientScript` has a `RegisterClientScriptResource` method that makes an embedded script file easy to use. When we load into the browser a web form that uses the `HilightPanel` control, we'll see that it's implemented with the following markup:

```
<script src="/WebResource.axd?d=XqzOS24AQmnMAnpnYgBkkaGxJ7CJjj9d96T1
➥E-AnBM4rsQyNADmOiV5ls3-PWEs_O&amp;t=633084819369290760"
    type="text/javascript">
</script>
```

The long query string in this URL provides all the information **WebResource.axd** needs to retrieve the **HilighPanel.js** from the custom control's assembly and return the contents of the file to the web browser. The first part of the query string is an encrypted identifier, while the second part is a time stamp. The time stamp ensures that the handler will always retrieve the most recent version of the resource.

Embedded resources help us build black-box components by hiding the complexity of the resources needed by a custom component. Instead of worrying about how to deploy images and script files, a web project needs only to reference the custom control. **WebResource.axd** also enables us to adhere to best practices, such as keeping our script file inside a separate resource.

Summary

This entire chapter has focused on applying abstractions to the user interface controls available in ASP.NET. These abstractions—properties, events, themes, and embedded resources—all help to make a project successful in the long run by improving the maintainability of the code base. It's easy to slap together master pages and user controls into a web site with the drag-and-drop designer, but taking the extra time to build these abstractions up front will always pay dividends later in the project's life cycle.

ASP.NET and Web Standards

The term **web standards** describes an approach to the use of client-side technologies—primarily (X)HTML, CSS, and JavaScript—that sees them applied in a best-practice manner. Generally, this application of standards means:

creating markup that's semantically meaningful

This includes practices such as using elements like h1 and h2 to specify headings and subheadings, and using div elements which have meaningful class names to demarcate parts of a page rather than using HTML tables.

achieving good separation of content, presentation, and behavior

This means using CSS for all presentational effects (including font settings, colors, and positioning) and using unobtrusive JavaScript rather than placing your scripts inline in the page.

coding for accessibility

Incorporating markup techniques to make a page as accessible as possible for users who may be vision-impaired or have difficulty using a mouse, or who may be browsing using a non-standard browser—whether that be a screen reader, a PDA, or a web-enabled mobile phone.

Web standards are important to web developers for a number of reasons. Firstly, the less markup an application produces, the smoother it will run—it no longer has to generate masses of extraneous markup, which saves both processor cycles and bandwidth. The separation of parts mentioned above makes your code easier to maintain, and search engines eat that clean semantic markup for breakfast! Finally, standards-compliance will give your application a competitive advantage—a drawcard that management types will doubtless appreciate.

By embracing web standards, you can enjoy the prospect of writing less code—you can offload the entirety of an application's skin onto a separate, loosely coupled file that you can edit easily without touching the core application. With a purely CSS-driven design, you can create an application that's easily alterable—in an aesthetic sense, at least. In addition, these changes can be handled entirely by the design team, rather than requiring developers to spend time making changes to the application itself.

Possibly one of the best—albeit sometimes horrifying—examples of the power of CSS is the social networking site MySpace.[1] Users of the site can customize their profile pages by modifying the colors, fonts, and images that are displayed. Since these customized pages are largely CSS-powered, the application can allow users to make these changes without having to generate a lot of extra markup.

ASP.NET—especially Visual Studio—has a poor reputation among standards-oriented developers. And as anyone who's spent significant time with Visual Studio 2003 can tell you, this reputation is not entirely unearned. It's not so easily justified these days, however: Visual Studio 2005 no longer takes creative liberties with your HTML. Microsoft's ASP.NET 2.0 web controls generate XHTML-compliant markup by default. The future is even more promising, as Microsoft now takes web standards very seriously. Orcas, the upcoming version of Visual Studio, takes CSS and JavaScript support to new levels within the development environment. Standards-oriented development is here to stay.

For the time being, however, we have to make an effort to ensure that our client-side code approaches best practice. This chapter will give you a few tips for doing just that.

---

[1] http://www.myspace.com/

What are all these **span tags doing in my HTML output?**

Visual Studio makes it very, very easy for a developer to drag controls onto a page, work through a few wizards, and produce a functional web form in a matter of minutes. But this ease of use has its costs, possibly the most significant of which is that the resulting application can produce lots of extraneous markup.

Creating a basic data-bound web page is easy: just drag a couple of Label controls onto the page in Design view, set up the data binding parameters, and call it a day. But take a look at the code that results:

ContentWithLabels.aspx *(excerpt)*

```
<h1>
  <asp:Label
      runat="Server"
      ID="PageTitleLabel"
      Text='<%# PageContent.Title %>'
  />
</h1>
<asp:Label
    runat="Server"
    ID="IsHotLabel"
    CssClass="hawt"
    Visible='<%# PageContent.IsHot %>'
  />
<asp:Label
    runat="Server"
    ID="ContentLabel"
    Text='<%# PageContent.ContentText %>'
/>
```

That code's nice and clean, right? Not quite! This example reveals a very common issue. The poorly planned use of server controls—such as the use of Label controls above—can lead to extraneous and invalid HTML output such as this:

```
<h1>
  <span id="PageTitleLabel">First Page</span>
</h1>
<span id="IsHotLabel" class="hawt">This is Hawt!</span>
<span id="ContentLabel"><p>Content ID 1.</p></span>
```

The output that appears in bold is directly attributable to the use of the `Label` controls to make the page. And it's very bad. It's bad for a couple of reasons:

- All the `span` elements are redundant.
- The placement of a `p` element (a block-level element) inside a `span` (an inline element) is invalid.

Solution

To avoid the unseemly introduction of all those unnecessary spans, modify your web form template to appear as follows:

```
                                              ContentNakedBound.aspx (excerpt)

<h1><%# PageContent.Title %></h1>
<p
    runat="server"
    ID="HawtParagraph"
    class="hawt"
    visible="<%# PageContent.IsHot %>"
>
    This is HAWT
</p>
<%# PageContent.ContentText %>
```

The HTML output produced by this form will be a vast improvement on that shown above:

```
<h1>First Page</h1>
<p id="HawtParagraph" class="hawt">
    This is HAWT!
</p>
<p>Content ID 1.</p>
```

Much cleaner, no?

Discussion

While all those `Label` controls are easy to manipulate within the **Design** view, they create extraneous HTML `span` elements within the markup. To solve that problem, we can quite easily replace each `Label` with a `Literal` control on the form, then recompile and redeploy our project.

But what if you didn't have the full source code handy—you had only the precompiled application? What if you wanted to distribute a work and let its users modify in a declarative manner the report templates that were used in the application?

In these advanced scenarios, inline data binding really begins to pay off. Using constructs like `<h1><%# PageContent.Title %></h1>` or `<%# PageContent.ContentText %>` allows developers to access server-side properties directly from the markup. So any variable or method that's available to that `Page` can be included in the markup.

Using the ternary operator can make this declarative binding much more powerful, as it allows us to include some small logical operations in the declarative markup. The operator itself looks like this:

```
<p><%# IsSunny() ? "It's sunny!" : "It rains!" %></p>
```

That statement translates to the following:

```
if (IsSunny())
{
  // output "It's sunny!"
}
else
{
  // output "It rains!"
}
```

We could have used this ternary operator to handle the question above, like so:

```
<%# PageContent.IsHot ? "<p class="hawt">This is HAWT!</p>" :
    string.Empty %>
```

What's the Difference Between <%# *i* %> and <%= *i* %>?

We can use two constructs to access page-level variables in an ASP.NET web template:

data binding syntax
> **Data binding**—the hierarchical mapping of control properties to data container values—is specified by the <%# ... %> tags. Code located within a <%# ... %> code block is only executed when the DataBind method of its parent control container is invoked.

code rendering syntax
> The <%= ... %> code tags output content to the browser. This content could be hard-coded, or it may contain page-level variables.

In most cases, either of these constructs could be used to achieve the same result, but there are some interesting nuances in the different ways in which each construct goes about its job.

For example, when we use data binding to place an object into a page, the ASP.NET parser actually creates a DataBoundLiteral control. It puts the control into the template, then fills in the value as appropriate. This control does have view state, so it can be persisted across postbacks. It makes sense to use this approach when we load data from a resource that's in high demand, and we want to keep it handy on the page. The disadvantage of using data binding is that we often need to call DataBind explicitly on the containing control to achieve the desired effect.

Displaying content to the browser, on the other hand, is a more lightweight solution, as it doesn't create a control the way data binding does. However, there are a couple of downsides to this approach. One is that the code within a code rendering block is executed on *every request* to the page—the lack of any caching may result in an increased server load.

Additionally, code rendering blocks occasionally produce an odd error that's difficult to debug. The error reads, "The Controls Collection cannot be modified because the control contains code blocks." This means that ASP.NET is trying to embed expressions into the output it generates, but is unable to do so because the output it's embedding is dynamic. Data binding expressions, on the other hand, are embedded at runtime, so they aren't affected by this limitation. Therefore, it's important to be very careful when using injection with dynamically created controls, and to be prepared to switch to using data binding or other expressions if necessary.

While this example is focused on `Label` controls, the theory of avoiding the use of server controls can be applied across the board—don't use them if you don't need them! Avoiding server controls wherever possible will help you keep your code cleaner.

How do I obtain `DataList`-style functionality without using a `table`?

A common requirement of many data-driven applications is that they display manipulable lists of data. However, many ASP.NET server controls output `table` elements as well as other potentially extraneous HTML. How can we best output our data lists without cluttering the page with layout tables and unnecessary markup?

Solution

An often-overlooked control in the ASP.NET toolbox is the trusty old `Repeater`. While it lacks the glitz of the `GridView`, `Repeater` can be very powerful, and produces clean, semantic HTML. Unlike its peers, the `Repeater` comes with no baggage—you, as a developer, can control exactly what lands on the page.

For example, let's say we have a list of `Person` data objects bound to the following `Repeater`:

RepeaterMagic.aspx *(excerpt)*

```
<asp:Repeater runat="Server" ID="ExemplarRepeater"
    DataSource="<%# Bloggers %>">
  <HeaderTemplate>
    <ul>
  </HeaderTemplate>
  <FooterTemplate>
    </ul>
  </FooterTemplate>
  <ItemTemplate>
    <li>
      <%# Eval("FirstName") %>
      <%# Eval("LastName") %>
      <asp:Button
          runat="Server"
          ID="SendReminderButton"
          Text="Send a Reminder"
```

```
        CommandArgument='<%# Eval("Id") %>'
        OnClick="SendReminder"/>
    <span
        runat="Server"
        id="SentLabel"
        visible="false"
        class="sent">
      SENT
    </span>
  </li>
</ItemTemplate>
</asp:Repeater>
```

The key to generating the code that provides us with DataList-style functionality lies in the event handler for the SendReminderButton:

RepeaterMagic.aspx.cs *(excerpt)*

```
protected void SendReminder(object sender, EventArgs e)
{
  IButtonControl sButton = (IButtonControl)sender;
  Guid id = new Guid(sButton.CommandArgument);

  // Actually send the reminder.
  PersonMailerService.SendMail(id);

  Control sControl = (Control)sender;
  Control c=sControl.NamingContainer.FindControl("SentLabel");
  c.Visible = true;
  sControl.Visible = false;
}
```

Discussion

Each of the objects and actions we used above is very simple, but when they're put together, they form a potent combination. Let's walk through it:

```
IButtonControl sButton = (IButtonControl)sender;
Guid id = new Guid(sButton.CommandArgument);
```

This snippet takes a reference to the sending object—in this case the `SendReminder-Button` for each `Repeater` item—and casts it as an `IButtonControl` object. Doing so allows us to access the `CommandArgument` attribute of our button, which is the most important part: it tells us which button was clicked. This approach is akin to using the `DataKeys` property of a `GridViewRow`. You can also use server-side `HiddenFields` or invisible `Literal` controls to store variables. Those variables are then available for you to use in your event handling logic.

```
Control sControl = (Control)sender;
Control c=sControl.NamingContainer.FindControl("SentLabel");
c.Visible = true;
sControl.Visible = false;
```

In the code listing above, the sender is cast as a generic control, so that we can access its `NamingContainer`—which, in the case of `Repeaters`, is the `RepeaterItem` that contains the control in question and all its peers. Once this property is available, calls to `FindControl` can obtain references to other controls in the row, and manipulate their properties and methods.

Finally, remember that just about any sort of control can be placed within a `Repeater`. For example, you could develop a fancy Ajax-powered `Person` user control that allowed us to view and edit a person's details, and which could be bound to a `Repeater` should user interface requirements call for it. See Chapter 8 for information about creating componentized user controls.

How do I use ASP.NET's fancy menus without the fancy HTML?

As a rule of thumb, the more complex a stock ASP.NET control is, the more verbose its output will be. The trusty old menu is a case in point. Let's build one, starting with the following sitemap:

Web.sitemap *(excerpt)*

```
<siteMap
    xmlns="http://schemas.microsoft.com/AspNet/SiteMap-File-1.0" >
  <siteMapNode url="~/Default.aspx" title="Home">
    <siteMapNode url="~/Products/Default.aspx"
        title="Products List">
```

```
            <siteMapNode url="~/Products/Books.aspx" title="Books" />
            <siteMapNode url="~/Products/CDs.aspx" title="CDs" />
            <siteMapNode url="~/Products/DVDs.aspx" title="DVDs" />
            <siteMapNode url="~/Products/Software.aspx"
                title="Software" />
        </siteMapNode>
        <siteMapNode url="~/About/Default.aspx" title="About Us">
            <siteMapNode url="~/About/OurFound.aspx"
                title="Our Founder" />
            <siteMapNode url="~/About/Investors.aspx"
                title="Investor Information" />
            <siteMapNode url="~/About/Careers.aspx"
                title="Career Opportunities" />
        </siteMapNode>
        <siteMapNode url="~/ContactUs.aspx" title="Contact Us" />
        View/edit User Control
    </siteMapNode>
</siteMap>
```

Let's combine the sitemap with the following menu declaration:

Site.master *(excerpt)*

```
<asp:SiteMapDataSource
    ID="WebSitemap"
    runat="server"
    ShowStartingNode="False"
/>
<asp:Menu
    ID="SampleMenu"
    runat="server"
    DataSourceID="WebSitemap"
    CssSelectorClass="StyledMenu"
/>
```

That code produces the following HTML:

```
<a href="#SampleMenu_SkipLink"><img alt="Skip Navigation Links"
    src="/CssFriendly/WebResource.axd?d=_9HAj-Fpl4_U3KC59gRMDw2&amp;
    ➥t=632966801392656250" width="0" height="0"
    style="border-width:0px;" /></a>
<table id="SampleMenu" class="SampleMenu_2" cellpadding="0"
```

```
      cellspacing="0" border="0">
<tr>
<td onmouseover="Menu_HoverStatic(this)"
    onmouseout="Menu_Unhover(this)" onkeyup="Menu_Key(event)"
    id="SampleMenun0"><table cellpadding="0" cellspacing="0"
    border="0" width="100%">

<!--[snip 2 pages of similarly obtuse and explicit HTML]-->

<img src="/CssFriendly/WebResource.axd?d=Bg6dmRXIOk258EPvRBAhHvMBlsz
➥JJFEJxW1KeGUAYjM1&amp;t=632966801392656250"
    alt="Scroll up" />
</div>
<div class="SampleMenu_0" id="SampleMenun1ItemsDn"
    onmouseover="PopOut_Down(this)"
    onmouseout="PopOut_Stop(this)" style="text-align:center;">
<img src="/CssFriendly/WebResource.axd?d=xK-_eiNXxMy41lKm3BdePL2PwrX
➥7KVf_qJT9YSSxQFY1&amp;t=632966801392656250"
    alt="Scroll down" />
</div>
</div><a id="SampleMenu_SkipLink"></a>
```

In total, this markup weighs in at 5.65KB—that's rather hefty for a very basic, un-styled menu. Had I spruced it up using the standard design properties, the file would have been even larger—all of the style information is included inline, which makes each menu item more resource-intensive to generate and send down the wire, which makes the task of generating and displaying each menu item even more resource-intensive than it is now. And, when this menu finally arrives at the client, JavaScript had better be enabled, or ASP.NET's fancy menus will be useless.

What's a responsible developer to do?

Solution

Probably the best way to tame ASP.NET 2.0's more complex server controls is to use the CSS Friendly Control Adapters Kit. Originally created by Microsoft, these adapters were released to the community on March 7, 2007. The project now lives on the CodePlex site,[2] and includes more than just an updated menu system—adapters abound for the most infamous of the server controls. You can drop these ad-

---

[2] http://www.codeplex.com/cssfriendly/

apters into your project without needing to modify a line of your existing code, as Figure 9.1 illustrates.

Figure 9.1. Adding CSS Friendly Controls to a Web Site project

Previously, adding the kit to your project required you to use a special template, or to jump through several hoops in an effort to add a jumble of files. Now the kit can easily be added to any ASP.NET project, thanks to Brian DeMarzo.[3] Just download the two files—**CSSFriendly.dll** and **CssFriendlyAdapters.browser**—from the CodePlex site. Then, add a reference to the **.dll** and add the **.browser** file to your **App_Browsers** folder.

How much of a difference can two little files make? Well, if we use them in conjunction with the menu declaration we saw above, the markup that's generated is a mere 1.57KB of somewhat intelligible menu code:

```
<div class="StyledMenu" id="ctl00_SampleMenu">
  <div class="AspNet-Menu-Vertical">
    <ul class="AspNet-Menu">
      <li class="AspNet-Menu-WithChildren">
        <a href="/CssFriendly/Products/Default.aspx"
           class="AspNet-Menu-Link">Products List</a>
        <ul>
          <li class="AspNet-Menu-Leaf">
            <a href="/CssFriendly/Products/Books.aspx"
               class="AspNet-Menu-Link">Books</a>
          </li>
            ⋮
        </ul>
      </li>
      <li class="AspNet-Menu-Leaf">
```

---

[3] http://www.demarzo.net/

```
            <a href="/CssFriendly/ContactUs.aspx"
                class="AspNet-Menu-Link">Contact Us</a>
        </li>
      </ul>
    </div>
</div>
```

Discussion

The kit works by taking advantage of ASP.NET 2.0's control adapters: convenient intercepting filters that inject themselves near the end of the rendering cycle to override the final output. The kit allows you to retain all the rich logic of the controls, which output much cleaner HTML. I should add that the controls are brutally efficient at this task—almost none of the visual properties of the adapted controls make it to the browser.

After you download the kit, don't forget to read Microsoft's excellent whitepaper on CSS Friendly Control Adapters.[4] This very readable document sheds light on the use of Control Adapters in general, and the use of the menu's styles in particular.

 What if I'm Stuck on ASP.NET 1.1?

The short answer to this question is that, if you care about standards support, you should really consider upgrading. Control adapters are a 2.0-only feature, and the Visual Studio 2003 designer's habit of mangling HTML in a semi-random fashion does not help developers embrace standards compliance. That, and the Framework itself, work against you.

ASP.NET 1.x features its own version of adaptive rendering, which uses the browserCaps element in the **machine.config** file to determine what sort of HTML—4.01 or 3.2—should be served to particular clients. Unfortunately, it makes the presumption that any browser it doesn't recognize wants HTML 3.2 output. And, in the default configuration, it doesn't recognize any modern browser except IE 7.

There is a fix—visit http://slingfive.com/pages/code/browserCaps/ to get an updated configuration that will, at least, let you serve adequate HTML to non-IE visitors.

---

[4] http://www.asp.net/CSSAdapters/WhitePaper.aspx

How do I make sense of the CSS maze produced by the CSS Friendly menu?

Visually speaking, the CSS Friendly menus aren't terribly appealing straight out of the box. An unstyled vertical menu can easily end up looking like Figure 9.2.

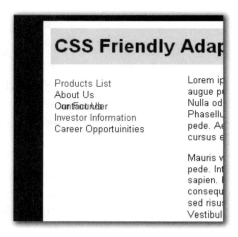

Figure 9.2. An unstyled menu displaying as a jumbled mess

Solution

It's time to roll up our sleeves and dive into some CSS coding! We're required to employ some advanced techniques in order to take advantage of the CSS API exposed by the CSS Friendly menu. The whitepaper I mentioned in the section called "How do I use ASP.NET's fancy menus without the fancy HTML?" is a great place to get started, but it covers far more than just styling the Menu control.

Instead of trying to cover all of the aspects of how each menu item could be styled, I've trimmed the menu styles down to the most important aspects of CSS—the parts that control the size, shape, and general behavior of the vertical menu:

StyleSheet.css *(excerpt)*

```
ul.AspNet-Menu {
  width: 160px;
  border-top: 1px solid red;
}
ul.AspNet-Menu ul {
```

```
    width: 180px;
    left: 155px;
    top: -1em;
    z-index: 400;
    border-top: 1px solid red;
}
ul.AspNet-Menu ul ul {
    left: 175px;
}
ul.AspNet-Menu li {
    background:teal;
}
ul.AspNet-Menu li a,
ul.AspNet-Menu li span {
    color: white;
    padding: 4px 2px 4px 8px;
    border: 1px solid red;
    border-top: none;
}
AspNet-Menu li:hover,
AspNet-Menu li.AspNet-Menu-Hover {
    background: #7795BD;
}
```

This markup produces a much more palatable system with very usable fly-out menus, as Figure 9.3 reveals.

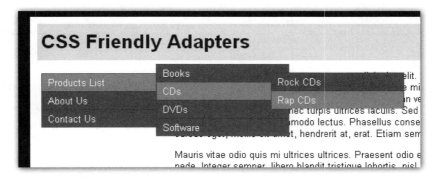

Figure 9.3. The menu is much prettier, especially considering JavaScript is disabled!

Discussion

For a fairly concise style sheet, this is a fantastic result! Let's see how we arrived at this outcome.

Simple CSS Inheritance

Similar to the way an object is extended in C#, an HTML node's child nodes inherit many of their parents' CSS properties—a concept known as **inheritance**. We can use CSS selectors to apply styles to specific children of a given HTML element. Let's look at an example:

```
div#mainContent h2 {
  border-bottom: 1px solid blue;
  font-size: 1.5em;
}
```

This style rule would make any h2 element contained within a div with the id of mainContent display at 1.5 times the page body's default font size, with a blue bottom border.

Now, if you wanted to, you could have generated the same visual effect by applying a new class attribute to the heading. The style rule accompanying your new markup would look something like this:

```
h2.bigBlueHeader {
  border-bottom: 1px solid blue;
  font-size: 1.5em;
}
```

But that would be the wrong way to approach the problem, for several reasons. For instance, what happens when you decide the headers should be red, and slightly smaller? Should you change any reference to the CSS class? Or should you just change the bigBlueHeader class to be small and red?

Had we used the first approach—taking advantage of the cascading aspect of Cascading Style Sheets by applying styles to elements within a given element—the change would be easy, not to mention all the bandwidth you'll save by not having class="bigBlueHeader" all over the place.

CSS Inheritance and Tables

CSS inheritance proves very handy in a number of cases. For example, if you wanted to display alternating row colors on a table, you could declare your style rules like so:

```css
td.headerCell {
  border: solid 1px navy;
  padding: 3px;
  color: #e2e2e2;
  background: navy;
}

td.dataCell {
  border: solid 1px black;
  padding: 3px;
  color: navy;
  background: white;
}

td.altDataCell {
  border: solid 1px black;
  padding: 3px;
  color: navy;
  background: #e2e2e2;
}
```

These style rules create cells with navy text and white or gray backgrounds, depending on which class is applied, but these rules require that a class be applied to each cell in the table. So, if you had a 50-row `GridView`, with ten columns, you'd have to generate class values of `dataCell` and `altDataCell` 500 times in your HTML—that's a total of 8750 characters for a presentational effect, once you factor in the `class` attribute.

A better way to approach this task is to declare a class for the overarching table, and use CSS inheritance to handle the job of styling rows:

```css
table.dataGrid {
  border-collapse: collapse;
  margin: 10px auto;
}
```

```
table.dataGrid td {
  padding: 3px;
  border: solid 1px black;
  color: navy;
  background: white;
}

table.dataGrid tr.headerRow td {
  color: #e2e2e2;
  background: navy;
}

table.dataGrid tr.altRow td {
  background: #e2e2e2;
}
```

Now all you have to do is set the `class` of the overarching `table` to `dataGrid`, the header row's `class` to `headerRow`, and the alternate row's `class` to `altRow`, and your work is done! If we applied this approach to styling the 50-row grid we discussed above, we'd use a mere 700 characters for the CSS rule sets, saving 8KB every time that page was sent down the wire. Inheritance can be very powerful and very useful indeed, and we'll make use of it to style our menu.

In fact, several layers of CSS have already been inserted into our menu by the CSS Friendly Adapters—why else do you think the menu is an illegible jumble, rather than a plain unordered list? The first step we're going to have to take is to figure out what we need to override. To do this, you *could* start reading through the style sheets included in the CSS Friendly Adapters project, but that's hardly very exciting, is it? There must be a better approach …

There is! Install some tools to help make the situation a little more intelligible.

CSS Development Tools

CSS debugging used to be a terribly manual process—essentially, it involved reading CSS, looking at output, and figuring out what was wrong with your web site by touch and feel. Recently, however, the suite of tools available to develop and debug CSS has improved dramatically:

Firebug

Firebug is a powerful Firefox extension that allows the tracing, profiling, and editing of CSS and JavaScript. This incredibly useful tool has become an indispensable aid for any serious client-side web developer. Thanks to Firebug, we have the ability to see exactly what the browser sees. Firebug includes a wealth of features, including graphs showing network activity, rulers and guides for lining up elements, an advanced DOM browser, and more.

Download the extension, and access a quick introduction to its capabilities at the Firebug web site.[5] You can also download a lightweight version of Firebug for use with other browsers such as Safari, Opera, and Internet Explorer.

Internet Explorer Developer Toolbar

IE is not without its own client-side development tools, however. Microsoft recently released the Internet Explorer Developer Toolbar, which provides IE with a subset of the functionality provided by Firebug.[6] Given that client-side CSS implementations differ significantly between browsers, it's quite necessary to have tools specific to each platform.

Debuggers are key to squashing CSS bugs, but having a powerful editor is never a bad idea. Consider these options:

Top Style Pro

Visual Studio 2005's CSS editor is good, but personally I prefer Top Style Pro,[7] mainly for one feature: its integrated CSS preview pane. The live preview eradicates many cycles of the all-too-common CSS development dance—updating a style sheet, saving to disk, and refreshing the browser—to significantly speed the CSS testing cycle. And, for the purposes of cross-browser testing, the tool allows you to view pages using any available rendering engine.

Visual Studio: code name "Orcas"

Last but not least, Orcas, the upcoming version of Visual Studio, features greatly enhanced CSS support, including the world's first-ever set of CSS refactoring tools.

---

[5] http://www.getfirebug.com/

[6] http://www.microsoft.com/downloads/details.aspx?familyid=e59c3964-672d-4511-bb3e-2d5e1db91038

[7] http://www.bradsoft.com/topstyle/

Getting Back to that Menu ...

Now that we have the preliminaries out of the way, let's walk through each of the CSS selectors in this solution and see how they shape the menu. First up is this apparently innocuous selector:

```
                                                    StyleSheet.css (excerpt)

ul.AspNet-Menu {
  width: 160px;
  border-top: 1px solid red;
}
```

This selector sets up the width of the statically visible parts of the menu—in this case, **Products List**, **About Us**, and **Contact Us**. This might seem to be an obvious place to attach global visual properties, but it's not—the root unordered list renders as a 1px line. The only visual property we could add here is a top border.

Next we have the second level of our menu:

```
                                                    StyleSheet.css (excerpt)

ul.AspNet-Menu ul {
  width: 180px;
  left: 155px;
  top: -1em;
  z-index: 400;
  border-top: solid red 1px;
}
```

This selector is the key to the menu's positional magic. The styles above will be applied to any unordered list that's contained within another unordered list. Since our menu exists as a series of nested, unordered lists, this means that every single tier of the menu (apart from the top level) will receive the styles.

Let's see what each of those CSS properties does:

width   This property sets the width of the submenu items. If it's not set explicitly, the width will inherit from the element's parent selector.

left   This property positions the fly-out menu on the *x* axis. The value it takes should be slightly less than that of the initial width, as it's offset from the left-hand side of the menu structure.

top   This property positions the fly-out menu on the *y* axis, and is measured relative to the top of the parent menu item.

z-index   Setting a large value for this property ensures that the menu will appear on top of the other elements on the page.

border   This property creates a border for submenu items, as can be seen in Figure 9.3.

Next, let's look at the list nested at the next level of our menu:

StyleSheet.css *(excerpt)*

```
ul.AspNet-Menu ul ul {
   left: 175px;
}
```

This style rule overrides our previous rule for `ul` elements that sit three levels deep or more. The rule sets the horizontal offset to 175 pixels. Why? Because this offset value should be slightly less than the width of menu items on the next level up, and in this case, that width value is 180 pixels. You could continue in this way to position lists further down the menu hierarchy, using more and more specific CSS selectors.

Continuing on, we arrive at the list item styles:

StyleSheet.css *(excerpt)*

```
ul.AspNet-Menu li {
   background: teal;
}
```

This little visual flourish sets the background color of our menu to a lovely shade of teal. And, just like the ul elements that we styled previously, selecting further nested li elements just delves another layer deeper into the menu. For example, consider this rule, which would make the second level of menu items display with a tan background:

StyleSheet.css *(excerpt)*

```
ul.AspNet-Menu li li {
  background: tan;
}
```

To round out our menu's basic CSS, we describe the menu item links:

StyleSheet.css *(excerpt)*

```
ul.AspNet-Menu li a,
ul.AspNet-Menu li span {
  color: white;
  padding: 4px 2px 4px 8px;
  border: 1px solid red;
  border-top: 0;
}
AspNet-Menu li:hover,
AspNet-Menu li.AspNet-Menu-Hover {
  background: #7795BD;
}
```

The first style rule sets the text to white and applies a border to links (or, in the case of items without links, to span elements). The second rule applies a different background color to menu items; this background displays when the mouse hovers over them.

Summary

In this chapter, we've explored a number of techniques to tweak the HTML output of ASP.NET in order to make that output more standards compliant. We discussed avoiding the use of server controls entirely, before learning how to use a lightweight Repeater, rather than a heavyweight GridView, to display an interactive list.

The second theme of this chapter focused on taking advantage of CSS to style your pages the modern way. First, we examined the process of wiring up the CSS Friendly Adapters. We then discussed a number of CSS techniques—particularly CSS inheritance—that we used to style a menu.

By resisting the temptation to use default ASP.NET controls out of the box, you're well on your way to producing standards-compliant code. Having taken this step forward, you can begin to bask in the glory of the benefits that come with such an achievement—an application that uses less bandwidth, code that is easier to maintain, and the glowing admiration of your peers.

Ajax and JavaScript

Before we begin to enhance our web applications with JavaScript, some context is needed. Thus I invite you to accompany me through a brief history of the web browser!

The first web browsers began to appear in the early 1990s, and their displays were limited to text documents that linked to other text documents. These first web browsers were relatively simple, but the ability to browse documents that were linked together made them powerful enough to start a revolution in the way people find and consume information.

Over the years, browsers continued to add features, such as the ability to display images and videos. The most important new features, however, were the features that made the web browser more *interactive*.

In 1995, Netscape introduced a scripting language into its web browser that today is called JavaScript. Client-side JavaScript code could respond to events, like button clicks, and the code could also manipulate the browser display via the browser's Document Object Model (DOM). JavaScript quickly became a standard feature in all major desktop web browsers, although even today there are still minor variations in each browser's implementation of the language. Those discrepancies aside, JavaScript was a huge leap forward, as it gave web developers the ability to build web applications that could rival desktop applications.

Another step forward for the Web occurred when Microsoft released Internet Explorer 5 in the year 2000, but this particular browser feature didn't really gather steam until 2005. In that year, Microsoft included a new component with the browser called the **XMLHttpRequest** (sometimes referred to as XHR) object. This object enabled JavaScript code to exchange text (be it XML, plain old ASCII, or some other format) with a server using HTTP—and it allowed this exchange to be performed *asynchronously*. A web developer could therefore use JavaScript and `XmlHttpRequest` to provide fresh data to a web page without having to go through the standard full-page refresh that had become an inevitable part of browsing the Web.

`XmlHttpRequest` eventually became a standard component in all the popular desktop browsers, and a new programming paradigm arose—**Ajax**. Ajax originally stood for *A*synchronous *J*avaScript *A*nd *X*ML, but has since come to be used to refer to any technique that communicates with the server without refreshing the page and causing that annoying page flicker. The result is a highly interactive and responsive web application whose user-friendly interface can, in some cases, rival that of a desktop application.

In this chapter, we'll look at common scenarios that involve JavaScript and Ajax. In some cases, we'll explore scenarios that relate to programming with JavaScript in a general sense, while in other discussions we'll assume that we're using the Microsoft web development tools.

We'll kick off by answering a question that's frequently asked by JavaScript programmers—how can I do it better?

How can I write better JavaScript?

As user expectations of web applications have increased, so has the amount of JavaScript that the average ASP.NET developer is asked to produce. The problem is that many web developers adopt a "quick and dirty" approach to scripting—they stuff some JavaScript functions into a file, add a few events, and move on. However, as the amount of client-side script in our web applications grows, this approach soon produces a tangled mess of code that's difficult to maintain.

It's already difficult to work efficiently in the JavaScript environment—the tools for writing JavaScript are less mature than those for other popular languages such as C# and Java, and the slight variations in the ways in which web browsers implement the language require us to test our code on several combinations of browsers, versions, and platforms. As a result, we need to develop an organized approach to writing client-side code.

Before I introduce such an approach, let's look at some code that highlights a few of the issues that arise from traditional approaches to writing JavaScript. Consider the following form. It includes a button that attaches its `onclick` event to a JavaScript function by the name of `getServerTime`:

GetServerTime.aspx (excerpt)

```
<head runat="server">
  <title>Get Server Time</title>
  <script type="text/javascript" src="GetServerTime.js"></script>
</head>
<body>
  <form id="form1" runat="server">
    <input type="button" id="getContentButton"
        onclick="getServerTime();" value="Get Server Time" />
    <div id="content">
    </div>
  </form>
</body>
```

When the user clicks the button, the page should retrieve the current time from the web server and display it inside the `div` element. The following JavaScript, which lives in an external file and can be referenced from our document using a `<script>` tag, shows how a typical inexperienced developer might implement this functionality. This script has numerous technical and style problems, which we'll address in a moment:

GetServerTime.js (excerpt)

```
var xmlHttp;
function getContent()
{
  xmlHttp = new XMLHttpRequest();
  xmlHttp.onreadystatechange = onReadyStateChange;
```

```
  xmlHttp.open("GET", "../ServerTime.ashx", true);
  xmlHttp.send();
}
function onReadyStateChange()
{
  if (xmlHttp.readyState == 4 && xmlHttp.status == 200)
  {
    updateContent(xmlHttp.responseText);
  }
}
function updateContent(text)
{
  var content = document.getElementById('content');
  content.innerHTML = text;
}
```

Let's dissect this script. When the user clicks the button inside the form, the getServerTime function executes. This function kicks off an asynchronous request to the server, using the XMLHttpRequest object. The server returns the current time, and when the client receives the result, the script updates the innerHTML property of the div element.

 The readyState Property

> The onreadystatechange event handler will fire when the XmlHttpRequest object's readyState property changes. When readyState is equal to the value 4 (loaded), all data has been received and complete data is available. We also check the status property to ensure the server returned a 200 (OK) status.
>
> For more details on the values that readyState takes and what they mean, refer to Cameron Adams's seminal article on Ajax and remote scripting.[1]

Now, let's isolate the first problem we want to address: our script doesn't expose a nice API for the page's developers. Should they call updateContent? Should they call getServerTime? We'd like to hide some of these implementation details and expose an obvious API that any page could use.

---

[1] http://www.sitepoint.com/article/remote-scripting-ajax/

Solution

Let's refactor our existing script so that the functionality is encapsulated in more modular packages. Newcomers to JavaScript don't often appreciate the extensive (and powerful) object-oriented capabilities that JavaScript possesses. If you fall into that category, allow me to enlighten you! Consider the following, and slightly different, version of our form:

RefactoredGetServerTime.aspx *(excerpt)*

```
<head runat="server">
<title>Get Server Time</title>
<script type="text/javascript" src="RefactoredGetServerTime.js" />
<script type="text/javascript">

  var contentManager;

  window.onload = function()
  {
    contentManager = new ContentManager();
    contentManager.updateServerTime();
  }

  function getContent()
  {
    contentManager.updateServerTime();
  }
</script>
</head>
<body>
  <form id="form1" runat="server">
    <input type="button" id="getContentButton"
        value="Get Server Time"
        onclick="getContent();" />
    <div id="content">
    </div>
  </form>
</body>
```

Notice that our JavaScript is now using an object named `contentManager`. Our document invokes a method named `updateServerTime` on this object, the implementation of which we can place in a separate file, as follows:

```
                                              RefactoredGetServerTime.js
function ContentManager()
{
  this.updateServerTime = function()
  {
    xmlHttp = new XMLHttpRequest();
    xmlHttp.onreadystatechange = onreadystatechanged;
    xmlHttp.open("GET", "../ServerTime.ashx", true);
    xmlHttp.send();
    return false;
  }
  var onreadystatechanged = function()
  {
    if (xmlHttp.readyState == 4 && xmlHttp.status == 200)
    {
      updateContent(xmlHttp.responseText);
    }
  }
  var updateContent = function(text)
  {
    document.getElementById('content').innerHTML = text;
  }
  var xmlHttp;
  var content = document.getElementById('content');
}
```

The above code uses a **constructor function** named ContentManager. A constructor
function works with the new operator in JavaScript to create a new object, defining
its methods and properties. This object hides many of its implementation details—in
this case, the updateContent and onreadystatechanged functions—from the outside
world.

Since these methods aren't visible to other objects, the following script would fail:

```
<script type="text/javascript">
window.onload = function()
{
  var contentManager = new ContentManager();

  // This is an error!
```

```
   contentManager.updateContent('hello');
}
</script>
```

We have, however, exposed the `updateServerTime` function by prefixing the definition with the `this` reference. When we use the `var` keyword in the `ContentManager` constructor function, we're declaring a local variable that will remain private to the `ContentManager` object. To define any public property or method in JavaScript, we prefix the relevant definition with the `this` keyword, as we've done here.

 Functions Are Objects!

In JavaScript, functions themselves are objects—we can pass functions as arguments, and use functions as return values.

Discussion

The goal of our refactoring exercise was to encapsulate the details of our client-side code into a package that was clearly defined and loosely coupled to the page on which it acts.

One improvement we made was to use constructor functions to hide the details of methods that didn't need to be public. Clearly defining the scope of our methods makes the object's intended use obvious to other developers who might interact with our code.

Our solution is less than ideal, though. We still have JavaScript code mixed up with our markup—ideally the two would be contained within completely separate files for ease of maintenance and reusability. We also have a major problem in terms of the way we instantiate the `XmlHttpRequest` object—the approach we've used will only work on a subset of web browsers (most notably, this approach will not work on Internet Explorer 6). We'll address these issues in the coming topics.

How can libraries make writing robust, cross-platform JavaScript easier?

One of the greatest challenges of writing JavaScript code is to write scripts that will work on *all* of the various browsers available in the wild: Internet Explorer, FireFox, Safari, Opera, and others. This challenge is made even more difficult by the fact that scripts which work on Internet Explorer 7 aren't guaranteed to work on Internet Explorer 6, so testing and fixing your scripts to flesh out all the idiosyncrasies can take a considerable amount of time.

There's no doubt about it: writing robust, cross-platform scripts is tough. Luckily, there's help available.

Solution

As JavaScript has matured as a language (and browsers have better and more reliable support), so have a number of toolkits and frameworks of well-tested JavaScript code. One of these many toolkits is the Prototype JavaScript Framework.[2] Prototype includes Ajax features and DOM extensions that you can rely upon to work across all popular browsers. Prototype is freely distributable under an MIT-style license, and can be obtained with a single download of the **prototype.js** file. Once you've downloaded Prototype, you can use it by inserting a simple script reference in any **.aspx** page, like this:

```
                                                    Prototype.aspx (excerpt)

<html>
<head runat="server">
  <title>Prototype</title>
<script type="text/javascript"
    src="../scripts/prototype/prototype.js"></script>
  <script type="text/javascript"
    src="PrototypeGetServerTime.js"></script>
</head>
<body>
<form id="form1" runat="server">
  <input type="button" id="getContentButton"
      value="Get Server Time" />
```

---

[2] http://www.prototypejs.org/

```
    <div id="content"></div>
</form>
</body>
</html>
```

Notice that this version of our document doesn't include any JavaScript mixed up alongside HTML—our code and markup are kept quite separate, as they should be. Let's look at a new version of our script that retrieves the current server time. This version assumes the Prototype framework is included in the page:

PrototypeGetServerTime.js *(excerpt)*

```
var contentManager;
Event.observe(window, 'load', windowLoad); ❶
function windowLoad()
{
  contentManager = new ContentManager();
  contentManager.updateServerTime();
  Event.observe($('getContentButton'), 'click', getContent); ❷ ❸
}
function getContent()
{
  contentManager.updateServerTime();
}
var ContentManager = Class.create(); ❹
ContentManager.prototype.initialize = function() ❺
{
  this.content = $('content');
}
ContentManager.prototype.updateServerTime = function()
{
  var ajax = new Ajax.Request( ❻
  "../ServerTime.ashx",
  {
    method: 'get',
    onComplete:
    function(response)
    {
      contentManager.updateContent(response);
    }
  });
}
ContentManager.prototype.updateContent = function(response)
```

```
{
  this.content.innerHTML = response.responseText;
}
```

This solution looks radically different from the previous script, so let's take some time to examine the code.

Prototype defines a number of objects that make it easy for developers to perform Ajax calls, define classes, and manipulate the DOM:

❶ The Event object is one of the cornerstones of the Prototype framework. Events are triggered when the user performs an action, such as clicking a button or hovering over a link, and the Event object is Prototype's gateway to interaction with the user.

❷ The Event.observe method is able to subscribe to events in a non-destructive manner, and works across multiple browsers. The above line of code will attach the window's load event to the windowLoad function. Inside the windowLoad event, we use Event.observe again to subscribe to a button-click event. This line of code also demonstrates another popular feature of the Prototype toolkit: the $ function.

❸ The $ function in Prototype is a convenience mechanism. You can use the $ function to reference an HTML element without using the carpal-tunnel-inducing document.getElementById method. Prototype includes a number of these shortcuts—for example, the $F function returns the value property of an input given the id of the input, or even the input element itself.

❹ The Class.create method creates a new class object and works behind the scenes to assign an initialize method as the object constructor. We merely need to define the initialize method and include the setup instructions. The initialize method is the first function defined in our script, and sets up a public property by the name of content.

❺ Notice that we use a prototype property when defining the initialize method. Although this JavaScript feature is presumably where the Prototype toolkit found its name, it isn't specific to the toolkit. *Every* object in JavaScript has a `prototype` property. Any methods or properties defined by an object's prototype appear to be properties and methods of the object itself.

❻ Another feature of Prototype is the cross-browser Ajax functionality exposed by the `Ajax` object. The `Ajax.Request` instance encapsulates the `XmlHttpRequest` object. We now have an Ajax solution that works in all popular web browsers. Also, note that we use an anonymous function in the above code to handle the `onComplete` event. This anonymous function forwards the response to the `updateContent` method of the `ContentManager`.

Prototype-based Languages

Object-oriented programming languages generally fall into one of two camps. There are class-based languages (like C#, Visual Basic, and Java), and prototype-based languages (like JavaScript, Squeak, and REBOL).

Prototype-based languages don't instantiate a new object on the basis of a class definition. Instead, they generally construct a new object by cloning the object's **prototype**—a skeleton of that object. Modification of the `ContentManager`'s prototype means that we modify the template the runtime will use when it creates new `ContentManager` objects.

Discussion

Some form of JavaScript library or toolkit is almost *de rigeur* when it comes to building the best web applications these days, as it's such a difficult task to figure out all the different browsers' quirks. Even if you target just a single browser, libraries provide you with tested code to build on, which lets you avoid having to reinvent the wheel.

Prototype isn't the only popular toolkit in use today. The following are mature, popular frameworks:

scriptaculous (http://script.aculo.us/)
scriptaculous builds on top of the Prototype toolkit to offer animation, drag-and-drop functionality, Ajax controls, and more.

Yahoo! User Interface Library (http://developer.yahoo.com/yui/)
YUI includes a powerful library of user interface controls, as well as CSS tools and utilities.

Dojo (http://dojotoolkit.org/)

Dojo includes UI widgets and Ajax wrappers, and supports client- and server-side storage of data.

You'll want to evaluate the JavaScript library to find the best fit for your project. One area to assess is the feature set—some libraries go far beyond simple Ajax wrappers to provide animations and widgets that you can use in the browser. You should also evaluate the libraries' documentation—some of the freely available libraries don't offer extensive documentation and examples from which to learn.

Finally, consider the download size of the JavaScript library. Generally, the more features a library offers, the larger the JavaScript file your client will need to download. You might be able to get away with using large files for intranet applications, but you'll certainly want to think long and hard before putting a 150KB JavaScript file on the front page of your web site—although the browser will cache the file so that it's not downloaded with every request, first-time users on a slow connection will experience a considerable wait.

So far, all of the libraries and toolkits we've mentioned are strictly collections of JavaScript code. If you want to look for an Ajax toolkit that integrates with ASP.NET server controls and Microsoft Visual Studio, you might consider Microsoft's own ASP.NET AJAX Extensions. We'll cover these extensions in the coming sections.

How do I use Microsoft's ASP.NET AJAX?

Microsoft released the first version of an Ajax toolkit, code-named "Atlas," in early 2005. After several versions and a name change, the toolkit now supports all modern browsers and integrates with Visual Studio 2005. You can download the setup package from the ASP.NET AJAX site.[3] Once the package is installed, you'll be able to build a new Ajax-enabled web site within Visual Studio using a special project template for the job, as shown in Figure 10.1.

---

[3] http://ajax.asp.net/

Figure 10.1. Starting an ASP.NET AJAX-enabled web site

The project template ensures that we have in our **Web.config** file all the assembly references and sections that are required to use the ASP.NET AJAX libraries.

Consider this question: how would you build a page that retrieves the current time from the server, like the one we explored in the previous two solutions, using ASP.NET AJAX? Well, we could take one of many different approaches. The following sections will examine two possible solutions.

Solution

One noteworthy feature of ASP.NET AJAX is that it gives us the ability to make web service calls from client-side script. Let's say we implemented the following web service in the code-behind file **ServerTime.cs** for **ServerTime.asmx**:

```
                                                          ServerTime.cs
using System;
using System.Web.Services;
using System.Web.Script.Services;
[ScriptService]
[WebService(Namespace =
```

```
    "http://sitepoint.com/books/aspnetant1/getservertime")]
public class ServerTime : WebService
{
  [WebMethod]
  public string GetServerTime()
  {
    return DateTime.Now.ToLongTimeString();
  }
}
```

As you can see, our web service class is decorated with a `ScriptService` attribute. The `ScriptService` attribute allows ASP.NET AJAX to generate a client-side proxy object that represents this web service. Before we see how the proxy works, let's take a look at our **.aspx** page:

GetServerTime.aspx *(excerpt)*

```
<head runat="server">
  <title>ASP.NET AJAX</title>
</head>
<body>
  <form id="form1" runat="server">
    <asp:ScriptManager ID="ScriptManager1" runat="server">
      <Services>
        <asp:ServiceReference Path="~/ServerTime.asmx" />
      </Services>
      <Scripts>
        <asp:ScriptReference Path="GetServerTime.js" />
      </Scripts>
    </asp:ScriptManager>

    <input type="button" id="getContentButton"
        value="Get Server Time" />

    <div id="content">
    </div>
  </form>
</body>
```

The `ScriptManager` control that appears in the code above is a new, important control in ASP.NET AJAX. The `ScriptManager` is responsible for sending the correct Ajax libraries and other JavaScript files to the client. The `ScriptManager` also coordinates partial page updates, timeouts, error messages, and many other key features needed for an Ajax-style application. Adding a `ServiceReference` service inside the `ScriptManager`, as we've done above, will result in the generation of client-side proxies for the web service. Likewise, the `ScriptReference` will make sure our own script file (**GetServerTime.js**) is included in the page.

The **GetServerTime.js** code is as follows:

MSAjaxGetServerTime.js *(excerpt)*

```javascript
var contentManager;
function pageLoad()
{
  contentManager = new SitePoint.ContentManager();
  contentManager.updateServerTime();
  $addHandler($get('getContentButton'), 'click', getContent);
}
function getContent()
{
  contentManager.updateServerTime();
}
Type.registerNamespace("SitePoint");
SitePoint.ContentManager = function()
{
  this.content = $get('content');
}
SitePoint.ContentManager.prototype.updateServerTime = function()
{
  ServerTime.GetServerTime
  (
    function(result)
    {
      contentManager.updateContent(result);
    }
  );
}
SitePoint.ContentManager.prototype.updateContent = function(text)
{
  this.content.innerHTML = text;
}
SitePoint.ContentManager.registerClass('SitePoint.ContentManager');
if (typeof(Sys) !== 'undefined')
  Sys.Application.notifyScriptLoaded();
```

Our first function in the script is a `pageLoad` function. ASP.NET AJAX will automatically invoke this function when the `body` of the document finishes loading. Inside this method, we find a shortcut used to attach event handlers—the `$addHandler` function. Like the `$` function in Prototype, the `$addHandler` function is non-destructive (it doesn't override any built-in JavaScript functions) and works in all popular browsers.

The `Type.registerNamespace` method call creates a new **namespace**—a domain with which variables are associated in order to avoid conflicts with other variables of the same name. Although technically JavaScript doesn't have namespaces, many JavaScript libraries (ASP.NET AJAX included) simulate namespaces using objects. Using a namespace is a good way of ensuring that your class names are globally unique in a world where the amount of client-side code continues to grow.

ASP.NET AJAX, like Prototype, makes use of an object's inner `prototype` property. In our example, we've defined a constructor function immediately after the namespace registration. This constructor function uses a `$get` method, which is a shortcut for `document.getElementById`.

Notice the `updateServerTime` method uses a `ServerTime` object. This is the client-side proxy that's included in the page by the `ScriptManager`'s web service reference. In the call to `GetServerTime`, we pass an anonymous function for use when the web service call successfully completes. This anonymous function forwards the call to a `SitePoint.ContentManager` object, which will update the page with the new time.

This solution has illustrated just a small example of how web services can be consumed using ASP.NET AJAX. We could have built a more complex web service that accepted parameters, yet still have had the ability to exchange information between client and server. As easy as this solution seemed, there's an even easier programming model for ASP.NET. We'll look at this model in the next section.

How do I perform partial page rendering?

ASP.NET AJAX includes a powerful **partial page rendering** feature. Partial page rendering allows an ASP.NET developer to select regions of a page that can be updated asynchronously, without a complete page reload.

Sound familiar? That's right—partial page rendering provides all the benefits of Ajax, without the need to write JavaScript code. The secret lies in the server-side controls provided by ASP.NET AJAX. These controls are found in the AJAX Extensions section of the Toolbox, as shown in Figure 10.2.

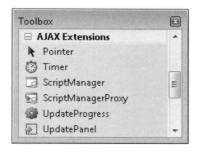

Figure 10.2. Server-side controls in ASP.NET AJAX

So, how can we implement our `GetServerTime` functionality using only server-side controls? We use the `UpdatePanel` control, which we'll explore now.

Solution

To use partial page rendering, we first need to identify the areas of a page that we want to update asynchronously. We then place the content of those sections inside the `ContentTemplate` area of an `UpdatePanel` control, as shown below:

UpdatePanel.aspx *(excerpt)*

```
<form id="form1" runat="server">
  <asp:ScriptManager ID="ScriptManager1" runat="server"
      EnablePartialRendering="true">
  </asp:ScriptManager>
  <div>
    <asp:UpdatePanel ID="UpdatePanel1" runat="server">
    <ContentTemplate>
      <asp:Button ID="Button1" runat="server"
          Text="Get Server Time" />
      <asp:Label ID="Label1" runat="server" Text="" />
    </ContentTemplate>
    </asp:UpdatePanel>
  </div>
</form>
```

Notice that we have a `ScriptManager` control in play again; this time we've explicitly set the `EnablePartialRendering` property of the `ScriptManager` control to `true`. The `ContentTemplate` element of the `UpdatePanel` contains the `Button` and `Label` controls that will participate in the partial page rendering.

With these controls in place, we can perform all of the updates we need from the page's code-beside file:

```
UpdatePanel.aspx.cs
using System;
public partial class updatepanel_Default : System.Web.UI.Page
{
  protected void Page_Load(object sender, EventArgs e)
  {
    if (!Page.IsPostBack)
    {
      UpdateServerTime();
    }
  }
  protected void Button1_Click(object sender, EventArgs e)
  {
    UpdateServerTime();
  }
  private void UpdateServerTime()
  {
    Label1.Text = DateTime.Now.ToLongTimeString();
  }
}
```

Now when the user clicks the button on the page, the ASP.NET AJAX client-side scripts will asynchronously contact the server, retrieve the updated page, and update the portion of the page inside the `UpdatePanel`. Our code doesn't need to be aware of the partial page rendering—we would have written the same code if an `Update-Panel` were not in place. In contrast to our previous solution, though, we haven't written any JavaScript code to achieve this—ASP.NET AJAX takes care of all the JavaScript code, asynchronous callback functions, and DOM manipulations.

Discussion

Any postback that originates from inside an `UpdatePanel` will result in an asynchronous postback that updates just the portion of the page inside the `UpdatePanel`. In the page we demonstrated, the button that forces the refresh lives *inside* the `UpdatePanel`; however, in a more sophisticated user interface we mightn't be able to place the postback controls inside the same `UpdatePanel` as the content. In those scenarios, we can explicitly identify the controls that will force an `UpdatePanel` to refresh by specifying the controls as **triggers**:

```
                                              Triggered.aspx (excerpt)
<div>
<asp:Button ID="Button1" runat="server" Text="Get Server Time"
    OnClick="Button1_Click" />
  <asp:UpdatePanel ID="UpdatePanel1" runat="server">
    <ContentTemplate>
      <asp:Label ID="Label1" runat="server" Text="" />
    </ContentTemplate>

    <Triggers>
    <asp:AsyncPostBackTrigger ControlID="Button1" />
    </Triggers>
  </asp:UpdatePanel>
</div>
```

As you can see, the above form has a button that lives *outside* the `UpdatePanel`, but the `UpdatePanel` specifies the button as a trigger, so our partial page rendering functions just fine.

UpdatePanels Behaving Badly

The `UpdatePanel` isn't 100% compatible with all server-side controls. For instance, the `Menu` and `Tree` controls in ASP.NET don't work correctly inside an `UpdatePanel`, and neither do the ASP.NET Web Parts controls. These controls register JavaScript blocks in a manner that's incompatible with ASP.NET AJAX, which can lead to erratic behavior, such as tree nodes and menu choices not displaying. We can reasonably expect, however, that future releases of ASP.NET will address this issue.

How do I show progress during a partial page render?

Not every call to the server will be as simple as retrieving the current time. There'll be many occasions when you'll need to perform database queries or calculations that'll take longer than just grabbing the current time. One tricky problem with asynchronous postbacks is that they don't give the user any indication that they're actually working behind the scenes. As a result, some users might click a button repeatedly, thinking that the page isn't responding. We need to provide some visual feedback that lets a user know that the page is refreshing.

Solution

The `UpdateProgress` control, which we saw in the section called "How do I perform partial page rendering?", is designed to provide status information for asynchronous postbacks. We can specify the content of this control inside its `ProgressTemplate` section, as follows:

```
                                                    Slow.aspx (excerpt)
<div>
  <asp:UpdateProgress ID="UpdateProgress1" runat="server">
    <ProgressTemplate>
      <img src="spinner.gif" alt="Loading..." />
    </ProgressTemplate>
  </asp:UpdateProgress>
  <asp:UpdatePanel ID="UpdatePanel1" runat="server">
    ⋮
  </asp:UpdatePanel>
</div>
```

We're free to add any HTML or other server-side controls to this template—we've added an animated **GIF** image, **spinner.gif**, inside the progress control. A spinning or moving graphic is a well-established convention for the representation of computer-processing time. The `UpdateProgress` control itself will display this content while an asynchronous postback is taking place, and it will hide the content when the postback is complete. We don't need to add any code!

When we view the page in Design view, we see a display like the one in Figure 10.3.

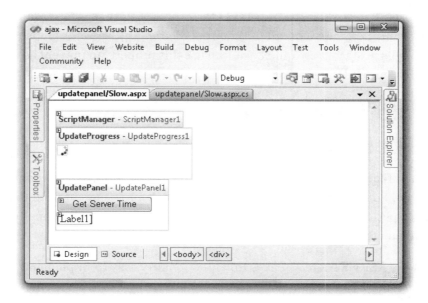

Figure 10.3. Viewing the `ProgressControl` in the Design View

Discussion

We've placed the `UpdateProgress` control outside the `UpdatePanel` control on our page, but the progress control would also work if we nest it inside the `UpdatePanel`. The control also has some additional properties that we can use, as the code below demonstrates:

Slow.aspx (excerpt)

```
<asp:UpdateProgress ID="UpdateProgress1" runat="server"
    AssociatedUpdatePanelID="UpdatePanel1"
    DisplayAfter="200" >
  <ProgressTemplate>
    <img src="spinner.gif" alt="Loading..." />
  </ProgressTemplate>
</asp:UpdateProgress>
```

An `UpdateProgress` control will display its contents when *any* asynchronous postback occurs on a page—unless the control is associated with a *specific* `Update-Panel` control. This specific association is made via the `UpdateProgress` control's `AssociatedUpdatePanelID` property.

Another useful property is the `DisplayAfter` property. `DisplayAfter` won't display its content until *after* an amount of time specified in milliseconds elapses. If your asynchronous postbacks are quick, you can use this property to prevent an annoying flicker of the progress indicator.

How do I periodically refresh an UpdatePanel?

We're often required to create pages that must make periodic asynchronous calls to the sever. For instance, a page that displays stock quotes might need to refresh its content periodically. Another example is a page that must occasionally call a server-side method in order to keep a user session alive.

Fortunately, ASP.NET AJAX makes this functionality easy to implement.

Solution

Periodic updates provide the perfect opportunity to use the ASP.NET AJAX `Timer` control. The `Timer` control uses JavaScript to force a postback from the browser after a specified number of milliseconds have elapsed. We control the timing with the control's `Interval` property, and during the postback, the timer control raises a `Tick` event on the server.

Let's revisit our familiar example for retrieving the time, and update the current server time every five seconds with the following `UpdatePanel`:

AutoRefresh.aspx *(excerpt)*

```
<asp:UpdatePanel ID="UpdatePanel1" runat="server">
  <ContentTemplate>
    <asp:Button ID="Button1" runat="server" Text="Get Server Time"
        OnClick="Button1_Click" />
    <asp:Label ID="Label1" runat="server" Text="" />
      <asp:Timer ID="Timer1" runat="server" Interval="5000"
          OnTick="Timer1_Tick">
    </asp:Timer>
  </ContentTemplate>
</asp:UpdatePanel>
```

As the code above shows, we've attached the timer's `Tick` event to a `Timer1_Tick` event handler on the server. This event handler calls our `UpdateServerTime` method, as shown below:

```
private void UpdateServerTime()
{
  Label1.Text = DateTime.Now.ToLongTimeString();
}
protected void Timer1_Tick(object sender, EventArgs e)
{
  UpdateServerTime();
}
```

Discussion

We've placed the `Timer` control inside the `ContentTemplate` of our `UpdatePanel`. Placing the `Timer` here makes the `Timer` a trigger for the `UpdatePanel`, so when the timer expires, the `UpdatePanel` will asynchronously update its content.

We can also use a single `Timer` to update multiple `UpdatePanels` by listing the timer as a trigger. In the following code sample, a single timer will update two `UpdatePanels`:

```
<form id="form1" runat="server">
  <asp:ScriptManager ID="ScriptManager1" runat="server" />
  <asp:Timer ID="Timer1" runat="server" Interval="5000"
      OnTick="Timer1_Tick" />
  <asp:UpdatePanel ID="UpdatePanel1" runat="server">
    <ContentTemplate>
      <asp:Label ID="Label1" runat="server" Text="" />
    </ContentTemplate>
    <Triggers>
      <asp:AsyncPostBackTrigger ControlID="Timer1" />
    </Triggers>
  </asp:UpdatePanel>
  <asp:UpdatePanel ID="UpdatePanel2" runat="server">
    <ContentTemplate>
      <asp:Label ID="Label2" runat="server" Text="" />
```

```
      </ContentTemplate>
      <Triggers>
        <asp:AsyncPostBackTrigger ControlID="Timer1" />
      </Triggers>
    </asp:UpdatePanel>
  </form>
```

Note that setting the `Interval` property to lower values than we've used in this example could create a tremendous amount of traffic and load on the server. Be careful to choose a value for this property that will provide users with the information they need, but won't tax the server heavily.

How do I work with generated IDs?

One problem that developers writing JavaScript face with ASP.NET is how to deal with the automatically generated ID properties that ASP.NET places on page elements.

The reason that ASP.NET generates IDs is to ensure that every element on the page has a unique ID. However, this feature causes difficulty for client-side scripts that rely on these IDs to reference elements, as they can't easily predict what that generated ID will be. Client-side IDs are generated for page elements whenever a server-side control on the page implements the INamingContainer interface. User controls, master pages, and many of the data-oriented controls (like `GridView` and `Repeater`) are examples of controls that implement INamingContainer.

Let's take a look at a concrete example. Imagine that you've designed a user control to display a joke. The punchline of the joke won't be visible until the user moves the cursor over the joke. Such a control might look like this:

JokeHost.aspx *(excerpt)*

```
<%@ Control Language="C#" AutoEventWireup="true"  %>
  <div onmouseover="jokeMouseOver();">
    <div>
      What does a proud computer call his son?
    </div>
    <div id="answer" runat="server" style="display:none;">
```

```
      A microchip off the old block ...
  </div>
</div>
```

The script that handles the `onmouseover` event might look like this:

```
<script type="text/javascript">
function jokeMouseOver()
{
  $get('answer').style.display = '';
}
</script>
```

Unfortunately, this script doesn't work. Since the `div` with ID of `answer` is a server-side control located within a user control, ASP.NET will assign it a different client-side ID from the one we specified in the **.aspx** file. You can use the **View Source** feature of your web browser to see what this ID will be:

```
<div onmouseover="jokeMouseOver();">
  <div>
    What does a proud computer call his son?
  </div>
  <div id="Joke1_answer" style="display:none;">
    A microchip off the old block..
  s</div>
</div>
```

As you can see, the `div` element that contains the answer to our joke has an `id` of `Joke1_answer`. ASP.NET has prefixed the ID we assigned our element with the ID of the user control, because a user control is an INamingContainer. In this code, our user control has an ID of `Joke1`.

The naïve solution to this problem is to simply change our script to reference the element by its generated ID, as follows:

Joke1.ascx (excerpt)

```
<script type="text/javascript">
function jokeMouseOver()
{
```

```
    $get('Joke1_answer').style.display = '';
}
</script>
```

The above script will work; however, it's dependent on the ID of the user control. This is less than ideal—the page developer could easily rename the control and break our script. So what's the best way to manage client-side IDs?

Solution

There are quite a number of solutions for dealing with generated IDs, and almost all of them revolve around the `ClientID` property of a server-side control. The `ClientID` property, as its name suggests, represents the ID that ASP.NET will use for an element on the client. Here's one approach we could take to improving our code:

Joke2.ascx *(excerpt)*

```
<%@ Control Language="C#" AutoEventWireup="true"  %>
<div onmouseover="jokeMouseOver();">
  <div>
    Why do computer programmers confuse Halloween and Christmas?
  </div>
  <div id="answer" runat="server" style="display:none;">
    Because oct31 = dec25.
  </div>
</div>
<script type="text/javascript">
function jokeMouseOver()
{
  $get('<%= answer.ClientID %>').style.display = '';
}
</script>
```

Notice that we now inject the `ClientID` property of the `answer` element into our JavaScript. This solution ensures that we'll always use the proper ID; however, it does come with some drawbacks.

The biggest issue is that we rarely embed our JavaScript code directly into an **.aspx** or **.ascx** file, like we've done here. In fact, as we discussed in the section called "How can libraries make writing robust, cross-platform JavaScript easier?", it's considered best practice to keep our code in an external **.js** file for the sake of maintainability and caching. One way to address this issue would be to use a single line of JavaScript to add a variable with the `ClientID` to our page:

Joke3.ascx (excerpt)

```
<script type="text/javascript">
  var answerId = '<%= answer.ClientID %>';
</script>
```

The rest of the script could then be placed in an external **.js** file:

```
function jokeMouseOver()
{
  $get(answerId).style.display = '';
}
```

Another similar approach is to place the required `ClientID` in a hidden form field. We can perform this task from our code-behind file, and leave the executable code in the **.ascx** file, as follows:

Joke4.ascx.cs (excerpt)

```
ScriptManager.RegisterHiddenField(
  this, "answerId", answer.ClientID
);
```

Our JavaScript code could then retrieve this value to find the element it needs, like so:

Joke4.ascx (excerpt)

```
// retrieve id from hidden field
var id = form1.answerId.value;
$get(id).style.display = '';
```

Another common solution to this problem is to use the `ScriptManager` class's `RegisterArrayDeclaration` method to place multiple `ClientID` values into a page.

This technique is extremely useful when we need the IDs of controls that are located inside a `GridView` or `Repeater`. Since our `GridView` or `Repeater` control is likely to contain multiple instances of each element, any assistance in managing the IDs of these elements is welcome.

Discussion

We've discussed several techniques that make use of the `ClientID` property, and these solutions can be effective if they're used sparingly. However, the addition of global JavaScript variables to a page can sometimes lead to maintainability problems. Some alternative approaches avoid using IDs altogether. Let's look at one more version of the joke control:

Joke5.ascx (excerpt)

```
<%@ Control Language="C#" ClassName="joke5" %>
  <div id="joke" onmouseover="jokeMouseOver(this);">
    <div>
      There are 10 kinds of people in this world ...
    </div>
    <div id="answer" runat="server" style="display:none;">
      Those who can count in binary and those who can't.
    </div>
  </div>
  <script type="text/javascript">
  function jokeMouseOver(sender)
  {
    var divs = sender.getElementsByTagName("DIV");
    divs[1].style.display = '';
  }
  </script>
```

In this code, we use the `getElementsByTagName` method (and the knowledge that our `div` is the second of the two nested `divs`) to locate the `div` we're after. While it's not always applicable, this approach can work well in many scenarios, and doesn't require any global variables, hidden form fields, or array declarations.

Where can I get some fancy ASP.NET controls?

These days, the fun part of writing web applications is finding ways to make web interfaces exciting.

In the past, ASP.NET developers have had to rely on custom ActiveX controls and technologies like Adobe's Flash Player for animations and interactive controls—plugins that aren't guaranteed to be installed on a client's machine. However, the combination of JavaScript, style sheets, and the DOM has given us the ability to write advanced controls that remain lightweight and easily distributable, and are guaranteed to be supported by all modern browsers.

Of course, we don't always want to write these controls from scratch, and we'd like the controls to integrate well with the ASP.NET server controls and Visual Studio development environment. So where can we find some existing controls?

Solution

The ASP.NET AJAX Control Toolkit is both a collection of ready-to-use controls and a toolkit for creating new controls.[4] The toolkit is an open source community project, featuring contributors from inside and outside Microsoft.

Once the toolkit is unpacked and set up, you'll be able to choose from a plethora of controls in the Web Forms Toolbox, which is illustrated in Figure 10.4.

---

[4] http://www.codeplex.com/AtlasControlToolkit/

Figure 10.4. Controls of the ASP.NET AJAX Control Toolkit

The toolkit comes with a sample web site that can be installed locally, and demonstrates how to use each control in the toolkit. Figure 10.5 shows the demonstration page for the Tabs control.

Figure 10.5. The demonstration page for the Tabs control

The controls in the toolkit use the same declarative markup we've become accustomed to with ASP.NET. Any scripts that the control requires will be taken care of by the control itself, so we don't need to worry about registering additional JavaScript files for the page.

The following code shows the AutoCompleteExtender control in use in an **aspx** page. This control attaches to a text box and, as the user types into the box, the control displays a popup containing words that begin with the letters the user has entered. The control can retrieve a list of possible words by making a web service call:

```
<asp:TextBox runat="server" ID="myTextBox" Width="300"
    autocomplete="off"/>
<ajaxToolkit:AutoCompleteExtender
    runat="server"
    ID="autoComplete1"
    TargetControlID="myTextBox"
    ServicePath="AutoComplete.asmx"
    ServiceMethod="GetCompletionList"
    MinimumPrefixLength="2"
```

```
        CompletionInterval="1000"
        EnableCaching="true"
        CompletionSetCount="12"
/>
```

As this example indicates, using these controls is often as simple as adding the name of the control to your page and setting the control's attributes.

You'll notice that most of the controls in the toolkit are not standalone ASP.NET server controls. Instead, the controls refer to existing ASP.NET server controls via a `TargetControlID` property. The Ajax controls use script to add behaviors to this target control.

The developers who work on the control toolkit are constantly adding controls, features, and fixes to the toolkit. Subscribe to the toolkit homepage's RSS feed to keep informed of updated versions.[5]

How can I debug JavaScript?

Sooner or later, you'll need to figure out what's going wrong with your JavaScript code and Ajax calls. As we mentioned back in the section called "How can I write better JavaScript?", the tools available for developing client-side scripts aren't as developed as those created for other languages, but there are a few approaches you can use to troubleshoot JavaScript bugs.

Solutions

The need to debug is an unfortunate consequence of software development, and no doubt many readers will have relied heavily on the `alert` function to debug their JavaScript in the past. Come on, own up—we've all done it. We'd scatter multiple calls to the JavaScript `alert` function throughout the page, and each call would display the value of a variable at a given point in the script. It's a painful technique, but it's all that was available at the time.

Fortunately, the use of more powerful tools can make the job of debugging JavaScript much easier.

---

[5] http://www.codeplex.com/AtlasControlToolkit/

Using Visual Studio

Visual Studio 2005 possesses a feature for debugging client-side script, which can only be used in Internet Explorer. To enable script debugging, visit the **Tools** menu in Internet Explorer, and select **Internet Options**. Click on the **Advanced** tab, and un-check the **Disable Script Debugging (Internet Explorer)** checkbox, as I've done in Figure 10.6.

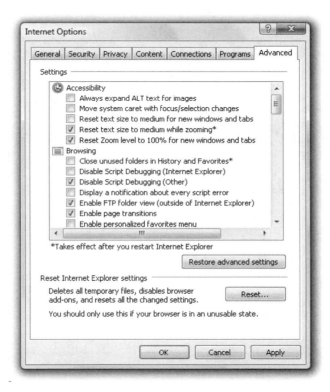

Figure 10.6. Enabling script debugging in IE 7

Once script debugging is enabled, we use the debugger to launch a web site or application in Internet Explorer (F5), and to set breakpoints in our JavaScript code. We can use Visual Studio to watch, inspect, and modify JavaScript objects and their properties. The tools in Visual Studio for debugging JavaScript are very similar to those for debugging C# and Visual Basic code.

Using Firebug

Another excellent tool is Firebug, a free extension for Firefox that's dedicated to JavaScript debugging and profiling.[6] Open your site in Firefox, then press F12 to launch the Firebug console and begin a debugging session, which will look like Figure 10.7.

Figure 10.7. The Firebug JavaScript debugger

Firebug provides you with the ability to watch variables and set breakpoints in JavaScript code. But Firebug is actually more than just a JavaScript debugger—you can also use it to inspect and manipulate the DOM, tweak style sheets, and measure download times.

---

[6] http://www.getfirebug.com/

Using Framework Tools

A third option when you come to debugging JavaScript is to make use of the features present in the JavaScript framework that you're using. For example, ASP.NET AJAX includes a `Sys.Debug` class that can be used to trace execution, display objects, and step into the debugger. Trace messages appear in the Output window of Visual Studio during a debugging session, but the runtime will also send trace messages to the page if it finds a `textarea` element with an `id` of `TraceConsole`.

Using Fiddler

Sometimes it's useful simply to capture the traffic between a web browser and a web server in order to discover how many requests are passing back and forth, or get an idea of the sheer amount of data being transmitted between client and server. A perfect tool for this purpose is Fiddler, a free HTTP debugging proxy.[7] Fiddler allows you to inspect the request and response parts of web server interaction, and includes powerful logging and scripting filters to recreate and track down problems.

As we've seen, a number of excellent tools are available to debug JavaScript code. So, the next time you catch yourself adding an `alert` message to your page to debug a script, consider one of these tools instead—it may save you a tremendous amount of time.

Summary

Many of the solutions we've explored in this chapter required us to push beyond the level of JavaScript that most ASP.NET developers are accustomed to using. It's true that a learning curve is associated with exploring the new libraries and toolkits that we've discussed, but the payoff is huge—with these new libraries, you can ensure that you produce robust client-side code with minimum effort.

This chapter also gave us a chance to discuss the new techniques you can use to take advantage of the object-oriented features of the JavaScript language, and we touched on some new tools that will help you to manage the complexity inherent in scripting. These new libraries, new tools, and new techniques are quickly revolutionizing the world of client-side scripting!

---

[7] http://www.fiddlertool.com/

If you're still a little puzzled by the world of JavaScript, and feel the need for a book that provides a solid foundation for this subject, then I strongly recommend you seek out *Simply JavaScript*, by Kevin Yank and Cameron Adams. As with all SitePoint books, you can download sample chapters of the book for free from the book's web site.[8]

---

[8] http://www.sitepoint.com/books/javascript1/

Working with Email

Although the word *email* is seen by many to be synonymous with *spam*, email remains the primary means of direct, person-to-person communication on the Internet. In some situations, technologies such as RSS and instant messaging have proven popular alternatives, but nothing has eclipsed the classic SMTP and POP mail protocols. Despite its problems, email is here to stay. Fortunately, dealing with email from within ASP.NET is relatively painless.

How do I send a plain-text email?

In .NET 1.1, sending email relied upon a creaky old component called CDONTS (short for *C*ollaboration *D*ata *O*bjects for Microsoft Windows *NT S*erver), on which the `System.Web.Mail` class was dependent. It was awkward to use, had serious performance issues, and was difficult to troubleshoot.

Sending email in .NET 2.0 is far more straightforward because this version provides us with access to the `System.Net.Mail` class. The first rule of thumb when sending mail in .NET 2.0 is therefore to *avoid* `System.Web.Mail` *like the plague!* It's still there for the sake of backwards compatibility, but don't use it—use `System.Net.Mail` instead.[1]

> **Email and .NET 1.1**
>
> If you have an application that still uses .NET 1.1, and you need to send email, you might consider using a third-party email library. One such library is FreeSMTP.Net from Quiksoft.[2]

Solution

Before you even begin sending any mail, you'll need to configure your SMTP settings to indicate which mail server you'll be talking to. It's possible to configure SMTP programmatically, but I find it easiest to set it up once, in my **Web.config** file, and forget about it.

SMTP is configured via the `mailSettings` element:

Web.config *(excerpt)*

```
<system.net>
  <mailSettings>
    <smtp from="michael.bolton@initech.com">
      <network host="smtp.initech.com" port="25" userName="mbolton"
          password="pcloadletter" defaultCredentials="true" />
    </smtp>
  </mailSettings>
</system.net>
```

In the example above, we're configuring `System.Net.Mail` to connect to a remote server (`smtp.initech.com`) that requires a username and password for authentication.

That reasonably verbose solution might be used on your production server. However, if your SMTP server happens to live on the same machine as your web server (as may be the case in your development environment), you can probably get away with a much simpler version:

---

[1] If you'd like a crash course in the difference between `System.Web.Mail` and `System.Net.Mail`, the community-run web sites http://www.systemwebmail.com/ and http://www.systemnetmail.com/ are both excellent resources.

[2] http://www.quicksoftcorp.com/freesmtp/

```
Web.config (excerpt)

<system.net>
  <mailSettings>
    <smtp>
      <network host="localhost" />
    </smtp>
  </mailSettings>
</system.net>
```

This "set and forget" configuration approach is sufficient for most web applications. However, if your application sends mail through several different servers, you may need to configure your SMTP settings in your application code using the properties of the `System.Net.Mail.SmtpClient` class. More information about this class can be found in the MSDN documentation.[3]

To send mail, make sure that your project has a reference to `System.Net.Mail`, and use the `MailMessage` and `SmtpClient` classes, as shown in the following example:

```
SendMail.aspx.cs (excerpt)

MailMessage m = new MailMessage();
m.From = new MailAddress("manager@tchotchkes.com");
m.To.Add("joanna@tchotchkes.com");
m.Subject = "Your Flair";
m.Body = "I need to talk to you about your flair.";
SmtpClient sc = new SmtpClient();
sc.Send(m);
```

The code above will deliver the following email to Joanna's inbox:

```
mime-version: 1.0
from: manager@tchotchkes.com
to: joanna@tchotchkes.com
date: 29 Mar 2007 22:59:24 -0700
subject: Your Flair
content-type: text/plain; charset=us-ascii
content-transfer-encoding: quoted-printable
I need to talk to you about your flair.
```

---

[3] http://msdn2.microsoft.com/en-us/library/system.net.mail.smtpclient.aspx

The `Mail` class is very discoverable, so I won't bog you down by discussing all the various options and methods available for sending email. Whatever you want to do with email, `System.Net.Mail` is a solid starting point. You can read more about this class at the unofficial System.Net.Mail FAQ[4] or the official MSDN documentation.[5]

How do I send an HTML email?

While everyone has an opinion about which is better—plain-text or HTML email—there's one group of people who will always push for emails to be sent in fancily formatted HTML: your clients.

You might think that the easiest way to send an HTML-formatted email is just to write some markup into the body of your email. The problem with this approach is that not all email clients are able to display HTML. Users of some clients won't be able to read your message easily because they'll have to wade through raw HTML to find it.

A better solution is to provide the HTML version of the message as an alternative view. Email clients that are capable of displaying HTML can then display the fancy HTML view, while less capable email clients can still view the plain-text version.

Solution

The following code sets up both plain-text and HTML content. We provide the HTML content using the `AlternateView` class:

SendMultipart.aspx.cs *(excerpt)*

```
MailMessage m = new MailMessage();
m.From = new MailAddress("manager@tchotchkes.com");
m.To.Add("joanna@tchotchkes.com");
m.Subject = "Your Flair";
m.Body = "I need to talk to you about your flair.";
AlternateView html = AlternateView.CreateAlternateViewFromString(
"I need to talk to you about <b>your flair</b>.", null,
    "text/html");
```

---

[4] http://www.systemnetmail.com/
[5] http://msdn2.microsoft.com/en-us/library/system.net.mail.aspx

```
m.AlternateViews.Add(html);
SmtpClient sc = new SmtpClient();
sc.Send(m);
```

This code delivers to Joanna's inbox a slightly larger email than the one we created in the section called "How do I send a plain-text email?":

```
mime-version: 1.0
from: manager@tchotchkes.com
to: joanna@tchotchkes.com
date: 29 Mar 2007 22:59:24 -0700
subject: Your Flair
content-type: multipart/mixed; boundary=boundary0
--boundary0
content-type: multipart/alternative; boundary=boundary1
--boundary1
content-type: text/plain; charset=us-ascii
content-transfer-encoding: quoted-printable
I need to talk to you about your flair.
--boundary1
content-type: text/html; charset=us-ascii
content-transfer-encoding: quoted-printable
I need to talk to you about <b>your flair</b>.
--boundary1--
--boundary0--
```

The email is a **multipart MIME** message, meaning that this single email encapsulates multiple packages of content. Our email has two content packages: one is plain text, and the other is HTML. The content is functionally equivalent in each case. If Joanna's email client understands the content type of text/html it can render that message. If not, her email client can fall back to the plain-text message.

Discussion

You should be aware of the following issues before you send HTML-formatted email:

■ Support for HTML and CSS among the many different mail clients is extremely limited when compared to the support offered by web browsers. For example, Outlook 2007 moved away from using Internet Explorer as its HTML rendering engine for security reasons. Unlike Outlook 2003, Outlook 2007 therefore supports a *restricted* subset of HTML, and offers very little support for CSS. It's unwise to assume that the user's email client—whatever it may be—has browser-equivalent, rich HTML support.

- For privacy reasons, modern email clients won't automatically retrieve images from an HTML-formatted email. Retrieving graphics via HTML necessitates that a request be sent from the user's computer to a remote web server. These requests are tracked as key metrics by misguided email marketers who want to monitor the success of their marketing campaigns. It's a good thing that this behavior is disabled by default, but it does mean that users must explicitly allow images before they will display in any HTML email.

- You should *always* send a plain-text version of your email, in case the user's client can't (or just won't) render HTML.

The general rule of thumb when using HTML inside an email is to keep your content (and layout) simple. Your email might be read with a web mail client, a mobile phone, or a five-year-old desktop application. It's impossible to test all the devices and programs in the world, so aim for the lowest common denominator.

How do I attach a file to my email?

When you want to send content such as a Microsoft Word file, or a PDF file, you'll need to send that file as an attachment to a mail message. Fortunately, .NET 2.0 makes sending attachments easy.

Solution

The following code sends as an attachment a file named **Flair.doc** that exists in the root of the web application:

SendAttachment.aspx.cs *(excerpt)*

```
MailMessage mail = new MailMessage();
mail.From = new MailAddress("manager@tchotchkes.com");
mail.To.Add("joanna@tchotchkes.com");
mail.Subject = "Flair guidelines";
mail.Body = "See the attached file for more details";
string path = Server.MapPath("~/Flair.doc");
mail.Attachments.Add(new Attachment(path));
SmtpClient client = new SmtpClient();
client.Send(mail);
```

Notice that we attach the file by creating an `Attachment` object and adding the object to the mail's `Attachments` collection. Alternatively, we could have created the `Attachment` object by passing a `Stream` instance to the constructor. Using a stream would mean we wouldn't necessarily need to save a file to disk. For instance, we could create a file attachment using data that's already in memory from a previous HTTP file upload.

Discussion

As with HTML email, there are a few issues to be aware of when sending attachments via SMTP:

- The recipient may not have installed the software necessary to open the attachment.

- Not every email client understands how to process attachments. Remember, it's possible that your email could end up on any number of ancient devices.

- To virus scanners, attachments are prime suspects—even harmless Microsoft Word files can be blocked by an overzealous anti-virus application wary of macros and other forms of embeddable code that may appear inside the document. Sending an attachment with an **.exe** extension, or an executable script extension like **.vbs**, will almost guarantee that your attachment will be quarantined by anti-virus software.

- Large attachments stand a good chance of being rejected by mail server software.

How do I send personalized form letters?

It's usually good practice when sending email—even messages that contain what is largely the same content, such as a newsletter—to personalize the message to some degree, rather than sending exactly the same email to every recipient. Including details that are specific to the recipient—be it a customer's order details, account information, or just the person's name—makes the process a lot more personal for each reader.

Solution

ASP.NET boasts a built-in component for sending templated emails. It can really save you development time.

To use the component, first create a template for the email like the one shown below. Name the file **mailtemplate.txt**, and place it in the root of your web site:

```
MailTemplate.txt

Dear <customer>,

A review of our records shows that your account was accidentally
debited by <amount>. We have credited your account for <amount> to
resolve the problem.

Regards,
INITech Technical Support
```

With this file in place, we can use the `MailDefinition` class, which provides methods for automatically merging templated content from a file:

```
SendTemplated.aspx.cs (excerpt)

MailDefinition md = new MailDefinition();
md.BodyFileName = "mailtemplate.txt";
Dictionary<string, string> d = new Dictionary<string, string>();
d.Add("<customer>", "ACME Global");
d.Add("<amount>", ".0002 cents");
MailMessage m = md.CreateMailMessage("finance@acmeglobal.com", d,
    new LiteralControl());
m.Subject = "account review";
m.From = new MailAddress("support@initech.com");
SmtpClient smtp = new SmtpClient();
smtp.Send(m);
```

Your email template can now be used to send personalized messages to multiple recipients!

Discussion

There are two issues to be aware of when you're using the `MailDefinition` class:

1. Creating a new instance of `MailDefinition` requires that a `Control` object be passed into the `CreateMailMessage` method. This `Control` is used to derive the

correct path for the template file. Passing in `null` doesn't work; instead, we've passed a new, empty `LiteralControl` class.

2. `MailDefinition` requires that the `From` property of the `smtp` node be populated. You can, of course, override the address, but it must be populated in **Web.config**.

Once we've accounted for these oddities, the properly merged email arrives as expected:

```
Dear ACME Global,

A review of our records shows that your account was accidentally
debited .0002 cents. We have credited your account for .0002 cents
to resolve the problem.

Regards,
INITech Technical Support
```

Of course, if this were a real-world example, we'd be sending these emails in a loop, building up our `Dictionary` with unique values from a database with each iteration.

How do I allow users to submit content via email?

The standard approach for accepting input from a web site's users is via an HTML form. However, you may want to allow users to interact with your web site through direct email (for example, to allow them to subscribe or unsubscribe from an email newsletter).

Each of the previous examples involved *sending* mail using the SMTP class in `System.Net.Mail`. Now, let's reverse the situation. We need our application to *receive* mail. Unfortunately, Microsoft doesn't provide any built-in methods in .NET for POP3, which is the receiving protocol. We'll have to look for a third-party component—either open source or commercial—to add the missing POP3 support.

Solution

Despite extensive research, I have yet to discover any active open source projects that I would recommend for use in this case. However, performing a search in Google for the phrase "C# POP3" reveals several C# code samples that developers have made available online. I'll explore one such .NET 2.0 code sample that I downloaded from CodeProject, named Pop3MailClient.[6]

Gotta Keep 'Em Separated!

I recommend that you don't mix personal mailboxes with machine mailboxes. So if you're planning to take advantage of unattended email accounts, for instance, to allow users to submit content to a site, set up a new email account explicitly for the purpose.

Begin your foray into the automated receiving of email by instantiating the POP3 object and letting it connect to the POP3 server. In the following example, I chose to use a free Google Mail account that I set up explicitly for this purpose. I then enabled POP3 support for the account via the Google Mail control panel. Now it's time to connect:

Program.cs *(excerpt)*

```
Pop3.Pop3MailClient p = new Pop3.Pop3MailClient(
"pop.gmail.com", 995, true, "someone@gmail.com", "password");
p.IsAutoReconnect = true;
p.ReadTimeout = 60000;
p.Connect();
```

Now that we have a connection, let's query the account to see how many new emails have arrived in our mailbox:

Program.cs *(excerpt)*

```
int mailcount;
int size;
p.GetMailboxStats(out mailcount, out size);
```

Bear in mind that these variables refer only to the number of *new* emails received by the account. The POP3 protocol was not designed for emails to be stored on the server—every time you connect, retrieve your mail, and disconnect, the Pop3Mail-Client code assumes that those emails have been successfully transferred to the

---

[6] http://www.codeproject.com/cs/internet/Pop3MailClient.asp

client and removed from the server. So the next time you connect, those messages won't be counted.

Now that we have the count of new emails, let's iterate through those messages and determine which ones we need to handle. We'll do this by looking at the Subject and Body content of each:

```
                                                        Program.cs (excerpt)
for (int i = mailcount; i > 0; i--)
{
  if (p.GetEmailSize(i) < 131072)
  {
    p.GetRawEmail(i, out email);
    if (MatchesSubject(email, "subcription change"))
    {
      if (MatchesBody(email, "unsubscribe"))
      {
        // do something with the email here..
        p.DeleteEmail(i);
      }
    }
  }
}
p.Disconnect();
```

In the above code, we've prevented the retrieval of any emails that are over a certain size, just in case our inbox receives an email that's too big for us to process. The criteria we've specified ensure that we only process an email when:

- The size of the email is less than 128KB (131,072 bytes).

- The email subject line contains the phrase "subscription change."

- The email body contains the word "unsubscribe."

If we see any emails that match these criteria, we'll take action in the code, then delete the emails in question.

The actual parsing of an email's subject header and body is handled by a few regular expressions:

```
                                              Program.cs (excerpt)
static Boolean MatchesSubject(string email, string subject)
{
  return Regex.IsMatch(email, @"^subject:\s.*" + subject + ".*$",
  RegexOptions.Multiline | RegexOptions.IgnoreCase);
}
static Boolean MatchesBody(string email, string text)
{
  // the body starts after the first blank line
  int bodystart = Regex.Matches(email, "^\r\n",
  RegexOptions.Multiline)[0].Index + 2;
  string body = email.Substring(bodystart);
  return Regex.IsMatch(body, text, RegexOptions.IgnoreCase);
}
```

While this code won't account for all types of, and variations in, content, it should serve as a good foundation from which you can experiment further.

Discussion

Parsing email is a complex topic that we've discussed only briefly in this solution, although an entire chapter could easily be written about it. It's difficult to know the email format your site's visitors will use, and practically impossible to force them to send only plain-text messages. The regular expressions we used above are basic, but they should work for simple "contains" tests on any email. If you need more sophisticated tests, I strongly recommend using a proper MIME parser to deal with the full breadth of the MIME format. One such formatter is the Pop3MimeClient, written by the author of the mail client I used in the above example.[7]

Heavy-duty email parsing is certainly not for the faint of heart, so be sure to equip yourself with the proper tools if you need to head down this path.

---

[7] http://www.codeproject.com/cs/internet/Pop3MimeClient.asp

Somebody Call Security!

For those processing form data in a web application, ASP.NET provides a level of protection against malicious users who try to break the application by injecting strange values, scripts, and other evil inputs into form fields. ASP.NET tries to detect cross-site scripting attacks, and its event validation feature will make sure a form receives the values it expects.

There are no such security measures in place for the acceptance of input via email. Treat all input as if it could be malicious, and *never* place the content of an email into a SQL command string, for example. Chances are that, sooner or later, someone will try to break your software via your email gateway.

How do I send an email without waiting for it to complete?

Allowing a user to send an email from a web page is simple enough, but the actual process of sending the email introduces unwanted network dependency to the page. What if the remote SMTP server is down or not responding? What if the SMTP server is responding extremely slowly? Your page won't finish loading or displaying until the email is sent, or until an error is returned from the SMTP server. This could spell disaster for the responsive user experience that the rest of your application provides!

Solution

ASP.NET 2.0 provides built-in logic for handling asynchronous events at the page level. To make use of this logic, you'll need to enable the Boolean `Async` directive in the `Page` element:

SendAsync.aspx (excerpt)

```
<%@ Page Language="C#" AutoEventWireup="true"
    CodeFile="SendAsync.aspx.cs" Inherits="_Default" Async="true" %>
```

Once you've enabled asynchronous support on the ASP.NET page, sending email asynchronously is as easy as setting up a delegate and calling the `SendAsync` method, like this:

```
MailMessage m = new MailMessage("mwaddams@initech.com",
                                "blumbergh@initech.com",
                                "Stapler",
                                "I believe you have my stapler.");
SmtpClient sc = new SmtpClient();
sc.SendCompleted +=
    new SendCompletedEventHandler(MailSendCompleted);
sc.SendAsync(m, m);
```

At first glance, this code appears to be passing the mail message twice to the `SendAsync` method, but it's not. The second parameter to `SendAsync` is a generic object token that will be passed back to the handler. We can actually pass any object we like as the second parameter, but it's convenient to use the mail object itself there so that we can refer to it later if something goes wrong.

Within the handler, we need to check the `Cancelled` and `Error` properties of the `AsyncCompletedEventArgs` object to ensure that nothing went wrong. If the `Error` property is `null`, as it is here, the email went through:

```
public static void MailSendCompleted(
object sender, AsyncCompletedEventArgs e)
{
  MailMessage m = e.UserState as MailMessage;
  if (e.Cancelled)
  {
    Debug.Write("Email to " + m.To + " was cancelled.");
  }
  if (e.Error != null)
  {
    Debug.Write("Email to " + m.To + " failed.");
    Debug.Write(e.Error.ToString());
  }
  else
    Debug.Write("Message sent.");
}
```

You can see how convenient it is to have passed in the `MailMessage` object for troubleshooting and logging purposes.

Since we've created an asynchronous operation delegate, we can't predict exactly *when* this code will run. The code could run 15 milliseconds after the user clicks **Send**, or two minutes after. So updating the user interface to provide feedback to the user about what's happening is more complicated than usual (read more about this topic in Chapter 10)—a factor that you should keep in mind when you're implementing this functionality from scratch.

 Side-stepping the Issue where Possible

I recommend that you use a logging technique—where a record of the steps taken to send the email is written to an external file—for asynchronous emails. The external file can then be used to display the status of the email when queried by the user.

With this approach, you conveniently avoid the technical hurdles involved in providing up-to-date feedback on the status of an asynchronous action.

Summary

Email support presents a unique set of challenges for a web application. Armed with the techniques outlined in this chapter, you'll be fully equipped to take advantage of the dated-but-still-useful POP3 and SMTP email protocols in your ASP.NET application.

Rendering Binary Content

Developers who spend much of their time building web applications tend to start thinking that all content is text. After all, what does our code really do other than render text to be shuttled back and forth between a web browser and the web server?

As it turns out, `text/html` is not the only MIME type that matters on the Web. There are plenty of other types of web content besides text: video files, various document files, and images, for example. Most developers think of images as static content—they're simply files that are placed in a directory and served up by the web server.

But you, intrepid reader, are not "most developers." Let's look at some of the ways in which we can take charge of this binary content.

How do I write binary content?

Let's jump right into a simple example of writing binary content. Afterwards, we'll take a step back to look at other ways of writing binary content to the browser, and to discuss what's happening under the hood.

Solution

To kick off our very simple example, add a new Web Form (.**aspx** file) to your project and implement the following code as the `Page_Load` method:

SimpleBinaryExample.aspx.cs (excerpt)

```
protected void Page_Load(object sender, EventArgs e)
{
  Byte[] binaryData = new byte[]
  {
    0x48, 0x65, 0x6C, 0x6C,
    0x6F, 0x20, 0x57, 0x6F,
    0x72, 0x6C, 0x64, 0x21
  };
  Response.OutputStream.Write(binaryData, 0, binaryData.Length);
}
```

Compile that and view the page in a browser. What happens?

Discussion

Figure 12.1 shows the results of the code.

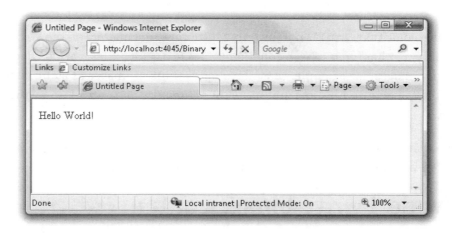

Figure 12.1. The classic Hello World example

It's not very exciting, of course, but what this code demonstrates is that we've been working with binary data all along!

All the data sent from a web server is ultimately just a stream of 1s and 0s. How the browser ends up interpreting it depends on the MIME type of that binary data. For example, by default, an ASPX page has a content type of text/html. Thus content sent from an ASPX page is interpreted by the browser as text—or, more specifically, HTML text.

How Does the Browser Interpret Binary Data?

If a web server simply returns binary data to a browser, how does the browser know how to interpret that data—how does it know to render a GIF image rather than an HTML page, for example?

When an HTTP response is returned from the web server, the header of the response contains that information. The browser knows to interpret the header as ASCII text.

This is a cut-down explanation, but that's all the detail we need for the purposes of this discussion. The point of this little exercise is to take a look under the hood of ASP.NET!

The ASP.NET team worked very hard to abstract the underlying mechanisms that come into play during a web application's development, as evidenced, among other things, but the names they gave to various objects. As you develop a new page, you might add a Web Form to your project. In Design view, you'll drag controls onto the form—a button, for example. Double-click the button and the IDE takes you to an event handler for the button click event. In some respects, building an ASP.NET page is not much different from building a Windows Forms application. However, the end result is very different. Windows Forms and Controls ultimately render bitmaps on the screen. In contrast, an ASPX page and its controls are compiled into a series of System.Web.HttpResponse.Write statements, which write text to a stream in response to a browser request.

How do I write raw data to the response?

This solution marks a slight diversion from the main topic of this chapter, but it's an important one. Whether you're writing binary content or raw (non-HTML) text content to the browser, it doesn't usually make sense to use an ASPX page to respond to such a request. What should you use?

Solution

One efficient approach is to use an `HttpHandler`. An `HttpHandler` is a class that inherits directly from `System.Web.IHttpHandler` and is responsible for responding to an HTTP request. For example, `System.Web.UI.Page`, the base class for ASPX pages, is an `HttpHandler` that typically handles requests for ***.aspx** files.

Here's the interface definition for `IHttpHandler`:

```
Interface IHttpHandler
{
  void ProcessRequest(System.Web.HttpContext context);
  bool IsReusable {get;}
}
```

The `IsReusable` property indicates whether ASP.NET can keep the handler in memory to service multiple requests, or if it must create a new instance of the handler for every request.

IsReusable Generally Shouldn't Return `false`

Unless you maintain some sort of state in the handler, which is uncommon, there's generally no reason for `IsReusable` to return `false`.

The `ProcessRequest` method is responsible for handling the request by executing any logic necessary and writing the resulting content to the `Response` stream. You'll do most of your work in the `ProcessRequest` method.

The following is an example of an `HttpHandler` that writes a short text message to the response:

```
using System.Web;

public class MyHandler : IHttpHandler
{
  public void ProcessRequest(HttpContext context)
  {
    context.Response.Write("Hello SitePoint!");
  }
  public bool IsReusable
  {
```

```
    get{return true;}
  }
}
```

Discussion

If the base class of an ASPX page is itself an `HttpHandler`, why wouldn't we just use an ASPX page to handle requests for raw data? The short answer is: it's overkill.

An ASPX page is an abstraction used to generate an HTML response to a request. When it's compiling and executing an ASPX page, ASP.NET builds up an entire control hierarchy, executes a series of events as part of the Page and Control life cycle, and writes the output to the response in order to respond to the request.

If you're sending raw content, you don't need to use this structure just to write the content to the response—you can write the content directly by implementing an `HttpHandler`.

How do I request an `HttpHandler`?

In the previous section, we discussed how to build an `HttpHandler`. But your work doesn't stop there. Once you've built your handler, how will you make a request to it?

Solutions

We can take either of two approaches to make a request to an `HttpHandler`. The first approach is to map a file extension to the handler—a process that involves two steps if you're hosting your site in IIS 5 or IIS 6. The second, which we'll cover later in this chapter, is to use a generic handler.

Using a Custom `HttpHandler`

First, you need to map the file extension you choose to the ASP.NET ISAPI DLL. Otherwise, IIS will not hand off the request to ASP.NET.

Wildcard Mappings in IIS 6

In IIS 6, ASP.NET is implemented as an ISAPI extension. Hence, only requests that IIS recognize as being handled by ASP.NET are sent along to the ASP.NET runtime.

However, it's possible to introduce wildcard mapping by mapping "*" to the ASP.NET runtime. Doing so will cause IIS to send every request to ASP.NET, including requests for static files such as images.

Although powerful, this approach can be more trouble than it's worth, as it makes you responsible for writing the code to handles requests for all file types, which can cause performance problems for your web site.

Note that if you're using IIS 7 and above you can run your ASP.NET web site in Integrated Mode. In Integrated Mode, ASP.NET is integrated into the IIS 7 pipeline, allowing you to use the **Web.config** file to choose the extensions you want to handle.

As a demonstration, let's suppose that we want to use the extension **.spt** for our custom handler. First, let's open the IIS **Default Web Site Properties** dialog—as seen in Figure 12.2—and click on the **Home Directory** tab.

Click on **Configuration...** to see the existing application extension mappings, as shown in Figure 12.3.

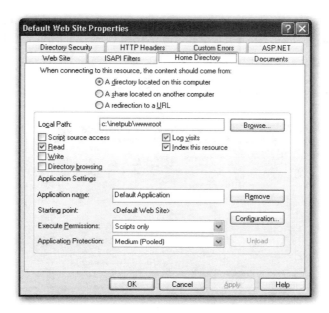

Figure 12.2. The **Default Web Site Properties** dialog

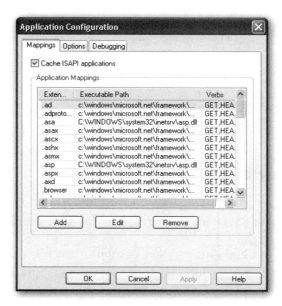

Figure 12.3. Inspecting the existing configuration of extension mappings

Click **Add** and, in the dialog that appears, which is shown in Figure 12.4, fill in the details necessary to map the **.spt** extension to the ASP.NET ISAPI DLL. For ASP.NET 2.0, the path to the extension should be:

%SystemRoot%\microsoft.net\framework\v2.0.50727\aspnet_isapi.dll

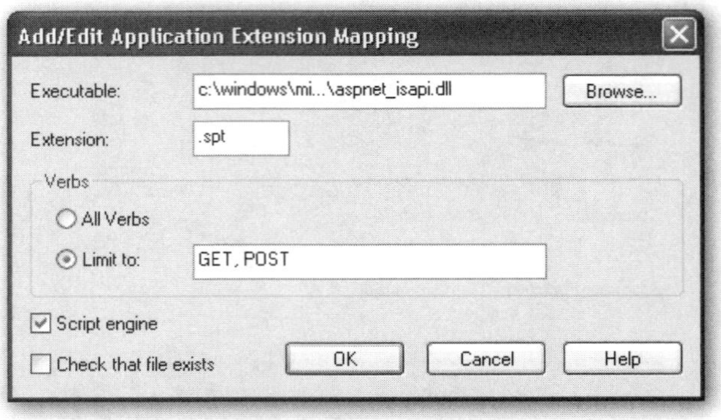

Figure 12.4. Setting up our custom mapping

To finish up, we simply need to add an appropriate entry to the `httpHandlers` section of **Web.config**, like so:

Web.config *(excerpt)*

```
<httpHandlers>
  <add verb="*" type="TypeName, AssemblyName" />
</httpHandlers>
```

Using a Generic Handler

If the ability to use a custom file extension isn't important to you, there's a much easier way to set up an `HttpHandler`—by using a generic handler.

This approach was available in ASP.NET 1.1, but it wasn't well documented or supported by VS.NET 2003, which left many developers unaware of its existence.

Fortunately, VS.NET 2005 has made it very easy to create a Generic Handler. Simply right-click on your project and select **Add New Item**. In the resulting dialog, which is depicted in Figure 12.5, select **Generic Handler**, enter the filename, and click **Add**.

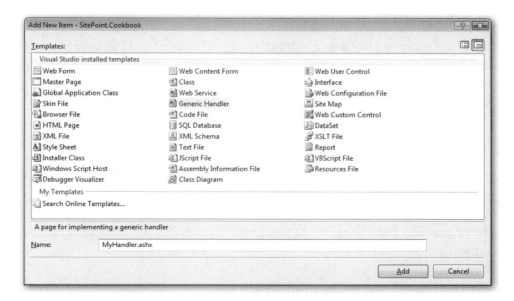

Figure 12.5. Adding a Generic Handler

This process will add a **.ashx** file to your project, as well as a **.ashx.cs** code behind file. The code behind file contains a class definition that implements `IHttpHandler`. Just implement the class, and make a request for the `.ashx` file, and you're done! There's no need to fiddle with IIS and **Web.config** settings.

We'll use this approach to set up `HttpHandlers` elsewhere in this chapter.

How do I write non-text binary data?

The past few sections have laid the groundwork. Now we're ready to really dig into the finer details of writing binary content—and this time, we'll go beyond boring text content, I promise!

Solution

Writing binary content from ASP.NET involves two key steps:

1. Set the content type.

2. Choose the proper method to write the binary content to the `Response`.

Understanding Content Types

The content type (or MIME type) indicates to the browser what kind of content is being sent. As I mentioned before, all content is sent as a stream of 1s and 0s, so we have to indicate to the browser exactly what those 1s and 0s mean.

A MIME type is a text string in two parts:

content type/subtype

For example, a MIME type of text/html indicates that the content type is text, of the subtype HTML.

Table 12.1 shows some common MIME types, though this list is by no means exhaustive (it's not even close).

Table 12.1. Some Common MIME Types

MIME Type	Description
text/html	the most common mime type on the web; represents HTML content
text/plain	defines plain text
application/vnd.ms-excel	Microsoft Excel document
image/gif	GIF-encoded image
video/mpeg	MPEG-encoded video
audio/mpeg	MPEG-encoded audio

To set the content type, we set the ContentType property of the HttpRequest instance. For example, within an HttpHandler, the following code will set the content type to image/gif and send the contents of a GIF image to the response:

ImageExample.aspx.cs (excerpt)

```
protected void Page_Load(object sender, EventArgs e)
{
  Response.Clear();
  Response.ContentType = "image/gif";

  // binary data as a base64-encoded string.
  string encoded = "R0lGODdhFAAUAIACABMTOkJCWiwAA"
```

```
                  + "AAAFAAUAAACKISPocvowGJ4S"
                  + "S567MVQT+59WMh1WkmCHrq"
                  + "qp2ux79jSM5XaMSzJVgEAOw==";
    // convert to raw bytes.
    byte[] binary = Convert.FromBase64String(encoded);
    Response.BinaryWrite(binary);
    Response.Flush();
}
```

Give that a try and see what happens. If nothing else, you'll soon understand why I'm not an artist!

 Forcing a Download Dialog to Display

If your browser is capable of rendering the content type (or has a plugin that does so), it will render the binary content when you click on a link to the handler.

However, if you'd prefer to have a **Download** dialog appear instead, you need to set the `Content-Disposition` header like so:

```
Response.AddHeader("Content-Disposition",
      "attachment; filename=\"MyFile.doc\"");
```

This code will display a **File Save** dialog in which the filename is defaulted to **MyFile.doc**.

Writing Binary Content

The approaches summarized in Table 12.2 are available for us to use to write binary content to the response. In the example above, I called the `HttpResponse.BinaryWrite` method, but we can also choose to write directly to the output stream via the `HttpResponse.OutputStream` property.

The `HttpResponse.WriteFile` method will write the contents of a file to the output stream. ASP.NET 2.0 introduces the `HttpResponse.TransmitFile` method, which is recommended over the `WriteFile` method because it incorporates streaming and avoids buffering the file in memory (`WriteFile` loads the whole file into memory).

Choose `TransmitFile` over `WriteFile`

In general, use `TransmitFile` instead of `WriteFile`, as `TransmitFile` makes better use of system memory.

Table 12.2. Four Approaches to Writing Binary Content

Method	Description
`HttpResponse.WriteFile( string )`	writes the file specified by the filename to the response; for large files, it's better to use `TransmitFile` instead
`HttpResponse.TransmitFile( string )`	streams the file to the response
`HttpResponse.BinaryWrite( byte[] )`	writes the set of specified bytes to the output stream
`HttpResponse.OutputStream`	allows you to write directly to the stream

How do I render simple bars?

For the creation of most images on a web site, you'll want to talk to Sally in the graphics team (or your graphic designer). However, there are many circumstances in which you'll want a graphic to be dynamic, either because you want to customize it for the user, or you want to regenerate it to reflect changing data. For example, if you wanted to use a bar graph to represent responses to a poll, it wouldn't make much sense to have Sally create images for every possible outcome.

Another possible application of dynamic images includes dynamically rendering skewed text as in an image CAPTCHA control (for instance, Jeff's CAPTCHA Server Control).[1] For now, we'll start with a really simple image example: drawing a bar graph.

Solution

Now we're starting to get into the world of GDI+. **GDI** stands for Graphics Device Interface—a Microsoft standard for the graphical representation of objects and for

---

[1] http://www.codeproject.com/aspnet/CaptchaControl.asp

the display of those objects on an output device such as the screen, a printer, and so on.

The plus sign in GDI+ means Microsoft has had a lot of time to improve GDI and make it easily accessible via the .NET Framework. But enough talk; let's look at how we can actually render images using this standard.

Release GDI+ Resources

GDI+ is built on unmanaged code. So when you create a reference to a `Graphics` instance or a `Bitmap`, you're dealing with an unmanaged system resource. It's important to release the resource, by calling the `Dispose` method, when you're finished with it.

In the code examples you're about to see, you'll notice we're accessing resources within `using` blocks. The `using` block is a construct provided by the compiler, and is equivalent to the more common `try/finally` pattern. It's a good idea to use `using` blocks liberally when dealing with unmanaged code; we'll see more of the `using` block later in this chapter.

We'll use a generic `HttpHandler` like the one we saw earlier in the section. For this example, we'll keep things simple by hard-coding some values and making only the width of the graphic configurable via the query string. Of course, it wouldn't be difficult to turn this into a more generally useful configurable handler, but for now, we'll stick with this simple example.

If we were to naïvely assume that all user input is safe, and directly fed the query string value to `Bitmap` constructor, we would create an open door for the entry of all sorts of invalid input. So, here's a method we'll use to grab the width (and other positive non-zero integers) from the query string:

SimpleBarHandler.ashx.cs (excerpt)

```
int GetSizeFromQueryString(HttpContext context, string key)
{
  string intText = context.Request.QueryString[key];
  int parsedInt;
  if (int.TryParse(intText, out parsedInt) && parsedInt > -1)
    return parsedInt;
  return 1;
}
```

Now we can write the body of our `ProcessRequest` method:

SimpleBarHandler.ashx.cs (excerpt)

```
public void ProcessRequest(HttpContext context)
{
  int width = GetSizeFromQueryString(context, "width");
  int height = 20; // hard-code for now.
  using(Bitmap graph = new Bitmap(width, height))
  using(Graphics g = Graphics.FromImage(graph))
  {
    g.Clear(Color.Blue);
    context.Response.ContentType = "image/gif";
    graph.Save(context.Response.OutputStream, ImageFormat.Gif);
  }
}
```

The first step we take in this code is to create an instance of a `Bitmap`. The width of the bitmap is determined by the query string parameter *width*. From that `Bitmap`, we can obtain an instance of the `System.Drawing.Graphics` object. The `Graphics` object represents a drawing surface.

For this example, we simply clear the bitmap, setting its background color to blue. We then set the content type to `image/gif` and save the bitmap to the output stream by calling the `Bitmap.Save` method.

Let's now make a simple test page in a separate HTML file:

SimpleBarTest.htm (excerpt)

```
<html>
  <head>
    <title>Bar Example</title>
    <style type="text/css">
      img {padding: 4px;}
    </style>
  </head>
  <body>
    <img src="SimpleBarHandler.ashx?width=200" />
    <br />
    <img src="SimpleBarHandler.ashx?width=175" />
    <br />
    <img src="SimpleBarHandler.ashx?width=225" />
```

```
    <br />
  </body>
</html>
```

This markup produces the page shown in Figure 12.6.

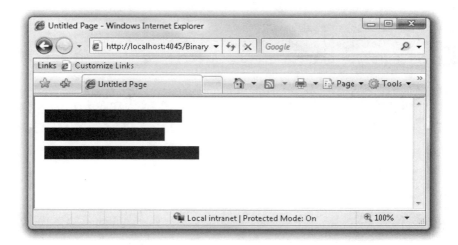

Figure 12.6. Testing our bar graph

Voilà! A bar graph!

How do I create a real bar graph handler?

The previous example was intended to give you a taste of what we can achieve with GDI+, but we didn't really do any drawing: we simply rendered a bitmap to the screen. Let's take the next step and render a full bar graph.

Solution

This example is a little more involved, and highlights a few more features of GDI+, than the last example. For the bar graph, we need three parameters: the width of the image, the scale of the data, and the data points themselves.

By "scale of the data" I mean the highest possible value that we'd want to graph. Every data point should have a value that's less than or equal to the scale. Since the scale could be larger than the width of the image, we'll have to scale the graph to fit the image's width. Let's learn how to do that now.

First, we need to grab some values from the query string; this snippet should be placed at the beginning of `ProcessRequest`:

BarGraphHandler.ashx.cs *(excerpt)*

```
int width = GetSizeFromQueryString(context, "width");
int scale = GetSizeFromQueryString(context, "scale");
int[] dataPoints = GetDataPoints(context);

// These values hard-coded for now
int barHeight = 20; // height of an individual bar
int padding = 4; // Padding between bars
```

Now, let's introduce a new method that extracts the data points from the query string:

BarGraphHandler.ashx.cs *(excerpt)*

```
int[] GetDataPoints(HttpContext context)
{
  string data = context.Request.QueryString["datapoints"];
  if (String.IsNullOrEmpty(data))
    return new int[] {};
  string[] dataPoints = data.Split(','); // Could throw an exception
  return Array.ConvertAll(dataPoints,
      new Converter<string, int>(int.Parse));
}
```

Next, we need to ensure that the scale is at least as large as the largest data point. Let's write a method for this task:

BarGraphHandler.ashx.cs *(excerpt)*

```
// Scale needs to be larger than the largest data point.
private int AdjustScaleToLargestDatapoint(int[] dataPoints,
    int scale)
{
  foreach(int dataPoint in dataPoints)
  {
```

```
    scale = Math.Max(dataPoint, scale);
  }
  return scale;
}
```

The following code calculates the total height of the image. Notice that we factor in some padding before, after, and between the bars:

BarGraphHandler.ashx.cs *(excerpt)*

```
// Get the height.
int height = (barHeight + padding) * dataPoints.Length + padding;
```

As in the previous example, we create instances of the `Bitmap` and `Graphics` classes. In this case, we set the background color to white using the `Clear` method of the `Graphic` class and draw a black border around the image using the `DrawRectangle` method. Notice that I left out the code that actually draws the data points:

BarGraphHandler.ashx.cs *(excerpt)*

```
// Create the bitmap using the scale, later
// we'll scale it down to the requested width.
using (Bitmap graph = new Bitmap(width, height))
using (Graphics g = Graphics.FromImage(graph))
{
  g.Clear(Color.White);
  // Draw a border.
  g.DrawRectangle(new Pen(Color.Black), 0, 0, graph.Width - 1,
      graph.Height - 1);
  // Draw the data paints
  // ...
  context.Response.ContentType = "image/gif";
  graph.Save(context.Response.OutputStream, ImageFormat.Gif);
}
```

We're finally ready to draw the actual data points! The code below replaces the `//` ... comment above.

Earlier I mentioned that we would need to scale the data points to fit the image. For example, suppose my data points come from a sample that contains values between

1 and 1000, but I want to render a graph that's 600 pixels wide. I'll need to scale the bar graphs to fit within the image area.

Fortunately, this task is very easily achieved with GDI+. We simply need to calculate a scaling value, and apply that scaling to the graphic's surface. Let's add a simple method to do this:

BarGraphHandler.ashx.cs (excerpt)

```
// Scale the graph to the image width.
private void ScaleGraphToImageWidth(int scale, Bitmap graph,
    Graphics g)
{
  float scaling = graph.Width /
      (float)scale;g.ScaleTransform(scaling, 1);
}
```

By calling the `Graphics.ScaleTransform` method, we can specify *x*-coordinate and *y*-coordinate scaling factors. In this case, the *x* scaling is equal to the quotient of the image width divided by the scale. Since we don't want to scale on the *y* axis, we simply set the *y* scaling factor to 1.

Now we're ready to draw the bars:

BarGraphHandler.ashx.cs (excerpt)

```
int y = padding;
foreach(int dataPoint in dataPoints)
{
  Brush brush = new SolidBrush(Color.Blue);
  g.FillRectangle(brush, 0, y, dataPoint, barHeight);
  y = y + barHeight + padding;
}
```

With GDI+, we use a `Pen` or a `Brush` to draw. A `Pen` is typically used to draw outlined shapes, whereas a `Brush` is used to draw filled shapes.

To have a little more fun, let's tweak the code that draws each bar so that it produces a slight drop-shadow effect. To do this, we'll use another `Brush` to draw a dark rectangle slightly offset from the bar. Let's go ahead and encapsulate this code in a method:

```
                                          BarGraphHandler.ashx.cs (excerpt)
private static void DrawBars(int barHeight, int[] dataPoints,
    Graphics g, int padding)
{
  int y = padding;foreach(int dataPoint in dataPoints)
  {
    Brush brush = new SolidBrush(Color.Blue);
    Brush shadow = new SolidBrush(Color.Black);
    g.FillRectangle(shadow, 0, y + 1, dataPoint + 2, barHeight);
    g.FillRectangle(brush, 0, y, dataPoint, barHeight);
    y = y + barHeight + padding;
  }
}
```

The result of our work is shown in Figure 12.7.

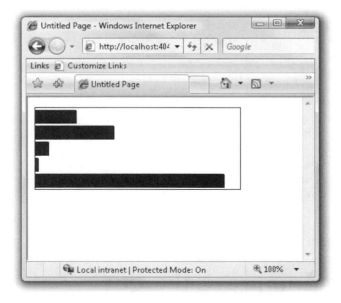

Figure 12.7. The second iteration of our bar graph

Pretty nifty, eh? Here's the full listing for the `ProcessRequest` method of the handler, not including the helper methods we just wrote:

```
public void ProcessRequest(HttpContext context)
{
  int width = GetSizeFromQueryString(context, "width");
  int scale = GetSizeFromQueryString(context, "scale");
  int[] dataPoints = GetDataPoints(context);

  // These values hard-coded for now.
  int barHeight = 20; // height of an individual bar.
  int padding = 4; // Padding between bars.
  scale = AdjustScaleToLargestDatapoint(dataPoints, scale);

  // Get the height.
  int height = (barHeight + padding) * dataPoints.Length
      + padding;

  // Create the bitmap using the scale, later
  // we'll scale it down to the requested width.
  using (Bitmap graph = new Bitmap(width, height))
  using (Graphics g = Graphics.FromImage(graph))
  {
    g.Clear(Color.White);

    // Draw a border.
    g.DrawRectangle(new Pen(Color.Black), 0, 0, graph.Width - 1,
        graph.Height - 1);
    ScaleGraphToImageWidth(scale, graph, g);
    DrawBars(barHeight, dataPoints, g, padding);
    context.Response.ContentType = "image/gif";
    graph.Save(context.Response.OutputStream, ImageFormat.Gif);
  }
}
```

How can I improve the quality of my dynamic images?

As exciting as it is to see dynamically created images display in your browser for the first time, you may be disappointed by the quality of those images. Your image handler won't be complete until you spend some time with image rendering formats and image quality.

Solution

There are two parts to this solution: picking the right image format, and using the appropriate rendering settings to optimize the image quality.

The PNG (Portable Network Graphic) format is usually the best for general-purpose web images, and its default settings will provide you with a good quality output at a reasonable file size. There's one gotcha in the process of rendering PNGs to the response stream, though: the PNG renderer requires a **seekable stream** (one that is not forward-only).

Unfortunately, `Response.OutputStream` is not seekable, so one has to employ a seekable `MemoryStream` to bridge the gap. Allow me to explain with an example.

Most image formats can be saved directly to the output stream, like this:

```
Response.ContentType = "image/jpeg";
image.Save(Response.OutputStream, ImageFormat.Jpeg);
```

However, when you render a PNG, you need to copy it to a memory stream, and output that to the browser:

ProtectedImageHandler.ashx *(excerpt)*

```
using (Bitmap bitmapCopy = new Bitmap(image))
{
  System.IO.MemoryStream memoryStream =
      new System.IO.MemoryStream();
  Response.ContentType = "image/png";
  bitmapCopy.Save(
      memoryStream,
      System.Drawing.Imaging.ImageFormat.Png
  );
  memoryStream.WriteTo(Response.OutputStream);
}
Response.End();
```

JPEG is generally a good format for photographs, but the default JPEG encoder settings might not give you sufficient image quality. You can change the quality of the image by modifying the encoder parameters like this:

```
                                    ProtectedImageHandler.ashx (excerpt)
ImageCodecInfo[] codecs = ImageCodecInfo.GetImageEncoders();
ImageCodecInfo jpegFormat = Array.Find(codecs,
    delegate(ImageCodecInfo ic)
    {return ic.MimeType == "image/jpeg";});
EncoderParameters ep = new EncoderParameters();
ep.Param[0] = new EncoderParameter(
    System.Drawing.Imaging.Encoder.Quality,90L);
Response.ContentType = "image/jpeg";
image.Save(Response.OutputStream,jpegFormat,ep);
```

GIF is the most difficult of the major image formats to get right. Unless you have some very good reasons to use GIF, I'd recommend using PNG format instead. There are only a few reasons why you might use GIF instead of PNG:

▓ GIF is the only widely supported image format that supports animation.

▓ GIF is the only widely supported image format that supports transparency. While PNG's transparency support is better than GIF's, Internet Explorer 6 doesn't support 24-bit PNGs properly without a CSS hack to invoke a DirectX filter.

▓ You may be sending the images as file downloads or interacting in other ways with systems or users who expect or require GIF images.

Discussion

If you need to support GIF, you'll need to use a different quantizer to improve the image quality. GIF image encoding condenses the color spectrum from the original image to a 256-color (eight-bit) palette, and the process of selecting the color palette and mapping individuals to the correct palletized color is called **quantization**. The default GIF quantizer that ships with System.Drawing isn't going to help you win any design awards, though—unless you're going for a really bad retro look.

What's Wrong with the Default GIF Encoder?

The main problem with the `System.Drawing` GIF quantizer is that it uses the same palette for every image—the standard Windows 256-color palette. That might have made sense ten years ago, but now that virtually all computers have 16-bit color as a minimum, it doesn't make much sense. The end result of using this quantizer is that more than 99% of viewers with decent video cards see ugly images as we strive to improve slightly the image quality for a few ancient computers with eight-bit graphics (whose owners clearly don't care much about graphic quality anyway).

Fortunately, a number of freely available quantizers will appear in the results of a web search for **gif system.drawing quantize**. Morgan Skinner wrote a great article for MSDN in May 2003, titled "Optimizing Color Quantization for ASP.NET Images."[2] The article shows how to use Octree Quantization to build a custom palette of 256 colors for your image.[3]

Morgan's `OctreeQuantizer` is fairly simple to use. Here's an example:

```
Response.ContentType = "image/gif";
OctreeQuantizer quantizer = new OctreeQuantizer (255,8);
using (Bitmap quantizedImage = quantizer.Quantize(image))
{
  quantizedImage.Save (Response.OutputStream ,ImageFormat.Gif);
}
```

How can I use a handler to control access to the images on my site?

HTML wasn't designed to protect your images. An image element's `src` attribute clearly displays the image's location, and can reference any image on the Internet.

Since images are so exposed online, it's very easy for others to use our images in ways we might not have anticipated:

---

[2] http://msdn2.microsoft.com/en-us/library/aa479306.aspx

[3] For a short summary of the research, see Brendan Tompkins's article, which includes some sample code, at http://codebetter.com/blogs/6103.aspx.

- They can download our images and use them in ways we don't want to allow (displaying them on their sites, for instance, defacing them, and so on).

- They can show our images on their sites, a practice referred to as **hotlinking**, which looks like this:

```
<body>
  <div>Here is Google's logo:</div>
  <img src='http://www.google.com/intl/en_ALL/images/logo.gif' />
</body>
```

Hotlinking causes two problems—in addition to the fact that others are using our image as if it were theirs, the image thieves are using our bandwidth to serve the image on their sites! This can be a real problem when your image is hotlinked from a popular site, as the extra bandwidth required to serve the image can cause site outages and additional bandwidth fees.

Ultimately, we'd like to allow the legitimate use of our images within our site, but discourage others from using our images.

Solution

We'll use an `HttpHandler` to serve our protected images. The handler will perform the following tasks:

- It will add a watermark to each image.

- It will issue with each image a key that expires after a set number of seconds as a means to discourage hotlinking. Images that are shown within our site will be issued fresh keys and will display correctly, but the use of those image links after they've been issued will cause the display of downgraded images over which our site's URL is written.

- Since the above operations will add some overhead to the site, we'll cache the processed images.

This discussion will be easier to follow if we look at how the handler will be used in an ASPX page first. Here's an example page that will display images using our protected image handler:

```
<%@ Page Language="C#" AutoEventWireup="true" %>
<script runat="server">
  void Page_Load(object sender, EventArgs e)
  {
    System.IO.DirectoryInfo dir =
        new System.IO.DirectoryInfo(Server.MapPath("images"));
    imageRepeater.DataSource = dir.GetFiles();
    imageRepeater.DataBind();
  }
</script>
<html>
  <head>
    <title>Image Handler Example</title>
    <style type="text/css">
      img {padding: 4px; float: left; clear: both;}
    </style>
  </head>
  <body>
    <asp:Repeater ID="imageRepeater" runat="server">
      <ItemTemplate>
        <img src='<%# "ProtectedImageHandler.ashx?image=images\\'+
            Eval("Name")+ '&key=" + HotlinkProtection.GetKey() %>'
            />
      </ItemTemplate>
    </asp:Repeater>
  </body>
</html>
```

Not too bad, huh? Here, we're just data binding a `Repeater` to a list of files in a directory, and passing each filename to our `ProtectedImageHandler`. We're also passing a key in the query string, which is supplied by the `HotlinkProtection` class.

`HotlinkProtection` is fairly simple: it issues and validates time-sensitive keys. This way, we'll allow images to be requested when our page is requested, not separately. The class exposes two public methods:

GetKey   GetKey returns a key. Our keys are timestamps that identify the number of seconds that passed between January 1st, 2005 and the point at which the key was generated, multiplied by an arbitrary value that makes it harder to guess the keys. Note that the level of security we chose here is commensurate with the value of the content we're protecting. If we were protecting the access details for a database, we'd choose a stronger level of security.

IsKeyValid   IsKeyValid validates that the key was issued recently. It takes two parameters: a key and a timeout. The method converts the key into a timestamp, then checks whether or not that timestamp occurred within the range specified by *timeoutSeconds*. We're using an absolute value difference to prevent guessing; otherwise, our application could be tricked by a very large *key* value.

Here's HotlinkProtection:

HotlinkProtection.cs *(excerpt)*

```csharp
public class HotlinkProtection
{
  // Site specific multiplier - might want to keep in Web.config
  private const long multiplier = 298467;
  public static long GetKey()
  {
    int minutes = GetSecondCount();
    return (multiplier * minutes);
  }
  private static int GetSecondCount()
  {
    TimeSpan span = DateTime.Now - new DateTime(2005, 1, 1);
    return (int)span.TotalSeconds;
  }
  public static bool IsKeyValid(long key, int timeoutSeconds)
  {
    try
    {
      int seconds = (int)(key / multiplier);
      int difference = Math.Abs(GetSecondCount() - seconds);
      return (difference < timeoutSeconds);
    }
    catch
    {
      return false;
```

```
      }
    }
  }
```

The `IsKeyValid` method makes it really easy for our image handler to check if the image is hotlinked:

```
                                            HotlinkProtection.cs (excerpt)
bool hotlinked = true;
long key;
// A key is only good for 30 seconds after it is issued
if (long.TryParse(context.Request.QueryString["key"], out key))
  hotlinked = !HotlinkProtection.IsKeyValid(key, 30);
else
  hotlinked = true;
```

Figure 12.8 depicts how an image looks when it's displayed from within our site. Notice that there's a discreet watermark in the lower left-hand corner.

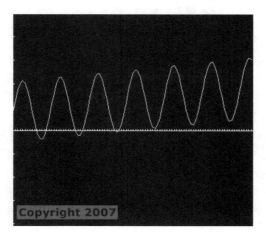

Figure 12.8. Applying a watermark to a hotlinked image

That image was referenced with a key that was generated when the HTML page was rendered. Each time the page is viewed, a new key is issued; it's valid for 30 seconds (which should be plenty of time for the browser to download the HTML and start to request the image).

Here's what a valid image request might look like:

http://localhost:2480/ImageHandler/ProtectedImageHandler.ashx?image=images\
➥sampleImage.png&key=19278441079911

Attempting to view the image via the above link (or without a key) will trigger our hotlink protection mechanism, which paints over the image with a hatched brush, and writes the domain of our web site over the degraded image. The effects of this mechanism can be seen in Figure 12.9.

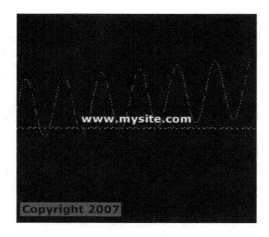

Figure 12.9. The result of loading our image from an external site

Let's look at the `ProcessRequest` method to get an idea of the overall flow of the code; we'll then dig into the hotlink and watermark methods in more detail:

ProtectedImageHandler.ashx *(excerpt)*

```
public void ProcessRequest(HttpContext context)
{
  string imagePath = context.Request.QueryString["image"];
  bool hotlinked = true;long key;

  // A key is only good for 30 seconds after it is issued
  if (long.TryParse(context.Request.QueryString["key"], out key))
    hotlinked = !HotlinkProtection.IsKeyValid(key, 30);
  else
    hotlinked = true;

  // Check if image is cached to avoid extra graphic processing
```

```csharp
Image cachedImage =
    context.Cache[GetCacheKey(imagePath,hotlinked)] as Image;
if (cachedImage != null)
{
  // We have a valid cached image, so just write it and return
  context.Response.ContentType = "image/jpeg";
  cachedImage.Save(context.Response.OutputStream,
      ImageFormat.Jpeg);
  return;
}
Image image = null;
Graphics graphics = null;
try
{
  string watermark ="Copyright " +
      GetCopyrightYear(image,DateTime.Now.Year.ToString());
  string sitename = "www.mysite.com";
  image = ConvertFromIndexed(Image.FromFile(
      context.Server.MapPath(imagePath)));
  graphics = Graphics.FromImage(image);

  // Pick an appropriate font size depending on image size
  int fontsize = 16;if (image.Width > 400) fontsize = 24;

  // Set up the font
  graphics.TextRenderingHint = TextRenderingHint.AntiAlias;
  Font font = new Font("Verdana",
      fontsize, System.Drawing.FontStyle.Bold,
      System.Drawing.GraphicsUnit.Pixel);
  if (hotlinked)
  {
    WriteHotlinkMessage(context, image, sitename,
        graphics, font);
  }
  WriteWatermark(image, watermark, graphics, font);

  // Add image to cache.
  // Must clone image since it will be disposed
  context.Cache.Insert(GetCacheKey(imagePath,hotlinked),
      image.Clone());

  // Output as PNG
  using (Bitmap bitmapCopy = new Bitmap(image))
  {
    System.IO.MemoryStream memoryStream =
```

```
        new System.IO.MemoryStream();
      context.Response.ContentType = "image/png";
      bitmapCopy.Save(
          memoryStream,System.Drawing.Imaging.ImageFormat.Png);
      memoryStream.WriteTo(context.Response.OutputStream);
    }
    context.Response.End();
  }
  finally
  {
    if(graphics!=null)
      graphics.Dispose();
    if(image!=null)
      image.Dispose();
  }
}
```

Let's look at the general graphics handling, as implemented above. It's important
to dispose of our graphics objects, since they use system resources. That's always
important, but it's especially important in server code:

```
Image image = null;
try
{
  image = Image.FromFile(imagePath);
  // WORK WITH IMAGE
}
finally
{
  image.Dispose();
}
```

Here's what's happening in the code:

■ Declare the GDI object.

■ Wrap the code that creates and uses the object in a `try` block.

■ Dispose of the object in a `finally` block.

We're using the same pattern for both the `Graphics` and `Image` objects:

```
Image image = null;
try
{
  image = GetImage();
  // WORK WITH IMAGE
}
finally
{
  if(image != null)
  image.Dispose();
}
```

Making Use of using

C# offers a shorthand syntax for the above pattern—the `using` block. `using` is a construct provided by the compiler; it expands from `using` to the `try/finally` pattern we saw in the previous example. Even cooler is that you can stack up `using` blocks, and the compiler will make sure that it disposes of each of the objects in the proper order:

```
using (Image image = Image.FromFile(imagePath))
using (Graphics g = Graphics.FromImage(image))
{
  // WORK WITH GDI OBJECTS
}
```

I highly recommend the `using` syntax—it's clean, and it's foolproof since we can rely on the compiler to dispose of the right object at the right time. Why on earth didn't I use that syntax in the example, then? Well, I wanted to pass the `Image` and `Graphics` objects by reference to a function that could modify them, and that's not allowed within a `using` block.

Let's look at the watermark generation code:

ProtectedImageHandler.ashx *(excerpt)*

```
private static void WriteWatermark(Image image, string watermark,
    Graphics g, Font font)
{
  // Determine size of watermark to write background
  SizeF watermarkSize = g.MeasureString(watermark, font);
  int xPosition = 5;
```

```
    int yPosition = image.Height - (int)watermarkSize.Height - 10;

    // Draw a translucent (alpha = 100) background for watermark
    g.FillRectangle(
      new SolidBrush(
        Color.FromArgb(100, Color.GhostWhite)
      ),
      new Rectangle(
        xPosition, yPosition,
        (int)watermarkSize.Width,
        (int)watermarkSize.Height
      )
    );

    // Write watermark
    g.DrawString(
      watermark,
      font,
      new SolidBrush(Color.Blue),
      xPosition,
      yPosition
    );
}
```

Here, we're using the same GDI+ features we used in the section called "How do I create a real bar graph handler?". But this time, we've added some simple text operations, which are handled by MeasureString and DrawString. Both of these operations require a Font object; we'll use the one we created in ProcessRequest:

ProtectedImageHandler.ashx *(excerpt)*

```
Font font = new Font("Verdana", 16,
    System.Drawing.FontStyle.Bold,
    System.Drawing.GraphicsUnit.Pixel);
```

This code is fairly straightforward. The first parameter is the font; it could be Verdana, Tahoma, Arial—whichever font you like. The font size is a Float value, which is used in conjunction with the GraphicsUnit. In this case, we're specifying the font size as 16 pixels. Any guesses what FontStyle.Bold does?

Let's use a TextRenderingHint to make the text smoother:

ProtectedImageHandler.ashx *(excerpt)*

```
g.TextRenderingHint = TextRenderingHint.AntiAlias;
```

Before we draw the text onto our image, we'll want to know how big the text will be. We need those dimensions for the watermark because we're going to put the text on top of a light-colored rectangular background; we'll also be using the rectangle's dimensions to center the hotlink message later. One other reason you might measure the text is to ascertain whether or not it's going to fit in the area you've got available; if it won't fit, you might shrink the font or decide to write a shorter text string.

MeasureString takes a string of text and a Font object:

ProtectedImageHandler.ashx *(excerpt)*

```
SizeF textSize = g.MeasureString(textToWrite, font);
```

The return value is a SizeF struct, which is a simple container for two Floats, Height and Width.

We want our watermark to be readable (but not obnoxious) over any image, be it light, dark, or in-between. In order to achieve that, we're drawing with a kind of dark brush (blue) on top of a light-colored translucent background. We'll make the light-colored background translucent by setting the *alpha* index to 100. The *alpha* index ranges from 0 (not visible at all) to 255 (fully opaque). A light background with an *alpha* index of 100 is sufficient to make sure that our blue text is readable on top of a black image:

ProtectedImageHandler.ashx *(excerpt)*

```
g.FillRectangle(
   new SolidBrush(Color.FromArgb(100, Color.GhostWhite)),
   new Rectangle(xPosition,
   yPosition,
   (int)watermarkSize.Width,
   (int)watermarkSize.Height)
);
```

Hotlinked images are overlaid with a hatched foreground which leaves the image viewable but ugly. The desired effect is to embarrass the hotlinker into removing the image from the site and, before it's removed, to direct viewers to our site to see the original. Here's how the `WriteHotlinkMessage` method works:

ProtectedImageHandler.ashx *(excerpt)*

```
private static void WriteHotlinkMessage(
    HttpContext context, Image image, string sitename,
    Graphics g, Font font)
{
  // If hotlinked, draw hatched overlay
  g.FillRectangle(
    new HatchBrush(HatchStyle.LargeConfetti,
        Color.FromArgb(90, Color.Blue)
    ),
    new Rectangle(0, 0, image.Width,
        image.Height)
  );

  // Write our site name in the center of the image
  SizeF siteSize = g.MeasureString(sitename, font);
  g.DrawString(sitename, font,
      new SolidBrush(Color.White),
      (image.Width - siteSize.Width) / 2,
      (image.Height - siteSize.Height) / 2);
  context.Response.Cache.SetCacheability(
    HttpCacheability.Public);
}
```

We're drawing the foreground using `FillRectangle` with a `HatchedBrush`. The `HatchedBrush` constructor takes a `HatchStyle` and a color, and `FillRectangle` is defined as the entire image size:

ProtectedImageHandler.ashx *(excerpt)*

```
g.FillRectangle(
  new HatchBrush(
    HatchStyle.LargeConfetti,
    Color.FromArgb(90, Color.Blue)
  ),
  new Rectangle(0, 0, image.Width, image.Height)
);
```

Our hotlink label is centered on the image. To achieve this, we measure the string, then subtract half the height and half the width from the center point of the image:

ProtectedImageHandler.ashx *(excerpt)*

```
SizeF siteSize = g.MeasureString(sitename, font);
g.DrawString(sitename, font,
    new SolidBrush(Color.White),
    (image.Width-siteSize.Width)/2,
    (image.Height-siteSize.Height)/2);
```

The `Image` object has the capability to expose metadata stored in the source image file. Though metadata may or may not be present in any JPEG image, it's most commonly available in images from a digital camera, and contains additional information that describes those images. Within the digital photography world, this kind of information is referred to as EXIF data. Some examples of common EXIF properties include the date the image was generated, the camera's make, and the shutter speed.

The `Image` object exposes metadata via the `GetPropertyItem` method. This method is as user friendly as a malnourished pit-bull. You have to pass in an integer identifier to the property you want; for example, the identifier for the date on which the image was created is 36867. An `enum` for these values would be much easier to work with, so we've provided one with this code.

EXIF Specifications

If you'd like to know more about specific EXIF fields (or you're having trouble falling asleep and would like some help), you can read the specifications online.[4]

We've included some very basic EXIF handling code to get you started if you want to read images' metadata properties. If you call `Image.GetPropertyItem` with the correct integer index, and the image doesn't have that property, the code will return `null`; if the property does exist, the code will return a `PropertyItem`. The `PropertyItem`'s `Value` is a byte array, so you'll need to convert it to the correct data type in order to work with it. We're working with all our data as strings, so we'll use the `System.UFT8.Encoding.GetString` method to convert the byte array:

---

[4] http://exif.org/specifications.html

ProtectedImageHandler.ashx *(excerpt)*

```
private bool GetExifString(
  Image image, ExifValues exifProperty, out string value)
{
  value = null;
  try
  {
    PropertyItem propertyItem =
        image.GetPropertyItem((int)exifProperty);
    if (propertyItem != null)
    {
      value = Encoding.UTF8.GetString(propertyItem.Value).Trim()
          as string;
    }
  }
  catch { }
  return !string.IsNullOrEmpty(value);
}
```

Summary

In this chapter we've seen how you can create more than just text/html content with ASP.NET code. It takes some work, but once you've learned the core concepts we've discussed in these pages, you'll be able to have your web site serve up a lot more than just text. Have fun, and remember to use your new-found powers for good!

Handling Errors

Sometimes it's hard to tell a professional programmer and an amateur programmer apart—both make mistakes in equal measure. However, there is a difference: professional programmers *know* when they've made a mistake; amateurs rarely do.

One of the first things a professional programmer does when setting up a new web project is to establish a strategy for receiving notifications of mistakes—some method of automatically handing the inevitable error messages that users will encounter as they using the web site.

It's not the user's job to tell you about problems with your web site—as a responsible software developer, *you* should know about problems with your web site before your users do!

How can I handle exceptions in my code?

Very few developers get exception handling right the first time. It's all too common to find code like this:

```
try
{
   // do something that may cause an error
}
catch (Exception ex)
{
   // handle any exception here
}
```

This is rarely the correct strategy. There are some circumstances in which you may need to catch *every* exception, but you should avoid doing so whenever possible.

Solution

Here are some guidelines that I've found useful when dealing with exceptions in my own code:

The golden rule of exception handling: unless you have a good reason to catch an exception, *don't!*

It's okay to catch exceptions in exceptional conditions. Exceptions are *supposed* to be exceptional, as the dictionary definition for the word (*uncommon, unusual*) indicates. When in doubt, let the calling routine—or the global exception handler—deal with the problem. The exceptions that are the most difficult to troubleshoot are those that don't exist, because a developer upstream from you decided it was a good idea to consume the exception, leaving you with nothing but a broken application and no visible symptoms. Once you've had to troubleshoot one of these monsters, you'll vow to never catch exceptions blindly again. So, always remember: when in doubt, do not catch any exceptions.

Catch the exception if you can correct the problem that it implies.

For example, if you try to write to a file that's marked as read-only, try removing the read-only flag from the file. In this case, you'd handle the exception and fix the problem, so you should eat the exception. It doesn't exist, because you fixed it.

Catch the exception if you can provide additional information to the user.

For example, if your application fails to connect via HTTP to a remote web site, you could provide details about why the connection failed. Was the DNS invalid? Did it time out? Was the connection closed? Did the site return 401 Unauthorized, which implies that credentials are needed? In these cases you want to catch the exception, and re-throw it as an inner exception with more information. This is a very good reason to catch an exception, but note that we are still re-throwing it.

Catch specific exceptions, but let the rest pass through.
Avoid catching System.Exception whenever possible; try to catch only the errors that are specific to a given block of code, and let the truly unusual rest become unhandled exceptions.

Of course, there will be times when you'll want to bend these rules for completely legitimate reasons—but at least consider the rules before you break them!

Also, if you need to re-throw an exception, be careful how you do it. Always re-throw the exception using the throw keyword with no parameters, like so:

```
try
{
  command.Execute();
  TransactionManager.Commit();
}
catch(Exception exception)
{
  TransactionManager.Rollback();
  throw;
}
```

Remember that the stack trace is created at the time you throw the exception, so using the throw keyword on its own like this (rather than using throw exception) preserves the stack trace of the original exception.

How can I handle errors in my web site?

This is one of the first questions you should think about when you set out to develop a web application. ASP.NET doesn't provide you with a global exception handling strategy out of the box. Fortunately, it does provide several different approaches for handling global exceptions in code. Each approach comes with its own advantages and disadvantages.

Solutions

The three options you can use to handle exceptions are:

- using the built-in health monitoring support
- setting exception handling settings in a **global.asax** and in the **Web.config** file
- using the `HttpModule` class

Let's look at each in turn.

Handling Exceptions Via Health Monitoring

One of the easiest ways to implement a global exception handler is to use the built-in ASP.NET health monitoring support.

Check the Event Log

In the absence of any other unhandled exception strategy, ASP.NET 2.0 does in fact log unhandled exceptions to the event log. It's not my favorite place to dig around for errors, but it's better than nothing.

To enable automatic email notifications of unhandled exceptions via health monitoring, simply add this section to your **Web.config** file:

Web.config *(excerpt)*

```
<healthMonitoring enabled="true">
  <providers>
    <add name="MailProvider"
        type="System.Web.Management.SimpleMailWebEventProvider"
        from="webserver@example.com"
        to="you@example.com"
        subjectPrefix="Unhandled Exception: "
        bufferMode="Critical Notification"
    />
  </providers>
  <rules>
    <remove name="All Errors Default"/>
    <remove name="Failure Audits Default"/>
    <add name="All Errors Default"
        eventName="All Errors"
        provider="MailProvider"
```

```
      />
    </rules>
</healthMonitoring>
```

For this code to work, you'll also need to set up `System.Net.Mail` SMTP email support in your **Web.config**. Here's a representative section that enables the most basic SMTP settings for a server named `localhost`:

Web.config *(excerpt)*

```
<system.net>
  <mailSettings>
    <smtp>
      <network host="localhost" />
    </smtp>
  </mailSettings>
</system.net>
```

And that's it! Now every unhandled exception will automatically generate an email that's sent to you. The email, shown in Figure 13.1, is not a paragon of great formatting, but it gets the job done.

Of course, ASP.NET doesn't limit you to using email notifications—you can use any of the built-in health monitoring event providers to direct your exception information to one or more of the following providers:

- `EventLogWebEventProvider`: This class writes events to the window's event log for posterity. Writing exceptions to this class is enabled by default.

- `SqlWebEventProvider`: This class writes events to your application's database.

- `WmiWebEventProvider`: This class publishes events to the Windows Management Instrumentation. Other applications can consume these WMI events in order to alert system administrators that an exception has occurred.

- `SimpleMailWebEventProvider`: This class sends an email (for example, to a system administrator) in response to application health events.

■ TraceWebEventProvider: This class publishes events to the
System.Diagnostics.Trace object. This data can then be collected by a
TraceListener for debugging purposes.

Conspicuously absent from that list is any sort of disk or file destination. You could
write your own provider, but that defeats the no-code advantage of the health
monitoring solution. Luckily, armed with the providers in the above list, we have
several good alternatives to writing to a file. The official MSDN documentation for
contains more information about these and other related classes.[1]

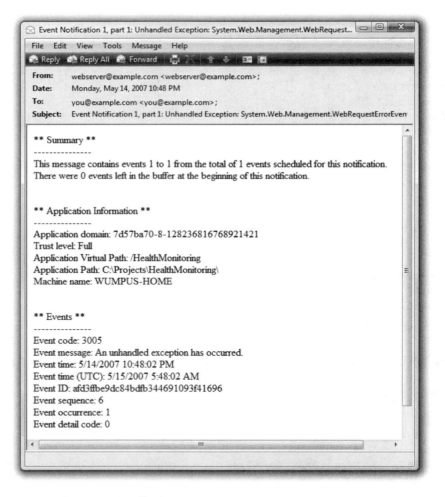

Figure 13.1. A notification email containing a list of unhandled exceptions

---

[1] http://msdn2.microsoft.com/en-us/library/system.web.management.aspx

Specifying Exception Handling in the global.asax and Web.config Files

The conventional way that you should implement a global exception handler is through **global.asax** and **Web.config**.

If your project doesn't contain a **global.asax** file, add one by accessing the **Add New Item** menu and selecting **Global Application Class**. Then locate the `Application_Error` method in this file and modify it to capture the error:

```
void Application_Error(object sender, EventArgs e)
{
  Exception ex =
  HttpContext.Current.Server.GetLastError();
  if (ex != null)
  {
    ErrorHandler.HandleException(ex);
  }
}
```

Next, create a new static class called `ErrorHandler` and add to it a new method called `HandleException` that deals with the exception:

```
public static class ErrorHandler
{
  public static void HandleException(Exception ex)
  {
    if (ex == null)
      return;
    Exception exceptionLayer = null;
    if (ex is HttpUnhandledException)
    {
      if (ex.InnerException != null)
        exceptionLayer = ex.InnerException;
    }
    else
    {
      exceptionLayer = ex;
    }
    StringBuilder sb = new StringBuilder();
    while (exceptionLayer != null)
    {
      sb.AppendLine(ex.ToString());
```

```
      sb.AppendLine("------------------------");
      exceptionLayer = exceptionLayer.InnerException;
    }
    Log(sb.ToString());
  }
}
```

The code is relatively straightforward. We make a point of discarding the outer `HttpUnhandledException`—it's a standard wrapper that comes with every ASP.NET exception. We have to peel that layer away to get to the `InnerException` (and *its* `InnerException`, and so on) that contains the *real* error.

Notice that, at this point in the code, I haven't populated the generic `Log` method, so the exception isn't being passed anywhere just yet. You could easily write your own `Log` method to send the exception via email, log it to a file, and so forth. But rather than write a whole lot of extra code, you might want to save some time by handing the exception off to the open source Log4net logging framework, which we'll cover in the section called "What's the best way to write a log file?" later in this chapter.

So we've satisfied our professional obligations as programmers, but what about those poor old users? It's bad form to let them see the Yellow Screen of Death shown in Figure 13.2.

If we're going to the trouble of implementing a global exception handling strategy behind the scenes, we might as well go the final mile and implement a friendlier user interface for users who are unlucky enough to encounter an exception.

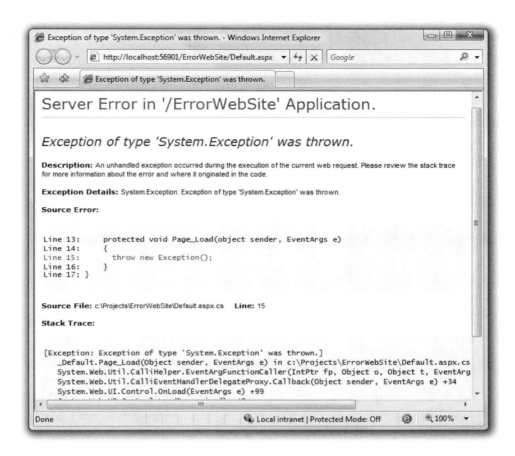

Figure 13.2. The Yellow Screen of Death—an ugly exception presented to the user

Implementing a custom error page is as simple as editing **Web.config** and adding a `customErrors` element within the **system.web** section that points to your custom file:

```
                                                            Web.config (excerpt)

<system.web>
  <customErrors mode="On" defaultRedirect="~/Error.aspx">
  </customErrors>
    ⋮
</system.web>
```

With this change, we've given the Yellow Screen of Death a friendlier face, as Figure 13.3 illustrates.

Figure 13.3. A more user-friendly error screen for users

As you can see, in this case, doing the right thing by users is very easy. They're already disappointed because your web site has crashed—don't make matters worse by scaring them with the awful default ASP.NET error page.

Handling Errors Via `HttpModule`

There's nothing wrong with the methods we've discussed so far, but by far the most *flexible* way to implement global exception handling is to use the `HttpModule` class.

First, let's create a class library project containing a new `HttpModule`:

```
public class ExceptionHandlingModule : IHttpModule
{
  public void Init(System.Web.HttpApplication app)
  {
    app.Error += new EventHandler(OnError);
  }
  private void OnError(object sender, EventArgs e)
  {
    HttpApplication app = (HttpApplication)sender;
    ErrorHandler.HandleException(app.Server.GetLastError());
  }
  public void Dispose()
  {
    // Nothing to Dispose()  }
}
```

Clean Up After Yourself!

It's not relevant in this example, but it's worth mentioning: if you're planning to present a custom interface to the user via code that utilizes the `Response.Write` method or something similar, you must clear the existing error before continuing. The following line of code will take care of that:

```
app.Server.ClearError();
```

Compile that class library, and add a reference to it from your web project or web site. Then edit **Web.config** as follows to reference our brand new `HttpModule`:

```
<httpModules>
  <add type="ExceptionHandlingModule,
       ExceptionLibrary"
       name="ErrorHandler" />
</httpModules>
```

The big advantage of this approach is that it doesn't require you to make any code changes in the web site that uses it.

The compiled `HttpModule`, along with the error handling logic, can be delivered in a single DLL file. Simply add that file to the web site path, then modify **Web.config**, and you have a perfectly portable and reusable global exception handling strategy to use across all of your web sites.

How can I use a pre-built exception handling strategy?

The exception handling strategies we explored earlier all require some coding on our part to deliver a complete solution. Luckily, there's a pre-built global exception handler that we can employ to avoid doing all that extra work—it even uses the flexible `HttpModule` model.

Solution

For a robust, global exception handling strategy that you can easily plug into a web site, look no further than the ELMAH (Error Logging Modules And Handlers) solution.[2]

Add a reference to the ELMAH binary in your web site or web application project. To enable ELMAH, edit your **Web.config** file and add a custom configuration section that instructs ELMAH on how we want it to handle errors, like so:

Web.config *(excerpt)*

```
<configSections>
  <sectionGroup name="elmah">
    <section name="errorLog"
        type="System.Configuration.SingleTagSectionHandler"/>
    <section name="errorMail"
        type="System.Configuration.SingleTagSectionHandler"/>
  </sectionGroup>
</configSections>
<elmah>
  <errorLog type="CodePlex.Elmah.MemoryErrorLog, CodePlex.Elmah"
      connectionStringName="ErrorDB"/>
  <errorMail from="webserver@domain.com"
      to="me@domain.com" subject="Application Error" async="true"/>
</elmah>
```

ELMAH supports a number of logging configurations, including the use of a SQL Server database, a MySQL database, and an XML file, but for this example we're going to use the in-memory database. We'll also want an email to be sent asynchronously when an error occurs.

Since we're sending mail, we'll need to add the SMTP configuration block for Sys-tem.Net.Mail to our **Web.config** file, like so:

Web.config *(excerpt)*

```
<system.net>
  <mailSettings>
    <smtp>
```

---

[2] http://code.google.com/p/elmah/

```
      <network host="localhost"/>
    </smtp>
  </mailSettings>
</system.net>
```

Finally, we need to configure the ELMAH `httpModules` and `httpHandlers`. Add these to the `system.web` section, as I've done here:

Web.config (excerpt)

```
<httpModules>
  <add name="ErrorLog"
      type="CodePlex.Elmah.ErrorLogModule, CodePlex.Elmah" />
  <add name="ErrorMail"
      type="CodePlex.Elmah.ErrorMailModule, CodePlex.Elmah" />
</httpModules>,
<httpHandlers>
  <add verb="POST,GET,HEAD" path="elmah/default.aspx"
      type="CodePlex.Elmah.ErrorLogPageFactory, CodePlex.Elmah" />
</httpHandlers>
```

Once this code is in place, fire up your web site and trigger an exception. I often find it useful to include a hidden method for generating an exception on any deployed web site, so I can periodically check and make sure the global exception handling is working properly.

Although ELMAH doesn't provide an interface for the unfortunate user who's experiencing the exception, it does provide an excellent web interface for developers to view exceptions. Simply browse to http://*localhost:nnnnn*/elmah/default.aspx (where *localhost* and *nnnnn* are replaced by your server and port number, respectively). From here you can browse through all the exceptions that have occurred in your web application, as shown in Figure 13.4.

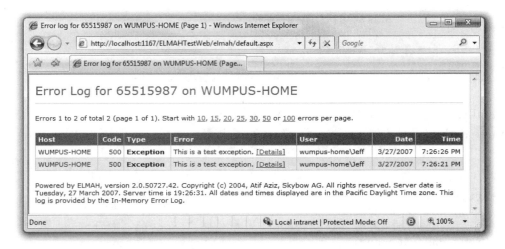

Figure 13.4. The ELMAH exception log

The interface lets you view details for each individual error. You can also subscribe to the RSS feed for this page, so that you can monitor your site's errors in the RSS feed reader of your choice.

Since we opted to use the in-memory logger, rather than a more permanent one, we can only view exceptions that have occurred since our application was last started. But this is usually enough for troubleshooting purposes, as we always have the exception email to fall back on.

What's the best way to write a log file?

One of the most popular solutions for logging debug information and exceptions is the **log4net** framework.[3] This open source logging framework is part of the popular log4j Java logging framework, yet, despite its popularity, many developers still struggle to get log4net to work properly within the context of an ASP.NET web site.

In this solution, I'll step you through the task of setting up the log4net framework. We'll use the best-practice technique of creating a separate configuration file, rather than dumping the log4net settings into **Web.config**.

At the time of writing, the latest release of log4net was version 1.2.10; I'll focus on that version here.

---

[3] http://logging.apache.org/log4net/downloads. html

Solution

First, add the **log4net.dll** reference to your web application or web site project.

With this file in place, we need to set up a log4net configuration file. While it would be possible to specify the log4net settings in **Web.config**, this is not the most desirable place to locate these settings. Any update to **Web.config** causes the AppDomain to recycle, which causes a performance hit as the sessions are dropped, cache is cleared, and pages are recompiled. So even a small change to a log4net setting would effectively restart the entire web site.

However, if we put our settings in a separate log4net configuration file, log4net will attach a FileSystemWatcher to that file and reload the logging settings any time that file changes, *without* reloading the AppDomain.

While this is a matter of preference, I like to put my log4net settings in a file named **log4net.config**, like so:

log4net.config

```
<?xml version="1.0" encoding="utf-8" ?>
<log4net>
  <appender name="RollingLogFileAppender"
      type="log4net.Appender.RollingFileAppender">
    <file value="..\\Logs\\CurrentLog" />
    <appendToFile value="true" />
    <datePattern value="yyyyMMdd" />
    <rollingStyle value="Date" />
    <filter type="log4net.Filter.LevelRangeFilter">
      <acceptOnMatch value="true" />
      <levelMin value="INFO" />
      <levelMax value="FATAL" />
    </filter>
    <layout type="log4net.Layout.PatternLayout">
      <conversionPattern
        value="%-5p %d %5rms %-22.22c{1} %-18.18M —%m%n" />
    </layout>
  </appender>
  <root>
    <level value="DEBUG" />
    <appender-ref ref="RollingLogFileAppender" />
  </root>
</log4net>
```

This sets up a `RollingLogFileAppender` to receive logging messages. As you might have guessed by the name, the `RollingLogFileAppender` logs messages to a file, rolling over to a new file every day, week or month, depending on your settings. For a more in-depth understanding of these settings, refer to the configuration section of the log4net manual.[4]

Now we need to tell log4net where its configuration file is located. We can do this in two ways. For Web Application projects, you can use an `XmlConfigurator` attribute within **AssemblyInfo.cs**:

```
                                          AssemblyInfo.cs (excerpt)

[assembly: log4net.Config.XmlConfigurator(ConfigFile =
    "Log4net.config", Watch = true)]
```

This code will look for a file named **log4net.config** within the web root.

This approach is fine for web application projects, but we can't use it for web site projects, as the code for a Web Site project isn't compiled into a single assembly by default. In Web Site projects, we can add a **Global.asax** file and add the following code to the `Application_Start` method:

```
                                             Global.asax (excerpt)

void Application_Start(object sender, EventArgs e)
{
  log4net.Config.XmlConfigurator.Configure(
      new System.IO.FileInfo(Server.MapPath("Log4net.config")));
}
```

Now we're ready to start logging. To use log4net, we simply create an instance of a logger and call its various logging methods. The most common practice is to create a static instance of the logger at the top of every class that requires logging, as I've done below:

---

[4] http://logging.apache.org/log4net/release/manual/configuration.html

```
                                          Log4Net.aspx.cs (excerpt)
public partial class _Default : System.Web.UI.Page
{
  private static readonly ILog Log =
    LogManager.GetLogger(MethodBase.GetCurrentMethod().DeclaringType);
  ⋮
}
```

Notice that we can pass *any* string to the `GetLogger` method, but by passing in `MethodBase.GetCurrentMethod().DeclaringType`, the logger will be initialized with the declaring type, which gives our log messages additional context.

Now we can start logging messages to our heart's content:

```
                                          Log4Net.aspx.cs (excerpt)
Log.Debug("Debug Message, only for debbuging.");
Log.Info("Informational message.");
Log.Warn("Warning Will Robinson!");
try
{
  // Some potientially exceptional operation
}
catch (Exception e)
{
  Log.Error("An unexpected exception occurred.", e);
}
```

How do I debug log4net?

Sometimes it feels like you've followed every instruction for configuring log4net to the letter, but it stubbornly refuses to log a message. What do you do then?

Solution

In order to log internal debug messages from log4net, we'll need to take advantage of ASP.NET's internal tracing mechanism. But first, we need to enable internal debugging for log4net. Add the following line to the `AppSettings` section in **Web.config**:

```
                                                    Web.config (excerpt)
<configuration>
  <appSettings>
    <add key="Log4Net.Internal.Debug" value="true" />
  </appSettings>
</configuration>
```

 Enabling Internal Debugging in your Code

You can also enable internal debugging programmatically by setting the static `log4net.Util.LogLog.InternalDebugging` property to `true`. There are two drawbacks to this approach, though:

1. Since it's a code change, turning internal debugging off again will require the recompilation of your project.

2. Any internal debug messages created before this line of code is reached will not be logged.

If you decide to enable internal debugging from your application code, keep these points in mind.

The next step is to ask a trace listener to listen for these messages, and log them to a file, like so:

```
<system.diagnostics>
  <trace autoflush="true">
    <listeners>
      <add name="Log4NetTraceListener"
           type="System.Diagnostics.TextWriterTraceListener"
           initializeData="C:\log4net.txt" />
    </listeners>
  </trace>
</system.diagnostics>
```

This approach will create a file named **log4net.txt** that contains your trace messages.

How do I perform tracing?

Before Visual Studio was released, the standard approach for debugging an ASP.NET application was to use `Response.Write` statements to display troubleshooting information to the screen—a technique known as **tracing**. ASP.NET has a built-in tracing facility, but unfortunately it's severely limited when logging from ASP.NET pages. This renders it unsuitable for proper logging duties, as I'll explain later.

With the arrival of Visual Studio's built-in debugger, tracing has been somewhat superseded. However it can still be a useful technique if you're troubleshooting an application—even if it's no replacement for a remote debugger and the log4net framework.

Solution

To enable tracing, add this line to **Web.config**:

Web.config *(excerpt)*

```
<system.web>
  <trace enabled="true">
</system.web>
```

Once you've enabled tracing, the **trace.axd** handler will be available on the local host machine. Navigating to http://*localhost:nnnnn*/trace.axd will, by default, show the last ten requests for your application, as Figure 13.5 indicates.

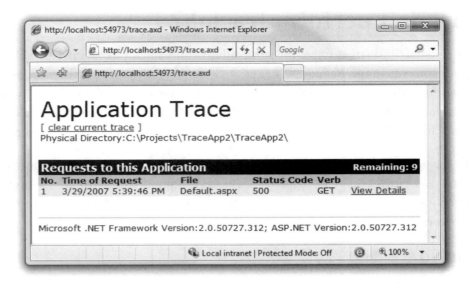

Figure 13.5. The last ten requests, as displayed by ASP.NET's built-in tracing log

Drilling down through each request reveals an option to view page-level tracing. On the page for which trace output is shown in Figure 13.6, I inserted the following code into the `Page_Load` event:

```
Trace.Write("Hello, World!");
throw new Exception("This is a demo exception.");
```

As Figure 13.6 shows, both calls to `Trace.Write` and unhandled exceptions are automatically logged in the per-request trace handler.

Exceptions Disappearing Without a Trace

Be careful when you're using the `Trace.Write` overloaded method that allows for the passing in of an exception—the exception is not actually written to the log by default, so it will appear to be swallowed up unless you tweak your trace logs to display it explicitly.

Figure 13.6. A log of all trace statements and unhandled exceptions

What you see in Figure 13.6 is a *bona fide* unhandled exception, not the result of a call to `Trace.Write`. The `Trace.Write` method allows you to group your trace messages by category:

```
Trace.Write(String message);
Trace.Write(String category, String message);
Trace.Write(String category, String message, Exception errorInfo);
```

If you'd like to see the trace output somewhere other than the **trace.axd** handler, you can choose from the five built-in `TraceListeners` in the `System.Diagnostics` namespace:

1. DefaultTraceListener

2. TextWriterTraceListener

3. EventLogTraceListener

4. DelimitedListTraceListener

5. XmlWriterTraceListener

To enable these outputs, you'll need to wire up a TraceListener. Here, I'm redirecting the trace output to a file named **log.txt** in the root of the current web site:

Web.config *(excerpt)*

```
<system.diagnostics>
  <trace autoflush="true">
    <listeners>
      <add name="log"
           type="System.Diagnostics.TextWriterTraceListener"
           initializeData="log.txt" />
    </listeners>
  </trace>
</system.diagnostics>
```

Be careful, however, because both the Page and System.Diagnostics classes include a Trace object. If you're calling methods like Trace.Write from within an ASP.NET page, you won't see any output at all until you add the Boolean attribute shown in bold below to the trace element:

Web.config *(excerpt)*

```
<system.web>
  <trace enabled="true" writeToDiagnosticsTrace="true"/>
</system.web>
```

Once you have this attribute in place, make some Trace.Write calls—you should find that your trace output is being written to the log file. Unfortunately, that file also includes all the other diagnostic tracing messages from the Page, which severely limits its usefulness. If you intend to use Trace.Write to build a log, you should call it from a Class Library project to avoid this limitation.

Summary

Only amateur programmers would build an ASP.NET web application without an exception handling strategy. With the advice we've provided here, hopefully you, too, can ascend to the hallowed ranks of professional programmers. You'll continue to make mistakes, of course. But you'll know about, and be able to act on, those mistakes—*before* your users give up and move on to greener pastures.

Configuration

It's true that .NET application deployment is a lot like tailoring a suit: one size does *not* fit all. Fortunately, ASP.NET comes with a rich and powerful configuration system that allows us to manage application settings very closely.

This chapter will briefly cover the basics of configuration, then step through a few tricks that you can use to get the most out of your configuration efforts.

How do I store and retrieve basic settings?

ASP.NET provides the **Web.config** file for the storage of application settings. So how exactly do we store and retrieve simple settings using this file?

Solution

The **appSettings** section of the **Web.config** file will be sufficient to store our configuration settings in many situations. This section contains name-value pairs that can be retrieved via the configuration API. The following snippet demonstrates the use of the appSettings section:

Web.config *(excerpt)*

```xml
<?xml version="1.0" encoding="utf-8"?>
<configuration>
  <appSettings>
    <add key="MySetting" value="MyValue"/>
    <add key="AnotherSetting" value="SomeValue"/>
  </appSettings>
</configuration>
```

Retrieving an application setting value is also very easy:

```csharp
using System.Configuration;
…
string setting = ConfigurationManager.AppSettings["MySetting"];
```

Changes in ASP.NET 2.0

The Configuration API has been moved into a new **System.Configuration.dll** assembly, so make sure your project references this assembly. Visual Studio.NET 2005 adds a reference to this class automatically as part of the ASP.NET project template.

Also note that in ASP.NET 1.1, you could retrieve the application setting value like so:

```csharp
string setting =
    ConfigurationSettings.AppSettings["MySetting"]
```

While this approach still works in ASP.NET 2.0, it has been deprecated and is not guaranteed to work in future versions of ASP.NET.

How do I store connection strings?

Most web sites use data, and they find that data through connection strings. Connection strings are some of the most important settings you'll be storing in your **Web.config** file.

What's the best way to store connection strings?

Solution

In ASP.NET 1.1, we didn't have much choice but to stuff our connection strings into the appSettings element. But ASP.NET 2.0 introduces a new configuration section explicitly for storing connection strings, as this **Web.config** example demonstrates:

```
                                                    Web.config (excerpt)

<configuration>
  <connectionStrings>
    <add name="sqlDb"
        connectionString="…your conn string here…" />
  </connectionStrings>
</configuration>
```

The following code shows how we retrieve a connection string programmatically from the connectionStrings section:

```
//   indicates line-break caused by formatting
string connection = ConfigurationManager.
    ConnectionStrings["sqlDb"].ConnectionString;
```

How do I retrieve settings declaratively?

While building an ASPX page, you might want to set the value of a control to the value of an application setting, or to set the connection string of a SqlDataSource to one stored in the connectionStrings section. Wouldn't it be nice if you could do so declaratively without having to resort to the code-behind model? You can!

Solution

ASP.NET 2.0 introduces new syntax that allows us to bind to values within the configuration file. For example, insert the following markup into your ASPX page to render a label with the value of the setting that has the key `MySetting`:

```
<asp:Label ID="sample" Text="<%$ AppSettings:MySetting %>"
    runat="server" />
```

Connection strings can be retrieved in a similar fashion. The following code sets the connection string for a `SqlDataSource`:

```
<asp:SqlDataSource ID="ds" runat="server"
    ConnectionString="<%$ConnectionSTrings:sqlDb%>" />
```

How do I create a custom configuration section?

For many applications, the `appSettings` section of **Web.config** is a suitable place to store configuration settings. However, there are a few drawbacks to this approach.

The first is that the list of application settings can become quite long. It would be very helpful to be able to group them into coherent categories using something other than comments and whitespace.

Another issue—and this is a bigger one for many developers—is that application settings are accessed via a string key, so the entry of an invalid key will not be caught by the compiler, and could result in a runtime error.

A third problem is that all the values in the application settings section are returned as strings. We need to cast these values to their appropriate types when we access them, which can clutter up our code.

Fortunately, the Configuration API built into ASP.NET provides rich support for the addition of your own custom configuration sections to **Web.config**.

Solution

In ASP.NET 1.1, creating your custom configuration section was a slightly involved process that required you to write a configuration section handler as well as your configuration class. This task becomes easier in ASP.NET 2.0, thanks to the new `ConfigurationProperty` attribute.

Let's dig right in, shall we? Suppose I want to create a class to store settings for my blog engine. I might want to store any of a number of settings, but let's just add two for now—the title and the number of posts on the first page. Here's the beginning of the skeleton for our class:

BlogSettings.cs (excerpt)

```
public class BlogSettings : ConfigurationSection
{
  //implementation goes here.
}
```

The first thing you'll notice is that this class inherits from `System.Configuration.ConfigurationSection`. This class provides a container in which to store our configuration settings; it's retrieved using the `this[key]` syntax.

For each setting we wish to store, we add a property getter and a setter that stores and retrieves the value from the property container. For example, we'll add the property `FrontPagePostCount` to store the number of posts, which will be displayed on the front page:

BlogSettings.cs (excerpt)

```
public int FrontPagePostCount
{
  get { return (int)this["frontPagePostCount"]; }
  set { this["frontPagePostCount"] = value; }
}
```

We're not done yet, though! We need to decorate this property with the
ConfigurationProperty attribute. This attribute indicates which element of the
configuration section corresponds to FrontPagePostCount:

```
[ConfigurationProperty("frontPagePostCount"
    , DefaultValue=20
    , IsRequired=false)]
public int FrontPagePostCount
{
  get { return (int)this["frontPagePostCount"]; }
  set { this["frontPagePostCount"] = value; }
}
```

Note that the first quoted parameter is the name of the configuration property. This
is the same value we use to store and retrieve the value from the property container.

To declaratively define valid property values, we can add to the property a validator
attribute that inherits from ConfigurationValidatorAttribute. As you can see in
the list below, the validator attribute specifies a corresponding class, which inherits
from ConfigurationValidatorBase, to perform the validation check.

CallbackValidatorAttribute

 specifies a CallBackValidator object that's used to validate the property value

IntegerValidatorAttribute

 specifies an IntegerValidator that provides some basic integer validation such
 as minimum and maximum values

LongValidatorAtribute

 as for IntegerValidatorAttribute, but for long (64-bit) integers

PositiveTimeSpanValidatorAttribute

 specifies a PositiveTimeSpanValidator that provides some basic validation
 for positive time spans

RegexStringValidatorAttribute

 allows you to specify a regular expression that the RegexStringValidator uses
 to validate the property

StringValidatorAttribute

specifies a StringValidator that provides some basic string validation, such as maximum and minimum string length and allowed characters

SubclassTypeValidatorAttribute

specifies a SubclassTypeValidator that .NET will use to validate that the property value is of a specified type

TimeSpanValidatorAttribute

specifies a TimeSpanValidator that provides basic validation for any time spans, positive or negative

Let's make sure that the only values considered valid for the frontPagePostCount property lie within the range from 1 to 100:

BlogSettings.cs (excerpt)

```
[ConfigurationProperty("frontPagePostCount"
    , DefaultValue=20
    , IsRequired=false)]
[IntegerValidator(MinValue=1, MaxValue=100)]
public int FrontPagePostCount
{
  get { return (int)this["frontPagePostCount"]; }
  set { this["frontPagePostCount"] = value; }
}
```

Next, we'll follow a similar process to add the Title property, then we'll wrap both properties in a neat BlogSettings class:

BlogSettings.cs (excerpt)

```
public class BlogSettings : ConfigurationSection
{
  [ConfigurationProperty("frontPagePostCount"
      , DefaultValue = 20
      , IsRequired = false)]
  [IntegerValidator(MinValue = 1, MaxValue = 100)]
  public int FrontPagePostCount
  {
    get { return (int)this["frontPagePostCount"]; }
    set { this["frontPagePostCount"] = value; }
```

```
    }
    [ConfigurationProperty("title", IsRequired=true)]
    [StringValidator(InvalidCharacters =
        " ~!@#$%^&*()[]{}/;'\"|\\"
        , MinLength=1
        , MaxLength=256)]
    public string Title
    {
      get { return (string)this["title"]; }
      set { this["title"] = value; }
    }
}
```

Now that we have this code in place, we need to add the corresponding XML to
Web.config—a fairly straightforward process.

First, let's add a `section` element within the `configurationSections` element:

Web.config *(excerpt)*

```
<configuration>
  <configSections>
  <section name="MySection"
      type="Fully.Qualified.TypeName,
      AssemblyName" />
  </configSections>
  ...
</configuration>
```

We then add the XML for our class:

Web.config *(excerpt)*

```
<BlogSettings frontPagePostCount="10"
    title="Sitepoint Stirrings" />
```

Finally, we need to work out how to access our new custom configuration section.
It's quite simple:

```
using System.Configuration;
    ⋮
BlogSettings settings =
    ConfigurationManager.GetSection("BlogSettings")
    as BlogSettings;
```

One small pattern I always follow with my custom configuration classes is to add a static property that I can use to access the setting—it just makes the setting easier to discover:

BlogSettings.cs *(excerpt)*

```
private static BlogSettings settings =
    ConfigurationManager.GetSection("BlogSettings")
    as BlogSettings;
public static BlogSettings Settings
{
  get { return settings; }
}
```

Now, accessing the title of the blog is as easy as this:

```
String title = BlogSettings.Settings.Title;
```

 Accessing Built-in Configuration Sections

You can access other built-in configuration sections using strongly typed configuration section classes. For example, to access authentication settings within the `system.web` configuration group, use the following code:

```
AuthenticationSection auth =
    ConfigurationManager.GetSection(
        "system.web/authentication")
    as AuthenticationSection;
```

For a full list of such sections, you'll have to pick through the list of classes derived from `System.Configuration.ConfigurationSection` within MSDN.[1]

---

[1] http://msdn2.microsoft.com/en-us/library/435zhefd.aspx

How can I simplify my Web.config file?

One of the strengths of ASP.NET is its configurable extensibility. We can hook up new features—many of which we've demonstrated in this book—simply by dropping binaries in the **bin** folder and wiring them up in **Web.config**.

But that's a bit of a problem. With each new feature or option we use (ASP.NET, Ajax, providers, ASP.NET membership, ASP.NET monitoring, log4net, urlrewriting.net, SubSonic, and so on), the **Web.config** file keeps growing until it's an unruly mess of XML.

How can we gain control over the **Web.config** file without giving up all the great features in ASP.NET?

Solution

We can use the `configSource` attribute to reference external configuration files from our **Web.config** file. This approach allows us to place any configuration section into its own separate file, which can turn our enormous, cluttered **Web.config** into a lightweight file that references simple configuration files, each of which meets a single purpose.

In ASP.NET 1.1, a **Web.config** file's `appSettings` element can reference an external file via the `file` attribute:

```
<appSettings file="DevSettings.config">
  <add key="Common" value="External file settings are
      merged with Web.config values" />
</appSettings>
```

This approach suffered a big limitation, though—the `file` attribute was only available for the `appSettings` element. Given that ASP.NET 2.0's new features have caused our **Web.config** files to balloon in size, we can be glad that these features also include the new `configSource` attribute, which is available for all elements in a **Web.config** file.

For example, here's a simplified **Web.config** file that uses external configuration files to handle specific configuration elements:

Web.config *(excerpt)*

```xml
<?xml version="1.0"?>
<configuration
    xmlns="http://schemas.microsoft.com/.NetConfiguration/v2.0">
  <appSettings configSource="config/appSettings.config"/>
  <connectionStrings configSource="config/connections.config"/>
  <log4net configSource="config/log4net.config"/>
  <urlrewritingnet configSource="config/log4net.config"/>
  <system.web>
    <compilation debug="true" />
    <authentication mode="Windows"/>
    <identity impersonate="true"/>
    <pages configSource="config/pages.config"/>
    <profile configSource="config/profile.config"/>
    <httpHandlers configSource="config/httpHandlers.config"/>
    <httpModules configSource="config/httpModules.config"/>
  </system.web>
</configuration>
```

Web.config Will Restart on External Changes

ASP.NET monitors your application's **Web.config** file, and will restart your application when it's updated. This measure is necessary to allow your application to adopt the new configuration values, but it may disrupt your users unless your servers are load balanced.

External configuration files that are referenced by the `configSource` attribute won't cause application restarts if their `restartOnExternalChanges` attributes are set to `false`, however.

To check which files will trigger an application restart, look at the **machine.config** file—elements with `restartOnExternalChanges="false"` will not trigger a restart. If you'd like those elements to trigger a restart, you can override the `restartOnExternalChanges` setting in your **Web.config** like so:

```xml
<appSettings
    configSource="config/appSettings.config"
    restartOnExternalChanges="true" />
```

Two Options for External Files in `appSettings`

As noted earlier, `appSettings` supported external configuration file references with the `file` attribute back in ASP.NET 1.1. That support is also provided in 2.0, so we now have two options for including external files for the `appSetting` element (`file` and `configSource`). Which should you use?

Well, there's a tradeoff. If you use `configSource`, you can decide whether or not you want to monitor the external **config** file and, when the external file changes, trigger application restarts with the `restartOnExternalChanges` element. External files that are referenced by the `file` attribute aren't monitored for changes.

The upside to using the `file` attribute is that you can merge settings from the **Web.config** element with an external file. For example, you could employ the following settings in your **Web.config** file:

```
<?xml version="1.0"?>
<configuration xmlns="http://schemas.microsoft.com/.NetConfi
➥guration/v2.0">
  <appSettings file="config/appSettings.config">
    <add key="KeyOne" value="LoadedFromWebConfig" />
    <add key="KeyTwo" value="LoadedFromWebConfig" />
  </appSettings>
</configuration>
```

Values from the file referenced in the `file` attribute could be merged with the **Web.config** `appSettings` values like so:

```
<appSettings>
    <add key="KeyTwo" value="LoadedFromExternalFile" />
    <add key="KeyThree" value=" LoadedFromExternalFile" />
</appSettings>
```

This approach differs from the way `configSource` source works—`configSource` doesn't merge at all. For that reason, you may choose to reference `appSettings` as a file, rather than a `configSource`.

Discussion

The way file references are merged hints at an interesting aspect of the way the ASP.NET configuration has been developed. The entire system is based on inheritance:

- The root is the **machine.config** file, in the **C:\Windows\Microsoft.NET\Frame-work\v2.0.50727\CONFIG** directory.

- The default settings for all ASP.NET sites on the server are stored in a **Web.config** file that resides in the same folder as **machine.config**. This **Web.config** file overrides the settings in **machine.config**.

- The **Web.config** folder in the root of each web site directory inherits from the **machine.config** file and the default **Web.config** file, and overrides those settings as necessary. If you wanted to, you could give your site's **Web.config** file a blank root element, in which case it would simply inherit all the default settings.

- You can further override these settings within your web site's subfolders—an approach that can be useful if your site has an **Admin** subfolder that requires **Admin**-specific settings. But, while this technique can be helpful, keep in mind that it can make site maintenance and troubleshooting slightly more complex, because settings in the **Web.config** file are in effect for all but that specific sub-folder.

- You can continue to override **Web.config** settings by adding **Web.config** folders to subfolders further down through the levels of your web site's hierarchy.

How can I manage Web.config values between deployment environments?

Many of the settings in your **Web.config** file, such as the connection details for your development and production databases, will vary between deployment environments. However, since your **Web.config** is one of the most vital components of your ASP.NET application, you should keep it under version control.

We need a solution that allows us to extract the environment-specific settings into separate files so that we can use the same **Web.config** file in all deployment environments, along with the external **config** file that's appropriate to the specific environment we're using.

Solution

If you've read the section called "How can I simplify my Web.config file?", you probably already have a good idea of what this solution will involve! We use the `configSource` attribute contained within the **Web.config** file to reference external files that vary between environments.

Let's look at the most obvious example—connection strings. Here's a stripped-down **Web.config** file that references connection strings in an external file:

Web.config *(excerpt)*

```
<configuration
    xmlns="http://schemas.microsoft.com/.NetConfiguration/v2.0">
  <connectionStrings configSource="Config\connections.config"/>
</configuration>
```

This **Web.config** file will remain the same in all environments (including development, testing, and production), so we can add it to version control; the aspect that varies between environments is the **Config\configurations.config** file. Notice that we store our external configuration files in a separate folder, just to indulge our desire to keep the web site's root folder clean.

Now here's the neat trick—let's add to the **Config** folder a subfolder called **Environments**. Inside that folder, we'll create a separate folder for each environment—**Dev**, **Test**, **Prod**. Each folder will contain the **config** files appropriate to that environment. Now, this is hardly rocket science, but the cool thing about it is that we can add the entire **Config** folder to source control. The only items that we don't add to version control are the files at the root of the **Config** folder, which will differ for each environment.

This is probably easier to visualize if we look at the actual folders involved. Figure 14.1 shows the site's root directory, including the **Config** folder.

Figure 14.1. The site's root directory structure

Inside the **Config** folder, we find the **connections.config** file, as shown in Figure 14.2, which is referenced in our **Web.config** file. We also have a folder for each target environment (**Development**, **Production**, and **Test**), each of which contains the version of **connections.config** file appropriate to that environment. Every single folder and file—except **Config\connections.config**—is checked into version control and is deployed to all environments.

Figure 14.2. Inside the **Config** folder

The important point here is that we can track the **Web.config** file and the **Config***Environment* folder via version control. The only aspect that changes between environments is the **connections.config** file, but the environment-specific **config** file is stored in that environment's folder.

When you deploy a site to an environment, you'll need to copy **connections.config** (and any other **config** files) from the applicable environment folder into the **Config** folder. You can automate this procedure by including it in your deployment process—for instance, you can include the file copy action in a build event.

How can I encrypt a section of my Web.config file?

Sensitive information may reside in several configuration areas—for instance, the `connectionStrings` section may contain database usernames and passwords, and the `identity` section will contain a username and password if you need the runtime to impersonate a fixed identity. You may even keep a password for a third-party web service in **appSettings** or a custom section of **Web.config**.

Consider encrypting the sections where secrets like these reside, instead of leaving sensitive details in plain text.

Solution

Encrypting an entire section of a configuration file is straightforward, thanks to the ASP.NET 2.0 configuration API.

The easiest way to encrypt a section of the configuration file is to call **aspnet_regiis.exe** from a .NET command line using the –pe argument. To do so, launch the Visual Studio 2005 command prompt, found in the **Visual Studio Tools** folder in your **Start** menu, then enter this command:

```
C:\>aspnet_regiis -pe "connectionStrings" -app "/MyKillerSite"
```

In this case, we're using the –app argument to select the application. You can use the –pef argument to point directly to the application directory, which is handy if you're using the Visual Studio 2005 Web Server (formerly known as Cassini):

```
C:\>aspnet_regiis -pef "connectionStrings" "C:\Projects\My Site"
```

We use –pd (specifying an IIS application) or –pdf (specifying a file path) to decrypt the config section:

```
C:\>aspnet_regiis -pdf "connectionStrings" "C:\Projects\My Site"
```

The WebConfigurationManager makes it fairly easy to encrypt or decrypt site configuration settings from within an ASP.NET application. The following code shows how easy it is to protect (encrypt) and unprotect (decrypt) an entire configuration section using WebConfigurationManager:

```
protected void toggleEncryption(object sender, EventArgs e)
{
  Configuration config;
  config = WebConfigurationManager.OpenWebConfiguration("~");
  ConnectionStringsSection section;
  section = config.GetSection("connectionStrings")
      as ConnectionStringsSection;
  if (section.SectionInformation.IsProtected)
  {
    section.SectionInformation.UnprotectSection();
  }
  else
```

```
{
    section.SectionInformation.ProtectSection(
        "DataProtectionConfigurationProvider");
}
config.Save();
WriteMessage("connections protected = " +
    section.SectionInformation.IsProtected);
}
```

 Leave Decryption to the Runtime

You don't need to unprotect a section in order to read the configuration settings in that section—the runtime will perform the decryption necessary for your application to read the plain text values. The `UnprotectSection` method call in this sample demonstrates how to return a section to its unencrypted form.

If we were to examine our **Web.config** file after we turned encryption on, we'd notice that the configuration API has added some information to it:

Web.config *(excerpt)*

```
<?xml version="1.0"?>
<configuration
    xmlns="http://schemas.microsoft.com/.NetConfiguration/v2.0">
  <protectedData>
    <protectedDataSections>
      <add name="connectionStrings"
          provider="DataProtectionConfigurationProvider"
          inheritedByChildren="false" />
    </protectedDataSections>
  </protectedData>
  <appSettings configSource="appSettings.config"/>
  <connectionStrings configSource="connections.config"/>
  <system.web>
    <compilation debug="true" />
    <authentication mode="Windows"/>
    <identity impersonate="true"/>
  </system.web>
</configuration>
```

In addition, our **ConnectionStrings.config** file would contain a `CipherValue` instead of plain text connection strings, as you can see in the code snippet shown here.

Note that we don't need to use an external configuration source to take advantage of encryption—the configuration API would have happily encrypted the connection strings section if it lived inside **Web.config**, like so:

```
                                          ConnectionStrings.config (excerpt)
<connectionStrings>
  <EncryptedData>
    <CipherData>
      <CipherValue>AQAAANCMnd8BF…</CipherValue>
    </CipherData>
  </EncryptedData>
</connectionStrings>
```

At runtime, the configuration API will decrypt configuration sections on the fly. We can still use `WebConfigurationManager.ConnectionStrings` to return connection strings that can be used by our application without our having to worry about whether or not they're encrypted.

To understand what we're seeing in the configuration file, we first need to realize that the runtime turns to a configuration encryption provider to carry out encryption and decryption work. The two providers that ship with .NET 2.0 are the `DataProtectionConfigurationProvider` and the `RSAProtectedConfigurationProvider`, though you can also implement your own protected configuration provider if need be. We specify the provider we want to use in the string passed to the `ProtectSection` method, as seen in the earlier source code snippet for our `toggleEncryption` function. In that example, we used the `DataProtectionConfigurationProvider`.

Under the hood, the `DataProtectionConfigurationProvider` uses the Windows Data Protection API (DPAPI). This provides a machine-specific secret key for encryption and decryption work. As the `DataProtectionConfigurationProvider` relies on this machine-specific key, you can only use your computer to decrypt cipher text that was encrypted on the same machine.

If you need to move configuration files with encrypted sections from machine to machine, you'll need the `RSAProtectedConfigurationProvider`. As its name implies, the `RSAProtectedConfigurationProvider` uses RSA public key encryption. You can work with the `RSAProtectedConfigurationProvider` from the command line tool `aspnet_regiis`, which provides options that allow you to create a keypair (`-pc`), export a keypair (`-px`), import a keypair (`-pi`), grant access to a keypair (`-pa`), remove access from a keypair (`-pr`), and more. Command line arguments also allow you to specify the encryption provider you want to use.

Some Sections Can't be Encrypted

Some sections, such as the `processModel` section and the `configProtectedData` element, contain data that you cannot encrypt. However, you can use the **Aspnet_setreg.exe** tool to store a password for this section securely.

Summary

As ASP.NET's feature set continues to grow, more and more of your work will involve hooking up and controlling functionality from within the configuration system. In this chapter, we've shown you some essential tips that will help you smooth the configuration of ASP.NET functionality, and use the Configuration API more effectively to configure your own applications.

15

Performance and Scaling

Now that you've added the finishing touches to your web site and unleashed it onto the world, fame, fortune, and success will surely follow—won't it?

Unfortunately, your web application's success can lead to something less desirable—performance and scaling problems. On a traditional desktop application, one thousand users translate to one thousand client computers chugging away, sharing the load of running your application. The application is effectively spread among all the users' machines. When it comes to a web application, though, those same thousand users are usually serviced by a *single machine*—your web server.

Success can come at a cost for web applications: a cost in bandwidth and server hardware. However, there are a few clever ways you can reduce—and sometimes eliminate—these problems. We'll take a look at some of the different approaches to improving the performance of an ASP.NET site in this chapter.

How do I determine what to optimize?

You want your web application to be the best, right? Like all of us, by "best" you mean "fastest." And what better way to create a blazingly fast application than to optimize everything? Optimize, optimize, optimize—right? Wrong.

Premature optimization refers to the fixing of a performance problem before you understand the problem, or before there even *is* a problem, and it's a bad idea.

That's not to say that you should write sloppy, inefficient code. My point is that you should trust the ASP.NET Framework, and make use of the features that make it such a terrific environment in which to develop, until you hit a problem. Once you hit a problem, you should take the time to understand what that problem is, and only then should you start to look at how best to address it. Dr. Joseph M. Newcomer's essay, "Optimization: Your Worst Enemy," gives a fascinating overview of the perils of optimizing in the dark.[1]

The tips in this chapter propose fairly lightweight solutions for some common performance issues. I've steered away from dramatic changes, because I don't want you to end up doubling your development or maintenance time in order to shave a meagre 2% off your page load time. While it is possible to bypass the in-built ASP.NET Page mechanism completely (by using `Response.Write`, or building an ASHX-based sites), I'm not a fan of these approaches. The ASP.NET system as a whole has been tuned and improved for more than half a decade, and it's reasonably fast straight out of the box. There's a good chance that trying to improve on it will result in a slower and less maintainable web site.

So, with all that out of the way, let's assume that some of your pages are running slowly. How do you figure out what to fix?

Solution

Isolate the bottleneck in your site by measuring the actual speed of the site. This exercise can be performed using logs, database profiling, and tracing.

We've discussed the task of logging using log4net in Chapter 13. If you suspect that the database is the cause of the slowdown (for example, you know that your applic-

---

[1] http://www.flounder.com/optimization.htm

ation makes use of some large queries), you can either step through the page in debug mode to see whether the database calls are taking a long time to return, or you can use the SQL Server Profiler discussed in the section called "How do I speed up my database queries?" later in this chapter. For a very basic analysis of what's going on in your pages, you can use the ASP.NET trace; while it's not nearly as good as a full-featured logging system, it's easy to implement and will provide you with plenty of timing information.

The first step in using the trace is to get into the habit of adding trace statements. Write to the trace whenever you think there's something you might want to see when you debug future problems. Tracing doesn't have any real performance impact on your site until it's enabled in the **Web.config**, and when you need to troubleshoot a problem, you'll be glad it's there.

There's more information on tracing in Chapter 13, but the general idea is that you can write to the `Trace` object like this:

```
Trace.Write("Here's a trace message.");
```

Tracing is disabled by default; when you want your `Trace.Write` statements to actually do something, you'll need to turn tracing on in the **Web.config** file, as follows:

Web.config *(excerpt)*

```
<?xml version="1.0"?>
<configuration>
  <system.web>
    <trace enabled="true"
        mostRecent="true"
        localOnly="true"/>
  </system.web>
</configuration>
```

In this solution, we'll look at a sample page that performs a few different actions—it makes a call to a web service, retrieves some data from a database, and throws an exception. Each function that we'll use writes a trace message when it begins and ends, via a straightforward utility method called `writeTrace`. However, it has one slightly complex aspect—it uses the `System.Diagnostics` object to figure out the method name, so we don't have to pass it in. The code for our sample page is as follows:

Trace.aspx.cs *(excerpt)*

```csharp
using System;
using System.Web;
public partial class _Default : System.Web.UI.Page
{
  protected void Page_Load(object sender, EventArgs e)
  {
    hitAWebservice();
    getSomeData();
    doSomeProcessing();
    breakSomething();
    displayTheResults();
  }
  private void getSomeData()
  {
    writeTrace(true);
    simulateWaiting(8000);
    writeTrace(false);
  }
  private void hitAWebservice()
  {
    writeTrace(true);
    Trace.Write("A message to demonstrate tracing.");
    simulateWaiting(2000);
    writeTrace(false);
  }
  private void doSomeProcessing()
  {
    writeTrace(true);
    simulateWaiting(1000);
    writeTrace(false);
  }
  private void displayTheResults()
  {
    writeTrace(true);
    simulateWaiting(500);
    writeTrace(false);
  }
  private void breakSomething()
  {
    writeTrace(true);
```

```
      try
      {
        int superBig = int.MaxValue;
        superBig += 1;
      }
      catch (Exception ex)
      {
        Trace.Warn("Exception", "Oops", ex);
      }
    }
    private void writeTrace(bool enteringFunction)
    {
      if (!Trace.IsEnabled)
      return;
      string callingFunctionName = "Undetermined method";
      string action = enteringFunction ? "Entering" : "Exiting";
      try
      {
        //Determine the name of the calling function.
        System.Diagnostics.StackTrace stackTrace =
        new System.Diagnostics.StackTrace();
        callingFunctionName =
        stackTrace.GetFrame(1).GetMethod().Name;
      }
      catch { }
      Trace.Write(action, callingFunctionName);
    }
    /// <summary>
    /// Wait a bit.
    /// </summary>
    /// <param name="waitTime">Time in milliseconds to wait.</param>
    private void simulateWaiting(int waitTime)
    {
      System.Threading.Thread.Sleep(waitTime);
    }
}
```

Right, we've got our trace statements in place. Now, let's assume that this page is taking abnormally long to load, and we'd like to get to the bottom of the problem. With tracing enabled, we can simply load the page, then browse to **Trace.axd** within our web site; it's at http://localhost:1209/*MySite*/Trace.axd.

Figure 15.1 shows the first part of the **Trace.axd** output that was returned from the previous code.

Request Details

Request Details			
Session Id:	ozudhu45fm2umo454zzstmfq	**Request Type:**	GET
Time of Request:	4/24/2007 12:34:01 AM	**Status Code:**	200
Request Encoding:	Unicode (UTF-8)	**Response Encoding:**	Unicode (UTF-8)

Trace Information			
Category	**Message**	**From First(s)**	**From Last(s)**
aspx.page	Begin PreInit		
aspx.page	End PreInit	6.31365159538433E-05	0.000063
aspx.page	Begin Init	9.13523925526848E-05	0.000028
aspx.page	End Init	0.000117333348232806	0.000026
aspx.page	Begin InitComplete	0.000137168271386447	0.000020
aspx.page	End InitComplete	0.000157003194540088	0.000020
aspx.page	Begin PreLoad	0.000176000022349209	0.000019
aspx.page	End PreLoad	0.00019555558038801	0.000020
aspx.page	Begin Load	0.000214552408197131	0.000019
Entering	hitAWebservice	0.00155019702224724	0.001336
	A message to demonstrate tracing.	0.00159992401268876	0.000050
Exiting	hitAWebservice	2.00507857842268	2.003479
Entering	getSomeData	2.0063647754114	0.001286
Exiting	getSomeData	10.0068631627763	8.000498
Entering	doSomeProcessing	10.0075219057171	0.000659
Exiting	doSomeProcessing	11.0077434422531	1.000222
Entering	breakSomething	11.0082876454968	0.000544
Entering	displayTheResults	11.0086061217278	0.000318
Exiting	displayTheResults	11.5088845090647	0.500278
aspx.page	End Load	11.5089764201875	0.000092
aspx.page	Begin LoadComplete	11.509011620192	0.000035
aspx.page	End LoadComplete	11.5090440265453	0.000032
aspx.page	Begin PreRender	11.5090755948032	0.000032
aspx.page	End PreRender	11.5091113535379	0.000036
aspx.page	Begin PreRenderComplete	11.509143201161	0.000032
aspx.page	End PreRenderComplete	11.5091739313237	0.000031
aspx.page	Begin SaveState	11.5094795567593	0.000306
aspx.page	End SaveState	11.5132453985074	0.003766
aspx.page	Begin SaveStateComplete	11.5132937286722	0.000048
aspx.page	End SaveStateComplete	11.513327252486	0.000034
aspx.page	Begin Render	11.5133797731276	0.000053
aspx.page	End Render	11.5149662876148	0.001587

Figure 15.1. Trace output for our sample page

Table 15.1 shows the relevant portion of the trace output.

Right away, we can see which aspect of our page load is taking the majority of time—getSomeData takes eight seconds to execute. Without this information, we might have assumed the web service call was at fault and spent valuable time solving the wrong problem. This example shows how, armed with some real information, we can begin to fix the *right* problem.

Table 15.1. A Snapshot of Trace Output for our Sample Page

Category	Message	From Last(s)
aspx.page	Begin Load	0.000019
Entering	hitAWebservice	0.001336
	A message to demonstrate tracing.	0.000050
Exiting	hitAWebservice	2.003479
Entering	getSomeData	0.001286
Exiting	getSomeData	8.000498
Entering	doSomeProcessing	0.000659
Exiting	doSomeProcessing	1.000222
Entering	breakSomething	0.000544
Entering	displayTheResults	0.000318

How can I decrease the size of the view state?

One convenience of ASP.NET controls is that they can preserve state across post-backs—a topic we've covered in depth in Chapter 6. This, of course, is a feature that comes at a price—to implement it, we add a hidden field to the page to store the control settings for transmission between the client and server, but depending on the controls the page uses, the view state can sometimes become quite large.

One obvious way to reduce the size of view state is to *turn it off if you don't need it*. This adjustment can be performed either at the page level, or at the control level. If, for whatever reason, you *can't* disable the view state (for example, your page uses controls that are dependent upon the view state), there are a few other steps you can take to at least reduce its impact on your page size.

Solutions

You have two options for reducing the impact that view state has on your page size—either compress the view state, or store it on the server.

Compressing the View State

The following simple `CompressedViewStatePage` class implements basic GZIP compression on the page's view state. It reduced the size of the `ViewState` object on my sample page from 20,442 bytes to 6,056 bytes—an impressive 70% reduction in size! Here's the class in all its glory:

CompressedViewStatePage.cs *(excerpt)*

```
using System;
using System.IO.Compression;
using System.IO;
using System.Web.UI;
public class CompressedViewStatePage : System.Web.UI.Page
{
  static public byte[] Compress(byte[] b)
  {
    MemoryStream ms = new MemoryStream();
    GZipStream zs = new GZipStream(ms, CompressionMode.Compress);
    zs.Write(b, 0, b.Length);
    return ms.ToArray();
  }
  static public byte[] Decompress(byte[] b)
  {
    MemoryStream ms = new MemoryStream(b.Length);
    ms.Write(b, 0, b.Length);
    // last 4 bytes of GZipStream = length of decompressed data
    ms.Seek(-4, SeekOrigin.Current);
    byte[] lb = new byte[4];
    ms.Read(lb, 0, 4);
    int len = BitConverter.ToInt32(lb, 0);
    ms.Seek(0, SeekOrigin.Begin);
    byte[] ob = new byte[len];
    GZipStream zs = new GZipStream(ms, CompressionMode.Decompress);
    zs.Read(ob, 0, len);
    return ob;
  }
  protected override object LoadPageStateFromPersistenceMedium()
  {
    byte[] b = Convert.FromBase64String(Request.Form["__VSTATE"]);
    LosFormatter lf = new LosFormatter();
    return lf.Deserialize(Convert.ToBase64String(Decompress(b)));
  }
  protected override void SavePageStateToPersistenceMedium(
      object state
```

```
  )
  {
    LosFormatter lf = new LosFormatter();
    StringWriter sw = new StringWriter();
    lf.Serialize(sw, state);
    byte[] b = Convert.FromBase64String(sw.ToString());
    ClientScript.RegisterHiddenField("__VSTATE",
    Convert.ToBase64String(Compress(b)));
  }
}
```

To use GZIP compression, simply inherit a specific page from the class, like this:

```
public partial class MyPage : CompressedViewStatePage
```

If you're worried about the performance implications of compressing your view state, don't be. It's far more likely that bandwidth is a greater bottleneck than CPU time on any given web server. Although there are exceptions to this rule, the GZIP algorithm is blazingly fast on the CPUs of today. Besides, if your server's CPU operates at 100% all the time, you have far graver problems to worry about than the size of a handful of pages.

This compression algorithm could also be implemented as an HTTP module, which could then be applied to an entire site with a simple `Web.config` modification. I suggest you try implementing this module as an exercise, if you're keen. The MSDN article on building an HTTP module is a good place to start.[2]

Storing View State on the Server

The second option for reducing view state's impact on page size is to prevent view state data from being sent to the client altogether, and instead store the data on the server.

The following `ServerViewStatePage` class allows us to use the `Session` object to store the view state:

---

[2] http://support.microsoft.com/kb/307996/en-us

```csharp
using System;
using System.Web.UI;
using System.Configuration;
using System.IO;
public class ServerViewStatePage : System.Web.UI.Page
{
  private const string _configKey = "ServerViewStateMode";
  private const string _formField = "__SERVERVIEWSTATEKEY";
  private string ViewStateData
  {
    get { return Request.Form[_formField]; }
    set { ClientScript.RegisterHiddenField(_formField, value); }
  }
  private string PersistenceType
  {
    get { return (ConfigurationManager.AppSettings[_configKey]
    ?? "").ToLower(); }
  }

  private object ToObject(string viewstate)
  {
    byte[] b = Convert.FromBase64String(viewstate);
    LosFormatter lf = new LosFormatter();
    return lf.Deserialize(Convert.ToBase64String(b));
  }
  private string ToBase64String(object state)
  {
    LosFormatter lf = new LosFormatter();
    StringWriter sw = new StringWriter();
    lf.Serialize(sw, state);
    byte[] b = Convert.FromBase64String(sw.ToString());
    return Convert.ToBase64String(b);
  }
  private string ToSession(string value)
  {
    string key = Guid.NewGuid().ToString();
    Session.Add(key, value);
    return key;
  }
  private string FromSession(string key)
  {
    string value = Convert.ToString(Session[key]);
    Session.Remove(key);
```

```
      return value;
    }
    protected override object LoadPageStateFromPersistenceMedium()
    {
      switch (PersistenceType)
      {
      case "session":
        return ToObject(FromSession(ViewStateData));
      default:
        return base.LoadPageStateFromPersistenceMedium();
      }
    }
    protected override void SavePageStateToPersistenceMedium(
        object ViewStateObject
    )
    {
      switch (PersistenceType)
      {
        case "session":
          ViewStateData = ToSession(ToBase64String(ViewStateObject));
          break;
        default:
          base.SavePageStateToPersistenceMedium(ViewStateObject);
          break;
      }
    }
  }
}
```

To use `ServerViewStatePage`, simply inherit a specific page from this class, like this:

```
public partial class MyPage : ServerViewStatePage
```

This class is configured via a single setting in **Web.config**: `ServerViewStateMode`. Once you've configured this setting, you'll notice that the `ViewState` object disappears from the page—in its place is a simple ID that's used to look up the contents of the page's view state on the server, in the `Session` object. If you feel uncomfortable storing view state in `Session`, this class could easily be extended to store view state wherever you like—in the file system, in the ASP.NET cache, or in a database.

As usual, there's no free lunch here. The decision to push view state to the server and store it in `Session` has its own drawbacks. For example, the `Session` object could be lost if the IIS worker process recycles (a loss that does occur every so often in IIS, unless you've disabled this default behavior). Furthermore, any change to the underlying application files (such as editing **Web.config**, or adding new binaries to the **bin** folder of your application) will also cause the web application to recycle and Session data to be lost. And if you use more than one web server (such as in a web farm environment) you'll need to manage any shared session state that's stored in a database.

How can I decrease the bandwidth that my site uses?

ASP.NET abstracts a lot of traditional web development details from the developer. Just drag and drop a few controls on a form, set some properties, write a little bit of code, and—*bam!*—you've got a functioning web site.

However, that doesn't mean the resulting HTML markup will necessarily be efficient or small. It's not unusual to see ASP.NET pages that contain more than 100 kilobytes of markup. I recommend that you keep a close eye on the HTML markup that results from your ASP.NET web pages—to keep these file sizes in check can sometimes require additional effort, which is one reason we covered the topic of web standards in Chapter 9.

Solutions

The first rule of ASP.NET bandwidth control is to *know how large your pages are.* In Internet Explorer, the **File** > **Properties** dialog will tell you how many kilobytes of HTML markup the current page has produced, as Figure 15.2 shows. Firefox has a similar dialog, pictured in Figure 15.3, which can be accessed by selecting **Tools** > **Page Info**.

Figure 15.2. Viewing page information in Internet Explorer

Figure 15.3. Viewing page information in Firefox

However, note that the **Size** field in Firefox reports a much smaller number than does IE 7—13,976 bytes versus 49,774 bytes. That's because Firefox shows the actual number of bytes that came down over the wire, whereas IE 7 shows the size of the page after it has been received by the browser.

How is such a discrepancy possible? Well, the ASP.NET web site uses **HTTP compression** to decrease the page size before sending the page. HTTP compression is a W3C standard that allows the server to provide a GZIP-compressed version of the HTML content to the client, at the cost of a very minor increase in CPU time. The client receives the compressed content, then decompresses it on the fly before rendering the page. Right off the bat, you can see that this is just one easy way to reduce the amount of bandwidth you use by an impressive 72%—simply flip the switch to enable HTTP compression for your web site.

You can enable HTTP compression in two ways. The first takes place at the web server level; the second is implemented via a custom HTTP module at the ASP.NET application level.

Enabling HTTP Compression Support in IIS 6

 Manual Configuration is Only Necessary in IIS 6

That's right: it's only necessary to configure IIS to enable HTTP compression in IIS 6 and earlier, as IIS 7 enables static compression by default. Windows Server 2008 (which had yet to be released at the time of this writing) may offer a user interface to configure dynamic HTTP compression, but Vista's IIS Manager doesn't.

Use the IIS Service Manager to enable HTTP Compression in IIS 6. Right-click the node for your web site and select **Properties**. The **Service** tab contains the settings relevant to compression, as Figure 15.4 shows.

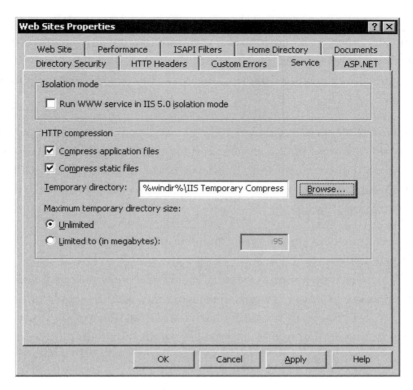

Figure 15.4. Configuring HTTP compression in IIS 6

The compression setting available in the GUI works; however, it only affects *static* content, such as HTML pages and CSS files. This setting won't do anything to compress *dynamic* content in ASPX pages. We must resort to editing the **meta-base**—the IIS database for configuration and metadata storage—to deploy dynamic content compression:

- Open the metabase in Notepad. For IIS 6, this is located at **C:\WINDOWS\system32\inetsrv\MetaBase.xml**. For IIS 5, the file is a binary file, so you'll need to download the Meta-data Edit tool instead.[3]

- Search for the `<IIsCompressionScheme>` tag. There should be two `<IIsCompressionScheme>` entries: one for `deflate` and one for `GZIP`—the two methods of compression that IIS supports. By default, IIS uses `GZIP`; `deflate` is rarely used.

---

[3] http://www.microsoft.com/downloads/details.aspx?FamilyID=48364A72-D54E-46DC-AACF-E3BE887D17A6

■ Search for the `HcScriptFileExtensions` section. Add to the list **aspx**, **asmx**, **php**, **cgi**, and any other file extensions that you want dynamically compressed. Follow the existing format carefully—it's return-delimited, and any extra spaces will prevent the file extensions from working. Make the same changes in both `deflate` and `GZIP`.

■ Set `HcDynamicCompressionLevel` to level 9 (it has a default value of 0, which means "no compression"). I recommend level 9, based on several reports that I've read on the Web suggesting that level 10 requires much more CPU time, while offering only a minimal reduction in file size over level 9. Make this change for both `deflate` and `GZIP`.

Note that this is a global compression rule that will affect all web sites. This setting is usually what you'll want, since HTTP compression is so effective and the cost is nominal. However, some poorly coded ASP.NET web sites may be incompatible with compression. In those circumstances, you may want to enable or disable compression on a per-site or per-folder basis—a setting that's also supported by IIS. The easiest way to configure this setting is to use the command line **adsutil.vbs** utility:

```
C:\Inetpub\AdminScripts\>adsutil.vbs set w3svc/ (site#) /root/DoStat
➥icCompression False
C:\Inetpub\AdminScripts\>adsutil.vbs set w3svc/ (site#) /root/DoDyna
➥micCompression False
```

The *(site#)* number can be obtained from the log properties dialog in the IIS server properties, and usually takes the form W3SVC*n*, where *n* is an arbitrary site number.

Enabling HTTP Compression Support in an ASP.NET Application

Perhaps you don't have control over the IIS settings on your server. Or maybe you'd just like a way to enable compression for your specific ASP.NET application. That's possible too.

The open source HttpCompress library is very easy to incorporate into an ASP.NET web site. First, download the latest version of HttpCompress from the official web site.[4]

---

[4] http://www.blowery.org/code/HttpCompressionModule.html

Place the **blowery.Web.HttpCompress.dll** binary somewhere logical, and add a reference to it.

Next, add the following compression-specific configuration section to your site's **Web.config**:

Web.config (excerpt)

```
<configSections>
  <sectionGroup name="blowery.web">
    <section name="httpCompress"
        type="blowery.Web.HttpCompress.SectionHandler,
            blowery.Web.HttpCompress"/>
  </sectionGroup>
</configSections>
<blowery.web>
  <httpCompress preferredAlgorithm="gzip" compressionLevel="high">
    <excludedMimeTypes>
      <add type="image/png" />
      <add type="image/jpeg" />
      <add type="image/gif" />
    </excludedMimeTypes>
  </httpCompress>
</blowery.web>
```

Finally, bring the actual compression HTTP module into the pipeline:

Web.config (excerpt)

```
<system.web>
  <httpModules>
    <add name="CompressionModule"
        type="blowery.Web.HttpCompress.HttpModule,
            blowery.web.HttpCompress"/>
  </httpModules>
</system.web>
```

Once this is in place, you should see compressed ASPX content being returned to the browser. To verify that this is the case, use Port80 Software's convenient Real-Time Compression Checker.[5]

---

[5] http://www.port80software.com/products/httpzip/compresscheck/

One limitation of the `HttpCompress` module approach is that *only* ASPX content that forms part of your application will be compressed; the CSS and JavaScript aren't served through the ASP.NET ISAPI handler, and will therefore remain uncompressed. As such, I recommend that you enable compression at the web server level whenever possible, so that these files also gain the benefits of compression.

How can I improve the speed of my site?

Most ASP.NET web servers perform a lot of unnecessarily repetitive work.

For example, suppose you have a page with a `DataGrid` bound to a table called `Products`. Every time a user requests the `Products` page, ASP.NET has to:

1. Look up the products data in the database.

2. Process the page.

3. Databind the product data.

4. Render the results to HTML.

5. Output the results to the browser.

If we assume the products list changes infrequently in comparison to how often it is requested by a user, most of that work is unnecessary. Instead of doing all that work to send the same HTML to all users, why not just store the HTML and reuse it until the `Products` table changes?

Solution

The ASP.NET cache provides the key to efficient storage and reuse of our HTML.

There are several ways to use the cache; we'll focus on the easiest tricks to get you started, then point you toward some resources that will help you tackle more advanced ways to utilize the cache.

The simplest solution is to use the `OutputCache` directive on your pages or user controls. For example, the following page will be cached for one hour (3600 seconds). You can refresh the page all you like, but the value of `DateTime.Now` won't change until the page is cleared from the cache. Here's the code that retrieves the current time:

OutputCacheSimple.aspx *(excerpt)*

```
<%@ Page Language="C#" AutoEventWireup="true"
    CodeBehind="OutputCacheSimple.aspx.cs"
    Inherits="chapter_15_performance.Performance.OutputCacheSimple"
%>
<%@ OutputCache Duration="3600" VaryByParam="none" %>
<html xmlns="http://www.w3.org/1999/xhtml">
<head id="Head1" runat="server">
  <title>Output Cache Example</title>
</head>
<body>
  <form id="form1" runat="server">
    <h1>Output Cache Example</h1>
    <div>
      <%= DateTime.Now.ToLongTimeString() %>
    </div>
  </form>
</body>
</html>
```

Figure 15.5 represents our page at 11:01:41 p.m.

Output Cache Example

11:01:41 PM

Figure 15.5. Loading a cached page for the first time

Figure 15.6 shows what it looks like at 11:23:01 p.m.

Output Cache Example

11:01:41 PM

Figure 15.6. Subsequent reloads of a cached page showing no changes to the page content

Notice that the time didn't change, as the page wasn't re-rendered.

Now let's look at a slightly more complex caching example:

OutputCache.aspx *(excerpt)*

```
<%@ Page Language="C#" AutoEventWireup="true"
    CodeBehind="OutputCache.aspx.cs"
    Inherits="chapter_15_performance.Performance.OutputCache" %>
<%@ OutputCache Duration="30" VaryByParam="none" %>
<html xmlns="http://www.w3.org/1999/xhtml" >
<head id="Head1" runat="server">
  <title>Output Cache Example</title>
  <script type="text/javascript">
    var d = new Date();
  </script>
</head>
<body>
  <form id="form1" runat="server">
  <!-- Pausing 5 seconds to simulate a database hit -->
  <% System.Threading.Thread.Sleep(5000); %>
  <h1>Output Cache Example</h1>
  <div>
    Time written by ASP.NET:
    <%= DateTime.Now.ToLongTimeString() %>
  </div>
  <div>
    Time written by Javascript:
    <script type="text/javascript">
      document.write(d.toLocaleTimeString())
    </script>
  </div>
  <div id="divCached" style="margin-top:25px;width=300px;">
    <script type="text/javascript">
      var aspTime = new Date();
      aspTime.setSeconds(<%= DateTime.Now.Second %>);

      // If there are more than two seconds difference
      // between the ASP.NET render and the javascript
      // evaluation, the page is almost certainly cached.
      if(Math.abs(d - aspTime) > 2000)
      {
        document.write('Probably Cached');
        document.getElementById("divCached").style.backgroundColor =
          "Coral";
      }
      else
```

```
        {
          document.write('Not Cached');
          document.getElementById("divCached").style.backgroundColor =
            "Aqua";
        }
      </script>
    </div>
  </form>
  </body>
</html>
```

The above page writes out the current time according to both ASP.NET (server side, cached) and JavaScript (client side, not cached). Additionally, if the JavaScript time is more than two seconds after the ASP.NET time, the page will report that it has probably been cached.

The first time this page is viewed, there's a five-second delay (due to the call to `Thread.Sleep`), then the page shown in Figure 15.7 is displayed.

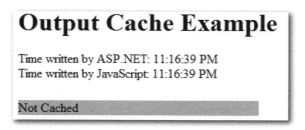

Figure 15.7. The page output on first load

But if you refresh the page within 30 seconds, you'll notice two differences. First, the page will return immediately. Second, it looks like Figure 15.8.

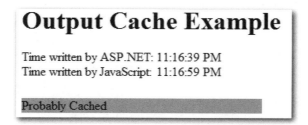

Figure 15.8. The page output 30 seconds after its initial load

Using `VaryByParam` to Cache Parameterized Pages

When you start to consider which pages in your application could be cached, you'll probably discover that many of them contain content that's 90% static. The remaining 10% of these pages is likely to contain one or two tiny portions that vary frequently. For example, consider a page in the example Northwind database that displays catalog information, including products filtered by category. The category is set by a parameter in the query string, so the following two URLs will yield different results:

- `http://www.contoso.com/Northwind/Products.aspx?Category=Seafood`

- `http://www.contoso.com/Northwind/Products.aspx?Category=Produce`

The novice programmer might apply the following code to cache these pages:

```
<%@ OutputCache Duration="30" %>
```

However, if you were to apply this code you'd quickly discover a problem—the category filter would stop working. The first version of the page that was displayed would be cached, so the filtering logic would be ignored on subsequent page views.

That's the exact function for which the `VaryByParam` attribute is used. In this case, we'd change the `OutputCache` directive to the following:

```
<%@ OutputCache Duration="30" VaryByParam="Category" %>
```

The `VaryByParam` attribute tells the cache system to store a *different* version of the page every time it sees a new value for `Category` in the URL. Once this attribute is in place, our users will be able to access a cached copy of the page for both the `Seafood` and `Produce` categories.

Keep in mind that storing different versions of the page for each parameter value isn't always the best idea—in cases where you have many different parameter values, you can quickly use a large amount of memory to hold all possible variations of the page. Use `VaryByParam` when your pages utilizes a limited number of parameter values.

Note that the number of seconds displayed in the JavaScript-generated time has updated to 59 seconds, while the ASP.NET time still shows 39. What this discrepancy suggests is that the server is sending the same HTML to the client for each request. Suppose that instead of just displaying the current time, we'd bound several GridViews to the results of several expensive database queries. With caching applied to such a page, the savings would be considerable.

You don't have to cache a page for long to see significant performance increases—a cache of one minute or less can improve your site's performance dramatically. For example, adding a cache to a simple page that just binds a GridView to the Products table in the example Northwind database will increase the performance of that page by about 500%, and for a page that performs a complex database query or processor-intensive calculation, this saving is likely to be amplified even further.

 Using Post-cache Substitution

While the OutputCache directive allows you to specify that the cache should vary with a specific parameter, it's not really efficient to cache a multitude of copies of one page that are nearly all identical.

Post-cache substitution, using the Substitution control, allows you to inject dynamic content into a cached page. The result is that you can cache some pages that you probably thought were unable to be cached. Read more on this subject in Scott Guthrie's article on the topic.[6]

One of the problems you might notice with this approach, however, is **latency**—the time delay between the point at which your data is updated and the moment when that same updated data reaches a user's browser. In the examples we've looked at in this solution, we displayed the same timestamp for 30 seconds after the page was rendered—this is great for performance, but might be a problem if your users require the data to always be up to date.

Fortunately, ASP.NET 2.0 has a solution to this problem, which we'll look at next.

---

[6] http://weblogs.asp.net/scottgu/archive/2006/11/28/tip-trick-implement-donut-caching-with-the-asp-net-2-0-output-cache-substitution-feature.aspx

How do I refresh my cache when the data changes?

As we saw in the previous tip, judicious use of output caching can provide dramatic improvements in your site's performance. Output caching works by saving the generated HTML for a rendered ASP.NET page. As long as the cache is valid, future requests for that page will just return that stored HTML, rather than processing the page again, which means no page parsing, hits to the database, data binding—any of those tasks that require precious bandwidth or processor cycles. Used correctly, caching can improve your requests-per-second on a high-traffic page by a factor of 100 or more.

For example, suppose you had a page that contained a `DataGrid` bound to a table called `Products`. Without caching, every page request would require ASP.NET to look up the product data in the database, process the page, data bind the product data, render the results to HTML, and output the results to the browser.

If the page was cached, only the first request for this page would require all that work; after that, ASP.NET would just skip all the hard work and serve up the HTML until the cache expired. The end result would be the same whether or not a cache was used: the same HTML would be sent to the browser. However, since a lot less work and network traffic is required to display cached HTML, the server can serve the cached page much faster and to more people.

One problem with cached pages is that they don't pick up data that has changed right away. To continue with the example above: if we were to add a new product to the `Products` table, it wouldn't show up on the page until the cache expired. Fortunately, ASP.NET 2.0 provides a good mechanism to refresh your cache automatically when the underlying data changes.

Solution

The SQL Cache Dependency was created to solve this problem. A few steps are required to set it up, but once it's up and running, you can use it throughout your whole application.

Using SQL Cache Dependencies with Older Versions of SQL Server

In this book I'll only cover the steps for configuring SQL Server Cache Dependencies on SQL Server 2005; there's a wealth of information on MSDN about how to set it up on SQL Server 2000:

- "ASP.NET SQL Server Registration Tool (Aspnet_regsql.exe)" (http://msdn2.microsoft.com/en-us/library/ms229862(VS.80).aspx)

- "Caching in ASP.NET with the SqlCacheDependency Class" (http://msdn2.microsoft.com/en-us/library/ms178604(VS.80).aspx)

- "Walkthrough: Using ASP.NET Output Caching with SQL Server" (http://msdn2.microsoft.com/en-us/library/e3w8402y(VS.80).aspx)

First, you'll need to make sure you've enabled SQL Server Service Broker for your database. You can confirm that with the following query:

```
ALTER DATABASE Northwind SET ENABLE_BROKER;
```

Next, you'll need to start the SQL Dependency event listener. The recommended place to make the change that triggers this listener is in the `Application_Start` method of **Global.asax**:

Global.asax (excerpt)

```
void Application_Start(object sender, EventArgs e)
{
  string northwindConnection = WebConfigurationManager.ConnectionStr
ings["NorthwindConnectionString1"].ConnectionString;
  SqlDependency.Start(northwindConnection);
}
```

Once the above code has been added to the **Global.asax** file, our connection can employ an SQL Cache Dependency.

To illustrate how an SQL Dependency is utilized, let's look at an example—a simple `GridView` that's bound to a table. We'll drag the good old Northwind `Products` table onto a new page, then set the following two attributes in the `SqlDataSource` control:

```
EnableCaching = "True" SqlCacheDependency =
    "NorthwindConnectionString1:Products"
```

With this simple line of code in place, the GridView won't read the Products table again until it changes. As soon as the Products table changes, though, SQL Server will notify ASP.NET to dump the cache, and the subsequent page request will reload the page from the database. The end result is that our application gains all of the performance benefits that come with caching, but our users will never see stale data.

How can I gain more control over the ASP.NET cache?

As we've seen, declarative caching provides a great return on investment—it's very easy to enable, and will give you some immediate performance benefits. However, you can gain even more benefit from the ASP.NET cache with only a little more work.

Solution

If you'd like to really take advantage of caching in ASP.NET, it's time you met the **Cache API**. Declarative caching might be easy to set up, but it can only take you so far. Unlike declarative caching, which stores and reuses rendered HTML, the Cache API allows you to store data efficiently in your application logic or code-behind code.

The simplest way to think of the ASP.NET cache is to compare it to the Application object. They're similar in that you can use both to store objects or values by a string key:

```
Cache["States"] = new string[] {"Alabama","Arkansas","Alaska"};
Cache["ProductData"] = GetProductDataset();
```

So what's the difference between the Application object and the cache for the storage of information? ASP.NET can remove items from the cache whenever it needs to free up memory. The cache has a limited amount of memory to work with, so when new content is added to the cache, the cache usually has to delete some older, cached data.

Different classes of information can be stored in your cache:

expensive data

Expensive data is information that you want to keep in the cache whenever possible. The term "expensive" refers to the fact that the generation of this class of data involves valuable resources (database or processing power).

inexpensive data

Inexpensive data refers to all of the other types of information that you'd like to put in the cache if there happens to be room, but is not particularly resource-intensive to generate.

The challenge is to prevent the inexpensive data from pushing the expensive data out of the cache.

The `Cache` object comes with some features that give you some control over which items are placed in the cache, and how long they stay there. Using the `Cache` object, you can apply custom cache dependencies, explicitly set cache expiration policies, and define callback events that fire when an item is removed from the cache (so you can decide whether you'd like to add it to the cache again).

One of my favorite features is the **sliding expiration**, which is a setting that lets you specify that an item should stay in the cache—as long as it has been used within a certain period of time:

```
Cache.Insert("ProductData", GetProducts(), null,
    System.Web.Caching.Cache.NoAbsoluteExpiration,
    TimeSpan.FromMinutes(10));
```

The above code tells the cache that we'd like it to keep our `Products` data set, as long as it has been used in the past ten minutes. The benefit of this approach is that frequently used data will stay cached, and infrequently used data will expire and stop taking up valuable space.

We can customize the settings for our cache, for example, setting a longer sliding expiration timeframe on data that's more expensive (such as that which results from a web service call). We could even add a cache dependency on the results of a `GetLastUpdateTimestamp` web service call to keep the data current if needed. Remember, though, that any data can still be removed from the cache at any time—our sliding expiration time setting is really just a suggestion to the cache system.

Discussion

Once you've begun to cache your data, you'll begin to see the benefit of what are some tried and true cache access patterns. Steven Smith wrote about the **cache data reference pattern** in his excellent MSDN article.[7] Here's some code that implements this pattern:

```
public DataTable GetCustomers(bool BypassCache)
{
  string cacheKey = "CustomersDataTable";
  object cacheItem = Cache[cacheKey] as DataTable;
  if((BypassCache) || (cacheItem == null))
  {
    cacheItem = GetCustomersFromDataSource();
    Cache.Insert(cacheKey, cacheItem, null,
        DateTime.Now.AddSeconds(GetCacheSecondsFromConfig(cacheKey),
        TimeSpan.Zero);
  }
  return (DataTable)cacheItem;
}
```

Smith's article explains the technique in more detail, but the most important point to note is the possibility that the object may not be in cache, or could potentially be removed at any time. The above code is safe because it loads the cached object, checks whether the object is null, and, if so, loads the object data and adds it back to the cache.

Another of my favorite cache patterns is one that Gavin Joyce uses on his Dot-NetKicks site—the **reluctant cache pattern**, which relies on his `ReluctantCacheHelper` class.[8] This pattern prevents an application from adding to the cache information that's unlikely to be used.

For example, when Google indexes your site, it will load every page that it can find. If your site implements a cache that is used by a large number of pages, your server will perform a lot of unnecessary work adding data to the cache, only for that data

---

[7] http://msdn2.microsoft.com/en-us/library/aa478965.aspx

[8] http://weblogs.asp.net/gavinjoyce/pages/The-Reluctant-Cache-Pattern.aspx

to be immediately dropped from the cache as other pages are added. Similar to the sliding expiration pattern, but in reverse, this pattern only adds data to the cache if it's been used a lot recently. Here's an example that implements this pattern:

```
public static List<Customer> GetCustomers() {
  string cacheKey = "Customers";
  int cacheDurationInSeconds = 5; // low number for demo purposes
  object customers = HttpRuntime.Cache[cacheKey] as List<Customer>;
  if (customers == null) {
    customers = CustomerDao.GetCustomers();
    if (new ReluctantCacheHelper(cacheKey,
        cacheDurationInSeconds, 2).ThresholdHasBeenReached)
    {
      HttpRuntime.Cache.Insert(cacheKey,
          customers,
          null,
          DateTime.Now.AddSeconds(cacheDurationInSeconds),
          System.Web.Caching.Cache.NoSlidingExpiration);
    }
  }
  return (List<Customer>)customers;
}
```

How do I speed up my database queries?

We've looked at a few ways to optimize your ASP.NET code, but if your queries are slow, you'll still have a site that drags its heels. You can hide the problem to some degree if you cache your data or add servers to your web farm, but eventually you will need to deal with your slow queries.

Of course, the best bet is to work with a good Database Administrator (DBA). We're ASP.NET developers, and while we can't help but learn about databases as we work with them, database administration is not our full-time job. A good DBA is by far the best solution to a database problem, but sometimes, it's just not an option. If you work on a team without a DBA, or you have limited access to your DBA, you need to do your best to solve problems when you can.

Slow Query or Slow Database?

It's important to decide whether you're dealing with one slow query or a whole slow database. Is one particular page slow, or is the whole site groaning? This solution will focus on the former; if you can narrow your database performance problems down to individual queries, refer to the section called "How can I troubleshoot a slow query?" later in this chapter.

Solution

Use the **SQL Profiler and Database Tuning Advisor**, located in the **SQL Server Performance Tools** folder.

Tuning a database server is hard. Initially, it can be difficult to find out what's responsible for slowing things down. Even then, fixing one problem (for example, applying indexes to a table to improve the speed of SELECT statements) can introduce new problems (such as slower INSERTs and UPDATEs).

Fortunately, the existence of the SQL Performance Tools means you don't have to bother with guesswork.

The SQL Profiler captures what's going on in your database, including which SQL statements are being executed, who's executing them, and how long they're taking. The profiler is the first step to determining what's actually happening on your server.

Note that the profiler captures both ad hoc and dynamic SQL. This means that the profiler is especially useful when control, library, or framework code is making a call in your database—you may not have access to the ASP.NET code, but the profiler will reveal exactly which queries are being executed, and how long they are taking.

It's best if you can run a profiler trace on your actual production system, but this may not always be possible—profiling a server slows the server down, and the site's regular users may not appreciate the extra delays. If you can't run on the production system, you can still gain a reasonable idea of server activity on a local or development server by simulating the way real users would using your site on the live server.

Running the profiler can be a bit daunting the first time—there are numerous advanced settings to monitor and tweak. It's best to start out with a predefined template like the one I've chosen in Figure 15.9. The two most useful templates for general performance diagnostics are the TSQL_Duration and Tuning templates.

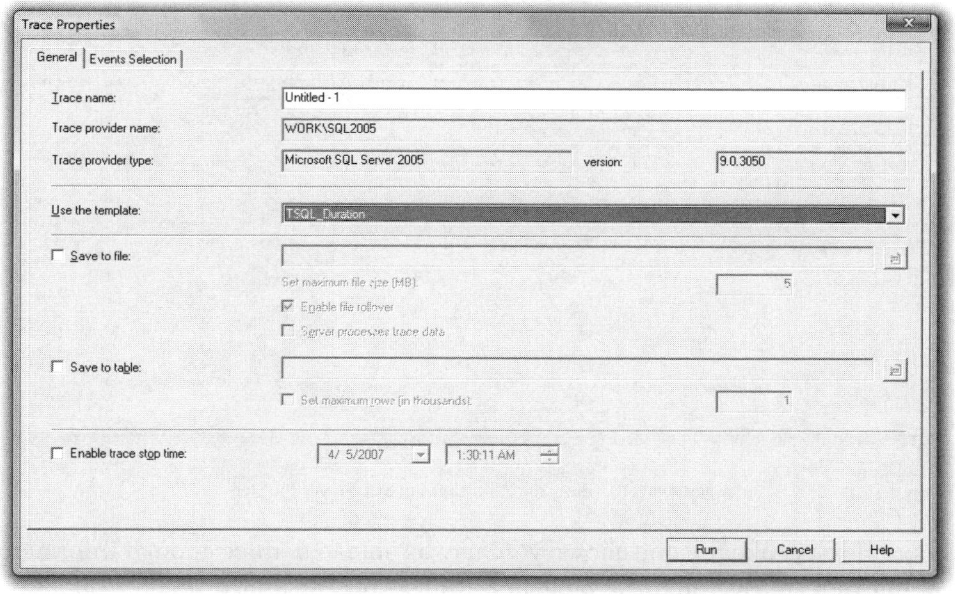

Figure 15.9. Selecting the TSQL_Duration template

The TSQL_Duration template is useful for giving you a quick snapshot of the queries and stored procedures that take the longest time to execute. Figure 15.10 shows some sample queries running against the Northwind example database. The slowest query—the query with the greatest duration value—is highlighted at the bottom of the list.

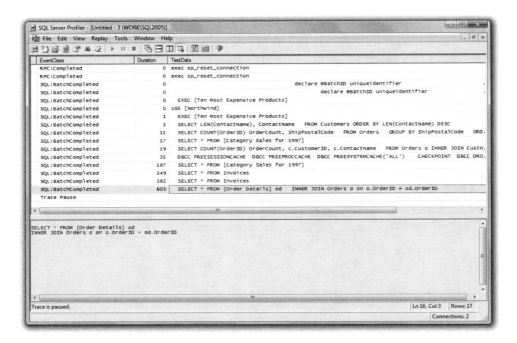

Figure 15.10. Query duration times in SQL Server Profiler

In a simple case like the one above, you may be able to deduce enough information from the TSQL_Duration trace to begin tuning a specific query. If you're at all in doubt, however, it's best to run the profiler with the Tuning template and analyze the results in the **Database Tuning Advisor** (also referred to as the DTA), a tool for analyzing database performance and suggesting which tables should be indexed.

To do this, first save your trace file from the profiler, as shown in Figure 15.11.

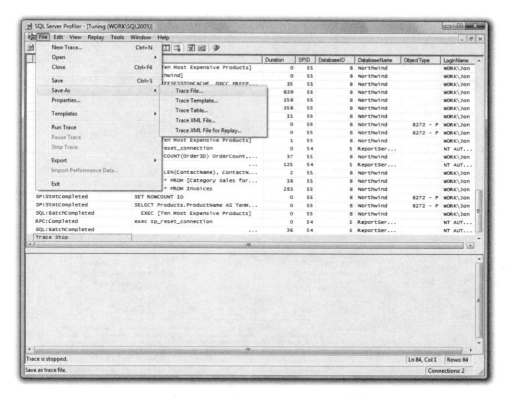

Figure 15.11. Saving a trace file from SQL Server Profiler

Now, we'll use the DTA to open the trace file that we just saved, as I've done in Figure 15.12, and click the **Start Analysis** button.

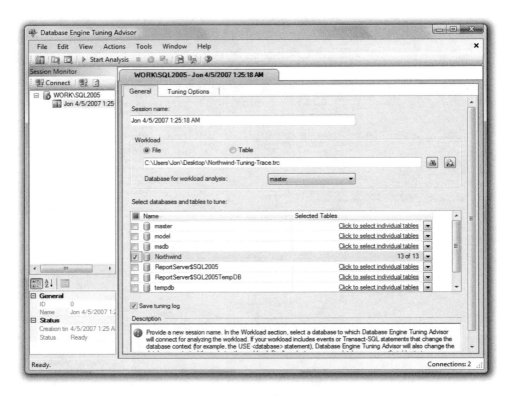

Figure 15.12. Loading the trace file in the Database Tuning Advisor

For my sample queries, DTA recommended that I apply a few indexes, to produce an estimated performance improvement of 5%, as shown in Figure 15.13. (The Northwind database is already more or less indexed; your estimated improvement should be a lot higher, with any luck.)

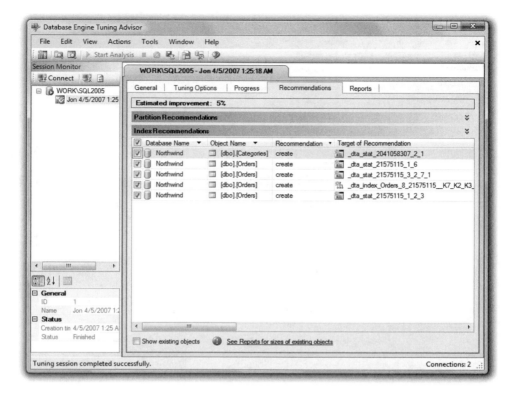

Figure 15.13. The index recommendations suggested by the DTA

If you scroll to the right, so that the `Description` column is visible, you'll see exactly which indexes and statistical changes the DTA recommends. Click on a recommendation to see a preview of the script that will add the proposed index, as shown in Figure 15.14.

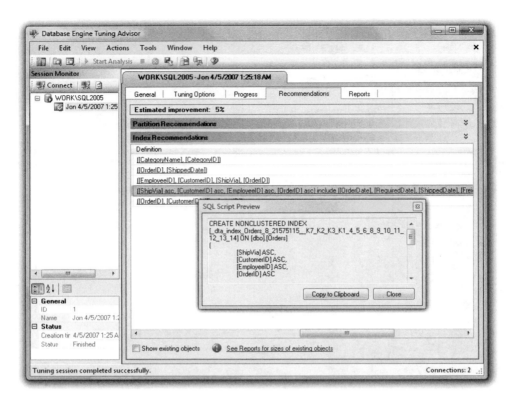

Figure 15.14. Viewing a preview of the script for applying one of the recommended indexes

To implement these changes, I suggest you save the recommendations (**Actions** >
Save Recommendations…), review them in SQL Server Management Studio (SSMS),
and apply them if you feel comfortable with them. Once you've done this, repeat
your original profiling test and verify that the changes have improved your database
performance.

Running the DTA with a SQL Workload Script File

Our walkthrough of the DTA used a SQL Server Trace file for the workload, but you can also use the DTA against a SQL script. Here's an abbreviated copy of the script I used for this walkthrough:

```
                                    SampleSqlWorkload.sql (excerpt)

USE [Northwind]
GO
SELECT * FROM [Order Details] od
INNER JOIN Orders o on o.OrderID = od.OrderID
GO
SELECT * FROM [Category Sales for 1997]
GO
SELECT * FROM Invoices
GO
SELECT COUNT(OrderID) OrderCount, ShipPostalCode
    FROM Orders
GROUP BY ShipPostalCode
ORDER BY COUNT(OrderID) DESC
GO
EXEC [Ten Most Expensive Products]
GO
SELECT COUNT(OrderID) OrderCount, c.CustomerID,
    c.ContactName
FROM Orders o INNER JOIN Customers c
    ON o.CustomerID = c.CustomerID
GROUP BY c.CustomerID, c.ContactName
sORDER BY COUNT(OrderID) DESC
GO
SELECT LEN(ContactName), ContactName
FROM Customers ORDER BY LEN(ContactName) DESC
GO
```

The important point to note is that there are GO separators between statements, which ensures that they're executed independently. You'll want your SQL workload script file to simulate actual usage, which means that you should include repeated calls to the most commonly used queries.

Using the Performance Dashboard

SQL Server includes **Dynamic Management Views** (DMVs)—database views that contain lots of useful management and troubleshooting information about your database. All the DMV views begin with the prefix `sys.dm_`; for example: `sys.dm_index_usage_stats`.

SSMS includes some built-in reports that leverage SQL Server Reporting Services as well as the DMVs. You can view these reports in SSMS if you right-click a database and select **Reports > Standard Reports...**.

SQL Server SP2 includes the ability to include custom reports, and one of the first to be released is the Performance Dashboard.[9] Once it's installed, the Performance Dashboard gives you a graphical snapshot that's visible in your browser, without you having to run a trace. Figure 15.15 shows the dashboard in action.

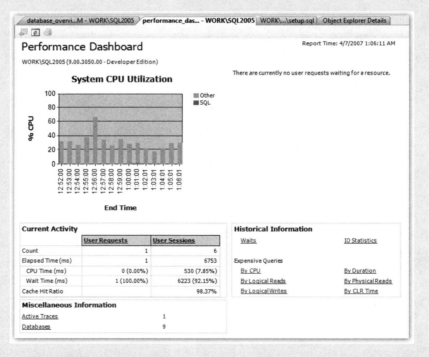

Figure 15.15. Viewing a handy third-party custom report in the Performance Dashboard

---

[9] http://www.microsoft.com/downloads/details.aspx?familyid=1d3a4a0d-7e0c-4730-8204-e419218c1efc

Discussion

One important aspect of troubleshooting a slow database is to understand what's making it run slowly. There are many potential causes of slow performance, but some common problems head the list. Let's look at a few of them.

Lack of Indexes

The ability to index data is one of the key benefits of storing information in a database. Imagine for a moment that you need to look up a name in a telephone book. You take advantage of the fact that the last names are sorted in alphabetic order—it would take forever to find a name if the entries were listed in random order. Databases take advantage of the way your information is sorted for the same reason. The default sort order in a table is called a **clustered index**.

Of course, you may want to search for your information in several different ways. To continue with the phone book example, you may want to look up businesses by zip code, business type, or name. The common approach to implementing this capability in a database is to order the data based on the most common search order, then place additional indexes to facilitate other search criteria. The data is sorted by the clustered index, but the database stores additional information to help it look up rows using other criteria. This additional lookup information is called a **nonclustered index**.

One of the most common reasons for slow queries is that the database is performing a **table scan**, which occurs when the database lacks an appropriate index to use to look up data. Asking your database to perform a table scan is equivalent to asking someone to look up a person in a phone book that lists entries in random order. To summarize, proper indexes are a necessity for database performance.

Incorrect Indexes

If indexes are good, more indexes are great, right?

Actually, no. There's a cost incurred when you add indexes to a database. Each time a row is added or updated, all the indexes need to be updated, and too many indexes can slow your database down. It's important to select a limited number of indexes that'll give you quick lookups without slowing down your updates. We'll be talking about some tools to help you with this task later in this chapter.

Poorly Written Queries

It's easy to land yourself in trouble if you don't really understand SQL. SQL is not just another programming language—it's a declarative, set-based query language. A lot of your standard programming tricks don't apply here.

We'll talk about troubleshooting query plans and poorly written queries in the section called "How can I troubleshoot a slow query?" later in this chapter.

Deadlocks

Databases use **locks** to prevent your data from being messed up by conflicting updates.

For example, we can't apply a 10% discount to all of our product prices *and* delete all products that are priced over $100 at the same time—we need to process one product at a time. Locks allow us to do this. The SQL Server engine is reasonably clever about how it uses database locks—it'll often lock portions of a table (called **pages**) and, sometimes, individual rows.

Yet there's always the potential for two transactions to arrive at a state where both are waiting for the freeing of a lock that's simultaneously held by the other transaction. This situation is called a **deadlock**.

For example, consider two queries that use the Products and Orders tables. The first query, which we'll call ProductsThenOrders, uses the Products table first; the second query, OrdersThenProducts, uses the Orders table first.

ProductsThenOrders locks the Products table and begins to make updates. Meanwhile, OrdersThenProducts locks the Orders table and performs its updates. No problems so far.

Now ProductsThenOrders is ready to update the Orders table, but it can't—the other query has it locked. Likewise, OrdersThenProducts wants to update the Products table, but is also blocked for the same reason. We're deadlocked!

When SQL Server eventually detects a deadlock, it will pick one query as the "deadlock victim" and kill it, while the survivors are released. The result of this conflict resolution process is that one of the queries will return with an error that it was unable to complete—not the most efficient use of resources.

Deadlocks don't happen too frequently—unless your application executes a lot of transactions. It's important to be aware of them and to fix deadlock conditions quickly. Deadlocks can be avoided by:

■ minimizing transaction length

■ accessing tables in the same order in competing queries

In the above example, accessing the `Products` table first in both queries would have prevented the deadlock.

 ### The NOLOCK Query Optimizer Hint

Even if you're not encountering deadlocks, locks have a definite performance impact. Locks restrict access to your data in such a way that only one query can use it at any time—an approach that's safe but slow.

In some cases, you mightn't need to lock your rows. You might query historical data that isn't subject to change, or it mightn't be crucial that the data returned in the query is perfectly up to date—comments on a weblog might fall into this category.

In these cases, you can use the `NOLOCK` hint to tell SQL Server you want to read directly from the table *without* honoring any locks. Note that this only makes sense for `SELECT` statements—any data modification will always require a lock. Best practices avoid using **table hints**—parameters that override the default behavior of a query—when possible. However, this one is relatively innocuous as long as you understand that you may be viewing uncommitted changes. Just don't use it when displaying critical information, such as financial data.

Here's how you'd use it:

```
SELECT COUNT(1) FROM Orders WITH (NOLOCK)
```

Since this statement places no locks on the data that it's reading, other queries won't be forced to wait for the query to complete before they can use the `Orders` table.

You can read more about deadlocks in the MSDN article, "Analyzing Deadlocks with SQL Server Profiler."[10]

Hardware Issues

As with any software application, SQL Server performs at its optimum when it's running on sufficiently powerful hardware.

If upgrading your server is an option, the first thing you should look at is memory, as SQL Server makes heavy use of available memory to cache frequently used data. And the cost of new memory is relatively cheap—often cheaper than the time required to tune an underpowered database server. Adding memory can compensate for slow CPU or drive access, since caching can significantly reduce the work that SQL Server needs to complete.

After you've exhausted your memory upgrade options, the next most common hardware issue is a disk read/write bottleneck. Database hardware configuration is a large topic and falls well beyond the scope of an ASP.NET book, but a great first step is to put your log files on a drive that's as fast possible, and is separate from the operating system and database files.

Using a production database server for other tasks—especially IIS—is a bad idea. It's often necessary in a development environment, but it will have a performance impact in production.

How can I troubleshoot a slow query?

Optimizing database performance is a complex topic that's the subject of numerous very thick books, so I'm not going to pretend that we can make you an expert in query optimization in a few short pages. Instead, I'll focus on some of my favorite "developer to developer" tips to point you in the right direction.

Solution

Before you begin to look for a solution, it's important to verify the problem at hand. You can then begin the process of elimination.

---

[10] http://msdn2.microsoft.com/en-us/library/ms188246.aspx

Verifying the Problem

First, verify that the SQL you *think* is being executed is actually being executed. The best way to confirm this is to duplicate the problem: run the query in SQL Server Management Studio (SSMS).

If you have any doubt about which SQL commands are being executed, run the SQL Profiler for confirmation (see the section called "How do I speed up my database queries?" earlier in this chapter for details on using the SQL Profiler). This tool is especially helpful when used with applications that make use of declarative data binding, or with frameworks that handle data access for you.

Clearing the SQL Cache when Testing in SSMS

SQL Server uses an intelligent caching system to enhance performance. If you run frequent queries against a certain table, SQL Server will recognize that fact and store the source (and result data) of those queries in its internal cache. By doing so, future matching queries won't need to look up this data until the next time it changes.

This functionality, while useful, can be confusing if you conduct your tests by running your queries from SSMS—some of your query information may be cached, so your queries will run faster the second time you execute them.

To ensure that you make valid comparisons that don't return cached information, clear your cache each time you run the query. The following script does just this—first it drops caches, then it calls a **CHECKPOINT** to flush pending changes from memory to disk, and finally it clears any data that has been stored in memory:

```
DBCC FREESESSIONCACHE
DBCC FREEPROCCACHE
DBCC FREESYSTEMCACHE('ALL')
CHECKPOINT
DBCC DROPCLEANBUFFERS
GO -- Your query goes here
```

Once you're able to duplicate the problem in SSMS, you can dig into the query itself.

Checking for Large Result Sets

If your query returns more rows than you expected it to, there are two main problems to look at—cross joins and incomplete WHERE clauses.

A **cross join** occurs when you fail to specify a join correctly. Here's an example:

```
SELECT * FROM Customers, Orders, [Order Details], Products
```

In the above query, we haven't specified how the tables should be joined, so the SQL interpreter will attempt to return every possible combination. That means that our result set will include *every Order* combined with *every Customer* (not just the Orders that each Customer made). So this query returns about 12.5 *billion* rows (91 Customers × 830 Orders × 2155 Order Details × 77 Products)—that's roughly 7.5GB of data.

That return is obviously way out of line, considering there are only 830 orders in the system. Of course, this is a slightly exaggerated example for demonstration purposes, but it's easy to see how a single cross join can waste a lot of database resources (CPU and memory) and delay network traffic between the database and web server.

An incomplete WHERE clause isn't quite as bad, but can still return more rows than you need. The following query returns 2155 rows:

```
SELECT * FROM [Order Details]
```

This one, on the other hand, returns three rows:

```
SELECT * FROM [Order Details] WHERE OrderID = 10252
```

ADO.NET makes it really easy to filter your data on the server, but unfortunately this feature is a double-edged sword—it can mask problems with a large result set. That's why it's important to verify the problem with real, systematic measurement rather than just assume that a Gridview displaying only a handful of rows couldn't possibly be the source of the problem.

Checking the Query Plan

If your query is indeed returning the correct number of rows, but still takes too long, the next step is to look at the **query plan**, which is a visual representation of the steps that your query takes to return its result set.

You can view the *estimated* query execution plan in SSMS if you first select the query, then select **Display Estimated Execution Plan** from the **Query** menu (tor use the toolbar button or the keyboard shortcut—**Ctrl-L**). You'll also have the option to include the *actual* query execution plan (also available from the **Query** menu, the toolbar, and via the keyboard shortcut **Ctrl-M**). The actual plan is a little more accurate than the estimated one, but requires that you actually execute the query and wait for it to complete.

Let's look at the actual execution plan for the `uspGetBillOfMaterials` stored procedure in the AdventureWorks sample database that comes with SQL Server. Enter the following text in the SSMS query window, then turn on the **Include Actual Execution Plan** option and execute the query:

```
EXEC dbo.uspGetBillOfMaterials 800, '2001-01-09'
```

Figure 15.16 shows the result.

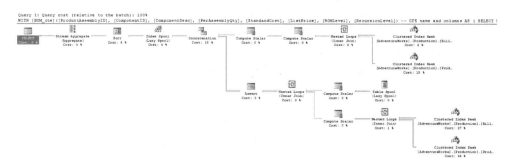

Figure 15.16. The execution plan for the `uspGetBillOfMaterials` stored procedure

Figure 15.17 shows a close-up of the bottom right-hand corner of our plan.

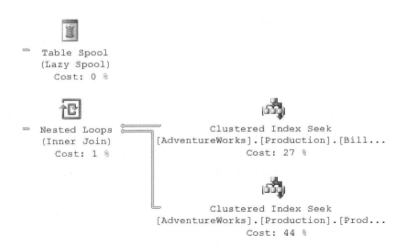

Figure 15.17. A close-up of the execution plan for the `uspGetBillOfMaterials` stored procedure

You'll need to look for a few important things when you're analyzing an execution plan:

thick lines

Thick lines in the execution plan indicate large amounts of data being passed between steps. I was once troubleshooting an extremely slow summary report query that returned only a dozen rows. When I looked at the execution plan, I saw that some of the lines between steps were an *inch thick*—this indicated *billions* of rows being passed between those steps, which were then filtered down to the final dozen rows displayed in the browser. The solution was to modify the query to ensure that the data was filtered as early as possible.

large values for `Cost`

Large percentage numbers indicate the most expensive operations—the value of 44% in Figure 15.17 is one example of this.

any operation containing the word "scan"

If one of the steps on your plan contains the word "scan" (or, in particular, "Table Scan"), this is an indication that the SQL engine had to step through every row in a table to find the data that it was after. This is usually associated with a high `Cost` value. There are occasions when a table scan is acceptable—such as when you're performing a lookup against a very small table—but in general they're best avoided.

If you see a problem, you can troubleshoot it in SSMS: modify the query and view the effect of your change on the execution plan.

If it looks as though your issue may be the result of an indexing problem, the best solution is to right-click the query and select **Analyze Query in Database Engine Tuning Advisor**. The DTA will launch with all the necessary options preselected, so all you need to do is click the **Start Analysis** button. Figure 15.18 shows the results of one such analysis.

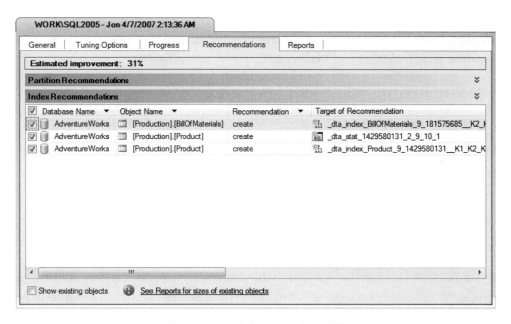

Figure 15.18. Analyzing a query in the DTA

As you can see, the DTA has recommended two index changes and one statistical change that should improve this query's performance by 31%. Of course, you'll need to consider the effect that these additional indexes will have on updates to the affected tables. In this case, since the tables in this particular example are probably updated rather infrequently, I think that these new indexes make sense. You can apply or save these changes via the **Actions** menu.

Eliminating Cursors

You'll want to look for and eliminate any unnecessary **cursors**—pointers for traversing records in the database.

Cursors let you write in a procedural style, applying logic to a single table row at a time. While it can be tempting to drop back to those skills that are most familiar to you in sticky situations, cursor-based queries will prevent the database engine from taking advantage of the index optimizations and set-based operations for which it was designed.

Resist the urge and get rid of your cursors!

I've written a lot of SQL in ten years of professional programming, and I've yet to encounter a case where cursors were required. I recently rewrote someone else's complex query from using cursors to standard SQL, and the time for the resulting operation dropped from eight hours to just over one minute.

Think about how to describe the problem as a bulk operation. For example, suppose your mode of thinking about a query was something like this:

> "I'll loop through the orders table, get the product ID, then grab the price, and compare it to …"

Instead, consider rephrasing it to something like this:

> "I want to find all orders for products that have prices greater than a certain amount …"

Remember that you can use common table expressions (CTEs), table variables, and temporary tables if you're stuck. While these fallback options aren't as efficient as performing a bulk operation, they at least allow the query engine to make use of indexes.

The Problem with SELECT *

Most developers will tell you that SELECT * queries are bad, but for the wrong reason.

The commonly understood reason is that SELECT * is wasteful because it returns columns that you don't need. While this is true, most normalized tables don't contain that many columns, so these extra rows usually won't have a noticeable impact on your site's performance unless they number in the millions.

Often, the bigger problem with SELECT * is the effect it will have on the execution plan. While SQL Server primarily uses indexes to look up your data, if the index happens to contain all of the columns you request, it won't even need to look in the table. This concept is known as **index coverage**.

Compare the following two queries (against the sample `AdventureWorks` database):

```
SELECT * FROM Production.TransactionHistoryArchive
  WHERE ReferenceOrderID < 100
SELECT ReferenceOrderLineID FROM
    Production.TransactionHistoryArchive
  WHERE ReferenceOrderID < 100
```

In both cases, we're returning the same number of rows, and the `SELECT *` query only returns 15KB more data than the second query. However, take a look at the execution plans shown in Figure 15.19.

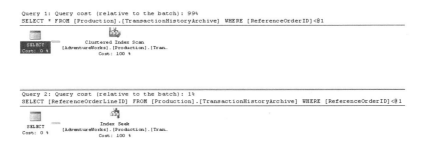

Figure 15.19. The execution plan for two queries—one using `SELECT *`, and one using the table name

You'll notice that the first query took 99% of the relative work for both queries. The second query was able to look up the values in the index via an **index seek**—a search that touches on only those rows that qualify. The first query, however, had to scan all the rows in the table. In this case, the fact that the requested columns were all contained in the search index resulted in a performance difference of nearly *one hundred-fold*.

It's important to include commonly queried data in your indexes—something that's simply not feasible if you're using `SELECT *`. If you just query the rows you need, the DTA will be able to recommend indexes to cover them.

Accessing More Information

There's a plethora of resources to which you can turn when you're stuck on a really difficult SQL database issue. Here are just a few of them:

- The Microsoft TechNet article on troubleshooting performance problems in SQL Server 2005 (http://www.microsoft.com/technet/prodtechnol/sql/2005/tsprfprb.mspx#E1BAG)
- SQLTeam.com—one of many SQL Server community forums (http://www.sqlteam.com/)
- The SitePoint Databases Forum (http://www.sitepoint.com/launch/dbforum/)

Summary

Performance optimization is an iterative process—be prepared to follow the repetitive steps of analyzing your site's performance, tuning your application, analyzing the performance again, then tuning some more, until your site performs the way you want it to. Premature optimization—tuning without understanding what's causing the slowdown—is likely to cause more problems than it solves.

ASP.NET and SQL Server 2005 power some of the most popular and powerful sites upon the planet, including MySpace, which serves billions of page views per day.[11] You've got all the tools you need to get the maximum possible use out of your web server—I hope the tips in this chapter will help you to put them to work.

---

[11] http://www.myspace.com/

16

Search Engine Optimization

The best web content in the world is worthless if nobody can find it.

On today's Web, a large percentage of your audience will find your site through a search performed on a major search engine, such as Google, Yahoo!, or MSN. Therefore, it should be your goal to rank on the first page of search results for the search keywords relevant to your content. The tasks involved in achieving this goal are known collectively as **Search Engine Optimization**, or SEO.

The first rule of SEO is very simple: *create compelling content*, and people will eventually find it, link to it, and increase its ranking. Nothing else you can do will matter as much as following this basic first rule. Put 99% of your effort into creating really great content—content that's useful to people, content that solves problems for people, content that provides helpful answers. Once you've done that, everything else *almost* takes care of itself.

That said, there are ways to make your content more accessible to search engines. That's the other 1% of SEO. To ensure that potential users or customers can find your web pages, you need to think like a search engine spider. Search engine spiders don't see images; they have a very limited understanding of Flash animations and

JavaScript; they certainly don't understand any fancy Ajax features. All they see is plain text and HTML.

To get yourself in the right frame of mind, open your page in a browser and view the source. That's what the search engine spider will see. Does your raw HTML look as good as the rest of your web site? Is it clean? Can you understand it?

It's not enough to make your web site look good for users who view it in a web browser. You need to make it look good as plain text for search engine spiders, too.

In this chapter, we'll look at how search engines index and rank content, and explore a number of solutions to specific issues that can hamper your search rankings.

How does Google rank pages?

Statistics—and common knowledge—show that Google is the most popular search engine. While the tips in this chapter are applicable to all major search engines, it's important that you have an understanding of how Google works.

Solution

Until recently, Google's PageRank algorithm was fairly easy to understand. Links to your site counted as votes, so if you linked the word "monkey" from your site to the San Diego Zoo's web site, you increased the chances that a user searching for the word "monkey" would see a link to the San Diego Zoo. Instead of search engines trying to figure out what we wanted to see, Google just directed traffic based on the road signs that content developers had set up.

This worked really well until everyone understood that links to their site meant high rankings, and unscrupulous people started to take advantage of the fact. You can still see the aftermath of these circumstances—especially in weblog sites, where automated systems litter blog comment areas with comment spam. Other automated systems copied content from legitimate weblogs and re-posted it on sites that included links to sites that were hoping for a higher Google rank, and hence more traffic and money. As this evidence suggests, abuse of the system was rife.

Google responded with a series of updates, codenamed "Florida" (in 2003) and "Jagger" (in 2005), which were intended to make the system a lot harder to abuse.

The exact algorithms are kept secret and regularly updated, but the basic ideas are reasonably well known.

Google has replaced the elegant but naïve PageRank system with the more cynical and world-weary TrustRank system. This system still counts links as votes, but it only counts votes from sites it trusts. A site is allocated trust ratings on the basis of links to that site from other sites that are already trusted. And trust propagates through the system, so if *The New York Times* web site links to my site, and I link to your site, your Google rank and trust rating within the system will both increase as a result of *The New York Times*'s TrustRank. This system also allows site owners to identify among their pages links that shouldn't count towards the linked site's search rank: the site owner simply adds `rel="nofollow"` to the relevant a elements. This facility has made the huge majority of comment spam completely useless (although unfortunately, the fact that it's useless doesn't mean it'll go away).

This system also punishes sites that attempt to abuse the system, removing their PageRank and TrustRank. If you follow SEO news, you'll regularly read about top corporations that tried to cheat the system and wound up banished from the search results for six months or more.

Once you understand how Google determines your site's rank, you'll see why everything we're advising is geared towards just making sure the search engines can find your pages and read the content. If you provide good content, you'll receive links from other sites, and advance up the Google rankings. You'll understand that stuffing your page with keywords is useless, because these don't count as votes towards your search ranking. And you'll know better than to waste your time trying to cheat the system, because it's difficult to do, and likely to see your site removed from search results.

How do I ensure search engines review only search-relevant content?

If you view the source of an ASP.NET page, the first thing you'll notice is a giant chunk of Base64-encoded text in a hidden `input` element at the top of the page. You can't miss it, as Figure 16.1 shows.

Figure 16.1. The `ViewState` input element at the top of an ASP.NET-generated web page

This is the container for view state data. In case you skipped Chapter 6, view state is a persistence mechanism that's built into ASP.NET to enable controls on the page to remember values between postbacks.

View state is both a blessing and a curse. It's convenient, because it keeps you from needing to write code to load and restore control values between postbacks. But it also increases the size of your page—sometimes dramatically.

View state can also interfere with search engine spiders. Most spiders will only retrieve the first *n* kilobytes of your page to index, where *n* is anything from 200 to around 1100 kilobytes.[1] If your `ViewState` object is 20 kilobytes in size, that's 20 kilobytes of meaningless, non-indexable binary data that the spider will ignore. You could have used those 20 kilobytes to present valuable content, boosting your search rankings in the process.

Solutions

There are three solutions to this problem. You can remove view state, move view state, or create an `HttpModule` class.

---

[1] http://www.sitepoint.com/article/indexing-limits-where-bots-stop/

Removing View State

My advice is to disable view state unless you really need it. If you're not using it, why not simplify your page? This can be done on a per-page or per-control basis; just set the ViewState property to false, and you're done.

No, Really: Try Disabling View State

You may have tried disabling view state in ASP.NET 1.0 or 1.1 and found that some of your controls ceased to function. The DataGrid was a prime example—when you disabled view state, all the events stopped firing.

ASP.NET 2.0 improved this situation with the introduction of *control state*. Control state holds the essential information that's required for the control to function, and it stays there even when you disable view state. So a GridView with view state disabled will still work—it just doesn't store all your bound data between postbacks.

So, give that "view state-free" thing another try. *Really*.

If you can't disable view state, the next best thing is to pick it up and move it to a place where it will do less damage: the bottom of the page.

Moving View State

The easiest way to move view state on a specific page is to override the Render method on the Page class. Just add the following code to any page in your ASP.NET project:

```
                                        MoveViewState.aspx.cs (excerpt)
protected override void Render(HtmlTextWriter writer)
{
  MoveViewState(writer);
}

protected void MoveViewState(HtmlTextWriter writer)
{
  StringWriter sw = new StringWriter();
  HtmlTextWriter hw = new HtmlTextWriter(sw);
  base.Render(hw);
  string html = sw.ToString();
  int ViewStateStart = html.IndexOf(
```

```
        "<input type=\"hidden\" name=\"__VIEWSTATE\"");
  if (ViewStateStart <= 0)
  {
    writer.Write(html);
    return;
  }

  // write the section of html before viewstate
  writer.Write(html.Substring(1, ViewStateStart - 1));
  int ViewStateEnd = html.IndexOf("/>", ViewStateStart) + 2;
  int FormEndStart = html.IndexOf("</form>");

  // write the section after the viewstate
  // and up to the end of the FORM
  writer.Write(html.Substring(ViewStateEnd, html.Length -
       ViewStateEnd - (html.Length - FormEndStart)));

  // write the viewstate itself
  writer.Write(html.Substring(ViewStateStart,
     ViewStateEnd - ViewStateStart));

  // now write the FORM footer
  writer.Write(html.Substring(FormEndStart));
}
```

Load the page into a browser, and view the source again. Note how clean your page looks now—Figure 16.2 shows how it appears.

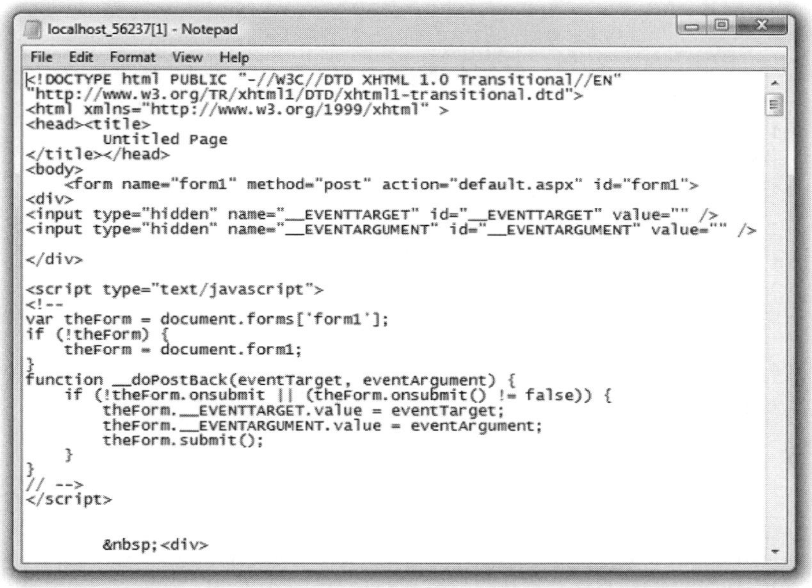


```
<!DOCTYPE html PUBLIC "-//W3C//DTD XHTML 1.0 Transitional//EN"
"http://www.w3.org/TR/xhtml1/DTD/xhtml1-transitional.dtd">
<html xmlns="http://www.w3.org/1999/xhtml" >
<head><title>
        Untitled Page
</title></head>
<body>
    <form name="form1" method="post" action="default.aspx" id="form1">
<div>
<input type="hidden" name="__EVENTTARGET" id="__EVENTTARGET" value="" />
<input type="hidden" name="__EVENTARGUMENT" id="__EVENTARGUMENT" value="" />

</div>

<script type="text/javascript">
<!--
var theForm = document.forms['form1'];
if (!theForm) {
    theForm = document.form1;
}
function __doPostBack(eventTarget, eventArgument) {
    if (!theForm.onsubmit || (theForm.onsubmit() != false)) {
        theForm.__EVENTTARGET.value = eventTarget;
        theForm.__EVENTARGUMENT.value = eventArgument;
        theForm.submit();
    }
}
// -->
</script>


         <div>
```

Figure 16.2. The page source after the view state data has been moved to the bottom of the page

This is a satisfactory solution, but it's a little tedious. Who wants to go through every page of their web site, adding this bit of code? This is copy-and-paste programming at its worst.

A slightly smarter approach would be to create a new base `Page` class and inherit all of our pages from that class. But that approach would still require us to edit every single page in our project. What are we to do?

Creating an `HttpModule`

The simplest way to move view state to the bottom of every page in your application, *without* editing every single page, is to implement this code as an `HttpModule`.

First, create a new class file to contain our `Filter`, and call it `MoveViewStateFilter`, as shown in the code below. The `Filter` inherits from `IO.Stream` and does the heavy lifting of moving strings around in the page. It's almost identical to the `MoveViewState` function we saw earlier:

```
public class MoveViewStateFilter : System.IO.MemoryStream
{
  System.IO.Stream _filter;
  readonly Encoding _encoding = Encoding.UTF8;
  bool _filtered = false;

  public MoveViewStateFilter(System.IO.Stream filter)
  {
    _filter = filter;
  }

  public override void Close()
  {
    if (!_filtered)
    {
      base.Close();
      return;
    }
    if (this.Length == 0)
    {
      _filter.Close();
      base.Close();
      return;
    }
    byte[] bytes;
    string html = _encoding.GetString(this.ToArray());
    int ViewStateStart = html.IndexOf(
        "<input type=\"hidden\" name=\"__VIEWSTATE\"");
    if (ViewStateStart <= 0)
    {
      bytes = this.ToArray();
    }
    else
    {
      System.IO.StringWriter writer =
          new System.IO.StringWriter();

      // write the section of html before viewstate
      writer.Write(html.Substring(1, ViewStateStart - 1));
      int ViewStateEnd = html.IndexOf("/>", ViewStateStart) + 2;
      int FormEndStart = html.IndexOf("</form>");

      // write the section after the viewstate
```

```
      // and up to the end of the FORM
      writer.Write(html.Substring(ViewStateEnd, html.Length -
      ViewStateEnd - (html.Length - FormEndStart)));

      // write the viewstate itself
      writer.Write(html.Substring(ViewStateStart,
          ViewStateEnd - ViewStateStart));I

      // now write the FORM footer
      writer.Write(html.Substring(FormEndStart));
      bytes = _encoding.GetBytes(writer.ToString());
    }
    _filter.Write(bytes, 0, bytes.Length);
    _filter.Close();
    base.Close();
  }

  public override void Write(byte[] buffer, int offset, int count)
  {
    // only do this for text/html responses
    if (HttpContext.Current.Response.ContentType == "text/html")
    {
      base.Write(buffer, offset, count);
      _filtered = true;
    }
    else
    {
      _filter.Write(buffer, offset, count);
      _filtered = false;
    }
  }
}
}
```

Now, create a class called `MoveViewStateModule`, which inherits from `IHttpModule`. It hooks up our `Filter` to the life cycle of the ASP.NET `Request`:

MoveViewStateModule.cs (excerpt)

```
public class MoveViewStateModule : System.Web.IHttpModule
{
  public MoveViewStateModule() { }
  void System.Web.IHttpModule.Dispose() { }
  void System.Web.IHttpModule.Init(
      System.Web.HttpApplication context)
```

```
    {
        context.BeginRequest +=
            new EventHandler(this.BeginRequestHandler);
    }
    void BeginRequestHandler(object sender, EventArgs e)
    {
        System.Web.HttpApplication application =
            (System.Web.HttpApplication)sender;
        application.Response.Filter =
            new MoveViewStateFilter(application.Response.Filter);
    }
}
```

Once we've added our `Filter` and `HttpModule` to the code, all we need to do is add the `MoveViewStateModule` to our **Web.config**'s `httpModules` section:

Web.config *(excerpt)*

```xml
<?xml version="1.0"?>
<configuration>
  <appSettings/>
  <connectionStrings/>
  <system.web>
    <compilation debug="true" />
    <authentication mode="Windows" />
    <httpModules>
      <add type="MoveViewStateModule, WebApp"
          name="MoveViewStateModule" />
    </httpModules>
  </system.web>
</configuration>
```

The net result is identical to the per-page method shown earlier: the view state is moved to the bottom of the page.

Using the `HttpModule` technique, all you have do to is:

▨ Add the precompiled assembly to your web site, or add the source code to your web site.

▨ Modify **Web.config** to include the new `HttpModule`.

The `HttpModule` approach is far more powerful than the previous solutions because it allows you to make global changes to the way your pages render *without modifying a single line of code on any of those pages*. Great stuff!

How do I rewrite my URLs for human readability?

If someone sent you an email that contained the URL below, would you click on it?

http://www.happy.com/view?v=JZCHpacxl4c

Now, would you click on the URL if it was reformatted to look like this?

http://www.happy.com/install/virulent-virus.do

That's just one example of how human-readable URLs make life easier for everyone. The text of the URL itself should hint as to the content users might expect to find at that location.

Human-readable URLs also boost the relevance of your page to the keywords for which you're trying to obtain a good ranking. When users perform a web search, they aren't just searching the content of the pages. They're also searching the title of the page, and the text of the URL itself. The inclusion of keywords in the URL is a powerful indicator that the user might find relevant content at that URL.

But forget SEO for a moment. If your URLs look like programming gobbledygook …

http://www.amazon.com/One-Fish-Two-Red-Blue/dp/0007173687/ref=sr_1_10/
102-5693857-5089762?ie=UTF8&s=books&qid=1179896923&sr=1-10

… then you've failed the user. We can, and should, do better than this today. Simplify your URLs via rewriting and make them human-readable. Take, for example, this URL:

http://mysite.com/category.aspx?id=refrigerators&subcat=stainless

We can rewrite the URL to express the same thing in a more human-readable way:

http://mysite.com/refrigerators/stainless/

Isn't that much nicer? For more evidence of the usability benefits of human-readable URLs, I refer you to a 1999 column by usability guru Jakob Neilsen titled "URL as UI."[2]

Solutions

ASP.NET 2.0 provides some basic tools for us to use to write our own URL rewriting engine, but before we talk about them, I need to point out that they have one serious limitation.

If you want to use .NET code to rewrite URLs, you can *only* do so for pages that end in **.aspx** or some other extension that's handled by the **aspnet_isapi.dll** ASP.NET handler in IIS. You can see which file extensions are mapped to each handler in the **Application Configuration** dialog in IIS, as shown in Figure 16.3.

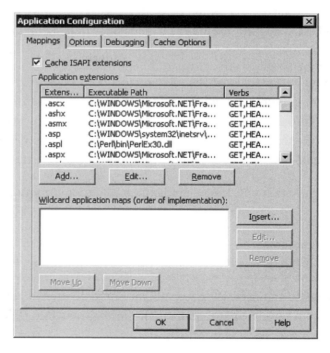

Figure 16.3. IIS file extensions and their handlers

[2] http://www.useit.com/alertbox/990321.html

The only available workaround is to remap file extensions in IIS so that *every single file type,* not just the ones ending in **.a??xx**, are handled by **aspnet_isapi.dll**. This undertaking is known as **wildcard mapping**, and it's a very invasive change. It means that every file—including static HTML files, images, CSS files, and so forth—will be passed through **aspnet_isapi.dll**. However, it doesn't work perfectly: wildcard mapping can't deal with URLs that refer to directories. In short, it's a scorched-earth solution with a lot of problems, which is why I don't recommend it.

So, what are our options? Well, I have some good news, and some bad news.

The bad news is that it's difficult to undertake proper URL rewriting using only .NET code. If you're serious about URL rewriting, you shouldn't be doing it in .NET code at all—you should be doing it at the web server level.

The good news outweighs the bad, though:

- In IIS 5.x and 6, you can install third-party ISAPI add-ins to enable proper URL rewriting.

- In IIS 7, .NET code can be hooked into the rendering pipeline, so you can write a true .NET URL rewriter at last.

URL Rewriting Via IIS

For IIS 6, a number of third-party products enable proper URL rewriting support:

- Ionic's ISAPI Rewrite Filter: http://cheeso.members.winisp.net/IIRF.aspx (free!)

- ISAPI_Rewrite: http://www.isapirewrite.com/

- IISRewrite: http://www.qwerksoft.com/products/iisrewrite/

These solutions typically support the de-facto standard Apache `mod_rewrite` rules, as documented in the Apache URL Rewriting Guide.[3] Note that you must be familiar with regular expressions to set up rewrite rules, whatever solution you choose. I have yet to see any URL rewriting tool that didn't use regular expressions as its *lingua franca.*

---

[3] http://httpd.apache.org/docs/2.0/misc/rewriteguide.html

Here's an example of some practical, basic URL rewriting rules that I use on my own web server.

The first rule prevents image bandwidth theft (you can blame MySpace for this one!).[4] Unless the `Referer` value of the HTTP request is in the whitelist (in this abbreviated example, only my own site and google.com are allowed), the users see a generic, small **block.gif** instead of the image they requested:

```
# Block external image linking
RewriteCond Referer: (?!http://(?:www\.codinghorror\.com|(?:.+\.)?go
↪ogle\.\w{2,3})).+
RewriteRule .*\.(?:gif|jpg|jpeg|png) /images/block.gif [I,O]
```

This next rule appends a trailing slash to the ends of folder names, so that, for instance, http://www.codinghorror.com/blog becomes http://www.codinghorror.com/blog/. This approach is slightly more efficient; the trailing slash prevents an extra HTTP round trip to determine whether or not the request is for a folder:

```
# fix missing slash on folders
RewriteCond Host: (.*)
RewriteRule ([^.?]+[^.?/]) http\://$1$2/ [I,R]
```

These rules remove the default files from the URL, so users don't bookmark the longer version of the URL (such as http://mywebsite/index.html). Instead, they bookmark the much simpler version (such as http://mywebsite/):

```
# remove index pages from URLs
RewriteRule (.*)/default.htm $1/ [I,RP,L]
RewriteRule (.*)/default.asp $1/ [I,RP,L]
RewriteRule (.*)/default.aspx $1/ [I,RP,L]
RewriteRule (.*)/index.htm $1/ [I,RP,L]
RewriteRule (.*)/index.html $1/ [I,RP,L]
```

---

[4] MySpace [http://myspace.com/] is a social networking site that's wildly popular with teenagers. MySpace users are often innocently ignorant of the trouble that linking to an image on another site from their own MySpace pages can cause.

I prefer the **canonical URL**—the definitive format to which each URL on a site resolves—for my site to use the `www.` prefix. The rule below forces requests for http://mywebsite.com/ to become http://www.mywebsite.com/:

```
# force proper www. prefix on all requests
RewriteCond %HTTP_HOST ^codinghorror\.com
RewriteRule ^/(.*) http://www.codinghorror.com/$1 [RP,L]
```

URL Rewriting Via .NET Code

If you want to perform URL rewriting in .NET, I strongly advise you *not* to write your own URL rewriting code—it's too easy to get it wrong (and I'm telling you that from personal experience!). Besides, why bother writing at all when there's a perfectly good open source solution like UrlRewritingNet?[5] Spending less time solving problems that have been solved by thousands of people before you enables you to focus your energies on other, more unique parts of your application.

 Implement URL Rewriting only for Extensions Handled by ASP.NET

As we mentioned at the beginning of this discussion, ASP.NET doesn't process all requests to your site by default and, for performance reasons, you probably don't want it to. For example, static resources like images and HTML files are served directly by IIS, so they end up on the user's screen faster than if they had had to pass through the ASP.NET system. If you want to use .NET code to rewrite URLs for resources it wouldn't normally process, you'll need to map those extensions to IIS using the **Application Configuration** dialog, as I mentioned earlier.

Let's walk through the task of setting up URL rewriting using the `UrlRewritingNet` module. Add to the **UrlRewritingNet.UrlRewriter.dll** a reference to our web project, then prepare to edit **Web.config** in a few places. First, add the rewriting `HttpModule`:

```
                                               Web.config (excerpt)
<system.web>
  <compilation debug="true" />
  <authentication mode="Windows" />
  <httpModules>my web pages are visible to search engines?
    <add name="UrlRewriteModule"
```

---

[5] http://www.urlrewriting.net/

```
            type="UrlRewritingNet.Web.UrlRewriteModule,
            UrlRewritingNet.UrlRewriter" />
    </httpModules>
</system.web>
```

Next, add the reference to the custom configuration section where we'll set up our URL rewriting preferences:

Web.config *(excerpt)*

```
<configSections>
  <section name="urlrewritingnet" restartOnExternalChanges="true"
      requirePermission="false"
      type="UrlRewritingNet.Configuration.UrlRewriteSection,
      UrlRewritingNet.UrlRewriter" />
</configSections>
```

Now we'll hook up an actual rewriting rule in the custom configuration section. We'll use the example I gave earlier, where a browser request of:

http://mysite.com/refrigerators/stainless/

results in a server request to:

http://mysite.com/category.aspx?id=refrigerators&subcat=stainless

Let's see what that looks like when it's expressed as a URL rewriting rule:

Web.config *(excerpt)*

```
<urlrewritingnet
    xmlns="http://www.urlrewriting.net/schemas/config/2006/07" >
  <rewrites>
    <add name="RewriteOnDomain"
        virtualUrl="/(\w+)/(\w+)$"
        destinationUrl="~/category.aspx?id=$1&amp;subcat=$2" />
  </rewrites>
</urlrewritingnet>
```

The namespace attribute (`xmlns`) is a nice touch, and it really reflects how polished this open source URL rewriting framework is. It's a fairly simple rule; any time we see an URL that *ends* with this:

(anything)/(word1)/(word2)

we replace it with:

/category.aspx?id=*(word1)*&subcat=*(word2)*

This is an intentionally simple rewrite example—there are many more knobs you can adjust and switches you can flip. For the complete rundown I recommend you read through the excellent documentation available at the URLRewritingNet site.[6]

Here's what our rewrite rule looks like in the browser. Figure 16.4 shows the old, ugly URL, and Figure 16.5 shows the new, friendlier, rewritten URL.

Figure 16.4. The original, messy URL

Figure 16.5. Our shiny, new, human-readable URL

---

[6] http://www.urlrewriting.net/download/UrlRewritingNet20.English.pdf

It's important to remember that the same `category.aspx` page is used in both cases, and behind the scenes, the URL is identical. The same query string parameters are passed in, but the rewritten form is much more readable by humans. And the best part is that we barely had to write any code at all!

 Don't Redirect Yourself out of Search Engines!

> By default, rewriting your URLs with .NET code does *not* generate an HTTP status code of 301 (Permanent Redirect). It is possible to redirect your users if you so choose, but you should take care with the status code that you send. By default, .NET returns a status code of 302, which can cause your redirected URLs to drop out of search indexes, according to Google's Matt Cutts.[7] If you opt to use redirects, make absolutely sure you set `redirectMode` to 301 (`permanent`), or you may regret it.

URL Rewriting with a Custom 404 Page

There are cases where you'll need to rewrite URLs that won't be handled by ASP.NET, though you can't install an ISAPI filter. For example, let's say you wanted to process requests for JPG files, but your site's running under a basic shared hosting plan at a hosting provider.

In such cases, you can use a sleazy hack to rewrite those requests. The technique requires that you have set a **custom 404 page**—a page that's displayed in place of the standard "missing resource" page when a requested URL can't be found. While most shared hosting providers won't let you monkey with IIS settings, many will at least allow you to specify a custom 404 page.

This technique takes advantage of the fact that we can actually include code to perform logic inside that custom 404 page. To perform the rewriting, we can intentionally link to a page that we know doesn't exist, then remap the client's request as required—all from within the 404 page. Yes, this is an ugly hack, but it does work. We don't recommend this approach if you can use an ISAPI filter-based rewriter, or if you only need to rewrite file extensions that ASP.NET knows about. However, when you're out of options, you can give this technique a shot.

---

[7] http://www.mattcutts.com/blog/asp-net-2-and-url-rewriting-sometimes-harmful/

First, we'll remap the missing page requests in IIS; then we'll configure ASP.NET to rewrite specific extensions. If you don't have access to the IIS Management Console, or you're using a web server other than IIS, ask your system administrator for assistance in configuring a custom 404 page.

1. If you're using IIS, launch the IIS Management Console. Right-click on your site, and select **Properties**. Click on the **Custom Errors** tab, select **404** from the list of HTTP errors, and click the **Edit Properties...** button.

2. Select **URL** for the **Message Type**, and enter the filename **404.aspx** in the **URL** text field.

3. We need to configure the **Web.config** file to handle requests that are routed through ASP.NET. Add the following to the `system.web` section of your **Web.config** file:

Web.config *(excerpt)*

```
<configuration>
  <system.web>
    <customErrors mode="On">
      <error statusCode="404" redirect="/404.aspx" />
    </customErrors>
  </system.web>
</configuration>
```

4. The next step is to create the page that will perform the rewriting. Create an ASP.NET page called **404.aspx** and add the following code to the `Page_Load` method:

404.aspx *(excerpt)*

```
protected virtual void Page_Load(object sender, EventArgs e)
{
  if (Request.QueryString != null
      && Request.QueryString[0] != null)
  {
    string queryString = Request.QueryString[0];

    // Note: The following is true for 404
    // requests that are NOT mapped to ASP.NET
```

```
    // IIS will send the string "404;intendedurl"
    // in the query string.
    int semiColonIndex = queryString.IndexOf(";");

    // The following line works whether
    // there's a semicolon or not.
    string url = queryString.Substring(semiColonIndex + 1);
    Trace.Write("Rewriting","Querystring = " + queryString);
    Trace.Write("Rewriting","Intended URL = " + url);

    // TODO: Add logic to Server.Transfer to correct page
    // based on intended URL.
  }
}
```

That last // TODO: part is up to you to fill in—you'll need to look at the requested
URL value and map it to the correct destination.

Adding Third-party Logic to your Custom 404 Page

Remember when I said earlier that writing your own custom URL rewriting code
was tough? Well, after leading you through that ugly custom 404 page hack, I have
a confession to make: there is actually an approach by which you can avoid putting
rewriting logic into your **404.aspx** page. However, it's a bit convoluted, so I'll just
skim the surface of this approach, and let you experiment on your own if you're
interested in pursuing it.

The basic premise is that it's possible to use a rewriting engine like URLRewritingNet[8] combined with the custom 404 page technique. To do so, we set up a rewriting rule that intercepts requests to **404.aspx** and redirects page requests based
on the rewriting rules we discussed earlier. In fact, there needn't even be a file
called **404.aspx**. Here's an overview of the flow:

- The user clicks on a link to a non-existent URL.
- IIS notices that there's no file with that name, and calls the custom 404 page.
- ASP.NET steps up to the plate to handle the request to **404.aspx**.
- The URLRewriting.NET handler intercepts the request to **404.aspx** and reroutes
  it based on the rewriting rules you've configured.

---

[8] http://www.urlrewriting.net/

How do I ensure my web pages are visible to search engines?

Since you're using ASP.NET, you're probably creating a dynamic web site. The web pages on a dynamic web site aren't rendered in advance—they're generated "on the fly," usually by a back-end database that holds input from the user.

This means that you probably have a bunch of pages that post back to themselves. The classic example of this approach is a search page, where users enter some search criteria in one or more form fields, and the form posts back to itself with the search results.

However, this is *not* the way major search engines work. Allow me to demonstrate: look at the URLs that are produced when performing a search for "lady sovereign" in each of the three major search engines:

- Here's the Yahoo! search:
  http://search.yahoo.com/search;_ylt=A0oGkmTghf9FeuYAawel87UF?&p=lady+sovereign

- Here are the search results from Live Search:
  http://search.live.com/results.aspx?q=lady+sovereign

- And here are the Google results:
  http://www.google.com/search?hl=en&q=lady+sovereign

Notice that all of the search terms are passed in directly via the URL. *All* three major search engines avoid postbacks in favor of URLs, and you'll find that most public web sites work in the same way. Why? Because search engine spiders can't follow postbacks. Any web pages behind a postback are therefore completely invisible to search engines—and thus, to search users.

Solution

Simply put, *don't hide your web pages behind postbacks!* It's okay to use postbacks in selected areas of your web site, but if you're interested in attracting public search traffic, avoid relying on postbacks as the primary method of navigation on your web site. The fact that postbacks are invisible to search spiders—which is a huge problem in itself—is not the only reason to avoid them. Postbacks are also problematic for users:

■ The browser's **Back** button no longer works as expected.

■ Bookmarking no longer works as expected.

■ The browser's **Refresh** button no longer works as expected.

With a postback, the page's URL never changes. The primary method of navigation for search spiders—and arguably for users as well—is the URL. Therein lies the disconnect.

Consider, for a moment, a search page created using the default web controls in Visual Studio 2005:

OldSearch.aspx *(excerpt)*

```
<form id="form1" runat="server">
  <div>
    <asp:TextBox id="SearchTextBox" runat="server" />
    <asp:Button id="SearchButton" runat="server"
        onclick="Button1_Click" Text="Search" />
    <br />
    <asp:Label id="SearchResultsLabel" runat="server"
        Text="Label" />
  </div>
</form>
```

This is a typical postback form, so it suffers from all the problems listed above.

One way to retrofit URL query string values into a form is to process them in the Page_Load event, like so:

NewSearch.aspx.cs *(excerpt)*

```
protected void Page_Load(object sender, EventArgs e)
{
  if (!String.IsNullOrEmpty(Request["q"]))
  {
    SearchTextBox.Text = Request["q"];
  }
}
```

Now we can prepopulate the search text box at the top of the results page with the query term. However, this quick fix may not be enough:

■ The page still does not display a link to the results page produced for the search term; the link *must* appear on the page in order for the web search spiders to find it. That's okay in this case, as the search form is open ended and doesn't need to be indexed, but we should include a link to the results page nonetheless.

■ The form still posts back by default, so the URL of the results page will never change. Although you can manually add query terms to the URL for inclusion in the search, they're not discoverable by spiders, because the silent postback takes precedence. Therefore the user has no way to bookmark a query URL resulting from the submission of search terms.

To fix these problems, we can add to our search page a piece of code that forces the button to perform a redirect instead of a postback:

NewSearch.aspx.cs *(excerpt)*

```
protected void Button1_Click(object sender, EventArgs e)
{
  if (String.IsNullOrEmpty(Request["q"]))
  {
    Response.Redirect("?q=" + SearchTextBox.Text);
  }
  SearchResultsLabel.Text = SearchResultsLabel.Text;
}
```

This solution's not terribly efficient, since we're now doing a postback *and* a redirect. But any deeper changes would mean a departure from the standard ASP.NET page life cycle model—a rich topic that's far beyond the scope of this chapter.

Watch Out for Paged Grids

Our example showed that pages can be "hidden" by button controls. Paged grid controls (the `DataGrid` and `GridView` controls) pose another common problem, since the page links require postbacks. If you have content in paged grids that you want search engines to find, you'll either need to implement custom, link-based paging,[9] or make sure that there's some other way to get to all the content without a postback (via links on other pages, or an updated **sitemap.xml** file, for example). See the tip that follows for more information.

---

[9] http://www.devx.com/dotnet/Article/26823

Want to Know what Search Spiders See? Just Ask!

You might be surprised to discover that it's really easy to find out what search spiders see when they look at your site. The two most popular search engines—Google and Yahoo!—both provide webmaster tools portals, which allow you to see which pages of your site are being spidered, what kinds of errors the engines encounter when they load your pages, and so on.

Both webmaster tools portals are very easy to use and are completely free. When you add a new domain to your account, you'll be required to verify that it's under your control by uploading a tiny HTML file to the root of your site. Once you've verified your access, you can look at in-depth information on both the search spidering process and what search users are doing.

I used this service recently to determine that Google wasn't able to browse a site of mine, due to a simple configuration issue that meant the site didn't show up on any Google searches. Once that issue was corrected, the site was the top hit for the target keywords, and of course the traffic picked up immediately. Give these tools a shot.

Using sitemap.xml

The **sitemap.xml** protocol allows you to notify search engines of your site catalog by placing an XML file (named, coincidentally, **sitemap.xml**) in the root folder of your web site). This protocol was originally developed by Google, but Yahoo! and MSN have announced support for it as well.

It's a good idea to use a **sitemap.xml** file and keep it up to date. Despite your best efforts to make your site easy for search engines to spider, the situation is always slightly beyond site owners' control: a page could time out or load incorrectly, causing the spider to miss all of its links. If that happens on a page near the top of your hierarchy, your entire site (or large sections of it) could drop out of a search index until the next time the spider returns, which could be weeks into the future. If you use a **sitemap.xml** file, the search spider will always try to load every page in your sitemap, in addition to following links.

Google has documented the **sitemap.xml** protocol in its Webmaster Tools portal.[10] I recommend that you find a system that automates the **sitemap.xml** generation process, though, since that will make it easier for you to keep the file up to date.

---

[10] https://www.google.com/webmasters/tools/docs/en/protocol.html

In addition to the list of available third-party systems,[11] you can also find
ASP.NET-specific systems, such as handlers and build providers, by performing
a simple search for **"google sitemap" ASP.NET**. I recommend GSiteCrawler.[12]
This donation-supported freeware application will spider your site, create your
sitemap.xml, and even FTP it to your web site.

How do I ensure my web pages produce descriptive search results?

Search engines gather three broad categories of information about your web pages:

1. the contents of the `title` element
2. the page's content
3. the text and "weight" of the links that point to your page

There are three main reasons why you should pay particular attention to the `title`
element:

1. Writing great content is very, very difficult. Getting people to link to your content
   is challenging. But writing good titles for your pages is as easy as falling off a
   bike.

2. The `title` element is weighted heavily in search results, which means a given
   keyword that appears in the `title` is more likely to influence a page's search
   engine ranking than a word appearing in the page's content.

3. The `title` element is the first thing users will see when they receive a search
   result hit on your web pages.

Every page on your site should have a unique, descriptive title—even those that
post back to themselves. Don't get this small but critically important detail wrong.

Solution

In ASP.NET 1.x, there was no way to access the `title` element of the page programmatically—a very strange oversight. Fortunately, in ASP.NET 2.0, this oversight

---

[11] http://code.google.com/sm_thirdparty.html

[12] http://gsitecrawler.com/

was corrected. We can easily set the `title` dynamically in the `Page_Load` event via the `Page` class:

```
protected void Page_Load(object sender, EventArgs e)
{
  Page.Title = "Custom Search For " + Request["q"];
}
```

Titles should be relatively short, so they can reasonably fit in the user's browser title bar—a rule of thumb is to keep your title to around 60 characters.

To provide a little more detail about the purpose of the page, we can add the `description` HTML meta tag to the page by making use of the `HtmlMeta` class:

```
protected void Page_Load(object sender, EventArgs e)
{
  HtmlMeta m = new HtmlMeta();
  m.Name = "description";
  m.Content = "A summary of links related to " + Request["q"]
  + " ordered by relevance";
  this.Header.Controls.Add(m);
}
```

Search engines universally ignore the information contained in `meta` elements when indexing content or categorizing your pages, and the `description` meta element is no exception. The text you put into the `description` won't be used to weight the search results, although the `description` *can* be displayed within the search results as the summary text. The actual rules about this are a little hazy, but at least one source at Google, Vanessa Fox, has confirmed this behavior in a posting to the Google Webmaster Help group on November 25th, 2006:

> Looking at your site in the search results, it appears that your pages would be well served by meta description tags. For most queries, the generated snippet is based on where the query terms are found on the page, and in those cases, your results are fine. But for some more generic queries, where a logical snippet isn't found in the text, the generated snippet seems to be coming from the first bits of text from the page—in this case, boilerplate navigation that is the same for every page.

The `title` element is the most important piece, so focus on getting that right first. However, if you have time, it's a good idea to expand the `title` into a couple of well-written summary sentences using the meta `description` element.

Summary

A great site isn't very useful if no one can find it. In this chapter, we've shown you some practical tips to ensure that search engine users can find your site, while minimizing the number of changes you have to make to your content.

Advanced Topics

This chapter covers some of the author team's favorite tips for working with ASP.NET. These nuggets of wisdom were either too complicated to include in a previous chapter or didn't quite fit the category, but were too good to leave out!

How can I tell what's going on behind the scenes?

Sometimes, you really need to know what's going on behind the scenes—especially if ASP.NET isn't behaving quite as you expect. For example, you might call `System.Web.DoSomeStuff` and find that it's not doing what you expected. Of course, your first step should be to perform a web search for **System.Web.DoSomeStuff**, but if that comes up empty, fear not—you still have options.

Solution

Use Reflector to look inside the ASP.NET runtime.[1]

---

[1] http://www.aisto.com/roeder/dotnet/

Reflector is a .NET assembly browser. It allows you to look through assembly code in a variety of languages, including C# and VB. None of the assembly code that comprises the .NET Framework is obfuscated, so you can look through all of it using a .NET disassembler. If you haven't used Reflector before, this might all sound a little scary. Don't worry; it's not.

Many plugins are available for Reflector, allowing you to do all kinds of things with the decompiled code—for instance, you can analyze it, or even export it to a .NET project.[2] We're going to concentrate on one of the simplest uses of Reflector in this solution: determining what System.Web is doing when a page executes. For example, why do <asp:literal> controls just write exactly what you send them, while <asp:label> controls seem to have a mind of their own and always wrap your markup in a span tag?

Let's take a look. Open Reflector and (if System.Web isn't already listed), select **File > Open** and search for the file **System.Web.dll**. The default location is **C:\WINDOWS\Microsoft.NET\Framework\v2.0.50727**, as shown in Figure 17.1.

Figure 17.1. Opening the **System.Web.dll** file in Reflector

---

[2] http://www.aisto.com/incoming/Reflector/AddIns/

We can now poke around the framework to gain a better understanding of the classes that we have, until now, used with blind faith. As demonstrated in Figure 17.2, the class System.Web.UI.WebControls.Label inherits from System.Web.UI.WebControls.WebControl.

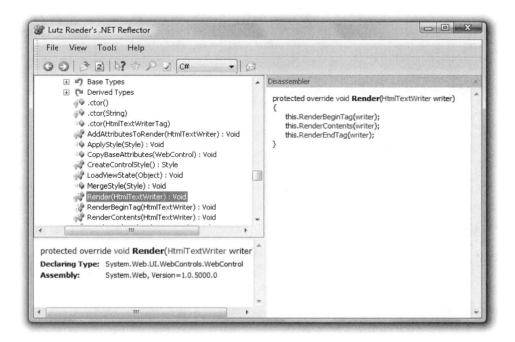

Figure 17.2. Opening the **System.Web.dll** file in Reflector

The significance of this hierarchy is that the default constructor for WebControl uses a span element by default:

```
protected WebControl() : this(HtmlTextWriterTag.Span)
{ }
```

The WebControl.Render method always wraps its contents in beginning and ending tags:

```
protected override void Render(HtmlTextWriter writer)
{
 this.RenderBeginTag(writer);
 this.RenderContents(writer);
 this.RenderEndTag(writer);
```

```
}

public virtual void RenderBeginTag(HtmlTextWriter writer)
{
  this.AddAttributesToRender(writer);
  HtmlTextWriterTag tag1 = this.TagKey;
  if (tag1 != HtmlTextWriterTag.Unknown)
  {
    writer.RenderBeginTag(tag1);
  }
  else
  {
    writer.RenderBeginTag(this.TagName);
  }
}
```

After looking through this code, you shouldn't be surprised that, when the Label control's constructor doesn't override WebControl's constructor, the Label is wrapped in a span.

What about Literal, then?

Well, Literal inherits from System.Web.Control, and it supplies its own render method:

```
protected override void Render(HtmlTextWriter output)
{
  output.Write(this._text);
}
```

We can see that the Literal control's Render method writes exactly what was supplied in the Literal's Text property—nothing more.

What was the point of this exercise? Aren't there other ways to find out how a Literal and a Label will render—ways that don't rely on third-party products? Of course there are! You could test it yourself, or you could read the documentation. In fact, these approaches are often easier than reading through the .NET Framework source code. However, it's always very nice to know that you *can* dig deep into the guts of the .NET Framework any time things aren't working the way you expect them to.

One more example—let's look at the `System.Web.Mail.SmtpMail.Send` class:

```
public static void Send(string from, string to, string subject,
    string messageText)
{
  lock (SmtpMail._lockObject)
  {
    if (Environment.OSVersion.Platform != PlatformID.Win32NT)
    {
      throw new PlatformNotSupportedException
      (SR.GetString("RequiresNT"));
    }
    if (Environment.OSVersion.Version.Major <= 4)
    {
      SmtpMail.CdoNtsHelper.Send(from, to, subject,
      messageText);
    }
    else
    {
      SmtpMail.CdoSysHelper.Send(from, to, subject,messageText);
    }
  }
}
```

So how does `System.Web.Mail` work? It just calls out to the CDO or CDOSYS built-in components, depending on which version of Windows you're running. This detail is good to know if, for example, your `Mail.Send` function is failing in Windows 2003 and Vista, but works on your Windows XP box.

How do I build a screen scraper?

Screen scraping—the process of parsing HTML content from another web site in order to retrieve (and potentially display) specific information for your own needs—should be a method of last resort when you can't obtain the same information via a more conventional and reliable technique.

Ideally, each web site would provide an API to allow us to access its displayed data, be that through some sort of web service, an RSS feed, or some other easily parsed format. This would certainly make our lives as developers nice and easy when it came to gathering information from other web sites!

Unfortunately, we don't live in such an altruistic world. Not every web site that publishes information has taken the time to make that information available in an easily consumable format. Sometimes screen scraping is the best we can do.

Many developers regard screen scraping as a dirty hack that's ethically questionable. However, there are many legitimate uses for the technique, such as consuming microformats or reading public domain information.[3] Just be aware that the process of screen scraping can be a bit unreliable—if the site you're scraping changes its layout, the process may fail.

Solution

Quite a lot of logic is required to parse an entire HTML page and process its information. Fortunately, a gentleman named Simon Mourier created and released the Html Agility Pack as an open source project hosted on CodePlex (Microsoft's open source repository).[4] Be sure to download the code and compile it—you'll need to reference the **HtmlAgilityPack.dll** assembly to follow along with this solution.

This class library makes it very easy to consume HTML content and transform it into XML. The solution for this section is divided into two parts. In the first part, we'll look at grabbing the HTML content over the Web and converting it to XML. In the second part, we'll render that XML content with a `Repeater` control bound to an `XmlDataSource`.

Scraping the Content

Before we begin, we need some content to scrape. For the purposes of this demonstration, I've created a simple ugly table of stock prices, which I've included in the code archive and displayed in Figure 17.3. I've also made the file available at http://haacked.com/Demos/Screen.html. Our goal will be to scrape this page, and change the display of the content on a new page.

---

[3] Make sure that you have legal access to the information you're using. The USA's Digital Millennium Copyright Act (DCMA) and the EU's European Union Copyright Directive, for example, have specific restrictions against screen scraping as a technical means of circumventing copyright protections.

[4] http://www.codeplex.com/htmlagilitypack/

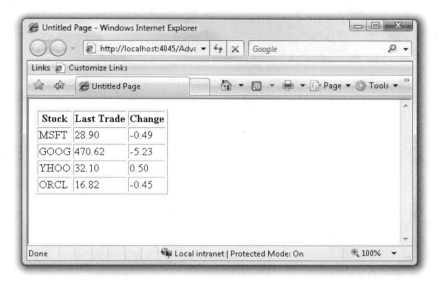

Figure 17.3. The table of stock quotes that will be screen scraped

First, let's add a static class named `HtmlScraper` with a static method `GetHtmlAsXml`:

```
                                                    HtmlScraper.cs (excerpt)
using System;
using System.IO;
using System.Text;
using System.Xml;
using HtmlAgilityPack;
public sealed class HtmlScraper
{
  public static XmlDocument GetHtmlAsXml()
  {
    // … implementation goes here.
  }
}
```

The implementation for `GetHtmlAsXml` is as follows:

```
                                                    HtmlScraper.cs (excerpt)
public static XmlDocument GetHtmlAsXml()
{
  // Set up an in-memory stream to hold the HTML.
```

```
    MemoryStream stream = new MemoryStream();
    XmlTextWriter writer =
        new XmlTextWriter(stream, Encoding.UTF8); ❶
    // Grab HTML over the web and convert to XML.
    HtmlWeb web = new HtmlWeb(); ❷
    web.LoadHtmlAsXml("http://haacked.com/Demos/screen.html", writer);
    // Now read from that in-memory stream
    // into a new XmlDocument class.
    XmlDocument xml = LoadFromStream(stream);
    return xml;
}
```

❶ The first step that this method takes is to set up an instance of `XmlTextWriter` wrapped around a `MemoryStream` instance, in which we store the XML.

❷ Next, we create an instance of the `HtmlWeb` class, one of the useful classes from the Html Agility Pack. Calling `LoadHtmlAsXml` makes an HTTP request for the specified URL, and writes the response to the specified `XmlTextWriter` instance, which in our case stores the result in a `MemoryStream`.

Choosing a Stream

In a real-world implementation, you might consider using a `FileStream` instead of an in-memory stream. That option would give you the potential to retrieve an archive of the data as something to fall back on if the site you're scraping is temporarily offline.

The final step in scraping our screen is to create an `XmlDocument` from the contents of the `MemoryStream`. The following method takes care of that for us:

HtmlScraper.cs *(excerpt)*

```
private static XmlDocument LoadFromStream(Stream stream)
{
  XmlDocument xml = new XmlDocument();
  stream.Position = 0;
  XmlReader reader = XmlReader.Create(stream);
  xml.Load(reader);
  return xml;
}
```

Displaying the Scraped Content

Now that we have a method to grab the HTML content, we need to transform and display that content. One method of doing so is to use an XSLT style sheet to transform the XML back into HTML.

XSLT is a powerful transformation language that would suit this task well. However, tackling XSLT for the first time can be incredibly daunting, so we'll look at an alternative solution here.

First, we create a new ASP.NET page and add an XmlDataSource instance using the **Design** view. Unfortunately, there doesn't appear to be a declarative way to specify that the XML for an XmlDataSource should come from a method call, so add the following to the Page_Load method in the code-beside file:

ScreenScraperDemo.aspx.cs (excerpt)

```
protected void Page_Load(object sender, EventArgs e)
{
  XmlDataSource1.Data = HtmlScraper.GetHtmlAsXml().OuterXml;
  XmlDataSource1.DataBind();
}
```

The next step is to configure the XmlDataSource with an **XPath** expression. XPath is a language for finding information in an XML document. The expression **html/body/table/tr** entered into the appropriate field in Figure 17.4 informs the XmlDataSource of the nodes to which we want to bind.

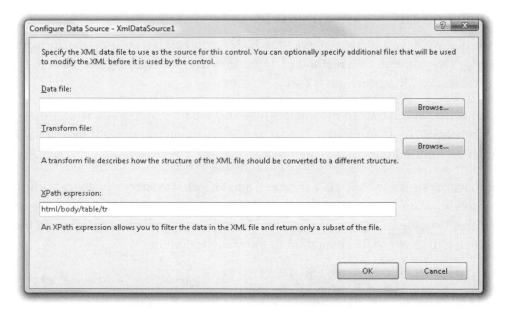

Figure 17.4. Locating the table rows using an XPath query

The expression **html/body/table/tr** selects every tr node (table row) in the table.

Now we'll add a Repeater to the page and choose the XmlDataSource1 as its data source, as shown in Figure 17.5.

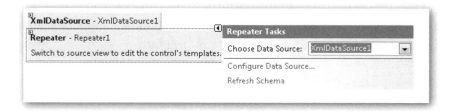

Figure 17.5. Setting a data source for our Repeater control

At this point, the repeater will repeat the contents of its ItemTemplate for each table row. Using this approach gives us a lot of control over how we want to render the data. Let's render the content in a horizontal table, just for fun. Here's the Repeater markup along with the XmlDataSource markup:

```
                                      ScreenScraperDemo.aspx (excerpt)
<asp:Repeater ID="Repeater1" runat="server"
    DataSourceID="XmlDataSource1">
  <HeaderTemplate>
    <table class="stocks">
      <tr>
        <td>
          <ul>
            <li><strong>Stock</strong></li>
            <li>Price</li>
            <li>Change</li>
          </ul>
        </td>
      </HeaderTemplate>
      <ItemTemplate>
      <td>
        <ul>
          <li>
            <strong><%# XPath("td[position() = 1]")%></strong> ❶
          </li>
          <li><%# XPath("td[position() = 2]")%></li> ❷
          <li><%# XPath("td[position() = 3]")%></li>
        </ul>
        </td>
      </ItemTemplate>
      <FooterTemplate>
      </tr>
    </table>
  </FooterTemplate>
</asp:Repeater>
<asp:XmlDataSource ID="XmlDataSource1" runat="server"
    XPath="html/body/table/tr[position() > 1]" />
```

Some comments about this code:

❶ Note that instead of generating a new table row for each corresponding row in the source page, we instead generate a new table cell.

❷ We can use the shorthand syntax `<%# XPath(xpath) %>` to evaluate the value of an XPath expression, using the current node as its base.

For example, notice that we use the following code to render the contents of the first table cell of the current row:

```
<%# XPath("td[position() = 2]") %>
```

This syntax is convenient shorthand for the XPathBinder.Eval method. The expression above is equivalent to the following:

```
<%# XPathBinder.Eval(Container.DataItem, "td[position() = 2]") %>
```

 Node Position Niceties

Notice that the position of each node in our XPath expression begins at 1, not 0 (as it would were we dealing with a regular array). Thus the first td node is referenced with the expression td[position() = 1].

All that's left to do is to add a dash of CSS to our page:

ScreenScraperDemo.aspx *(excerpt)*

```
<style type="text/css">
ul li {
  list-style-type: none;
  margin: 0;
  padding: 0;
}
table {
  border-collapse: collapse;
}
td {
  border: solid 1px #999;
  padding: 10px;
}
</style>
```

Figure 17.6 shows the result of our screen scraping.

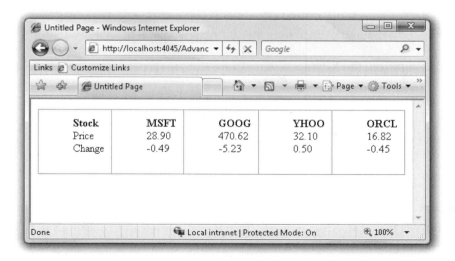

Figure 17.6. The final, screen-scraped stock quote content displaying in a new table

Discussion

One weakness about the `XmlDataSource` class is that it doesn't support XPath statements that use XML namespaces.

For example, if the HTML we were attempting to scrape had defined an HTML namespace (a common scenario with XHTML), the approach we used would not succeed. For example, the XPath statement we used in our `XmlDataSource` wouldn't work with the following HTML:

```
<!DOCTYPE html PUBLIC "-//W3C//DTD XHTML 1.0 Strict//EN"
    "http://www.w3.org/TR/xhtml1/DTD/xhtml1-strict.dtd">
<html xmlns="http://www.w3.org/1999/xhtml" lang="en" xml:lang="en">

<head>
<title>SitePoint : New Articles, Fresh Thinking for Web Developers
    and Designers</title>
    ⋮
```

There are a couple of workarounds for this issue. One solution requires a deep knowledge of XPath and is outlined in a blog post by Jason Follas, entitled "XmlDataSource: XPath Workaround For Default Namespaces."[5] This approach requires you to specify the namespace by way of the `namespace-uri` XPath method.

With this solution, the XPath we'd use to select the table rows in our example would be:

```
Xml/*[name() = 'tr' and
    namespace-uri() = 'http://www.w3.org/1999/xhtml']
```

As you can imagine, this solution can become quite cumbersome.

A second solution involves using an XSLT style sheet to strip out the namespaces and prefixes from the XML. This technique is outlined in Bill Evjen's blog post, "Namespaces and XmlDataSource Server Control."[6]

How do I build a data access layer?

This question might strike you as being slightly different from the others in this book—surely .NET comes with a data access layer built in? Before I jump into the solution, let me clarify exactly what it is that this question asks.

Many developers indeed believe that a data access layer is already provided by Microsoft in the subset of the .NET Framework we know as ADO.NET. When these (misguided, with all due respect) developers need to access the database, they may write code similar to this:

Simple.aspx.cs (excerpt)

```
string connectString =
    @"server=.\SQLEXPRESS;database=Orders;Trusted_Connection=yes";
using (SqlConnection connection = new SqlConnection(connectString))
using (SqlCommand sqlCommand = new SqlCommand())
{
  connection.Open();
  sqlCommand.Connection = connection;
  sqlCommand.CommandText = "SELECT * FROM Orders";
  using (SqlDataReader reader = sqlCommand.ExecuteReader())
  {
```

---

[5] http://jasonf-blog.blogspot.com/2006/08/xmldatasource-xpath-workaround-for.html

[6] http://www.geekswithblogs.com/evjen/archive/2005/10/10/56527.aspx

```
    // Do lots of stuff with the data that is hardcoded and highly
    // dependent upon the current schema, leading to maintenance
    // nightmares when your successor modifies the database.
  }
}
```

As an above-average developer who's nearing the end of this book, you've probably already spotted some of the problems that would result from implementing a "data access" layer that involves spreading the above code throughout an ASP.NET application. Let's identify some of those problems:

- Connection string management is difficult when the strings are hard coded and used in multiple locations.

- Database connections are precious resources—a cut-and-paste error that leaves a connection open could cause the application to exhaust all available connections.

- An **SQL injection attack** arises from a common loophole that malicious users aim to exploit—the culprits take advantage of poorly implemented validation to execute their own custom SQL commands. A cut-and-paste error or sloppy database access code can leave a web application vulnerable to SQL injection attacks.

- The code only supports SQL Server. Although applications that need to work with multiple databases are rare, they do exist. Regardless, tying one's application to a specific database is a bad idea, in case you need to switch or upgrade at a later date.

 Preparing for .NET 3.5

Aside from the obvious benefits of implementing a data access layer—security, productivity, and maintainability—there's another good reason to become accustomed to accessing your data through a data access layer: preparing yourself for .NET 3.5. The .NET 3.5 (Visual Studio 2008) release places a major focus on simplified data access. Begin working with data access layers now, and the jump to .NET 3.5 will be a much smoother process.

Understanding SQL Injection

A web application is vulnerable to SQL injection attacks when it passes unfiltered user input directly to a database. Here's an example:

```
SELECT * FROM Orders WHERE OrderId =" + TextBox1.Text
```

By using SQL escape characters, attackers may be able to place their own commands into `TextBox1` and have those commands executed on the database server.

If your site is ever hacked, it's most likely to occur via an SQL injection vulnerability. The ramifications of such a security breach can be disastrous, and every responsible developer needs to understand how an SQL injection works and how to defend against one. Paul Litwin's article on MSDN, "Stop SQL Injection Attacks Before They Stop You,"[7] provides a good run-down of the various types of attacks and how each can be prevented. The MSDN Security Developer Center article, "How to Protect from SQL Injection in ASP.NET,"[8] also contains numerous tips on how best to secure your application.

Of course, the example we've used in this solution is only a simple query—once you start to add parameters to queries and check return values, you begin to realize how mind-numbingly redundant the code becomes. Any time you see redundant code in an application, your brain should automatically begin to work out how that repetition can be prevented from occurring. We'll consider this goal of redundant code removal to be the first goal of a data access layer.

Solution

Microsoft's **Data Access Application Block (DAAB)** is a solid foundation for any data access layer. Use of this code library reduces the amount of custom code you need to write, test, and maintain, and follows best practices to avoid leaky connections and SQL injection attacks. This library also allows your application to support SQL Server, Oracle, and DB2 databases, and provides a configuration layer for the management of connection strings. The DAAB makes good use of the **provider pattern**, which establishes an API through which the business logic of an application and the database layer can communicate. As the DAAB utilizes this pattern, you

---

[7] http://msdn.microsoft.com/msdnmag/issues/04/09/SQLInjection/
[8] http://msdn2.microsoft.com/en-us/library/ms998271.aspx

can extend the library (or use extensions that other developers have written) to access data sources other than relational databases.

The DAAB is part of Microsoft's **Enterprise Library**, colloquially referred to as **EntLib**.[9] EntLib is a collection of application blocks designed to help developers with common challenges encountered when developing enterprise web applications.

 EntLib: Much More than a Data Access Layer

For the purposes of this solution we'll only be talking about EntLib's data access features, but you should keep in mind that EntLib provides an entire framework for developing enterprise applications. This framework includes caching, cryptography, data access, exception handling, logging, policy injection, security, and validation. What's particularly useful about EntLib is that all of these application blocks work well together, and all are configured using the same conventions.

Once you've downloaded and installed EntLib, you can add to your application a reference to the DAAB assembly, the location of which will be the library's installation directory. The name of the assembly is **Microsoft.Practices.EnterpriseLibrary.Data.dll**, and once you've performed this step, other core assemblies will be included automatically.

EntLib includes a configuration management console that will add the necessary application configuration information to your application. In Figure 17.7, I've right-clicked connection strings and selected **New** to create a new connection string.

---

[9] All of the source code needed to build EntLib is available for download from http://www.codeplex.com/entlib/. The most recent version of EntLib at the time of writing was 3.1.

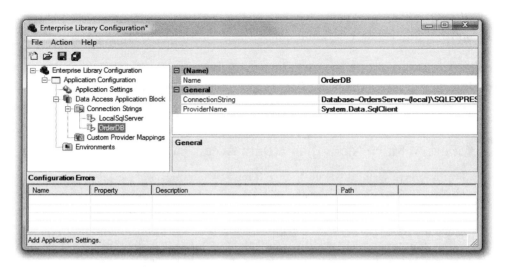

Figure 17.7. Adding a connection string for the DAAB

The connection string name is OrdersDB—we'll use that name in the code that follows:

```
                                                    Daab.aspx.cs (excerpt)
using System.Data;
using Microsoft.Practices.EnterpriseLibrary.Data;
// ...
string command = "SELECT * FROM Orders";
Database db = DatabaseFactory.CreateDatabase("OrderDB");
using (IDataReader dataReader
    = db.ExecuteReader(CommandType.Text, command))
{
    // Do lots of stuff with the data that is hardcoded and highly
    // dependent upon the current schema, leading to maintenance
    // nightmares when your successor modifies the database.
}
```

This code is certainly an improvement over our original attempt! We've abstracted both the connection string *and* the fact that we're using SQL Server. We still have to be careful to dispose of our data reader correctly, although EntLib will configure our database connection so that it automatically closes when we dispose of the data reader.

Discussion

EntLib is a good starting point for a data access layer; however, it places only a thin façade over the ADO.NET components. We still have to be careful not to let SQL commands become scattered throughout an application. Database schemas change; when they do, we need to know where to change the queries.

Many applications will require more functionality or flexibility than that provided by EntLib. Fortunately, there are other tools to use, some of which are free. For example, you can generate code to access database tables and stored procedures—thereby leaving your application free of hard-coded SQL strings—by building on top of the DAAB with SubSonic.[10] We'll discuss this tool in the next solution.

How do I automatically generate a data access layer?

When it comes to code, less is more—the more lines of code that you write, the greater the chance that you might introduce vulnerability.

For instance, the SQL injection issues that we explored in the section called "How do I build a data access layer?" are neutralized if you use simple ASP.NET declarative data binding. The reason why queries built using declarative data binding are safe from SQL injection attacks is that the `SqlDataSource` class passes parameter values as ADO.NET parameters rather than as SQL strings, so these parameters are checked for SQL Injection. Writing less code delivers a more secure application that can also benefit from other ASP.NET Framework features, such as caching and connection string management. There are, of course, downsides to declarative data binding (your code has the potential to become slightly more difficult to read and maintain), but my experience is that, more often than not, to work with declarative data binding results in an application that's far more secure than one written with custom data access logic.

Programmers are often tempted to judge their productivity and performance by how much code they write, but the only metric that's really valid is the quality of the application. If there is an approach to creating high-quality data-access work that

---

[10] http://www.subsonicproject.com/

uses minimal code, you owe it to yourself—and your clients—to investigate that approach.

Solution

Imagine that the ASP.NET team built you a custom version of the framework, designed to work with *your* database. That's what using the third-party SubSonic package feels like.[11]

Once you add SubSonic to your project (a process that's extremely easy), you gain immediate access to classes and controls that understand your data completely. The structure of these classes reflects properties like foreign keys and many-to-many mappings. Better still, SubSonic is really lightweight, so you can use it without feeling like it has taken over your project, as some data toolkits have a way of doing.

Oh, and SubSonic is completely free!

SubSonic is designed help you get your site up and running quickly. The best way to see what a SubSonic site looks like is to witness it in action, and fortunately, SubSonic ships with a sample web site designed to let you do just that. In this solution, we'll look at that site, SubSonic Central, to gain an idea of what it does. Then, we'll see how you can add SubSonic to your web site.

It Might be Called SubSonic, but it Moves Fast

While SubSonic's basic operation hasn't changed since its release in August 2006, the SubSonic team constantly adds new features and improvements. I make that statement based on my experience with SubSonic 2.0.3 and personal conversations with Rob Conery, the project's chief architect.

The AutoScaffold Page

SubSonic ships with a sample web site called SubSonic Central. You can download the project and run it as long as you have the Northwind database installed on a default instance of SQL Server. If you don't, you'll need to edit your **Web.config** file to point it to your Northwind database.

---

[11] http://www.subsonicproject.com/

Getting the Northwind Database

If you don't have Northwind installed, you can download it from the project's download site.[12]

Of course, you *could* use your own database if you wanted to, but SubSonic Central's Examples page relies upon queries run against the Northwind database. Everything else in the SubSonic Central example site will work, though.

Let's now take a look at the AutoScaffold page. This page is designed to let you administer your database via a web interface, with absolutely no setup required. The tables that form part of the scaffolding are all generated on the basis of the database configured in **Web.config**; therefore, when you're evaluating SubSonic for use on a project, you should picture how the page could be applied to your own database. Figure 17.8 shows how the AutoScaffold page looks when you first open it.

	Product	Product Name	Supplier	Category	Quantity Per Unit	Unit Price	Units In Stock	Units On Order	Reorder Level	Discontinued
Edit	1	Chai	Exotic Liquids	Beverages	10 boxes x 20 bags	18.0000	39	0	10	False
Edit	2	Chang	Exotic Liquids	Beverages	24 - 12 oz bottles	19.0000	17	40	25	False
Edit	3	Aniseed Syrup	Exotic Liquids	Condiments	12 - 550 ml bottles	10.0000	13	70	25	False
Edit	4	Chef Anton's Cajun Seasoning	New Orleans Cajun Delights	Condiments	48 - 6 oz jars	100.0000	53	0	0	False
Edit	5	Chef Anton's Gumbo Mix	New Orleans Cajun Delights	Condiments	36 boxes	100.0000	0	0	0	True
Edit	6	Grandma's Boysenberry Spread	Grandma Kelly's Homestead	Condiments	12 - 8 oz jars	100.0000	120	0	25	False
Edit	7	Uncle Bob's Organic Dried Pears	Grandma Kelly's Homestead	Produce	12 - 1 lb pkgs.	100.0000	15	0	10	False
Edit	8	Northwoods Cranberry Sauce	Grandma Kelly's Homestead	Condiments	12 - 12 oz jars	100.0000	6	0	0	False
Edit	9	Mishi Kobe Niku	Tokyo Traders	Meat/Poultry	18 - 500 g pkgs.	100.0000	29	0	0	True
Edit	10	Ikura	Tokyo Traders	Seafood	12 - 200 ml jars	100.0000	31	0	0	False
Edit	11	Queso Cabrales	Cooperativa de Quesos 'Las Cabras'	Dairy Products	1 kg pkg.	100.0000	22	30	30	False
Edit	12	Queso Manchego La Pastora	Cooperativa de Quesos 'Las Cabras'	Dairy Products	10 - 500 g pkgs.	100.0000	86	0	0	False

Figure 17.8. SubSonic's AutoScaffold page for the Northwind example database

---

[12] http://www.microsoft.com/downloads/details.aspx?FamilyId=06616212-0356-46A0-8DA2-EE-BC53A68034/

One nifty feature that you mightn't immediately notice about this grid is that it's not simply data-bound to the table to which you're referring—it follows foreign keys and retrieves that data as well. Figure 17.9 shows a closer view of the first five columns of the Products table.

	Product	Product Name	Supplier	Category	Quantity Per Unit
Edit	1	Chai	Exotic Liquids	Beverages	10 boxes x 20 bags
Edit	2	Chang	Exotic Liquids	Beverages	24 - 12 oz bottles
Edit	3	Aniseed Syrup	Exotic Liquids	Condiments	12 - 550 ml bottles
Edit	4	Chef Anton's Cajun Seasoning	New Orleans Cajun Delights	Condiments	48 - 6 oz jars
Edit	5	Chef Anton's Gumbo Mix	New Orleans Cajun Delights	Condiments	36 boxes

Figure 17.9. A close-up view of the AutoScaffold table

Table 17.1 shows the actual table data.

Table 17.1. The Data Retrieved

ProductID	ProductName	SupplierID	CategoryID	QuantityPerUnit
1	Chai	1	1	10 boxes x 20 bags
2	Chang	1	1	24 - 12 oz bottles
3	Aniseed Syrup	1	2	12 - 550 mL bottles
4	Chef Anton's Cajun Seasoning	2	2	48 - 6 oz jars
5	Chef Anton's Gumbo Mix	2	2	36 boxes

As you can see, the main difference between the data stored in the table and that retrieved on the scaffolding page is that SubSonic has filled in actual values for Supplier and Category.

Another nice feature you mightn't have noticed is that SubSonic formats your column names to display in a user-friendly way.

The **Edit** link in the far-left column of the scaffolding table takes you to a page where you can edit that particular row. Let's try it out! We'll look at the Orders table because it contains both foreign key and date values. Figure 17.10 shows how it looks in Edit mode.

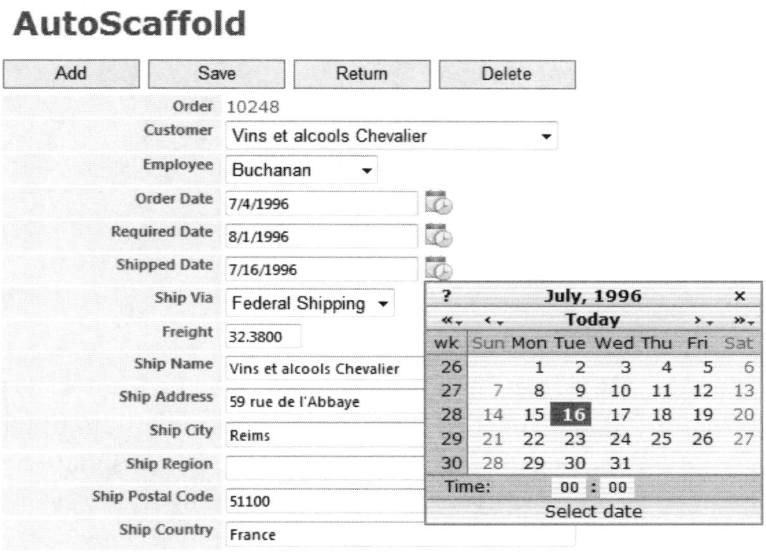

Figure 17.10. The edit page generated for one of the sample orders

Notice that the `DateTime` fields use a popup calendar—in Figure 17.10 I'm using this feature to edit the Shipped Date. Also notice that all of the values retrieved via foreign keys are displayed in drop-down menus, which is another nice touch that makes the page usable and minimizes the chance of invalid data being entered.

The Scaffold Control

The AutoScaffold page is great, but what if you'd like to allow one of your users to edit a single table within the administration section of your site? No problem—the `Scaffold` control does just that. Here's all the code that's needed to add a `Scaffold` to your page:

ScaffoldSample.aspx *(excerpt)*

```
<%@ Page Language="C#" AutoEventWireup="true"
    CodeFile="ScaffoldSample.aspx.cs" Theme="Default"
    Inherits="ScaffoldSample" %>
<%@ Register Assembly="SubSonic" Namespace="SubSonic"
    TagPrefix="subsonic" %>
```

```
<html xmlns="http://www.w3.org/1999/xhtml" >
<head runat="server">
  <title>Scaffold</title>
</head>
<body>
  <form id="form1" runat="server">
  <div>
    <subsonic:Scaffold runat="server"
        TableName="Products" GridViewSkinID="scaffold" />
  </div>
  </form>
</body>
</html>
```

We've used the `scaffold` skin that's included in the SubSonic Central site's `Default` theme, but take heart in knowing that this control has been built to fit into your site. It fits naturally with the ASP.NET theming system, so you should have no problem skinning the control to match the theme of your own site. Even better, the control produces markup that takes CSS-based design into account—all of the top level controls for both Grid and Edit mode have class attributes that you can use as hooks to style as you need. Figure 17.11 shows the result of the above code.

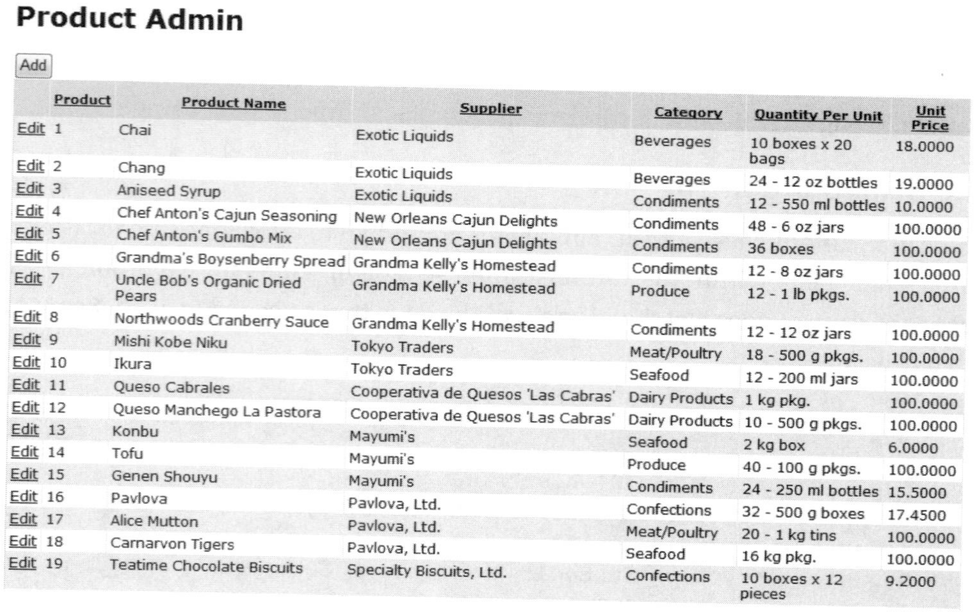

Product Admin

Add

Product	Product Name	Supplier	Category	Quantity Per Unit	Unit Price
Edit 1	Chai	Exotic Liquids	Beverages	10 boxes x 20 bags	18.0000
Edit 2	Chang	Exotic Liquids	Beverages	24 - 12 oz bottles	19.0000
Edit 3	Aniseed Syrup	Exotic Liquids	Condiments	12 - 550 ml bottles	10.0000
Edit 4	Chef Anton's Cajun Seasoning	New Orleans Cajun Delights	Condiments	48 - 6 oz jars	100.0000
Edit 5	Chef Anton's Gumbo Mix	New Orleans Cajun Delights	Condiments	36 boxes	100.0000
Edit 6	Grandma's Boysenberry Spread	Grandma Kelly's Homestead	Condiments	12 - 8 oz jars	100.0000
Edit 7	Uncle Bob's Organic Dried Pears	Grandma Kelly's Homestead	Produce	12 - 1 lb pkgs.	100.0000
Edit 8	Northwoods Cranberry Sauce	Grandma Kelly's Homestead	Condiments	12 - 12 oz jars	100.0000
Edit 9	Mishi Kobe Niku	Tokyo Traders	Meat/Poultry	18 - 500 g pkgs.	100.0000
Edit 10	Ikura	Tokyo Traders	Seafood	12 - 200 ml jars	100.0000
Edit 11	Queso Cabrales	Cooperativa de Quesos 'Las Cabras'	Dairy Products	1 kg pkg.	100.0000
Edit 12	Queso Manchego La Pastora	Cooperativa de Quesos 'Las Cabras'	Dairy Products	10 - 500 g pkgs.	100.0000
Edit 13	Konbu	Mayumi's	Seafood	2 kg box	6.0000
Edit 14	Tofu	Mayumi's	Produce	40 - 100 g pkgs.	100.0000
Edit 15	Genen Shouyu	Mayumi's	Condiments	24 - 250 ml bottles	15.5000
Edit 16	Pavlova	Pavlova, Ltd.	Confections	32 - 500 g boxes	17.4500
Edit 17	Alice Mutton	Pavlova, Ltd.	Meat/Poultry	20 - 1 kg tins	100.0000
Edit 18	Carnarvon Tigers	Pavlova, Ltd.	Seafood	16 kg pkg.	100.0000
Edit 19	Teatime Chocolate Biscuits	Specialty Biscuits, Ltd.	Confections	10 boxes x 12 pieces	9.2000

Figure 17.11. The default styling of the Scaffold control

Of course, you could write all of the ASP.NET code that generates this interface yourself; some of the tips in this book, particularly in Chapter 3, explained how to do just that. But why would you? Well, why *wouldn't* you want to have a fully functional administration system on the first day of your next project—especially when you've written almost no code?

Not convinced yet? Wait, there's more!

The Utility Controls

SubSonic ships with a growing list of exciting utility controls. I say "exciting" not because you couldn't write them yourself, but because you've probably *had to* write them yourself over and over, and no doubt you're heartily sick of it.

To illustrate how these utility controls work, we're going to set up a `DropDownList` bound to the `Employees` table, a `CheckBoxList` that allows many-to-many mapping (in this case, mapping of `Employees` to `Territories`), and a `RadioButtonList` bound to `Suppliers`. Figure 17.12 shows the design of our page.

The SubSonic Calendar Control

The `Calendar` control that I pointed out when we were looking at the `AutoScaffold` control is also included as a separate utility control.

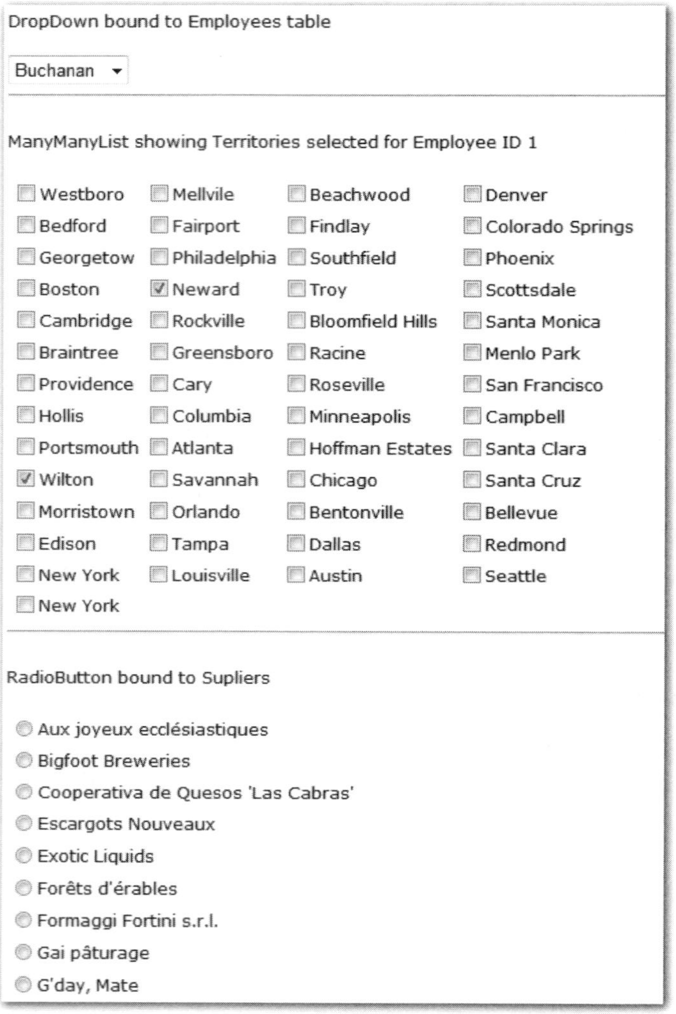

DropDown bound to Employees table

Buchanan ▾

ManyManyList showing Territories selected for Employee ID 1

☐ Westboro	☐ Mellvile	☐ Beachwood	☐ Denver
☐ Bedford	☐ Fairport	☐ Findlay	☐ Colorado Springs
☐ Georgetow	☐ Philadelphia	☐ Southfield	☐ Phoenix
☐ Boston	☑ Neward	☐ Troy	☐ Scottsdale
☐ Cambridge	☐ Rockville	☐ Bloomfield Hills	☐ Santa Monica
☐ Braintree	☐ Greensboro	☐ Racine	☐ Menlo Park
☐ Providence	☐ Cary	☐ Roseville	☐ San Francisco
☐ Hollis	☐ Columbia	☐ Minneapolis	☐ Campbell
☐ Portsmouth	☐ Atlanta	☐ Hoffman Estates	☐ Santa Clara
☑ Wilton	☐ Savannah	☐ Chicago	☐ Santa Cruz
☐ Morristown	☐ Orlando	☐ Bentonville	☐ Bellevue
☐ Edison	☐ Tampa	☐ Dallas	☐ Redmond
☐ New York	☐ Louisville	☐ Austin	☐ Seattle
☐ New York			

RadioButton bound to Supliers

- ◉ Aux joyeux ecclésiastiques
- ◉ Bigfoot Breweries
- ◉ Cooperativa de Quesos 'Las Cabras'
- ◉ Escargots Nouveaux
- ◉ Exotic Liquids
- ◉ Forêts d'érables
- ◉ Formaggi Fortini s.r.l.
- ◉ Gai pâturage
- ◉ G'day, Mate

Figure 17.12. The example page for demonstrating utility controls

Here's the code:

```
                                                    Utility.aspx (excerpt)

<p>DropDown bound to Employees table</p>
<subsonic:DropDown ID="ddlEmployees" runat="server"
    TableName="Employees" />
<hr/>
<p>ManyManyList showing Territories selected for Employee ID 1</p>
<subsonic:ManyManyList ID="manyEmployeesTerritories" runat="server"
```

```
    PrimaryTableName="Employees"
    PrimaryKeyValue="1"
    ForeignTableName="Territories"
    MapTableName="EmployeeTerritories"
    ProviderName="Northwind"
    RepeatColumns="4" />
<hr/>
<p>RadioButton bound to Suppliers</p>
<subsonic:RadioButtons ID="radiobuttons" runat="server"
    TableName="Suppliers"
    TextField="CompanyName"
    ValueField="SupplierID" />
```

The `QuickTable` is my favorite tabular control, because it makes it really easy to write good code when dealing with tables that are populated from the database. `QuickTable` looks like a simple `GridView`, except that its pager controls are prettier. It also includes one *really* cool feature: **database paging**. Unlike a data-bound `GridView`, which retrieves *all* of its rows from the database and then figures out which rows to show on the web server, the `QuickTable` uses smart queries so that it only retrieves the rows for the current page.

In our example, we're going to show three columns from the `Product` table. We'll filter discontinued items from the view, and configure paging to display a maximum of 15 rows per page. Figure 17.13 shows the result of this table as implemented using a `QuickTable`.

Product Name	Quantity Per Unit	Unit Price
Chai	10 boxes x 20 bags	$18.00
Chang	24 - 12 oz bottles	$19.00
Aniseed Syrup	12 - 550 ml bottles	$10.00
Chef Anton's Cajun Seasoning	48 - 6 oz jars	$100.00
Grandma's Boysenberry Spread	12 - 8 oz jars	$100.00
Uncle Bob's Organic Dried Pears	12 - 1 lb pkgs.	$100.00
Northwoods Cranberry Sauce	12 - 12 oz jars	$100.00
Ikura	12 - 200 ml jars	$100.00
Queso Cabrales	1 kg pkg.	$100.00
Queso Manchego La Pastora	10 - 500 g pkgs.	$100.00
Konbu	2 kg box	$6.00
Tofu	40 - 100 g pkgs.	$100.00
Genen Shouyu	24 - 250 ml bottles	$15.50
Pavlova	32 - 500 g boxes	$17.45
Carnarvon Tigers	16 kg pkg.	$100.00

`<< < Page 1 ▼ of 5 (69 total) > >>`

Figure 17.13. Using `QuickTable` to display tabular data—complete with paging and smart queries

We achieved all that with the following code:

QuickTable.aspx *(excerpt)*

```
<subsonic:QuickTable ID="ProductsTable" runat="server"
    TableName="Products"
    PageSize="15"
    ColumnList="ProductName,QuantityPerUnit,UnitPrice"
    WhereExpression="Discontinued=False" />
```

That's it! As you can see, a `QuickTable` requires less code than a `GridView`, it looks better, and it handles data access much more efficiently.

`QuickTable` takes the monotony of writing a custom tabular control out of your hands, so you can instead spend your time writing your application's custom business logic … which, incidentally, is also a task with which SubSonic can help you.

The SubSonic Data Access Layer

Every example of the SubSonic library that we've looked at so far is really just an application of the SubSonic **Data Access Layer (DAL)**. The SubSonic team is working hard to make your life easier, but once you've got a great automatically generated DAL, you might be tempted to think that they're just showing off how easy it is to build an application.

SubSonic lets you write your custom business logic with code like this:

```
                                          Examples.aspx.cs (excerpt)
GridView1.DataSource =
   new ProductCollection().
   Where(Product.Columns.UnitPrice, Comparison.GreaterOrEquals, 30).
   Load();
GridView1.DataBind();
```

I like this syntax because the components that comprise the query are all strongly typed. However, the code can be a bit verbose—especially for more complex queries. Luckily, the SubSonic DAL also supports the following, more concise, syntax:

```
                                          Examples.aspx.cs (excerpt)
GridView1.DataSource =
   Product.Query().
   WHERE("UnitPrice > 20").
   AND("CategoryID = 1").
   OR("UnitPrice > 20").
   AND("CategoryID = 5").
   ExecuteReader();
GridView1.DataBind();
```

While this syntax may look like inline SQL, it's definitely not. This style of coding is just a convenient shorthand—the strings are parsed and processed with the same scrutiny as they were in the first example. The result is the best of both worlds—you gain the benefit of simple SQL-like syntax, and the safety and power of a full DAL.

Here's an example of how you'd open, edit, and save a record:

```
SubSonic.Product product = new SubSonic.Product(1);
product.ProductName = "New Product Name";
product.Save("My User Name");
```

As you can see, working with the SubSonic DAL is fairly intuitive.

You're not only confined to operating on tables with SubSonic, by the way—you can also interact with your views and stored procedures. Here's an example:

Examples.aspx.cs *(excerpt)*

```
GridView1.DataSource =
  Northwind.SPs.CustOrderHist("ALFKI").GetReader();
GridView1.DataBind();
```

 The ActiveRecord Pattern

SubSonic uses the **ActiveRecord** pattern, a common approach to mapping data to objects. ActiveRecord is popular because it's simple: each table maps to a class, so each object maps to a single row in the table (the "active" record, hence the name).

If you'd prefer not to use ActiveRecord (or you're unable to, because of corporate standards, for example), fear not! The SubSonic code is generated using a template engine that uses standard ASP.NET syntax, so it's possible to customize the code that's generated to better suit your needs.

Adding SubSonic to your Project

To add SubSonic to your site, you need to follow three steps:

1. Install SubSonic.

2. Configure **Web.config**.

3. Generate your DAL.

Let's work through each of these steps now.

Installing SubSonic

Installing SubSonic is as easy as placing the **SubSonic.dll** file in your project's **bin** folder. You can download the latest version of this file (along with the SubSonic Central example application) from the project's download site.[13]

---

[13] http://www.subsonicproject.com/view/download-subsonic.aspx

Configuring Web.config

Next, we'll need to configure our **Web.config** file to specify which databases it should use. The easiest way to do this is to copy the **Web.config** file from the SubSonic Central example site (see the tip at the end of this section). However, if you have a custom **Web.config** file in place already, it's also relatively easy to add SubSonic to it. Let's walk through the process now.

SubSonic makes use of the custom configuration section `SubSonicService`. To add this section, enter the following code right below the `configuration` element at the very top of your **Web.config** file:

Web.config *(excerpt)*

```
<configSections>
  <section name="SubSonicService"
      type="SubSonic.SubSonicSection, SubSonic"
      allowDefinition="MachineToApplication"
      restartOnExternalChanges="true"
      requirePermission="false"/>
</configSections>
```

With this code in place, we can make use of the many configuration options available, a comprehensive list of which can be found on the SubSonic project site.[14] We'll look at a simple example using the Northwind database running on SQL Server. Add the following few lines to your **Web.config** file, right above the `appSettings` section:

Web.config *(excerpt)*

```
<SubSonicService defaultProvider="Northwind" >
  <providers>
    <clear/>
    <add name="Northwind"
        type="SubSonic.SqlDataProvider, SubSonic"
        connectionStringName="Northwind"/>
  </providers>
</SubSonicService>
```

---

[14] http://www.subsonicproject.com/view/config-options.aspx

Great! Now that SubSonic knows how to find your database, we can go ahead and generate our DAL.

Getting Set Up Quickly

In this solution we've seen how to add SubSonic to an existing project, but if you're setting up a new project you can take a shortcut by copying files from one of the two solutions that ship with the SubSonic distribution: SubSonic Central, or the SubSonic Starter Site.

- The SubSonic Central site includes a preconfigured installation of SubSonic, an AutoScaffold page, and a few of the control samples that we saw earlier in this solution.

- The SubSonic Starter Site is more comprehensive in that it includes some common JavaScript libraries, ASP.NET membership, and a simple CMS system.

You can copy either of these projects and remove from them the files that you don't need. An even simpler route would be to simply copy the **SubSonic.dll** and **Web.config** files from either of these files, and modify the `connectionString` value so that it points to your database.

Generating your DAL

A few tools are available to help you to generate your Data Access Layer:

- a custom build provider
- a web-based code generator
- a command-line code generator

Let's take a closer look at each of these tools.

The simplest way to use SubSonic is as a **build provider** in a Visual Studio 2005 Web Site Project. As the name suggests, a build provider is responsible for generating source code for different file types within an application. If you decide to use the SubSonic build provider, SubSonic will automatically build your DAL every time you build your site. Cool, huh?

The build provider is easy to set up. First, add a `buildProvider` entry to the compilation section of the **Web.config** file:

```
                                              Web.config (excerpt)
<system.web>
  <compilation debug="true" defaultLanguage="C#">
    <buildProviders>
      <add extension=".abp"
           type="SubSonic.BuildProvider, SubSonic"/>
    </buildProviders>
  <compilation debug="true" defaultLanguage="C#">
<system.web>
```

The above code tells ASP.NET that files with an extension of **.abp**—short for *a*pplication *b*uild *p*roject—should be built by SubSonic. It's an efficient way to kick off SubSonic every time your site is built.

Now we'll need an **.abp** file. Don't worry, it won't take much to set up this file—just create a text file called **builder.abp** in your **App_Code** folder. The contents of the file should be a single asterisk, and nothing more. Here's my entire **builder.abp** file:

```
                                              builder.abp (excerpt)
*
```

This file tells the SubSonic build provider to build classes for *all* tables, views, and stored procedures in our database. If you only want to generate classes for certain tables, just replace the asterisk with a list of tables, like this:

```
                                              builder.abp (excerpt)
Product
Categories
Orders
```

The Web Site Project Trade-off

The Web Site project model has some limitations, as we first saw back in Chapter 1. However, the SubSonic build provider works so well that I think the trade-off is often worth it. The SubSonic build provider is a huge productivity booster, especially when you're just getting started on your project and your database schema is changing frequently.

You may want to consider working with a Web Site project until your database design is stable, and converting your site to a Web Application project when the benefits of SubSonic diminish.

It's a lot easier to understand all these configuration entries in context. Here's a slightly simplified version of the **Web.config** from the SubSonic Central site, which uses the build provider method that we've just discussed:

Web.config *(excerpt)*

```
<?xml version="1.0"?>
<configuration
    xmlns="http://schemas.microsoft.com/.NetConfiguration/v2.0">
  <configSections>
    <section name="SubSonicService"
        type="SubSonic.SubSonicSection, SubSonic"
        allowDefinition="MachineToApplication"
        restartOnExternalChanges="true"
        requirePermission="false"/>
  </configSections>
  <appSettings/>
  <connectionStrings>
    <clear/>
    <add name="Northwind" connectionString="Data Source=localhost;
        Database=Northwind; Integrated Security=true;"/>
  </connectionStrings>
  <SubSonicService defaultProvider="Northwind"
      fixPluralClassNames="true" >
    <providers>
      <clear/>
      <add name="Northwind"
          type="SubSonic.SqlDataProvider, SubSonic"
          connectionStringName="Northwind"
          generatedNamespace="Northwind" />
    </providers>
```

```
    </SubSonicService>
    <system.web>
      <compilation debug="true" defaultLanguage="C#">
        <buildProviders>
          <add extension=".abp"
               type="SubSonic.BuildProvider, SubSonic"/>
        </buildProviders>
      </compilation>
      <authentication mode="Windows"/>
      <pages styleSheetTheme="Default">
        <controls>
          <add tagPrefix="subsonic" namespace="SubSonic.Controls"
               assembly="SubSonic"/>
        </controls>
      </pages>
    </system.web>
  </configuration>
```

SubSonic doesn't constrain you to the Web Site project model. You can also use a **web-based code generator**, which will churn through your database and create the code for your DAL in a folder you specify (C# and VB are supported).

You'll find the web-based generator on the SubSonic Central site. It's a long form, but you can leave most of the checkboxes blank when filling it out. The top half of the page, shown in Figure 17.14, generates classes.

Figure 17.14. The SubSonic Central web-based code generator

I selected **All** to select all of my database tables, and clicked the **Generate** button.
Figure 17.15 shows the resulting list of class files.

Order.cs
OrderController.cs
Product.cs
ProductController.cs
EmployeeTerritory.cs
EmployeeTerritoryController.cs
OrderDetail.cs
OrderDetailController.cs
CustomerController.cs
Employee.cs
EmployeeController.cs
Customer.cs
CustomerCustomerDemo.cs
CustomerCustomerDemoController.cs
CustomerDemographic.cs
CustomerDemographicController.cs
CategoryController.cs
Category.cs

Figure 17.15. The list of generated code files

The lower half of the code generator page, shown in Figure 17.16, generates editor controls.

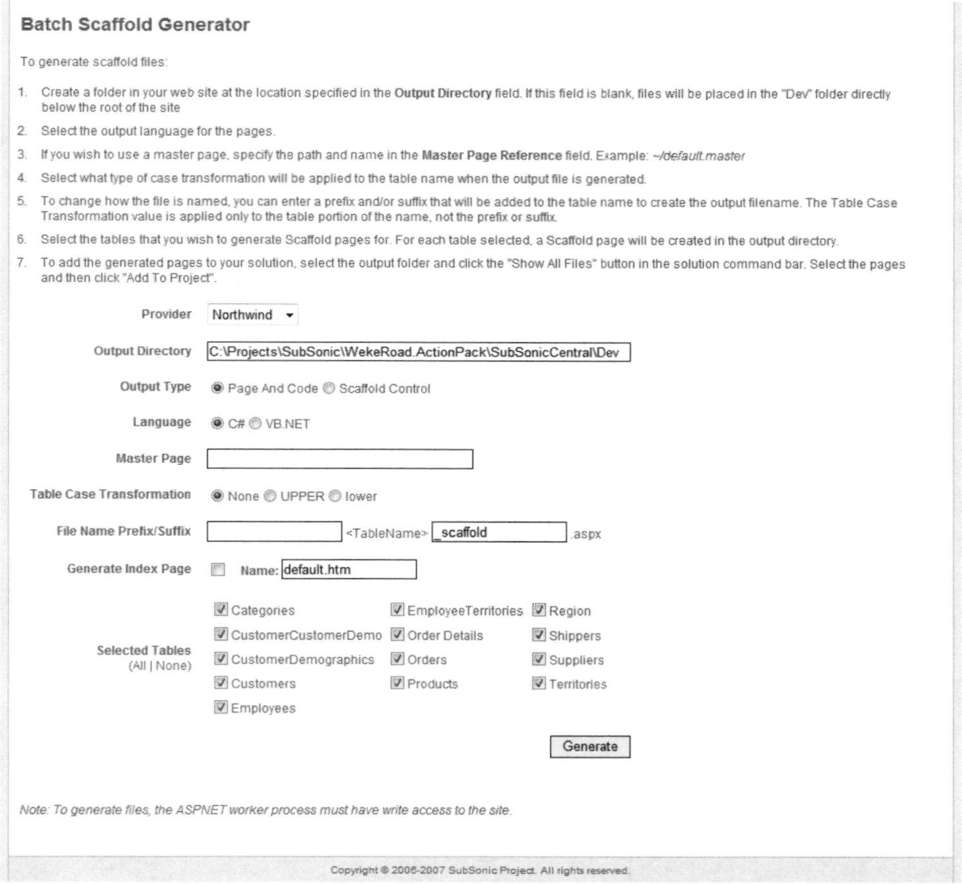

Figure 17.16. The SubSonic web-based form for generating editor controls

The most flexible way to build your DAL, however, is to use the command-line tool, **SubCommander**.

The smoothest way to set up SubCommander is to make the executable file **sonic.exe** visible from anywhere. Right-click on **My Computer** and select **Properties**. In the **Advanced** tab, click the **Environment Variables** button, and add the folder that contains the **sonic.exe** file to your path (for example, **C:\Projects\SubSonic**).

Then bring up a command prompt and change directories to your web site's directory:

```
cd C:\Projects\MyWebSite
```

There, you can generate the DAL with the following command:

```
sonic generate /out App_Code\Generated
```

The benefit of running SubCommander from within your web site's directory is that it automatically reads your **Web.config** file. Because of this, SubCommander inherits your SubSonic settings, including how to connect to your database.

If you want to specify your configuration separately, you can pass that information as a parameter on the command line:

```
sonic generate /out App_Code\Generated /server (local) /db northwind
```

We can also generate the code for a tabular control for editing data that exists in a specific table. This approach can be handy if you want to start by customizing an existing, working control, like this:

```
sonic editor /Products /out SiteAdmin
```

SubCommander has a bunch of other cool database utility functions, too. For instance, the *versiondb* command exports your entire database (schema and data) to a script:

```
sonic versiondb /out DatabaseScripts
```

When you factor in the power SubCommander provides us, there's no reason to limit your use of SubSonic to ASP.NET projects. This code works just great in other .NET project types—WinForm, Console, Code Library, and the like— too.

You can find all of the available options by typing **sonic.exe** at the command line, with no parameters:

```
sonic.exe v2.0.3.0 - Command Line Interface to SubSonic v2.0.3.0
Usage: sonic command [options]
Sample: sonic generate /server localhost /db northwind /out
    GeneratedFiles
```

```
Help: sonic help
TIP: SubSonic will read your App.Config or Web.Config - just select
   the project and run your command.
******************* Commands ********************************
version: Scripts out the schema/data of your db to file
scriptdata: Scripts the data to file for your database
scriptschema: Scripts your Database schema to file
generate: Generates output code for tables, views, and SPs
generatetables: Generates output code for your tables
generateODS: Generates an ObjectDataSource controller for each table
generateviews: Generates output code for your views
generatesps: Generates output code for your SPs
editor: Creates an Editor for a particular table
******************* Argument List ***************************
####### Required For all commands (these can be read from config
files) if you don't have a Web or App.config, these need to be set
/override SubCommander won't try to find a config - instead it will
   use what you pass in
/server - the database server - ALWAYS REQUIRED
/db - the database to use
####### Other Commands (some may be required for specific commands)
/userid - the User ID for your database (blank = use SSPI)
/password - the password for your DB (blank = use SSPI)
/out - the output directory for generated items. (default = current)
/lang - generated code language: cs or vb (default = cs)
/provider - the name of the provider to use
/includeTableList - used for generating classes. A comma-delimited
   list that defines which tables should be used to generate classes
/config - the path your App/Web.Config - used to instance SubSonic
/excludeTableList the opposite of tablelist. These tables will NOT
be used to generate classes
⋮
```

Discussion

I asked SubSonic's chief architect, Rob Conery, to review this solution for me.[15] He pointed out that there are a lot of smarts behind SubSonic's features that you mightn't initially notice—the DropDown and ManyManyList only query the two rows that they need, and the ManyManyList saves data within the scope of a transaction. These are simple examples, but they show the kind of detail and thought that has gone into creating this library.

---

[15] http://blog.wekeroad.com/

Rob also pointed out that the above features weren't just dreamed up by the development team—they were submitted by the community. The SubSonic community is very active, constantly submitting feature requests, bug fixes, and suggestions. More importantly, the development team is very responsive—one suggestion that I submitted was implemented and available for download less than two hours later!

Summary

This chapter's been a wild ride through some advanced applications of the ASP.NET toolkit. I hope you've found them helpful in your current projects, or can anticipate how you might apply them to your work in the future.

This concludes our coverage of the ASP.NET Framework. On this journey we've explored the ins and the outs of ASP.NET, Visual Studio, and a number of third-party tools—and hopefully along the way given you a new appreciation for the craft of web application development.

Of course, a good developer never stops learning—in Chapter 1 I listed a number of resources that can help you get the most out of ASP.NET. Read one of the books on that list, subscribe to one of the blogs I mentioned (or even start your own!) and get involved in the SitePoint .NET forums.[16]

It's impossible to learn everything there is to know about ASP.NET 2.0, but armed with the knowledge in this book, you're certainly well on your way.

---

[16] http://www.sitepoint.com/launch/dotnetforum/

Index

554

THE ART &
SCIENCE
OF CSS

BY **CAMERON ADAMS**
JINA BOLTON
DAVID JOHNSON
STEVE SMITH
JONATHAN SNOOK

CREATE INSPIRATIONAL STANDARDS-BASED WEB DESIGN

THE PRINCIPLES OF
BEAUTIFUL
WEB DESIGN

BY **JASON BEAIRD**

DESIGN BEAUTIFUL WEB SITES USING THIS SIMPLE STEP-BY-STEP GUIDE

SIMPLY
JAVASCRIPT

BY **KEVIN YANK**
& CAMERON ADAMS

THE CSS
ANTHOLOGY
101 ESSENTIAL TIPS, TRICKS & HACKS
BY **RACHEL ANDREW**
2ND EDITION

2ND EDITION

sitepoint

BUILD YOUR OWN
ASP.NET 2.0
WEB SITE
USING C# & VB

BY **CRISTIAN DARIE**
& ZAK RUVALCABA

THE JAVASCRIPT ANTHOLOGY

101 ESSENTIAL TIPS, TRICKS & HACKS

BY JAMES EDWARDS
& CAMERON ADAMS

THE MOST COMPLETE QUESTION AND ANSWER BOOK ON JAVASCRIPT